PSYCHOLOGICAL ASSESSMENT WITH THE MMPI

PSYCHOLOGICAL ASSESSMENT WITH THE MMPI

Alan F. Friedman, PhD
Northwestern University Medical School
Independent Practice
Chicago, Illinois

James T. Webb, PhD
Wright State University
Dayton, Ohio

Richard Lewak, PhD
Del Mar Psychiatric Clinic
Del Mar, California

1989

LAWRENCE ERLBAUM ASSOCIATES, PUBLISHERS
Hillsdale, New Jersey   Hove and London

Lawrence Erlbaum Associates, Inc., Publishers
365 Broadway
Hillsdale, New Jersey 07642

Library of Congress Cataloging in Publication Data

Friedman, Alan F.
  Psychological assessment with the MMPI.

  Includes index.
  1. Minnesota Multiphasic Personality Inventory.
I. Webb, James T. II. Lewak, Richard   III. Title.
RC473 · M5F75   1989   155 · 2'83   89–11662
ISBN 0-8058-0310-6

Printed in the United States of America
10 9 8 7 6 5

Dedicated to
Liz, Pat, and Linda

Contents

Code-Type Look-Up Table

List of Figures

List of Tables

Preface

This book has two broad purposes. The first is to provide beginning MMPI users with a basic understanding of the construction and application of the test. The second objective is to provide the more experienced MMPI user with a reference guide which will be useful in applied practice. Toward these aims the book covers a broad range of material. Some readers may elect to use only the code-type Look-up table which provides psychological descriptions of various MMPI configurations. Others may use the book to assist in their personality assessment report writing. For the beginning user in a class or involved in a self-directed study, there is an accompanying MMPI workbook. The authors attempted to fill a gap in the MMPI text area. We wanted to write a book that would both cover the important research literature as well as the rich clinical experience which many professionals bring to the task of interpreting MMPI profiles. An important occurrence in the field of assessment is the recent publication of the revised MMPI. Toward this end, we have included a descriptive chapter on the MMPI-2. However, we believe that it will be many years before the MMPI-2 can be properly evaluated through the necessary empirical research. It is likely that the MMPI-2 will continue to rest on the many decades of empirical findings that have formed the foundation of the original MMPI. Therefore, an understanding of the MMPI-2 rests on a thorough familiarity of the original MMPI. This book is intended to provide such a foundation.

ACKNOWLEDGMENTS

We would like to express our thanks to the many individuals who made contributions to this book, either in the form of critical review, the sharing of materials and ideas, and/or through encouragement which helped sustain our efforts. Philip

Marks reviewed early drafts of the beginning chapters and suggested many useful ideas, as did Peter Briggs. Alex Caldwell shared information and materials and was always available to impart his wisdom in the colorful manner that makes Alex unique. Jerry Wiggins was generous with his permission to reproduce his content scales as well as with his efforts in reviewing a part of the manuscript. Harrison Gough clarified much information about the history of the Ds scale and his interest is greatly appreciated. George Ritz shared materials, and his efforts are also much appreciated. Ken Serkownek helped to clarify facts about his subscales and gave permission to reproduce them. David Nichols worked on preparing his critical items list for this book as well as contributing his writings on the Goldberg Index. His receptivity and responsiveness to the many questions and requests for information helped this book progress. Philip Erdberg took an interest in this project and was supportive in many different ways. James Wakefield constructed several tables in the appendix, and his thoroughness, patience, and friendship are highly valued by us. We would like to also extend our thanks to Roger Greene for his interest in this project and his many clarifications about MMPI subtleties (or not so subtle) which helped us to write a clearer text. The material in chapter 9 was reviewed by Grant Dahlstrom, and his suggestions were appreciated, as was his support for the book. Robert Archer reviewed the entire manuscript in great detail and offered many useful suggestions that helped to improve the book. His support and thoroughness were important foundation stones in the making of this book. His graduate student, Ms. Lisa Lee, also carefully read the manuscript and made helpful suggestions. The efforts of Beverly Kaemmer at the University of Minnesota Press are greatly appreciated. She was responsive to the many permission requests that we are sure never seemed to end. Harold Sweet designed the graphs and cover of the book, and his dedication to the task is most appreciated. Jackie McLerran typed a large part of the book and was amazing in her patience. There were many weekends she contributed to this project and her skills were an important part of the finished product. Judith Suben and Robin Weisberg at our publisher were supportive and patient throughout the process and really a pleasure with whom to work.

Finally, the first author wishes to extend his heartfelt thanks to Goldine Gleser, who from the beginning offered words of encouragement and consultation over the years in the writing of this book. Her efforts are greatly appreciated.

Alan F. Friedman
James T. Webb
Richard Lewak

Foreword

There is certainly no scarcity of literature concerning the MMPI, and it has been estimated that over 10,000 articles, chapters, and books have been published related to this instrument. Therefore, the prudent reader might well ask whether a new publication in this area either offers new and relevant information, or serves to integrate the existing body of literature in a meaningful manner. The work of Alan Friedman, James Webb, and Richard Lewak certainly meets both of these criteria in an outstanding fashion. Beyond this, their text serves to provide very useful and well-organized information to individuals across a spectrum of experience with the MMPI.

This text serves as a comprehensive introduction to the MMPI. It provides a clear and concise review of the development of this instrument with specific and detailed attention to basic administration and scoring issues. In particular, the comprehensive discussion of administration criteria, including the importance of such often overlooked issues as test conditions and test instructions, forms a very solid foundation from which to begin an understanding of MMPI usage. This volume also contains an excellent step-by-step guide to profile interpretation and report writing, which includes an impressive review of the literature on validity scales, validity indices, the clinical scales and code-type configurations, and special scales categorized by test construction method.

There is a Code-Type Look-Up Table designed to direct the reader to various interpretations of single- and multiple-scale configurations. Clinicians will particularly find this section of value in aiding their interpretation of code-types. An attractive and additional feature of this volume is an accompanying workbook the authors have constructed to assist course instructors and/or clinical practitioners wishing to master the MMPI material in the text. The workbook for the MMPI is designed to provide exercises leading to report-writing and interpretation skills.

Throughout this text, a clear emphasis is placed on the provision of practical guidelines for the use of the MMPI which are well grounded in the empirical literature that has developed over the past 50 years.

In addition to meeting the needs of the novice user, this volume contains much information for the seasoned MMPI veteran. The discussion of the extensive item overlap on MMPI scales, and the implication of this phenomenon for interscale correlations, factor analytic findings, and differential diagnoses, is outstanding. The explicit emphasis on providing MMPI feedback to clients, accompanied by very useful suggestions in terms of meeting this crucial component of the assessment task, is certainly of use to MMPI users at any stage of experience. Further, the chapter on computerized interpretation approaches for the MMPI provides examples from an excellent cross section of the currently available MMPI services that should prove of use to anyone interested in MMPI assessment. Finally, the final chapter of this book provides a very comprehensive review of the current MMPI restandardization project at the University of Minnesota, including a thoughtful evaluation of the potential significance of this work for the practitioner.

In summary, the authors of this text have clearly drawn on their many years of MMPI assessment experience in clinical and research settings to provide specific and detailed recommendations for the use of the MMPI. These recommendations are consistently based on the uniquely rich research literature of this instrument. Their critical overview and evaluation of major MMPI assessment issues is characterized throughout this text by balance, thoughtfulness, and insight. This text should be of lasting value to a broad spectrum of clinicians learning, or improving their use of, the MMPI for clinical assessment purposes.

Robert P. Archer
Eastern Virginia Medical School

Development of the MMPI

GENERAL DESCRIPTION OF THE MMPI

The Minnesota Multiphasic Personality Inventory (MMPI) is the most widely used objective personality inventory in the world. According to Butcher and Owen (1978), 84% of the research in the personality inventory domain has been with the MMPI, and according to Reynolds and Sundberg (1976), the test is the undisputed leader in the number of test references produced each year. Dahlstrom, Welsh, and Dahlstrom (1975) listed close to 6,000 MMPI references in their book, *An MMPI Handbook,* and the *Eighth Mental Measurement Yearbook* by Buros (1978) contains more than 5,000 citations on the test (Greene, 1980). More recently, Butcher (1985) reported that over 8,000 books and articles have been produced on the MMPI.

The widespread use of the test is attributable to several factors including scoring and administration simplicity, an objective nature important for research designs, a large item pool (from which at least 700 additional scales have been derived), and many empirically established correlates and useful applications. Research and clinical settings are no strangers to the MMPI. In fact, it is difficult to imagine many settings in which psychologists perform assessment and treatment functions where the MMPI has not been used. Psychiatric inpatient and outpatient facilities often employ psychologists to make diagnostic and treatment decisions, and the MMPI is frequently included in psychological test batteries or even administered independently. Many clinical practitioners use the MMPI to screen new patients in their office practice for maladjustment and to help them formulate treatment plans. Psychologists use the test in medical settings to help evaluate any functional component in physical complaints and to assist in predicting response to various treatments (Osborne, 1979). Industrial and clinical psychologists, whose responsibilities involve matching individuals to particular employment positions or screening individuals for psychopathology, also routinely employ the test to aid in their tasks. For example, because the MMPI is sensitive to emotional maladjustment in individuals other than identified patient groups, it is often used in personnel selection situations where high-risk occupations require careful screening of applicants. Persons in public trust positions, such as airline flight crews, law enforcement officers, nursing staff, ministerial candidates, and nuclear power plant operators, are typically administered the MMPI (Butcher, 1979). Research applications, with the MMPI as either the sole subject of study or as one of the major dependent measures in an investigation, range from cross-cultural studies of response patterns to the use of the test in evaluating treatment effects and in making forensic decisions.

The MMPI consists of 550 self-reference statements, 16 of which are repeated, bringing the item pool to a total of 566. The repeated items were originally included to assist in the mechanical scoring of the inventory but are actually scored only once for the standard clinical scales. Persons respond to the items by marking true or false on an answer sheet or, in the original card deck form, test-takers sort their responses into "T for true," "F for false," or "cannot say" categories. An item is scored as "cannot say" if it is marked both true and false on the answer sheet, left blank, or sorted into the "cannot say" category in the card deck form.

There are several methods for scoring a completed test. The answer sheet is either hand-scored or "read" by a special scanner machine. Some MMPI users enter the responses from the answer sheet into a computer that is programmed to score and sometimes interpret the test. Fourteen basic scales are scored regardless of the scoring method. The following are the 4 validity scales and 10 basic clinical scales.

VALIDITY SCALES

? (cannot say)
L (lie)
F (frequency)
K (correction)

CLINICAL SCALES

Scale 1—Hypochondriasis (Hs)
Scale 2—Depression (D)
Scale 3—Hysteria (Hy)
Scale 4—Psychopathic deviate (Pd)
Scale 5—Masculinity-femininity (Mf)
Scale 6—Paranoia (Pa)
Scale 7—Psychasthenia (Pt)

Scale 8—Schizophrenia (*Sc*)
Scale 9—Hypomania (*Ma*)
Scale 0—Social introversion (*Si*)

The validity scales were developed to assist in recognizing invalid test records produced by uncooperative or deceptive subjects with various test-taking attitudes (e.g., faking good or faking bad). The clinical scales were developed primarily to assist in identifying the type and severity of abnormal psychiatric conditions. (The reader is referred to appendix A for a complete listing of the item composition for the validity and clinical scales.) A secondary goal was to provide an objective means of estimating therapeutic effects and other changes in the status of conditions across time (Dahlstrom, Welsh, & Dahlstrom, 1972). The raw scores on each of the validity and clinical scales are converted to *T*-scores by plotting them onto a profile sheet. This yields a series of comparable scores. It is the pattern of these scale scores that is usually clinically interpreted. The *T*-scores also provide the clinician an opportunity to examine how the test-taker compares to a normative and psychiatric population. A more detailed description of *T*-scores is provided in chapter 2.

HISTORICAL DEVELOPMENT OF THE MMPI

The MMPI was published in 1943 by the University of Minnesota Press. The authors and early developers of the test were Starke R. Hathaway, PhD, a psychologist, and J. Charnley McKinley, MD, a psychiatrist, both of the University of Minnesota. They began their work in the late 1930s. They were originally motivated to design a test that could serve as an aid "in diagnosing persons classified as constitutional psychopathic inferiors" (Hathaway, 1939, p. 117), assist "in assessing the psychological factors associated with physical problems or disease seen in a medical practice" (McKinley & Hathaway, 1943, p. 161), and as a corollary, "measure the effectiveness of insulin therapy" (Hathaway, 1964, p. 204), which had been gaining widespread use in the late 1930s. The test also came to be seen as an aid in determining levels of psychiatric impairment and changes in conditions over time as well as an estimate of the effects of psychotherapy (Dahlstrom, Welsh, & Dahlstrom, 1972). Currently, the MMPI is predominantly used to evaluate psychopathology in a variety of populations and to assess the structure of personality in both clinical and normal populations.

Hathaway and McKinley (1943) recognized many of the problems hampering the effectiveness of previously existing personality inventories, and they strove to correct these in developing the MMPI. Previous personality inventories were constructed with a *rational* basis or focus on content validity and lacked scales designed to measure the subject's test-taking attitude (e.g., defensiveness or overclaiming of symptoms). An example of a psychological inventory with such characteristics is the Woodworth Personal Data Sheet (1920), also called the Psychoneurotic Inventory. During World War I, there was a strong need to screen for maladjustment among draftees. Woodworth (1920) developed a 116-item self-rating scale to detect neurotic maladjustment. The items consisted of statements that the authors believed reflected neurotic symptomatology. If a subject answered a certain number of items in the deviant direction, a psychiatric interview was conducted. A fundamental assumption inherent in the test was that the items measured what the authors assumed they measured. Items were chosen on rational grounds; that is, if the items appeared content-relevant to neuroticism, they were included in the scale. Over time, it became clear that items selected on a rational basis were not always indicative of deviant behavior in the way the test constructors expected.

Another unwarranted assumption in the Woodworth Personal Data Sheet and similar tests was that the subject would and could honestly and accurately describe him- or herself. This is not always the case, as self-deception and social desirability factors operate to influence a person's responses to test items. Although the Woodworth Personal Data Sheet was not completed early enough to allow its operational use before World War I ended, it did set the stage for other similarly constructed inventories to gain some widespread use after the war (Anastasi, 1982). However, the Personal Data Sheet and other questionnaires failed to convince users that rationally constructed inventories were the most successful type of psychological test.

Hathaway and McKinley employed the empirical method (also called the criterion keying method) to construct the MMPI, and as Anastasi (1982) noted, the MMPI represents the outstanding example of this test construction methodology. According to this method, test items are administered to two or more groups of subjects—a criterion group selected for homogeneity of a certain diagnosis or cluster of characteristics (e.g., schizophrenia) and a normal comparison group that does not share the characteristics. Items to which the criterion and comparison groups respond differently are included on the scale being developed, and items to which the responses are similar are not included. Scales constructed in this fashion are typically named after the criterion group. Scoring the scales is accomplished by assigning one point to each item answered in a direction that is marked statistically more frequently by the criterion subjects; that is, if a higher proportion of hysterics than normals answered true to an item, a response of true to that item would be given one point on the hysteria scale, and a response of false would be given zero points. The higher the raw score a person receives on a scale, the more items he or she has answered in the direction of the criterion group.

Using this criterion keying method, Hathaway and McKinley began their construction of the MMPI by compiling more than 1,000 self-reference statements from a wide variety of sources including psychiatric examination forms, psychiatry textbooks, previously published attitude and personality scales, clinical reports and case summaries, and their own clinical experience. From these resources, the authors eventually adopted an item pool of 550 separate statements.[1] Using the rational method, the items were judged to be of simple readability and covered statements ranging from phobias, religious attitudes, and general health, to social attitudes and affect (Dahlstrom, Welsh, & Dahlstrom, 1972). Using this pool of 550 items, the authors proceeded to construct scales by contrasting the responses of normal and clinical criterion groups.

The normal criterion group consisted of relatives and friends visiting patients at the University of Minnesota Hospital (N = 724), who were willing to complete the test, as well as high school graduates attending precollege conferences at the University of Minnesota (N = 265), medical patients from the University hospital (N = 254), and work project administration workers (N = 265). Normal subjects (other than the medical patients) who were then under the care of a physician were excluded from the normative sample; all other subjects were included. A more detailed description of the normal sample is presented later in this chapter. Hathaway and McKinley found their original sample of normals to correspond well in age, sex, and marital status to the Minnesota population in the 1930s census (Dahlstrom, Welsh, & Dahlstrom, 1972).

The clinical criterion (abnormal) groups consisted of carefully selected psychiatric patients and subjects representing the following major diagnostic categories: hypochondriasis, depression, hysteria, psychopathic deviate, paranoia, psychasthenia, schizophrenia, and hypomania. Two other groups were later added to develop two additional scales for the MMPI. One of these groups consisted of normal college females used to develop a social introversion scale (*Si*), and the other group consisted of "homosexual invert males" (Hathaway, 1956, p. 110) used to develop the masculinity-femininity scale (*Mf*).

VALIDITY SCALE DEVELOPMENT AND USE

The validity scales are cannot say (*?*), *L, F,* and *K.* Their function is to aid in determining the test-taking attitude of the subject. According to Marks, Seeman, and Haller (1974), "The validity scales shed light upon factors which permit one to accept the clinical profile with some confidence or indicate that extreme caution must be exercised in the interpetation of the profile" (p. 9). Some individuals are motivated to distort their responses to the test items either to minimize the presentation of their psychological problems or to exaggerate their psychopathology. Others may give a distorted picture of themselves by answer-

---

[1]The item pool originally consisted of 504 items, to which the authors later added 55 items primarily related to masculinity-femininity (McKinley & Hathaway, 1943) but eventually eliminated 9 more items, resulting in a final pool of 550 separate items. Because 16 items were repeated to facilitate early machine scoring, the final published booklet version contains 566 items, with the 16 repeated items scored only once.

ing the items without fully comprehending their meaning or perhaps by simply not reading the items and responding randomly or with a true or false response bias. It is therefore important to ascertain the subject's test-taking disposition before interpreting the clinical scales. Although the validity scales were designed for this purpose, they have also been shown to correlate with personality traits and behaviors. Hence, the validity scales can enrich the clinical interpretation of the profile by providing the clinician with other psychological descriptors as well as an index of self-description accuracy. (See chapter 5 for further information.) The group booklet item numbers for each validity scale with the keyed responses are presented in appendix A.

Scale ? (Cannot Say)

The cannot say (?) scale is technically not a psychometric scale in the sense of having a consistent item pool or set number of items (Archer, 1987). Rather, it consists of the number of items for which a response is omitted from the answer sheet in the Form R booklet or group form of the test or the number of items sorted behind the cannot say category in the card deck form. The cannot say scale score also indicates the number of double-marked items (items marked true and false) or number of items to which respondents elected not to respond. The reasons for a lack of response are numerous. Perhaps some of the items lack personal relevance, or an individual filling out an answer sheet could accidentally skip an item. Different motivational factors, such as test-taking resistance or suspiciousness, have been associated with high cannot say scores (Dahlstrom, Welsh, & Dahlstrom, 1972). More recently, it was demonstrated that not answering an item may be related to decisional ambiguity, which is the inability of the subject to decide how to respond to an item (Fulkerson & Willage, 1980). Also, intellectual or reading deficits may make it difficult to comprehend an item, leading to its omission (Ball & Carroll, 1960). However, most subjects respond to all of the items, although some subjects may object to various items (Clopton & Neuringer, 1977).

Subjects in personnel selection situations are more likely to react negatively to items if they feel there is no job relevance. If a subject omits items, it is always desirable to encourage him or her to complete the omitted ones and assess why they chose to leave them out. Whereas in many cases the omission may have occurred accidentally, other omissions may have occurred because the item was ambiguous or offensive to the reader or, as implied earlier in the case of adolescents, semantically confusing.

Archer (1987) summarized the findings of Ball and Carroll (1960), who examined correlates of cannot say scores among 262 ninth-grade public school students in Kentucky. He stated that, in general, the adolescents who omitted greater numbers of MMPI items also had lower IQ scores and grades that were below average. This seems to suggest that intelligence and reading limitations are associated with cannot say scores more than are negativistic attitudes toward the testing.

Usually 10 omitted items or less will not affect the validity of the profile. Greene (1980) recommended a procedure, called "augmenting" the profile, when between 5 and 30 items are omitted. In this procedure, the items that were omitted are endorsed in the deviant direction, scored, and reinterpreted. The test should also be scored without the items marked in the deviant direction, so that the two profiles can be compared.

If enough items are omitted, then the scale on which they are scored will be lowered. Thus, the validity of the profile will be compromised (Marks, Seeman, & Haller, 1974). The omission of items can also change the MMPI's high-point pairs (highest two clinical scales), which could significantly alter the interpretation of the profile (Clopton & Neuringer, 1977).

Clopton and Neuringer (1977) conducted a two-phase study to address these issues. In the first phase, they examined the occurrence of omitted MMPI items from Veteran's Administration psychiatric patients being admitted to the hospital, outpatient MMPI answer sheets at a regional mental health center (MHC), and police and firefighter applicants who had completed the MMPI. In each of these three groups, the majority of test subjects completed the entire 566 items, with the percentage of subjects omitting five or less items being 93.7% for the job applicants, 88.9% for MHC clients, and 85.6% for the VA patients. The corresponding number of mean items omitted was 2.45 for job applicants, 2.24 for MHC clients, and 4.68 for the VA patients.

The second phase of Clopton and Neuringer's (1977) study involved inspecting the effects of randomly omitted items on profile elevation and configuration (high-point pairs). A subset of 180 randomly selected VA patient MMPI profiles, which were completely filled out, were then rescored with 5, 30, 55, 80, 105, and 130 items randomly omitted. The original MMPI profiles were compared to the different rescored profiles with different levels of omitted items. As more MMPI items were omitted, there was a corresponding reduction in the profile elevation and, perhaps more importantly, changes occurred in profile configurations. The mean reductions in T-scores across the clinical scales for the six levels of omitted items fell an average of .45, 2.74, 5.61, 7.70, 9.09, and 11.54, respectively. Their study shows that randomly eliminating 30 MMPI items from complete answer sheets leads to a change in the high-point pair in more than 25% of the profiles and an average reduction of nearly three T-score points in the mean profile. Profile configuration, rather than specific T-scale scores, is more importantly affected by large numbers of item omissions.

The T-score values for the cannot say scale, as well as for L and F, were arbitrarily set by Hathaway and McKinley and do not accurately reflect the frequency with which a specific raw score will be obtained. For example, the

profile sheet shows a raw score of 30 on the cannot say scale to correspond to a
T-score value of 50. This is a gross inaccuracy, as omitting 30 items would be
highly unusual. In fact, no study has reported a mean number of omitted items
close to 30 (Clopton & Neuringer, 1977). Greene (1980) pointed out in a review
of four population samples (clinic clients, medical patients, prison inmates, and
university students) that no more than 5% of the subjects in any given sample
omitted more than 30 items. Clopton and Neuringer (1977) recommended that
changes be made in the norms on the standard profile sheet so that a raw score of
5 be set equal to a T-score of 50. Such a score would reflect that most subjects
fail to omit more than five items. They also suggested that the next level of
T-score, 60, be equivalent to a raw score of 30 omitted items, which should
indicate caution in interpreting a profile with such a score. Omitting 30 items is
likely to render a profile invalid (Graham, 1987). Greene (1980) also suggested
using adjusted T-scores to more accurately indicate the frequency with which a
specific cannot say raw score will be obtained. He showed raw scores between 1
and 5 to correspond to T-score values between 45 and 49, raw scores between 6
and 30 to correspond to T-score ranges between 60 and 69, and raw scores of 31
and above to correspond to T-scores of 70 and higher. For the cannot say scale,
as well as for the other validity scales, male and female norms are equivalent.

Scale L

The L (lie) scale consists of 15 items. They are all scored in the false direction.
These items had their origin in previous research on honesty and deceit by
Hartshorne and May (1928). Because the items for scale L were borrowed from
previous work and rewritten, they represent the only scale in the original MMPI
that was not empirically constructed. The L scale items provide 15 opportunities
throughout the test for the subject to endorse certain virtues. The items represent
socially virtuous behaviors (e.g., denial of dishonesties) that may be desirable
for many people but are rarely true for most people. For this reason, the "items
constituted a fairly subtle trap for anyone who wanted to give an unusually good
impression of himself" (Meehl & Hathaway, 1946; cited in Dahlstrom & Dahlstrom, 1980, p. 97). Individuals are expected to claim some feelings of virtue, so
most do, in fact, answer some items in the "lie" direction. The mean number of
items answered in this direction by the Minnesota normals employed in
standardizing the test was four. The T-score values for scale L (and scales $?$ and
F) were arbitrarily established, with the result that a raw scale L score of 7 on the
profile sheet corresponds to a T-score of 60, and a raw score of 10 corresponds to
a T-score of 70. There is a problem with these values because they underestimate
the frequency of occurrence of these scores; Hathaway and McKinley (1983)
recommended adjustments. Chapter 5 more specifically addresses validity scale
elevation issues as they relate to interpretation.

Generally speaking, higher raw scores on scale L reflect a tendency to put oneself in a favorable light. Consequently, the clinical scales are expected to be suppressed because the individual is tending to deny basic human frailties and "look good." As mentioned previously, there are no separate male-female norms for scale L or the other validity scales. Because all the items on this scale are scored in the false direction, an all-false response set will elevate scale L as well as scales 1, 2, and 3, which are also predominantly keyed as false for a deviant response.

Moderator variables (e.g., socioeconomic status, education) greatly affect scores on scale L. The item content of the scale is apparent or obvious in terms of what it is measuring, so that test-sophisticated individuals rarely elevate the scale. This may be because they realize it would be unconvincing to give such a distorted response to the items (Greene, 1980). College-educated individuals and those with a higher socioeconomic status infrequently obtain raw scores above 4. An elevated L score in a college-educated individual should be carefully evaluated. Less-educated individuals and individuals of lower socioeconomic classes are more likely to obtain higher scale L scores.

The majority of the items on scale L ($N = 9$) do not overlap the other MMPI scales. The largest overlap occurs with scales 2 and 9 sharing two items in common with scale L. The reader is referred to appendix B for a presentation of the overlap content of scale L.

Test–retest correlation coefficients for psychiatric cases on scale L range between .74 and .78, with a 1- to 2-day interval between tests, and between .35 and .61 with a 1-year interval between administrations (Dahlstrom, Welsh, & Dahlstrom, 1975).

In a large-scale meta-analysis of MMPI reliability studies using a wide variety of populations conducted between 1970 and 1981, Hunsley, Hanson, and Parker (1988) reported an average internal consistency of .77 across 70 studies of the L scale. They also reported an average test–retest reliability of .63 for eight studies with time intervals from 1 day to 2 years.

Examples of scale L items are:[2]

*45. I do not always tell the truth—(False)
 60. I do not read every editorial in the newspaper every day—(False)
 75. I get angry sometimes—(False)
225. I gossip a little at times—(False)

---

[2]The item numbers refer to the group booklet form of the MMPI. The deviant response for the items are in parentheses following the items. The different forms of the MMPI are described in chapter 2.

*Credit: Minnesota Multiphasic Personality Inventory (MMPI). Copyright © The University of Minnesota 1943, renewed 1970. Reproduced by permission of the University of Minnesota Press.

Scale *F*

The *F* scale was designed to measure the tendency of an individual to respond to the test items in an unusual manner, such as in the case of not comprehending the items. It consists of 64 items, to which at least 90% of the normals in the original standardization group responded in the same direction (either true or false). Whether an *F* scale item is answered true or false is irrelevant; the point is that the items are said to have high community agreement in most cases.[3] "Every time a subject responds in a rare direction they are deviating from the community on some subject in which it is in exceedingly high agreement" (Marks, Seeman, & Haller, 1974, p. 12). For this reason, perhaps, the scale has come to be called the frequency or infrequency scale. The probability is .90 or better that for any given item the normal subject will answer in the popular direction. Because of this high community agreement, it is not surprising that the mean number of deviant responses for the *F* scale (three items) is relatively low. The items represent a broad range of content that is obviously suggestive of deviant behavior, making it relatively easy for subjects to deny symptoms or overclaim problems depending on their motives. Examples from scale *F* are:

*27. Evil spirits possess me at times—(True)
 31. I have nightmares every few nights—(True)
 42. When I am with people, I am bothered by hearing very queer things—(True)
 54. I am liked by most people who know me—(False)
113. I believe in law enforcement—(False)
156. I have had periods in which I carried on activities without knowing later what I had been doing—(True)

The item content of the scale includes psychotic-type experiences and strange sensations, social maladjustment, and unconventional beliefs. Because 21 of the 64 items on scale *F* overlap one or more of the so-called psychotic tetrad scales (scales 6, 7, 8, and 9), increasing elevations on *F* are usually associated with increasing psychotic scale elevations. Scale *F* is considered one of the most useful single scales in the MMPI for indicating severity of maladjustment (Meyer, 1983). Seriously or acutely disturbed individuals tend to obtain elevated scores on this scale. Also, individuals who exaggerate their concerns and psychological problems by overclaiming symptomatology elevate scale *F*.

---

[3]Greene (1980) pointed out that five of the *F* scale items do not meet the 10% or less criterion for males and females in the original normative sample.

Credit: Minnesota Multiphasic Personality Inventory (MMPI). Copyright © The University of Minnesota 1943, renewed 1970. Reproduced by permission of the University of Minnesota Press.

Test–retest correlation coefficients for psychiatric cases on scale F with a 1- to 2-day interval between tests range from between .80 and .81, and between .63 and .76 with a 1-year interval between tests (Dahlstrom, Welsh, & Dahlstrom, 1975).

In Hunsley et al.'s (1988) large-scale meta-analysis of MMPI reliability studies using a wide variety of populations conducted between 1970 and 1981, an average internal consistency of .77 across 70 studies of the F scale was reported. They also reported an average test–retest reliability of .70 for 15 studies with time intervals from 1 day to 2 years.

Scale K

The K scale is the fourth validity indicator developed for the MMPI. Because it "was derived as a correction scale or suppressor variable for improving the discrimination yielded on the already existent personality scales, it was not assumed to be measuring anything which in itself is of psychiatric significance" (Meehl & Hathaway, 1946, cited in Dahlstrom & Dahlstrom, 1980, p. 103). Experience with the MMPI showed that the cannot say, L, and F scales were not adequate in detecting certain response sets or outright deception. Specifically, the scale constructors wanted to reduce the number of psychiatric patients obtaining normal MMPI profiles (clinical scales under a T-score of 70) without reducing the number of test hits.[4] Their purpose was to reduce false negatives.

The K scale was developed by selecting 25 male and 25 female psychiatric inpatients who obtained normal scale elevations (no T-score over 70—i.e., false negatives). These patients had L scale T-scores of at least 60, indicating test-taking defensiveness. The psychiatric evaluations indicated that the patients were manifesting either alcoholism, personality disorders, or behavioral disturbances rather than psychotic or neurotic disorders (Greene, 1980). The profiles of these patients (who apparently were answering these test items in a defensive manner) were compared with the responses of some of the Minnesota normative cases

---

[4]A test hit is defined as a normal person or psychiatric patient yielding a normal and abnormal MMPI profile, respectively. It is a test hit when a test is accurately classifying the subject. When a normal individual obtains a nonelevated MMPI profile, his or her test is said to be a true negative, because it indicates the absence (negative) of psychopathology. When the clinical status of a patient indicates abnormality and the corresponding MMPI profile is elevated, the results are congruent with the observed clinical status, and a true positive result is obtained. This means that the test is accurately detecting the presence (positive) of abnormal behavior. A test miss is defined as a normal or abnormal individual yielding an abnormal or normal profile, respectively. It is a "test miss" because the MMPI is incorrectly classifying the subject. When a normal individual obtains an elevated or abnormal MMPI profile, he or she is being falsely identified on the test as having present (positive) psychopathology. His or her test is said, therefore, to be a false positive. When an abnormal person generates a normal profile, the test is falsely identifying the absence (negative) of abnormality and is therefore called a false negative.

used in the original standardization group. Item analysis yielded 22 items (common to males and females) that discriminated the "true and false negative profiles in their item endorsements by at least 30%" (Dahlstrom, Welsh, & Dahlstrom, 1972, p. 124). High scores on these items indicated more defensiveness and the greater likelihood of a "false negative"; that is, a patient who should have generated an abnormal profile actually obtained a normal one. Low scores on these items were important in detecting false positives; that is, the cases where normals obtained abnormal test scores. Because the 22-item K scale was insensitive to some depressed and schizophrenic patients who tended to score low, an additional 8 items were included to assist in separating the original normative group from these two patient groups. In addition to meeting the criterion of differentiating the normals from the abnormals (schizophrenics and depressives), the items also had to meet another criterion. Specifically, Marks, Seeman, and Haller (1974) stated that these items also had to be insensitive to subjects instructed to fake good or fake bad.

The main function of the 30-item K scale is to improve the discriminating power of the clinical scales. By adding differential proportions of the K raw scores to five different clinical scales, the test constructors were able to improve the ability of the scales to differentiate between the normal and criterion groups. Most MMPI experts advise test-users to make certain that they add the K-correction factor to the five clinical scales, as the standard profile sheet is based on T-scores corrected for the K additions. The raw K scale addition for scale 1 (Hs) is .5, and .4 for scale 4 (Pd). Scale 7 (Pt) and scale 8 (Sc) have one full raw score value of K added, and scale 9 (Ma) has .2K added to it.

As the K-corrections were developed with adult psychiatric patients, it may not always be appropriate to employ the K-corrections with dissimilar populations. Greene (1980) reviewed the literature on the use of K in various settings and concluded that "in general, however, little research justifies the continued widespread use of K-correction of the clinical scales" (p. 42). He continued, "clinicians probably need to avoid using K-corrections in settings in which normal persons are being evaluated with the MMPI, but they should use the K-corrections in settings in which psychopathology is suspected keeping in mind the potential inaccuracies the K-corrections may introduce" (p. 42). However, it does appear that most clinicians continue to use the K-correction despite its limitations. It is recommended for adults (i.e., subjects 18 years and over) that the reader apply the K-correction and plot T-scores with and without the K-correction with normal populations until future research determines the parameters of its misapplications. It is also recommended that MMPI users plotting adolescent profiles be aware that the most frequently used adolescent norms (Marks, Seeman, & Haller, 1974) do not use K-corrections. It is important to be aware of the limitations of scale K and its effect on profile configurations.

The K scale elevation by itself, as well as in conjunction with other validity scales, is a measure of the subject's test-taking attitude. Various elevations are also associated with personological and nontest correlates of the test. Very high scoring subjects generally are described as maintaining a defensive posture and unwilling to admit to psychological problems. Very low scoring subjects are seen as being overly self-critical in confessing many psychological difficulties. Individuals motivated to fake good often elevate K, and this suggests that their defensive attitude will generally tend to lower the clinical scale profile elevation. Also, when there are clinical scale elevations in a high K profile, they tend to be associated with the neurotic triad (Dahlstrom, Welsh, & Dahlstrom, 1972). Individuals faking bad tend to overclaim symptomatology, and the resultant low K scores are often associated with peaks on the psychotic tetrad scales (6, 7, 8, and 9) (Dahlstrom, Welsh, & Dahlstrom, 1972). Socioeconomic factors, age, race and culture, and intelligence all affect the interpretation of the clinical and validity scales and must be considered when interpreting a profile. These factors are discussed in chapter 4.

The K scale uses T-scores derived in the standardized manner, unlike the three other validity scales. The same norms are used for males and females. Some examples of K scale items are:

*39. At times I feel like smashing things—(False)

89. It takes a lot of argument to convince most people of the truth—(False)

124. Most people will use somewhat unfair means to gain profit or an advantage rather than to lose it—(False)

138. Criticism or scolding hurts me terribly—(False)

322. I worry over money and business—(False)

It is important to recognize that a high T-score on a clinical K-corrected scale could be due to a large K-correction added or due to a high raw score on that scale. Therefore, it is critical to examine the raw-score values on the elevated scales. For example, a T-score of 70 on scale 7 (Pt) could be achieved in several ways. One way would consist of a male subject endorsing 10 scale-7 items in the deviant direction and 23 K-scale items, or 28 scale-7 items and 5 K-scale items. Inferring worry or tension from the T-score values of 70 in each case could be misleading, as the individual with the lower raw score value on scale 7, in this case, is less likely to be experiencing worry and tension.

Most of the K items overlap the other clinical scales, and there are only five items that are considered unique to the scale.

Test–retest correlation coefficients for psychiatric cases on the K scale range between .46 and .56 for a 1- to 2-day interval between tests and between .42 and .72 with a 1-year interval between tests (Dahlstrom, Welsh, & Dahlstrom, 1975).

In Hunsley et al.'s (1988) large-scale meta-analysis of MMPI reliability studies using a wide variety of populations conducted between 1970 and 1981, an average internal consistency of .82 across 71 studies of the K scale was reported. They also reported an average test–retest reliability of .77 for 15 studies with time intervals from 1 day to 2 years.

CLINICAL SCALE DEVELOPMENT AND USE

The MMPI has 10 clinical scales that are universally scored when the MMPI is administered. These scales are numbered 1 through 9 plus 0. They were originally named after diagnostic criterion groups (e.g., depression, schizophrenia, etc.), but currently they are indicated by their numbers. The original diagnostic labels that named the scales are misleading, as the behaviors expected to be associated with elevations on specific scales are not always observed. Therefore, the naming of the scales by numbers tends to be less misleading in terms of what the scales are measuring. Appendix A contains the group booklet item numbers for each clinical scale with the keyed responses.

The clinical scales were the first scales to be constructed from the MMPI items and have been the focus of most of the MMPI research done in the past 45 years. They form the basis of all coding systems and the core of all clinical uses of the MMPI. Scales 1, 2, and 3 are referred to as the neurotic triad. Scales 6, 7, 8, and 9 are referred to as the psychotic tetrad.

Scale 1—Hypochondriasis (*Hs*)

Scale 1 was the first scale to be published on the MMPI and measures the degree of bodily complaints claimed by an individual or, said another way, the degree to which a person is denying good physical health. Hypochondriasis was a clinical syndrome studied by Hathaway and McKinley (1940) to construct scale 1, and their criterion group consisted of 50 inpatients with only pure, uncomplicated hypochondriasis. Hypochondriasis is a disturbance involving an unrealistic interpretation of physical signs or sensations as abnormal, which leads the person to fear that he or she has a serious disease (American Psychiatric Association, 1980). Patients with other coexisting disorders, like a psychosis or other physical disease, were excluded from the criterion group. Hypochondriasis was selected for study because of the large numbers of patients with this disorder, and because it was a relatively easy diagnosis to establish (Colligan, Osborne, Swenson, & Offord, 1983).

Several revisions of the scale were required before it could satisfactorily make discriminations. The first step in the construction of the scale after the criterion group was selected was to specify the normals. Various samples within the normal group used in constructing scale 1 were also included to various degrees in assembling the other clinical scales. The first sample consisted of 724 married men and women, ranging in age from 26 to 43, who were visitors at the University of Minnesota Hospitals. Subjects were eliminated if they were under the care of a physician at the time. The normals were all white and belonged to what was termed the underprivileged classes (McKinley & Hathaway, 1940). The second normal sample consisted of 265 unmarried entering freshmen who were receiving precollege guidance counseling at the University of Minnesota Testing Bureau (McKinley & Hathaway, 1940). A third normal sample consisted of 265 skilled workers from local works progress administration projects. The fourth sample involved 254 physically diseased hospitalized patients without frank psychiatric symptomatology. A fifth group consisted of inpatients in the psychiatric unit at the University of Minnesota Hospital with varied diagnoses (McKinley & Hathaway, 1940). The empirical method was primarily used to identify a list of items that discriminated the normals and physically ill people from the 50 patients in the hypochondriacal criterion group. An item was considered for inclusion on the scale if the normals and patients in the criterion groups differed in the frequency of responding to the item by at least twice the standard error proportions of true-false responses (Greene, 1980). However, McKinley and Hathaway (1940) rejected a few of the items in a nonempirical manner if they thought the item would not apply generally in the population. An initial version of the scale consisted of 55 items, but further work was required to refine the scale because of the high numbers of psychiatric patients without clinically observed hypochondriasis obtaining significant scale 1 elevations. To correct for this occurrence, 50 patients without hypochondriacal complaints, but with high scores on the initial version of scale 1, were compared to the original group of 50 hypochondriacal patients. Items that discriminated these two groups became known as the C_H (correction for hypochondriasis) scale. The C_H scale consisted of 48 items. Experimentation with these items by assigning them different weights failed to improve their performance, so the improved discriminating score on scale 1 was derived by subtracting the C_H scale from the Hs scale. As Greene (1980) described it, "for each of these correction items that an individual answered in the non-hypochondriacal direction, one point was subtracted from the total score on Scale 1" (p. 9). Cross-validation with the H-minus-C scale reliably separated normals from hypochondriacal patients. The hospitalized medical sample demonstrated that the presence of physical disease did not significantly raise scores on the scale. A final revision of scale 1 occurred when the authors attempted to improve the separation between scales 1 and 3. Many C items were dropped as were original scale 1 items that did not stand up on further analysis. The addition of a one-half K value helped to improve the ability of the scale to make accurate diagnostic discriminations, and commercially available profile sheets provide a space to add the one-half K value to scale 1.

The final scale consisted of 33 items related to various aspects of bodily functions including generalized aches and pains and concerns about different body regions. The content of the scale is considered obvious, with no subtle items, meaning that an individual wishing to deny good health could easily do so.

The item content of several MMPI clinical scales were classified by Wiener and Harmon (1946) as being subtle or obvious, with the former meaning that an item does not obviously appear related to the psychopathology it is measuring. The differential endorsement of subtle and obvious items has implications about the test-taking attitude of the subject and can be used as another validity measure. This topic is more fully presented in chapter 3. Where applicable, scale items classified as subtle versus obvious are indicated in parentheses next to the example items presented in this chapter. The obvious-subtle content of the clinical scales is discussed in the descriptive sections of the scales.

The following are examples of scale 1 items:

*29. I am bothered by acid stomach several times a week—(True)
189. I feel weak all over much of the time—(True)
243. I have few or no pains—(False)

The deviant direction for 67% (22 of the 33 items) is false. Most of the items on scale 1 overlap the other neurotic scales (D and Hy), and only four items overlap with scale 8 (schizophrenia) and one with scale 6 (paranoia) (Dahlstrom, Welsh, & Dahlstrom, 1972). Twenty of the 33 items on scale 1 are also scored on scale 3 (hysteria). Therefore, an elevated score on either scale tends to raise the other one. There are only 8 items unique (nonoverlapping) to scale 1. Appendix B contains a detailed presentation of the overlap and nonoverlap item content of scale 1. Increasing elevations on the scale correspond to increasing bodily complaints. Neurotics with bodily preoccupations tend to endorse a diffuse amount of item content relating to the body, whereas actual illness patients without psychological disturbance contain their item endorsements to the specific physical areas concerning them. Patients with actual physical illness are more likely to elevate scale 2 (depression) than scale 1. When examining scale 1 in a profile, it is important to note the amount of K being added. Because a one-half value of K is added to scale 1, a person may have important hypochondriacal concerns despite an unelevated score due to a low K value.

Although some MMPI experts consider scale 1 elevations to sometimes reflect transient symptoms such as the flu or a cold (Duckworth, 1979), it is generally considered to be a stable scale with test–retest coefficients for psychiatric cases ranging from .79 to .86 for up to a 2-week period and .38 to .65 for a 1-year interval (Dahlstrom, Welsh, & Dahlstrom, 1975).

In Hunsley et al.'s (1988) large-scale meta-analysis of MMPI reliability studies using a wide variety of populations conducted between 1970 and 1981,

---

an average internal consistency of .79 across 70 studies of scale 1 was reported. They also reported an average test–retest reliability of .78 for 16 studies with time intervals from one day to two years.

Scale 2—Depression (*D*)

Scale 2 was designed to measure symptomatic depression, which is a mood state typified by low morale, feelings of hopelessness and helplessness, general dissatisfaction, and sometimes preoccupations with death and suicide (Dahlstrom, Welsh, & Dahlstrom, 1972). Five subject groups were used to construct the scale, but most of the 60 items contained on the scale were derived by comparing normals, that is, subjects without observable depression, and a group of 50 patients who were carefully studied and diagnosed as being in the depressed phase of a manic-depressive psychosis (Hathaway & McKinley, 1942). Because some nondepressed subjects obtained elevated scores (false positives), a correction factor was derived (as was done in the construction of scale 1) by comparing item endorsement patterns of 40 normal individuals, who earned elevated depression scores on an early version of the scale, with a group of 50 patients without observable depressive signs, but who scored high on the early depression scale (Colligan, Osborne, Swenson, & Offord, 1983). A depressed normal group (i.e., the false positives) was used in the derivation of the scale "to help establish the meaning of more intermediate scale values between the normal and criterion groups, which would have been impossible if only the two extreme groups were contrasted" (Greene, 1980, p. 73). The 11 items that differentiated these two groups became correction items and were included in the final scale. Hathaway and McKinley (1942, as cited in Dahlstrom & Dahlstrom, 1980) described the final selection of scale items in the following way:

> First, each depressive item had to show a progressive increase in frequency from the normal groups through the depressed normal group to the criterion group since it was assumed that the depressed normals would be less depressed than the criterion cases but more than the general normals. In all items primarily indicating depression, the difference in percentage between the normal and the criterion was 2.5 or more times its standard error. Second, the nondepressed group percentage for the item was required to approach that for normals. After careful analysis of all percentages for each of the 504 items, 60 items were chosen as the final depression scale. (p. 26)

Scale 2 is considered to be a mood scale and is therefore sensitive to momentary and transient emotional states. It is useful in measuring treatment changes, because it is the most frequently elevated scale in the MMPI and the most frequent high point in an adult psychiatric population. Scale 2 appears second only to scale 4 in high-point frequency in adolescent patients (Marks, Seeman, & Haller, 1974). The majority of items on scale 2 are marked false (40 of the 60) for the deviant direction. Therefore, an all-false response set will inflate scale 2 scores as well as the other scales in the neurotic triad (scales 1, 2, and 3). Greene (1980) pointed out that it may seem odd that a psychotic criterion group was employed to develop a scale that is considered in the neurotic triad. He stated that the original test authors were most interested in the manifest characteristics of the manic-depressive illness and believed that these depressive features were similar to symptomatic depression stemming from reactive causes (e.g., loss of a loved one, financial difficulties, etc.). Consequently, they felt comfortable using patients suffering from the depressive symptoms of manic-depressive illness. In fact, these patients most likely met the criteria for major depression which today is not necessarily considered a psychotic illness.

Dahlstrom et al. (1975) reported reliability coefficients for psychiatric patients ranging between .88 and .96 for 1-day intervals and between .49 and .50 for 1-year intervals. Despite the sensitivity of the scale to transient mood shifts, it appears more stable than one would expect.

In Hunsley's et al. (1988) large-scale meta-analysis of MMPI reliability studies using a wide variety of populations conducted between 1970 and 1981, an average internal consistency of .81 across 74 studies of scale 2 was reported. They also reported an average test–retest reliability of .78 for 16 studies with time intervals from 1 day to 2 years.

There is extensive item overlap of scale 2 with other scales. Forty-seven of 60 items are about equally distributed on the other neurotic and psychotic scales, leaving only 13 items unique to scale 2 (Dahlstrom, Welsh, & Dahlstrom, 1972). Wiener and Harmon (1946) described the majority of items on scale 2 to be obvious in nature.

The following are examples of scale 2 subtle (*s*) and obvious (*o*) items:

*2. I have a good appetite—(False—*o*)
 5. I am easily awakened by noise—(True—*s*)
 30. At times I feel like swearing—(False—*s*)
178. My memory seems to be alright—(False—*o*)
236. I brood a great deal—(True—*o*)

Scale 3—Hysteria (*Hy*)

The description of the criterion group and normal sample used in the derivation of scale 3 is much more ambiguous and incomplete compared to the subjects used in constructing the other scales. Although no modal description or demographic data for hysteric patients were provided (Colligan et al., 1983), the 50 patients included in the criterion group did manifest the "neurotic defenses of the conversion form of hysteria" (Dahlstrom, Welsh, & Dahlstrom, 1972, p. 191).

These patients were seen as manifesting actual conversion hysteria symptoms involving an involuntary psychogenic loss or disorder of function (Graham, 1987) or hysterical personality features. In the former case, individuals developed physical symptoms that appeared to allow them to evade responsibilities and to escape from stressful and unpleasant situations. It was relatively easy for the test constructors to identify patients manifesting what they thought to be obvious conversion symptoms like the inability to use one's voice, but other cases with less dramatic symptomatology raised concerns about possible physical causes for the symptoms and made psychodiagnosis a more difficult and less certain task. It was thought that patients whose personality organization revolves around hysterical defenses tend to function adequately or even well under ordinary circumstances, but when faced with difficult situations a regression occurs with a breakdown of ego defenses. Dahlstrom, Welsh, and Dahlstrom (1972) noted that a need to detect such a predisposition for breakdown was necessary and was in part the motivation for the development of scale 3.

Scale 3 consists of 60 items, 47 (78%) of which are scored in the false direction for the deviant response. Therefore, like scales 1 and 2 in the neurotic triad, a tendency to endorse the MMPI items in the false direction will also elevate scale 3. Twenty items of scale 3 overlap with scale 1, the greatest degree of shared items for any of the scales on the MMPI. Other clinical scales share about equally in the item overlap distribution from scale 3. Greene (1980) pointed out that, "despite the absence of a K-correction value for Scale 3, the ten items shared between the K scale and Scale 3 operate to produce a result similar to K-correction" (p. 78). Examples of scale 3 subtle (s) and obvious (o) items are as follows:

*6. I like to read newspaper articles on crime—(False—s)

12. I enjoy detective or mystery stories—(False—s)

76. Most of the time I feel blue—(True—o)

238. I have periods of such great restlessness that I cannot sit long in a chair—(True—o)

The evenly split subtle and obvious content of the scale (Wiener & Harmon, 1946) consists of many somatic items overlapping scale 1 and refers to specific body regions such as the head or chest (Dahlstrom, Welsh, & Dahlstrom, 1972). A positive correlation exists between scale 1 and somatic scale 3 items due not only to extensive item overlap, but because of a common dimension in the elevated 1 and 3 scales, presumably neuroticism (Friedman, Gleser, Smeltzer, Wakefield, & Schwartz, 1983; Marks & Seeman, 1963). Initially, an attempt was made to reduce the overlapping somatic items between scales 1 and 3, but some items were returned to the *Hs* scale (Colligan et al., 1983).

A second subset of items within scale 3 indicates that an individual feels well-adjusted and comfortable with others, whereas a somewhat paradoxical third subset of items reflects sadness and lack of satisfaction, although not necessarily psychiatric involvement (e.g., I am worried about sex matters). The subsets of items describing somatic complaints and feelings of well-being and comfort are usually independent of each other or negatively correlated in normals but tend to be positively correlated in patients whose personality functioning is organized around hysteric psychodynamics. Generally, the more elevated and prominent the role of scale 3 in a code type, the less insightful the individual tends to be and the more likely it is that physical symptoms will emerge when under stress.

The test–retest correlation coefficients for psychiatric patients ranged between .66 and .80 for intervals between 1 and 2 weeks and between .36 and .72 for a 1-year interval between tests (Dahlstrom, Welsh, & Dahlstrom, 1975).

In Hunsley et al.'s (1988) large-scale meta-analysis of MMPI reliability studies using a wide variety of populations conducted between 1970 and 1981, an average internal consistency of .78 across 70 studies of scale 3 was reported. They also reported an average test–retest reliability of .74 for 15 studies with time intervals from 1 day to 2 years.

Scale 4—Psychopathic Deviate (*Pd*)

Scale 4 is named "psychopathic deviate" (*Pd*) and was developed to measure the "personality characteristics of the amoral and asocial subgroup of persons with psychopathic personality disorders." (Dahlstrom, Welsh, & Dahlstrom, 1972, p. 195). The criterion group consisted of more girls than boys ranging in age from 17 to 22, but the sample size was not reported (McKinley & Hathaway, 1944). The subjects were referred by the courts for study in a psychiatric setting; they had long histories of delinquent-type behaviors such as stealing, lying, alcohol abuse, promiscuity, forgery, and truancy (McKinley & Hathaway, 1944). They did not have histories of major crimes or a neurotic or psychotic diagnosis. The common denominator across subjects seemed to be that they had low anticipation of the consequences of their behavior and could not seem to "learn those anticipatory anxieties which operate to deter most people from committing anti-social behavior" (Marks, Seeman, & Haller, 1974, p. 25). Essentially, individuals with psychopathic traits were seen as lacking in their ability to form warm and stable bonds to others, to appreciate social customs and abide by societal rules, and to profit from experiences that had negative consequences. These individuals may appear free from disabling anxiety and not be perceived as particularly troubled or disturbed until found in a situation demanding the use of inner resources that the psychopathic individual lacks. The general social maladjustment that characterizes these individuals leads to dissatisfaction with the self and others and can result in strong feelings of social and self-alienation.

The normal comparison group consisted of college freshmen receiving guidance at the University of Minnesota and married Minnesota subjects who were considerably older. The average age of these latter subjects was 35, so the college sample tended to introduce some balance. Cross-validation procedures involved 100 prisoners and 78 psychiatric inpatients. Five preliminary scales were developed before the final items were selected for inclusion on the *Pd* scale. Scale 4 was termed the psychopathic deviate scale because it was viewed as being able to measure or detect some types of psychopathic deviation; specifically, the scale could correctly identify approximately half of the cross-validational criterion subjects (Greene, 1980). The addition of .4 of scale *K* to scale 4 improved its ability to make diagnostic discriminations, and this value (.4*K*) is generally added to the raw score on the *Pd* scale.

The item content on scale 4 is broad, covering areas from family and personal dissatisfaction to difficulties with authorities and paranoid proclivities. Some examples from the subtle (*s*) and obvious (*o*) items on scale 4 are as follows:

*21. At times I have very much wanted to leave home — (True — *s*)

24. No one seems to understand me — (True — *o*)

82. I am easily downed in an argument — (False — *s*)

110. Someone has it in for me — (True — *o*)

137. I believe that my home life is as pleasant as that of most people I know — (False — *o*)

The item content of the scale is multidimensional as opposed to the unidimensional content of scale 1, which measures an individual's perception of his or her physical health. Factor analytic studies on scale 4 typically identify four or five factors given the broad range of items (Greene, 1980). Dahlstrom, Welsh, and Dahlstrom (1972) described the results of Comrey's (1958) and Austin's (1959, 1961) factor analytic investigations and reported that hypersensitivity and poor impulse control were two of the many factors emerging from their work. Wiener and Harmon (1946) indicated somewhat more obvious than subtle items on scale 4. The critical or deviant direction for the items is almost evenly split between true and false. Ten out of 50 items are nonoverlapping or unique to scale 4, with the remaining 40 overlapping items being distributed over the clinical scales and scales *F* and *K*. Scale 4 shares only 1 overlapping item with scale 1 and 1 or 2 with scale 5, depending on whether male or female norms are being utilized. Scales 3 and 8 both share 10 items with scale 4, and scales 2 and 3 share 7 and 10 items, respectively, with scale 4. The fact that there are 7 scale 4 items overlapping with scale 2 (depression) may be consistent with the situational or

---

Credit: Minnesota Multiphasic Personality Inventory (MMPI). Copyright © The University of Minnesota 1943, renewed 1970. Reproduced by permission of the University of Minnesota Press.

state condition of the criterion subjects at the time of testing. Greene (1980) pointed out that because all the members of the criterion group were involved in legal proceedings and/or incarcerated, it is likely that they manifested depressive moods more reflective of their situation rather than an inherent tendency to feel depressed. The reader is referred to appendix B for a more detailed presentation of the overlapping item content of scale 4. Scale 4 typically is reported as the most frequently occurring high-point scale in adolescents and is often observed as one of the high-point pairs in adolescent psychiatric samples (Marks, Seeman, & Haller, 1974). It is also the high point (usually below a T-score of 70) for police applicants and psychology graduate students (Duckworth, 1979).

In psychiatric cases, test–retest correlation coefficients for 1- to 2-day intervals ranged between .69 and .75 and between .48 and .49 for 1-year intervals between tests (Dahlstrom, Welsh, & Dahlstrom, 1975).

In Hunsley et al.'s (1988) large-scale meta-analysis of MMPI reliability studies using a wide variety of populations conducted between 1970 and 1981, an average internal consistency of .81 across 71 studies of scale 4 was reported. They also reported an average test–retest reliability of .71 for 16 studies with time intervals from 1 day to 2 years.

Scale 5—Masculinity-Femininity (*Mf*)

The exact motivation of the test authors for developing scale 5 could be somewhat unclear to readers consulting different texts, as different accounts exist explaining the scale's origins. For example, Dahlstrom, Welsh, and Dahlstrom (1972), generally considered the most reliable historical chroniclers of the MMPI, stated that:

> Scale 5 was designed to identify the personality features related to the disorder of male sexual inversion. This syndrome is another homogeneous subgroup in the general category of psychopathic personality, sometimes called pathological sexuality. The group, like the psychopathic deviate group, shows considerably more uniformity than is found in the psychopathic personality category as a whole. Persons with this personality pattern often engage in homoerotic practices as part of their feminine emotional makeup; however, many of these men are too inhibited or full of conflicts to make any overt expression of their sexual preferences. (p. 201)

The individual with this type of personality pattern is viewed as psychopathological, yet Colligan et al. (1983) indicated that the 1943 *MMPI Manual* describes the *Mf* scale as intending to measure "the tendency toward masculinity or femininity of interest pattern in the direction of the opposite sex" (*MMPI Manual*, 1943, cited by Colligan et al., 1983, p. 40). Clearly, the manual's description differs from the more psychopathological account given by Dahlstrom, Welsh, and Dahlstrom (1972) in describing the origins and intent of scale

5. The test constructors (Hathaway, 1956) apparently discovered that it was too difficult then to obtain a large enough group of homosexual males and females possessing enough similar qualities to classify into a single criterion group. At least three subgroups of homosexuals were identified with different etiologies for their homosexuality. One subgroup was a pseudo-homosexual type with neurotic features related to inferiority, another subgroup was a psychopathic type who tended to elevate scale 4 (*Pd*), and a third subgroup became the final reference criterion group. This group consisted of 13 homosexual invert males (Hathaway, 1956). There were no demographic data reported for these subjects. However, they were screened for gross psychological abnormalities, like psychosis, and any clear neurotic tendencies. They were also considered free of psychopathy (Dahlstrom & Welsh, 1960). These individuals were seen as having a feminine emotional makeup. However, many were considered too inhibited or conflicted to express their homoerotic sexual preferences. Their feminism was believed to be apparent in their expressive styles, interests, and attitudes as well as in their sexual relationships (Dahlstrom, Welsh, & Dahlstrom, 1972). Greene (1980) stated that, "such persons were thought to engage in homoerotic behavior as a part of their feminine (i.e., inverted) personality characteristics" (p. 90).

Many of the items used to develop scale 5 were added after the original Minnesota normative group had already participated in the various scale constructions, consequently, newly formed normal groups were selected for comparison purposes. The latter group consisted of 67 female airline employees and 54 soldiers. Three basic comparisons resulted in the addition of 55 new items in the MMPI pool. When an item differentiated a soldier from a criterion group subject (male homosexual inverts), the item was said to be a trend in the direction of femininity on the part of male sexual inverts (Hathaway & McKinley, 1943). A second comparison step in item selection involved identifying a group of males scoring in the feminine direction on an invert index derived by Terman and Miles (1936). The item endorsements of these invert males were then compared to a group of normals. The use of the invert scale from Terman and Miles' (1936) Attitude Interest Analysis Test "represents the first time that items from one diagnostic test were used to select a contrast group that was then employed as an additional criterion group used for selecting items on an MMPI scale" (cited in Colligan et al., 1983, p. 44). A third comparison step that appears to have been conducted initially but is considered the least important by Hathaway (1956) involved comparing the normal males (soldiers) to normal females (airline employees) to determine the response frequencies by sex.

The 60 items that persevered through all three comparison steps became scale 5. Twenty-three of the scale 5 items are borrowed from Terman and Miles (1936), whereas the other 37 items came from the MMPI item pool.

Despite their efforts, the test authors were unable to successfully construct an independent scale measuring female homosexual inversion. The final *Mf* scale was believed to measure masculinity at one end of the scale and femininity at the opposite pole. The scale was seen as being bipolar. However, as other researchers (Bem, 1974) suggested, masculinity and femininity may be more accurately assessed using separate scales for each dimension. They may each represent a different construct. On the other hand, Bem's measures of sex role are not independent of masculinity vs femininity scales such as scale 5 of the MMPI (Wakefield, Sasek, Friedman, & Bowden, 1976). Also, the psychometric adequacy of Bem's femininity scale has been criticized (Kimlicka, Wakefield, & Friedman, 1980; Kimlicka, Wakefield, & Goad, 1982). Recent studies (e.g., Kimlicka, Sheppard, Wakefield, & Cross, 1987) suggest that bipolar *Mf* scales have not yet been, and may not be, replaced by separate *M* and *F* factors.

Factor analytic studies of scale 5 indicate the scale is composed of multiple factors (Sines, 1977). Given the multidimensional content of scale 5, Greene (1980) cautioned MMPI users about making inferences of masculinity and femininity based on scale 5 elevations. The item content of scale 5 is varied and to a degree does seem to reflect, among other things, masculine and feminine interest patterns. Items reflecting masculine-feminine interests appear to have the highest biserial correlations; that is, they tend to have the highest correlation with overall scale scores and therefore are considered the most differentiating items on the scale (Dahlstrom, Welsh, & Dahlstrom, 1972). Although the interest-type items are obvious or face-valid, there are other items on the scale with more subtle meaning. For example, group booklet item 213 "In walking I am very careful to step over sidewalk cracks" (Hathaway & McKinley, 1983) is keyed in the false direction for both males and females. A true response would earn both males and females a point in the masculine direction. Apparently, this item empirically differentiated the criterion groups, and no obvious theoretical explanation (except perhaps post hoc) can be offered. Serkownek (1975) identified six subscales that are named: narcissism-hypersensitivity, stereotypic feminine interest, denial of stereotypic masculine interest, heterosexual discomfort-passivity, introspective-critical, and socially retiring. These subscales indicate there is a range of item content on scale 5. Examples of scale 5 items, including similarity to and differences from the aforementioned subscales, are:

Sexual Proclivities:

*69. I am very strongly attracted by members of my own sex—(scored True for males and False for females)

Social Activities:

99. I like to go to parties and other affairs when there is a lot of loud fun—(False)

Credit: Minnesota Multiphasic Personality Inventory (MMPI). Copyright © The University of Minnesota 1943, renewed 1970. Reproduced by permission of the University of Minnesota Press.

Hobbies:

132. I like collecting flowers or growing house-plants—(True)

Types of Work:

219. I think I would like the work of a building contractor—(False)

Personal Sensitivities:

299. I think that I feel more intensely than most people do—(True)

The same 60 items are used to evaluate masculinity-femininity for males and females, with 55 items keyed in the same critical scoring directions for both males and females. For females, high T-scores on the profile sheet are associated with low raw scores, indicating a response to the items in a masculine direction. For males, the converse is true, with high raw scores associated with high T-scores. Therefore, a male with a high raw score or high T-score is said to be endorsing scale 5 items the way in which the opposite sex stereotypically responds. Low T-scores in males reflect a low endorsement of feminine-type items and indicates a more masculine interest pattern. The reason for reversing the raw scores on the profile sheet is to maintain uniformity with the other scales, in that high scores represent a form of deviation. In the case of scale 5, elevated T-scores represent endorsement patterns similar to the opposite sex.

Five items in the 60-item Mf scale deal with clear sexual concerns and represent a scoring exception in that they are not keyed in the same direction for both females and males. The critical scoring direction for these 5 items is opposite for males and females. For example, group booklet item 133 "I have never indulged in any unusual sex practices" is scored true for females and false for males. The other 4 items dealing with sexual concerns are keyed true for males and false for females (group booklet item 69, 179, 231, and 297). Because of the obvious nature of these 5 Mf items dealing with sexual concerns, someone wishing to conceal his or her sexual concerns could easily do so. Wiener and Harmon (1946) did not classify scale 5 items into obvious-subtle types, presumably because of the obvious or face-valid nature of the items.

The meaning of scale 5 elevations differs for males and females and is described in chapter 6. The scale does appear more sensitive to interest patterns than it does to sexual preferences, and therefore it is important not to infer homosexuality based on elevated Mf scores (Todd & Gynther, 1988). In fact, it is difficult to predict homosexuality solely from MMPI data.

Test–retest correlation coefficients for psychiatric cases range between .79 and .83 for a 1- to 2-day interval and between .77 and .91 for college students. The correlation coefficients for 1- to 2-week intervals between test administrations in psychiatric cases range between .76 and .79, and .72 is given for male college students (Dahlstrom, Welsh, & Dahlstrom, 1975).

In Hunsley's et al. (1988) large-scale meta-analysis of MMPI reliability studies using a wide variety of populations conducted between 1970 and 1981, an average internal consistency of .73 across 39 studies of scale 5 was reported. They also reported an average test–retest reliability of .69 for 10 studies with time intervals from 1 day to 2 years.

Scale 6—Paranoia (*Pa*)

There is no available information describing the exact way the paranoid criterion group was selected, nor are any data obtainable about the demographic character-istics of the subjects. It is assumed that the usual item selection procedures were employed as with the other MMPI scales. The criterion patients, according to Hathaway (1956), had a diagnosis of paranoid state, paranoid condition, or paranoid schizophrenia. The scale was developed to assess paranoid symptoms and features. The patients studied in the criterion group manifested various signs of paranoia including ideas of reference, feelings of persecution, grandiose self-concepts, hypersensitivity, rigid thinking, and suspiciousness. The content of scale 6 includes items of a frank psychotic nature consistent with the aforementioned paranoid characteristics, whereas other items are more subtle in nature. Wiener and Harmon (1946), found that 17 of the 40 scale 6 items are subtle in nature, with 23 judged to be obvious. The following are examples of subtle (*s*) and obvious (*o*) scale 6 items:

*15. Once in a while I think of things too bad to talk about—(True—*s*)

  35. If people had not had it in for me, I would have been much more successful—(True—*o*)

 111. I have never done anything dangerous for the thrill of it—(False—*s*)

 123. I believe I am being followed—(True—*o*)

 319. Most people inwardly dislike putting themselves out to help other people—(False—*s*)

Sixty three percent (25 items) are scored true to produce a deviant response with 37% (15 items) scored false to produce a deviant response. As with all the scales of the psychotic tetrad (scales 6, 7, 8, and 9) an all-true response set will elevate scale 6. There are 7 nonoverlapping items on scale 6, with the remaining 33 items sharing the most overlap with scales 8 (13 items) and scale *F* (9 items) (Greene, 1980).

   The test–retest correlation coefficients for psychiatric cases range between .61 and .71 with a 1- to 2-day interval between testing, and between .59 and .65 for a 1-year interval between testing (Dahlstrom, Welsh, & Dahlstrom, 1975).

Credit: Minnesota Multiphasic Personality Inventory (MMPI). Copyright © The University of Minnesota 1943, renewed 1970. Reproduced by permission of the University of Minnesota Press.

In Hunsley et al.'s (1988) large-scale meta-analysis of MMPI reliability studies using a wide variety of populations conducted between 1970 and 1981, an average internal consistency of .73 across 70 studies of scale 6 was reported. They also reported an average test–retest reliability of .69 for 15 studies with time intervals from 1 day to 2 years.

Scale 7—Psychasthenia (*Pt*)

Scale 7 was designed to measure a neurotic pattern called *psychasthenia,* a term introduced by Pierre Janet (Marks, Seeman, & Haller, 1974), but which is no longer generally used. The concept of psychasthenia involves an inability to resist undesired, maladapted behaviors, which McKinley and Hathaway (1942) described as deriving from the concept of a "weakened will" (p. 616). Individuals classified as having psychasthenic tendencies were described as having excessive self-doubts leading to tension, difficulties in making choices, various fears, obsessive preoccupations, compulsive urges and acts, vague anxieties, and feelings of low self-confidence and insecurity. These individuals might find themselves ruminating about meaningless facts (like repeatedly counting unimportant objects) leading to a sense of loss of control over their thought processes resulting in high anxiety levels. However, scale 7 does not contain items reflecting specific phobias and compulsions, because individual differences between subjects probably failed to permit an item to be endorsed with sufficient frequency to survive an item analysis. It is believed, therefore, that the underlying personality structure of psychasthenia, rather than specific fears and/or phobias, is reflected in the content of scale 7. Marks, Seeman, and Haller (1974) stated, "although the specific fears, preoccupations, and compulsive acts are different from individual to individual and are potentially innumerable, the personality makeup of such persons has sufficient homogeneity to comprise a recognizable common pattern" (p. 28).

Scale 7 consists of 48 items that were derived by using the usual empirical method of contrasting the criterion group to a mixed group of normals and by selecting additional items that correlated with a total scale score. Specifically, the scale constructors selected 20 psychiatric inpatients as their criterion subjects, a relatively small sample. It was apparently very difficult to locate outpatients with this syndrome, and few patients were so severely handicapped by their condition as to require hospitalization. McKinley and Hathaway (1942) admitted that even with the small group of carefully examined inpatients, there was at least one and possibly more incorrectly diagnosed subjects. The item endorsements of the 20 criterion cases were compared to a group of 139 normal married males ranging in age from 26 to 43 and 200 normal married females aged between 26 and 43. Additionally, 265 college students were included in a separate comparison to ascertain the effects of age on item endorsements. Once items were identified as differentiating the criterion group from the two normal groups, an additional item analysis was performed correlating each item with the total scale score in a sample of 100 randomly selected psychiatric patients and 100 normal persons. Due to the small number of criterion cases studied, the scale was not cross-validated at the time it was published (McKinley & Hathaway, 1942). However, the scale appears to be internally consistent with split-half values that are almost as high as the test–retest coefficients. The content of the scale seems to indicate an underlying personality structure for the various psychasthenic symptoms it is measuring. The 48 items on scale 7 measure feelings of low self-confidence and doubts about one's abilities, as well as anxiety, heightened sensitivity, and moodiness (Dahlstrom, Welsh, & Dahlstrom, 1972). The following are examples of scale 7 items:

*3. I wake up fresh and rested most mornings—(False)

86. I am certainly lacking in self-confidence—(True)

178. My memory seems to be alright—(False)

217. I frequently find myself worrying about something—(True)

317. I am more sensitive than most other people—(True)

337. I feel anxiety about something or someone almost all of the time—(True)

The items appear to be highly face-valid, that is, they lack subtlety. Because the items are obvious in nature, Wiener and Harmon (1946) did not develop obvious-subtle scales for scale 7. True is the critical scoring direction for 81% (39 of the 48 items), and therefore an all-true response set would elevate scale 7. The addition of a full K value (the entire raw K score) to scale 7 can help correct for a defensive response set affecting scale 7 elevation, and a space is provided on the profile sheet to add 1.0 K to the Pt raw score. Scale 7 has 9 nonoverlapping items, with most of its overlapping content being shared with scale 8 (17 items).

Test–retest coefficients for psychiatric patients on scale 7 range from between .83 and .86 for 1- to 2-week intervals between administrations and between .49 and .58 for 1-year intervals between tests (Dahlstrom, Welsh, & Dahlstrom, 1975).

In Hunsley et al.'s (1988) large-scale meta-analysis of MMPI reliability studies using a wide variety of populations conducted between 1970 and 1981, an average internal consistency of .84 across 70 studies of scale 7 was reported. They also reported an average test–retest reliability of .82 for 16 studies with time intervals from 1 day to 2 years.

Scale 8—Schizophrenia (*Sc*)

It is not surprising that the development of scale 8 was the most difficult of all the clinical scales to construct because schizophrenia involves diverse behavioral, emotional, and cognitive symptoms. Although more research time was devoted to this scale than the others, it is still considered one of the weaker diagnostic scales (Marks & Seeman, 1963). The best ability of the scale to detect schizophrenia after refinement was 60% (Hathaway, 1956). Four preliminary scales were derived before the final version, named *Sc,* was accepted and cross-validated. These preliminary scales were all based on a criterion group of 50 patients with a diagnosis of schizophrenia. Different subtypes of schizophrenia (catatonic, paranoid, simple, and hebephrenic) were included in the criterion group, and about 60% of the subjects were female and about 40% were males. Hathaway (1956) did not offer exact definitional features of the criterion subjects, but Dahlstrom, Welsh, and Dahlstrom (1972) stated the following:

> Most commonly persons showing this psychiatric reaction are characterized as constrained, cold, and apathetic or indifferent. Other people see them as remote and inaccessible, often seemingly sufficient unto themselves. Delusions of varying degrees of organization, hallucinations, either fleeting or persistent and compelling, and disorientation may appear in various combinations. Inactivity, or endless stereotypy, may accompany the withdrawal of interest from other people or external objects and relationships. These persons frequently perform below the levels expected of them on the basis of their training and ability. (p. 215)

Nichols (1988) pointed out that it is very likely that the criterion group of schizophrenics was contaminated with a large minority of affectively disordered subjects. Typically, schizophrenia has been grossly overdiagnosed in this country, whereas affective disorders have been underdiagnosed, especially in relation to each other. Because there is much symptom overlap between the two syndromes, many affectively disordered subjects were probably inaccurately classified as schizophrenics. In contrast, few false positive classifications were likely made in constructing the criterion group for scale 9 (hypomania), as manic patients with schizophrenic-like symptoms were excluded. Therefore, Nichols (1988) stated that scale 9 was probably rendered an "unusually valid measure of the core features of the manic syndrome" (p. 80).

Current psychiatric consensus recognizes schizophrenia as a group of disorders with a biogenic etiological basis (Eysenck, Wakefield, & Friedman, 1983; Gallagher & Jones, 1987). Diagnostic criteria for a schizophrenic disorder according to the *Diagnostic and Statistical Manual* (American Psychiatric Association, 3rd ed., 1980) include impairment in various psychological processes involving thinking, perceiving, feeling, and behaving, with no specific feature pathognomonic of the disorder. Often a deterioration from a previous level of functioning is observed, with continuous signs of the disorder necessary for at least 6 months during the individual's life. Various symptoms precede the illness (prodromal) or remain (residual) after the active phase of the disorder. These symptoms often vary between individuals and include social withdrawal, inappropriate affect, bizarre ideation, odd behavior, and digressive, vague, circumstantial speech. According to Marks and Seeman (1963), "As a result, the clinician talking to a schizophrenic patient often wonders 'how did we get to this?' because progression toward a goal of thought is so devious and so frequently interrupted" (p. 29).

Despite the many efforts to improve the detection ability of scale 8, it was not until the K scale was developed by Meehl and Hathaway (1946, cited in Dahlstrom & Dahlstrom, 1980) and used as a device to improve the discriminative ability of scale 8 that it was finally complete. The addition of one full K value to scale 8 helped to reduce the number of false positives or high-scoring normals from a high of 15% to 2%. By adding K to the raw score on scale 8, the T-scores for the criterion subjects (schizophrenics) and normals were both raised, but the T-scores of the criterion group were raised greater relative to the normals. Presumably, the reason the schizophrenics failed to be identified was the denial or minimizing of psychopathology associated with K. Adding K to their scores corrects for this minimizing tendency, which is not as pronounced in the normals. It is now customary to add the value of 1.0 raw K to the raw score of scale 8 before plotting the standard score on the patient's profile sheet. Because one full K value is added to scale 8, it is possible to obtain an elevated scale 8 score (above a T-score of 70) with approximately 20 scale 8 items endorsed in the deviant direction and an average score on the K scale (Greene, 1980). Therefore, it is important to examine the raw score on scale 8 as well as the endorsed item content before inferring any psychotic-type diagnosis from an isolated scale 8 elevation. Usually a diagnostic conclusion of schizophrenia cannot be made solely on the basis of a scale 8 elevation. The relationship of other scale elevations and patterns must be examined, as well as special indices, in order to confidently and accurately identify schizophrenic patients. The following are examples of scale 8 items that are all considered to be obvious in nature. Wiener and Harmon (1946) did not develop subtle-obvious categories for scale 8, as most of the items are obvious in nature.

*103. I have little or no trouble with my muscles twitching or jumping—(False)

305. Even when I am with people I feel lonely much of the time—(True)

334. Peculiar odors come to me at times—(True)

339. Most of the time I wish I were dead—(True)

---

350. I hear strange things when I am alone—(True)

358. I am worried about sex matters—(True)

Scale 8 is the longest scale, with 78 items. Consequently, there is a great deal of item overlap with other clinical scales, especially the other psychotic scales and scale *F*, with which it has 15 items in common. Scale 8 has the most overlap with scale 7, with 17 items in common. There are 16 items unique (nonoverlapping) to scale 8. As is the case for the other psychotic scales, the abnormal direction of endorsement for the majority of scale 8 items is true; specifically, 59 (76%) of the 78 items on the scale are scored as true.

Scale 8 test–retest coefficients for psychiatric cases ranged between .75 and .82 with a 1- to 2-day interval between tests and between .56 and .64 for a 1-year interval between tests (Dahlstrom, Welsh, & Dahlstrom, 1975).

In Hunsley et al.'s (1988) large-scale meta-analysis of MMPI reliability studies using a wide variety of populations conducted between 1970 and 1981, an average internal consistency of .82 across 73 studies of scale 8 was reported. They also reported an average test–retest reliability of .78 for 17 studies with time intervals from 1 day to 2 years.

Scale 9—Hypomania (*Ma*)

Scale 9 (*Ma*) consists of 46 items measuring the milder aspects of an elevated mood that often is accompanied by a flight of ideas, affective lability, and psychomotor excitement. The personality pattern the scale reflects is the affective disorder termed *hypomania*. Hypomania indicates heightened activity levels with accompanying symptoms or traits such as easy distractibility, insomnia, overoptimism, occasional grandiosity, suspiciousness, and irascibility. Less severe cases of the same or similar psychopathological condition were selected for study because florid, manic-type patients would be unable to focus their attention and behavior on sorting inventory items into appropriate categories. It is obviously not necessary to use a psychological test to identify full-blown manic cases, as their behavior speaks louder than words, but more subtle or moderate cases of the same disorder are best identified early so that treatment options and prognosis can be considered. Scale 9 is useful in identifying such forms of psychopathy, maladapted overactivity, and agitated depressions (Dahlstrom & Dahlstrom, 1980).

The selection of items for scale 9 was accomplished using basically the same procedures as for the other clinical scales. Normals and criterion group cases consisting of 24 psychiatric inpatients responded to 550 separate inventory items. Items that significantly differentiated the two groups were retained for preliminary inclusion on scale 9, with 46 items finally representing the scale. There are no available demographic data reported on the criterion subjects (Colligan et al., 1983). The 24 criterion patients were studied as psychiatric inpatients at the

University of Minnesota Hospital. Patients with severe conditions of mania were excluded, as they would be unable to cooperate adequately. Therefore, the diagnostic conditions were either mild acute mania or hypomania (Dahlstrom & Dahlstrom, 1980). Patients were excluded from study if they were delirious, confused, schizophrenic, or depressed with agitation. The test constructors recognized the small number of cases in their criterion group and conceded that "in spite of the small number of criterion and test cases available, a scale for hypomania is presented. It is the best that we could derive from the patients seen over a five-year period" (McKinley & Hathaway, 1944, cited in Dahlstrom & Dahlstrom, 1980, p. 57).

The heterogeneous item content in scale 9 covers the classic features of a hypomanic syndrome, such as excitement and heightened activity levels and grandiosity or expansiveness. Other items describe moral attitudes and family relationships as well as body concerns. The following examples are subtle (s) and obvious (o) items from scale 9:

*21. At times I have very much wanted to leave home—(True—s)

 97. At times I have a strong urge to do something harmful or shocking— (True—o)

105. Sometimes when I am not feeling well I am cross—(False—s)

166. My speech is the same as always (not faster nor slower, or slurring, no hoarseness)—(False—s)

250. I don't blame anyone for trying to grab everything he can get in this world—(True—o)

Wiener and Harmon (1946) determined that the scale has 23 obvious and 23 subtle items. The predominant deviant response to the items is true (35/46) as it is for the other psychotic scales (Greene, 1980). Therefore, an all-true response set would elevate scale 9 with the other scales in the psychotic tetrad. Other than scale 8, with which it shares 11 overlap items, scale 9 shares few overlap items relative to the other scales. Fifteen of the 46 items are unique to the scale. Commercially available profile sheets provide for adding .2 of the full K value to scale 9, as this value has been shown to increase the ability of the scale to make accurate diagnostic discriminations. Scores on scale 9 tend to be related to age, with older individuals obtaining lower scores (reflecting less energy and activity levels and more body concerns) and late-adolescent or younger subjects, such as teenagers, tending to score in the upper-normal to moderate range, which could be considered indicative of impulse control problems (Greene, 1980). Age should, therefore, be considered when examining scale 9. Consistent results have not emerged regarding the effects of race on scale scores. But Gynther (1979a) described various demographic effects on MMPI scales, and Blacks do appear to score higher on scale 9 compared to whites, although not dramatically so. The effects of demographic factors are more fully considered in chapter 4.

Test–retest correlation coefficients for psychiatric cases with a 1- to 2-day interval between tests ranged between .71 and .81 and between .43 and .52 with a 1-year interval between tests (Dahlstrom, Welsh, & Dahlstrom, 1975).

In Hunsley et al.'s (1988) large-scale meta-analysis of MMPI reliability studies using a wide variety of populations conducted between 1970 and 1981, an average internal consistency of .71 across 73 studies of scale 9 was reported. They also reported an average test–retest reliability of .65 for 17 studies with time intervals from 1 day to 2 years.

Scale 0—Social Introversion (*Si*)

The 70-item social introversion (*Si*) scale (scale 0) was designed to evaluate an individual's degree of introversion-extroversion (Drake, 1946). Its construction was motivated by the use of a test being routinely administered in the guidance program at the University of Wisconsin. This test was developed by Evans and McConnell (1941) and designated as the Minnesota *T-S-E* Inventory (*T*-thinking, *S*-social, and *E*-emotional). Evans and McConnell separated the character traits of introversion-extroversion into areas of thinking, social activity, and emotional expression. An individual could be considered as introverted or extroverted in any of these three areas. Because the MMPI was also part of the standard battery of tests being administered to students, Drake (1946) decided to devise a scale measuring social introversion from the MMPI that would produce data similar to the *T-S-E* Inventory. He began by establishing the criterion groups.[5] Two groups were selected, with the first group consisting of 50 female students ranking at the 65th percentile or higher on the social introversion-extroversion dimension of the *T-S-E* Inventory. The second group consisted of 50 female students who scored below the 35th percentile.[6] Although the scale was constructed with all

---

[5]The *Si* scale is the only clinical scale on the MMPI for which the criterion group was comprised of a nonpsychiatric (normal) sample (Marks, Seeman, & Haller, 1974). The reader may question whether the criterion subjects employed in constructing scale 5 were also normal, as the homosexual men employed in the criterion group were said to be free of psychotic, neurotic, and psychopathic tendencies. In assembling scale 5, the test constructors apparently viewed the personality traits associated with what they termed "male sexual inversion" (Dahlstrom, Welsh, & Dahlstrom, 1972, p. 201) as belonging to a category of pathological sexuality. Their intention in constructing the scale was to be able to detect sexual inversion patterns, and this seems to indicate that they viewed such patterns as psychopathological. This is a somewhat different view of a homosexual type of orientation by current psychiatric standards, as no homosexual personality disorder per se currently exists (American Psychiatric Association, 1980).

females, it was later validated with males. Because males and females scored so similarly, Drake considered them as a single group for purposes of establishing the normative base. The only other factor used in creating the two criterion groups of high- and low-scoring females on the *I-E* scale of the *T-S-E* Inventory was the elimination of three subjects scoring high on the *L* scale of the MMPI. The items in the MMPI pool that differentiated these two groups (after removing items with very high or very low endorsement frequencies in either or both groups) became the 70-item social *I-E* scale (Drake, 1946), later known as scale 0 (*Si*) on the MMPI. After the 70 items were identified that discriminated the two criterion groups, a new group of MMPI record sheets was scored with the new scoring key for social introversion-extroversion. "These MMPI record sheets contain the responses of a group of students who had cleared through the testing office after the group of students who provided the data for the Item Analyses" (Drake, 1946 as cited in Dahlstrom & Dahlstrom, 1980, p. 77). The scores were then correlated with the social *I-E* scores obtained on the *T-S-E* Inventory and yielded a correlation coefficient of $-.72$ for 87 females and $-.71$ for a sample of 81 male students.[7] Norms were reported in terms of T-scores and were based on the test records of 193 male students and 350 female students. As stated previously, male and female scores were so similar that the norms were combined for both sexes (Drake, 1946). In a subsequent study, Drake and Thiede (1948) obtained additional cross-validation for scale 0 by examining the level of high school and college activity participation in a sample of 594 female college students. Students tending to participate in more activities were shown to score higher on extroversion, whereas those with lower activity participation scores scored higher on introversion. The concept of introversion and extroversion has a rich history in psychology and is one of Jung's original personality types (Jacobi, 1968). The developers of the Minnesota *T-S-E* Inventory conceptualized social introversion as indicating a withdrawal from social responsibilities and contacts, with little real interest in people, and social extroversion as involving an interest in social contacts with a strong interest in others (Dahlstrom, Welsh, & Dahlstrom, 1972). The final *Si* scale may be limited by any of the biases inherent in the *T-S-E* Inventory because the criterion groups of social introverts and extroverts were derived from scores on the social *I-E* scale (Dahlstrom, Welsh, & Dahlstrom, 1972).

Elevated scores on scale 0 indicate introversion tendencies, whereas scores below a *T*-score of 50 indicate extroversion tendencies. Many researchers and

---

[6]The female students were studied in 1944 and 1945, and men were not included in further validation studies because of the danger that the war would most likely have left an extremely biased and atypical male sample on college campuses (Drake & Thiede, 1948).

[7]The correlation coefficients yielded negative values because a low score on the *T-S-E* Inventory indicates introversion, whereas a high score on the MMPI indicates introversion.

clinicians believe there are strong constitutional and biological factors contributing to the introversion-extroversion dimension of personality (Eysenck, 1967; Meyer, 1983; Wakefield, Wood, Wallace, & Friedman, 1978). The stability of scores on this scale over time seem to reflect this biological and/or constitutional component. Test–retest correlation coefficients tend to be in support of this contention, with generally high test–retest coefficients for the scale. The coefficients for psychiatric patients with a 1- to 2-week interval between tests ranged between .80 and .88 and between .63 and .64 for a 1-year interval between tests (Dahlstrom, Welsh, & Dahlstrom, 1975).

In Hunsley et al.'s (1988) large-scale meta-analysis of MMPI reliability studies using a wide variety of populations conducted between 1970 and 1981, an average internal consistency of .81 across 41 studies of scale 0 was reported. They also reported an average test–retest reliability of .86 for 16 studies with time intervals from one day to two years.

The item content of scale 0 broadly reflects a dimension of introversion-extroversion that strongly emerges as a primary dimension from statistical studies of the MMPI (Friedman, 1982; Gentry, Wakefield, & Friedman, 1985; Wakefield, 1979; Wakefield, Bradley, Doughtie, & Kraft, 1975). The items appear to reflect uneasiness in social situations, feelings of inferiority and discomfort, unhappiness, shyness, and hypersensitivity. Wiener and Harmon (1946) did not classify the items into subtle and obvious categories. The following are examples of scale 0 items:

*138. Criticism or scolding hurts me terribly—(True)

 201. I wish I were not so shy—(True)

 236. I brood a great deal—(True)

 371. I am not unusually self-conscious—(False)

Scale 0 has proportionately fewer overlap items than any other scale (Greene, 1980). Twenty-six nonoverlapping items appear on scale 0. Scales 7 and 2 share the most items with scale 0 (8 and 7 items respectively). Thirty-four of the 70 items are scored as deviant if marked true, whereas 36 items are scored as deviant if marked false.

FORMS

Various forms of the MMPI exist and are described in the *MMPI Manual* (Hathaway & McKinley, 1983). The most commonly used forms are discussed here. (All commercially available MMPI test forms can be purchased from

---

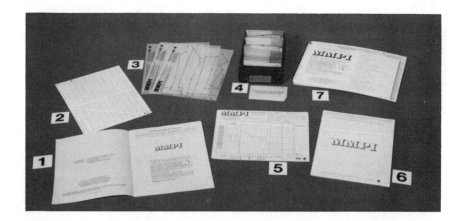

FIG. 1.1.   1. Group booklet form. 2. Group booklet answer sheet. 3. Plastic scoring templates. 4. Card form. 5. Profile sheet. 6. *MMPI Manual*. 7. Form *R* with answer sheet. (*Source:* Minnesota Multiphasic Personality Inventory [MMPI]. Copyright © The University of Minnesota 1943, renewed 1970. Reproduced by permission of the University of Minnesota Press.)

Professional Assessment Services of National Computer Systems [NCS], P.O. Box 1416, Minneapolis, MN 55440 [1-800-328-6759], the only authorized distributor of the test.) As the MMPI is a restricted instrument, only test users with proper qualifications may purchase materials through NCS. The purpose of such restricted availability is to insure, as much as possible, that the products are available to those who are professionally qualified. A user qualification form is contained in the NCS catalog.

The most commonly used administration forms of the MMPI are the Group Booklet Form and Form *R* (see Fig. 1.1). The reusable Group Booklet Form is the most popular form in use. It was originally published in 1947 by the Psychological Corporation. It consists of 550 statements, with 16 items from scales 6, 7, 8, and 0 repeated, increasing the total item pool to 566.[8] The 16 repeated items were included to facilitate early machine scoring of IBM answer sheets. An advantage in using the Group Booklet Form, as Greene (1980) pointed out, is that most of the discussion in the MMPI literature about specific items refers to the numbering system of items in the group booklet. Therefore, one would have to transform item numbers to group booklet numbers if another form was used. This problem, however, can easily be eliminated when computer scoring is used, as the programs can usually compute the transformations.

---

[8]MMPI group booklet item 13, which is repeated as number 290, is one exception in that it is scored only on scales 2 and 9.

Form R is a hardcover, spiral-bound booklet. The answer sheet is inserted over two pegs in the back of the book and follows a step-down format whereby each consecutive page reveals another column of answer spaces matched with the booklet column of corresponding questions. Previously, the items on the answer sheet were unnumbered, but NCS has now corrected that omission by making it easier to associate specific answers with the test questions. This is valuable to the clinician wishing to look up specific item responses. The Form R booklet is particularly suitable for use when the subject has no hard surface available on which to answer the test (e.g., bedridden patients). The fact that the step-down format reveals only one column of questions and answer spaces at a time reduces the possibility of misplacing a response to a specific question. This is especially useful when testing confused patients or individuals unaccustomed to taking tests. The last 200 items of Form R are reordered so that the first 399 items can be scored on all the clinical and validity scales. Thus, when a clinician is interested in reducing administration time, he or she can stop the subject at item 399 and still have completed answers to score all basic scales. However, eliminating the remaining items also reduces the number of special scales that can be scored. Stopping at item number 399 on Form R represents an abbreviated form of the test, and the same procedure can be followed on the Group Booklet Form by instructing the subject to stop at item number 366 and complete the following 33 additional items, which are scored on scales K and Si: 371, 374, 377, 383, 391, 397, 398, 400, 406, 411, 415, 427, 436, 440, 446, 449, 450, 451, 455, 461, 462, 469, 473, 479, 481, 482, 487, 502, 505, 521, 547, 549, and 564. As Graham (1987) pointed out, the hand-scoring templates for scales K and Si must be modified if using this abbreviated format. Of course, the same disadvantage is applied regarding the reduction of special scales that can be scored with any abbreviated format. If the test user administers the Group Booklet Form and instructs the subject to stop at item 366, he or she can estimate the long-form equivalents for scales Si and K by consulting a table constructed by Cochran (1975). However, this may be unnecessary, as the obtained correlations between the abbreviated 366-item Group Booklet Form and long form for Si and K were .95 and .96, respectively.

The Individual or Card Form (see Fig. 1.1) is another format available from NCS. This form is especially useful when testing individuals with visual impairments or in disturbed or confused states, which can make it possible to mix up answers on the answer sheet. The card format consists of a box containing 550 statements, each printed in large type on a $3\frac{1}{2} \times 2\frac{1}{4}$ inch card with a distinctive color on the top and right-hand edges. The examinee sorts the cards into three groups—true, false, or cannot say. Results are recorded on a separate recording sheet by the examiner and must be scored by hand.

An audiocassette version containing the entire Group Form is also available from NCS. This form is intended for individuals with visual impairments, reading difficulties, and physical handicaps (a proctor records the responses). The subject must be able to understand spoken English (the MMPI Group Booklet Form is also available in Spanish, with hand-scoring materials from NCS).

Some MMPI users have found the length of the MMPI too prohibitive, so short forms have been developed. Abbreviated versions of Form *R* and the Group Booklet Form that were described earlier could be administered without losing any clinical or validity scale information. But even shorter forms have been developed to eliminate administering the entire MMPI. One of the shorter forms, named the Mini-Mult (Kincannon, 1968), consists of 71 items and is scored for the standard clinical and validity scales, except for scale 0. A longer short version of the test is the MMPI-168 developed by Overall and Gomez-Mont (1974). It is scored for all the standard clinical and validity scales. Basically, the first 168 items in either the Group Booklet Form or Form *R* are scored using the standard hand-scoring templates. Tables are needed to convert the abbreviated raw scores to standard raw scores. Graham (1977) reviewed five abbreviated MMPI forms and concluded that the MMPI-168 is the most promising short form available due to: (a) its ability to match code types in the standard MMPI, and (b) the respectable correlation coefficients between standard MMPI scores and corresponding scores derived from the MMPI-168. Graham systematically reviewed the short forms in an easy-to-understand way, and interested readers should consult his text. Other abbreviated versions of the MMPI include the 86-item Midi-Mult (Dean, 1972), the 173-item Hugo Short Form (Hugo, 1971), the 166-item Faschingbauer Abbreviated MMPI (FAM) (Faschingbauer, 1974), the Maxi-Mult 104 (Spera & Robertson, 1974), and the Maxi-Mult 94 (McLachlan, 1974).

Recent investigations of abbreviated versions of the MMPI continue to support Alker's statement in the *Eighth Mental Measurements Yearbook* review (Buros, 1978) that "virtually no convincing evidence is available that the short forms make contributions to clinical decision-making in a fashion that compares favorably on statistical criteria with the full MMPI" (p. 934). Alker also stated that no one version is clearly superior over any other (cited in Buros, 1978, p. 934). Willcockson, Bolton, and Dana (1983) compared six MMPI short forms for their ability to identify code types and indices of psychopathology obtained from the full-length MMPI using renal dialysis patients and paranoid schizophrenics. Their results suggest that the accuracy of the short forms differ for different patient populations and diagnostic criteria. One problem common to all the shortened forms is the failure to recapture the exact profile obtained from the full-length MMPI (McLaughlin, Helms, & Howe, 1983). Whenever a test is shortened, the issue of the effects on its reliability is raised. In an examination of short forms, Streiner and Miller (1986) stated: "From the limited evidence that is available, it appears that there is some reduction in reliability of short forms due to shortening the individual scales" (p. 111). These authors concluded that no shortened scale will ever favorably compare to the full MMPI. Greene (1982) suggested that we treat abbreviated MMPI versions as new tests and attempt to validate them individually.

Too many factors mitigate against the use of any of the short forms for routine clinical use. The one exception is reducing Form *R* to 399 items, as doing so does not eliminate any validity or clinical scale information. The most important reason not to abbreviate the test is because code-type correspondence to the full-length MMPI is generally poor. In addition, in shortening the test, many items are eliminated that are needed for scoring the supplemental scales—for example, Wiggins content scales, Harris-Lingoes subscales, and various special scales (Ward, Ward, & Moore, 1983). Also, by eliminating items the test protocol is less useful for research purposes. In most situations, the entire test should be given, even if it requires completing the test in more than one session.

FOREIGN TRANSLATIONS

The MMPI is used in over 50 countries and has more than 100 foreign translations. These include Hebrew, Chinese, Dutch, Russian, Spanish, and Japanese, of which there are at least 15 translations (Butcher & Pancheri, 1976; Butcher, 1985). There are three Italian and two German adaptations, and at least five Spanish editions exist, with the Nunēz (1967) translation being the most widely used in Latin America. Although the Nunēz translation is extensively used, there have been few validity or standardization studies conducted with this translation in the United States. A recent investigation by Fuller and Malony (1984) concluded that the Nunēz translation cannot be used interchangeably with the English form of the MMPI. Specifically, 18 teenaged bilingual Hispanic female students in California took the English and Nunēz forms of the MMPI with a 2-month interval between administrations. Administration order was randomized, with half taking the Spanish form first and half taking the English form first. The results indicate that the Spanish means were larger than the English means on five scales, making the two tests nonequivalent. The reasons for the discrepancies can be many, and Butcher and Pancheri (1976) presented a comprehensive guide and description of general strategies for developing foreign translations of the MMPI. It is recommended that the reader contemplating using foreign translations or developing adaptations consult Butcher and Pancheri's book.

2

Administration, Scoring, and Coding

SUBJECT REQUIREMENTS

One of the most important determinants for taking the MMPI is reading level. *The MMPI Manual* (Hathaway & McKinley, 1983) suggests that at least a 6th-grade reading level is required, although recent reevaluations of the MMPI word-content have resulted in higher reading level recommendations. Ward and Ward (1980) suggested that at least a 7th-grade reading level should be required. Blanchard (1981) analyzed the MMPI for reading difficulty using readability formulas with various criteria for comprehension. Using a criterion for comprehension of items between 90% and 100%, he found several items requiring 10th-grade reading skills and recommended that alternate forms of presentation be employed for subjects with less than 10th-grade reading skills.[1]

Some subjects with less than a sixth-grade education possess the reading ability to complete the MMPI, whereas others with more education do not. Therefore, if the reading ability of subjects is suspect, they can be shown several items to read aloud to immediately assess their test suitability. Foreign-language-speaking subjects or minorities often speak more fluently than they read, so a careful check should be made of their reading ability. Some examiners choose to orally administer the test to subjects unable to read at the required sixth-grade reading level (inattentive, visually handicapped, or illiterate subjects) but whose receptive language abilities are adequate. A recent investigation of the effects of orally administering the MMPI showed that although statistical differences occurred between the standard and oral administration in a split-half design, clinically significant differences appeared minimal (Kendrick & Hatzenbuehler, 1982). Clinicians administering the test orally most likely will obtain results comparable to the standard administered tests, although more research is needed to confirm this conclusion. Variables like reading fatigue, which can influence the administrator's inflections and tone, may have some unknown impact on the

---

[1]Using the 550 MMPI item pool, Blanchard (1981) found that the MMPI contains 6,317 words, of which 4,467 are monosyllabic, 1,422 disyllabic, and 320 trisyllabic. Average sentence length was 11.2 words, with an average number of syllables per sentence being 15.4. There was about one polysyllabic word per sentence.

subjects. Consequently, it is recommended that the standardized audiocassette form rather than oral reading of the items be used.

Psychiatric impairment does not usually interfere with the administration of the MMPI unless the subject is too confused or agitated to cooperate. Because depressed patients or cognitively impaired subjects may take longer than usual to complete the test, it is important to note the test-taking time. This is useful for all subjects, as too much or too little time can be of diagnostic significance (e.g., too little time may indicate impulsiveness or uncooperativeness, whereas too much time may indicate obsessiveness). Usual administration time for the completion of the test varies between 1 and 2 hours, although subjects with limited reading ability or noncooperative attitudes may take considerably longer.

Functional intelligence as measured by a standardized IQ test (e.g., WAIS-R or WISC-R) should be at least 80 for successful completion of the MMPI, although somewhat lower scores may be possible (Williams, 1985). Although there is no actual ceiling on age, older adults too weak or disabled should not be given the test in one sitting, as it can be fatiguing. The lowest appropriate age for the test is considered to be 12 (Dahlstrom, Welsh, & Dahlstrom, 1972), although the norms actually are listed at 13. The Marks, Seeman, and Haller (1974) adolescent norms, which list age 14 and below, did include some younger subjects in their sample (see appendix E). However, below this age, the subject either lacks the reading level or life experience necessary to relate to the items (Williams, 1985). Also, there are no existing norms for subjects below this particular age.

Subjects with disadvantages, such as blindness, deafness, or even paralysis, can successfully complete the MMPI under certain conditions. However, special versions of the test are necessary, such as the audiocassette form or the card box form, usually with additional proctoring assistance. *An MMPI Handbook, Volume I* (Dahlstrom, Welsh, & Dahlstrom, 1975) should be consulted before testing subjects with disadvantages.

TEST CONDITIONS

The testing environment should be comfortable, with as few distracting in-fluences as possible. Extraneous noise should be minimized, and the subject should be isolated from others not involved in simultaneous testing. Testing is a matter involving personal or confidential issues, and whenever possible the subject is entitled to adequate privacy. Only the test administrator and test-taker should be able to see the test items and responses, in order to prevent inadvertent answer disclosure and to maintain a consistent test environment (American Psychological Association, 1986). Lighting should be adequate and seating comfortable. If the subject is seated in an office, a desk or tabletop is preferable to holding the booklet on the lap. Form *R*, which is hardcover, is usually indicated when a hard surface is not available. If a subject is bedridden (e.g., hospitalized), Form *R* is most helpful. Test administrators using computer equipment to administer the test should consult the *Guidelines for Users of Computer-Based Tests and Interpretations* (American Psychological Association, 1986). If a monitor screen is used to present the items, it should be free from noticeable glare. Correct positioning of the equipment can reduce reflections from windows and lights. An obvious but frequently neglected point is the importance of informing the subject ahead of time to bring reading glasses if necessary.

Whether the test is group or individually administered or presented on a monitor screen, a proctor should be available to monitor the test-taking and provide assistance when necessary and appropriate. A trained assistant to the examiner can successfully answer any questions a subject raises during the examination. Proctoring is especially necessary in group administrations to ensure the privacy of responses. Proctors should be careful not to linger near any particular subject for too long, so that the subject does not become overly concerned that his or her responses are being monitored. Help in writing answers in the appropriate places and discouraging conversations should be the major function of the proctor. When questions are asked about the specific meaning of a statement or a word in either a group or individual administration, the proctor or examiner should attempt to be helpful but neutral. Specifically, dictionary definitions should be given for misunderstood words (Dahlstrom, Welsh, & Dahlstrom, 1972). Commonly misunderstood words include *diarrhea, constipation, nausea, dramatics, journalist,* and *brood* (Dahlstrom, Welsh, & Dahlstrom, 1972). When subjects question the meaning of an item itself, it is best to encourage them to interpret it in their own way. Even though the MMPI is considered to be an objective instrument, the items pull from the subject a particular meaning that leads to an endorsement that is ultimately compared to a normative base of subjects who responded to the same items.

TEST INSTRUCTIONS

Because administering the MMPI is a relatively easy task, many professionals overlook important factors that influence the subject's test-taking attitude and hence contribute to invalid results. Clinicians are urged to thoroughly familiarize themselves with *The MMPI Manual* (Hathaway & McKinley, 1983) prior to administering and scoring the test. The MMPI should be presented to the test-taker in a serious manner; too often clinicans minimize the importance of the test in an attempt to alleviate any performance anxiety. As a result, subjects often believe the test is not important and thereby compromise their cooperation by reading the items too quickly, carelessly, skipping others, and generally lessening their investment in the task. Clearly explaining how the results will be used can help increase cooperation and fulfill the ethical responsibilities of the psychologist to inform consumers as to the nature and purpose of an evaluation. Psychologists unfamiliar with professional assessment guidelines should consult the following resources: "Ethical Principles of Psychologists" (American Psychological Association, 1981); *Standards for Education and Psychological Testing* (American Psychological Association, 1985); *Standards for Providers of Psychological Services* (American Psychological Association, 1977); and *Guidelines for Computer-Based Tests and Interpretations* (Committee on Professional Standards [COPS] and Committee on Psychological Tests & Assessment [CPTA]; American Psychological Association, 1986).

Instructions to the subject are printed on Form *R* and the Group Booklet Form. The instructions to subjects for the Card Form are in the cover of the box and are read by the examiner. These instructions basically direct the test-taker to decide whether an item is mostly true or mostly false as it applies to him- or herself. A question that commonly arises is, "Do I answer as I am currently feeling?" Most examiners encourage the subjects to answer as they are currently feeling, but sometimes, under special circumstances, an examiner may want to learn how subjects wish to perceive themselves when they feel better or are leaving the hospital or concluding psychotherapy. The examiner may then ask the subject to fill out the test looking ahead toward the completion of a therapy or hospital program and answer the items in the way they would expect to feel at that time. In some situations, the subject who is able to produce a less disturbed profile under such looking ahead instructions (called the *projected discharge profile*), as compared to their admission or initial profile taken under the usual instructions, is considered to have a better prognosis (Marks, Seeman, & Haller, 1974).

In addition to the standardized instructions printed on the MMPI forms, some test-users employ supplemental instructions and information to help answer commonly asked questions and to alleviate any test anxiety. Examples of such supplemental instructions include one taken from a form adopted from the *Caldwell Report* (Caldwell, 1977), and a second representing modified questions from a brochure given to subjects prior to the administration of the test at the Del Mar Psychiatric Clinic (Lewak & Nelson, 1986).

Questions People Ask When Taking
the Minnesota Multiphasic Personality Inventory[2]

1. *"How long will this take?"*
Answer: About an hour to an hour and a half, usually. Some people take longer, whereas some people finish in 45 minutes or less.

2. *"I'm tired and not feeling well; will that affect how I do on the inventory?"*

---

[2]Adapted from the Caldwell Report (Caldwell, 1977).

Answer: Probably not. But answer the statements in terms of how you feel most of the time. How you feel now may make you take a little longer to finish, but the results will be essentially the same as long as you answer truthfully.

3. *"Will it make any difference if I skip some questions and come back to them?"*

Answer: If you do it carefully, skipping some questions and returning to them probably will not make any difference. But it is easy to get mixed up in marking your answers, and that will make a difference. So it is better to do them in order, if possible.

4. *"What if I do not have time to finish all of the questions right now?"*

Answer: That is perfectly alright. But try to do them all now, or as soon as possible. Brief interruptions do not matter and will not change the results.

5. *"Suppose I cannot answer all of the questions?"*

Answer: Try to answer all of them. If you omit a few items, it will not matter, but try to do them all.

6. *"Why do some questions appear more than once?"*

Answer: In order for the old (original) IBM answer sheet to be machine scored, it was necessary to repeat 16 statements. The newer forms have retained these, so as not to discard any information.

7. *"Why do so many questions seem irrelevant or just plain stupid or silly?"*

Answer: Many may seem that way, but the wording of the question often has little to do with how the question is scored. Your answer is simply compared with those of others who have answered the same question.

Supplemental Instructions For Taking
the Minnesota Multiphasic Personality Inventory

1. Answer every question as truthfully as you can; that's very important for accuracy and the best use of the results.
2. Be sure to mark the correct number on the answer sheet for the question you are answering. Remember that a question marked both true and false may be scored as "not answered," or as answered in both directions.
3. If a question seems confusing, as if it could mean different things, answer it according to the meaning that is best for you at this time.
4. Phrases like *some of the time* and words like *often* and *seldom* should be answered according to how you feel about them; it's how *you* feel about the words that matters.

5. When you have finished, take a few minutes to check your answer sheet for any missing answers, incomplete erasures, or double-answered questions.

6. Above all, relax. Numerous people have taken the MMPI, and all have survived.

The Minnesota Multiphasic Personality Inventory
(MMPI): Questions and Answers[3]

You have been asked to take the MMPI. Here are some questions that are commonly asked about the test. Please read this booklet before you take the test. If you have other questions, feel free to ask.

1. *"What is it?"*

Answer: The MMPI is short for the Minnesota Multiphasic Personality Inventory. It is a tool used for the assessment of the personality. It is approximately 45 years old and is psychology's most researched instrument.

2. *"How do I answer the questions?"*

Answer: When you take the test, answer the questions as you currently feel. Work quickly, because no one answer is "vital." It is the pattern of answers that makes a difference.

3. *"Do I have to answer all of the questions even if I don't know the right answers?"*

Answer: Answer all the questions. If you cannot answer all the questions, leave no more than a few unanswered. If you are unsure about an answer, use the following rule: If the answer to a question is more true than false, answer true. If it is more false than true, answer false. For example, the item "I get headaches often" could be answered as follows: I get headaches but not that often; therefore I answer false.

4. *"Why am I taking this test? Does it mean that something is wrong with me?"*

Answer: We have asked you to take the test because it helps us to get to know you better in less time. Many who come to the clinic are asked to take it for this reason. Also, it is cost-effective.

5. *"But I don't have any problems. It is my child, whom I brought to the clinic, who has the problems. Why do I have to take the test?"*

Answer: You are asked to take the test so we know what kind of psychological environment your child lives in. For example, your child may possess extremely high energy and be very active, and you as a

---

[3]Del mar Psychiatric Clinic, Lewak & Nelson, 1986.

parent may have energy that is more in the average range. Knowing this helps us (and you) understand how your interactions with your child are affecting you both.

6. *"If my wife and I take the test, I'm afraid that you will blame one of us for the problems we're having, and that will make things worse."*

Answer: That is a reasonable concern, but the MMPI is not used to find out who has the most problems. What the MMPI can do is help us see how two people might be inadvertently "pushing each other's sensitive area" and so be unable to communicate. The test interpretation is not meant to judge either person nor leave either person feeling blamed.

7. *"The test has a lot of questions that seem very outdated. Can it still be valid?"*

Answer: One of the strengths of the test is that it has been used for a long time, so that it is extremely well-researched. The outdated questions have remained so as not to disturb the validity of the test. Many of the items are currently being examined for replacement in a new MMPI version.

8. *"Some of the questions repeat themselves. Is that meant to trick me?"*

Answer: The repeated questions were originally included to facilitate machine scoring of the test and are not intended to trick anyone.

9. *"I think I can outsmart the test. I probably can tell what the questions are getting at."*

Answer: The pattern of answers to questions rather than individual responses is what is important to the psychologist. Being as honest as possible will serve to make the test results more valid and useful to you and the psychologist interpreting the test. In fact, many questions that appear to be obvious are not measuring what people think they are measuring. People who try to outsmart the test might make it invalid, but often not in the direction they think and not without revealing their intention to do so.

10. *"Why does the test ask so many questions that clearly don't apply to me?"*

Answer: The test was constructed as a general inventory, so many questions may not apply to you. If a question does not apply to you, simply answer false or true, whichever direction is most applicable for you.

11. *"How can you tell anything about me from all of those questions anyway?"*

Answer: After your answer sheet is finished, it is scored and a graph is drawn to see how you score on different dimensions of personality and how your scores compare to others. There are also scales that tell how you answer the test (cautiously, candidly, denying problems, or even exaggerating them). Your configuration or pattern of scores is what is important to us.

12. *"Will I get feedback from my test?"*

   Answer: The actual test protocol and the graph will not be given to you in order to maintain test security. However, an explanation of the results will be provided.

13. *"What is the cost of the test?"*

   Answer: See the clinic fee schedule. The fee covers administration and scoring. Feedback will probably come in a regular session for which you pay your usual fee to your therapist.

14. *"What if I disagree with the feedback?"*

   Answer: That is something you and your therapist can discuss. When you get feedback, you may want to bring a tape recorder so that you can listen to the feedback and take some time to formulate questions that you might want to ask your therapist. Remember, the test is for your own benefit.

TEST SCORING

Scoring the MMPI can be accomplished using hand-held scoring templates; more recently, computers have been utilized in scoring and drawing (and interpreting) MMPI profiles. There are several services available to score MMPI answer sheets. For example, National Computer Systems in Minneapolis, Minnesota offers a scoring service for the Group Booklet Form and Form *R* utilizing both adult and adolescent norms. As previously mentioned, The Group Booklet and Form *R* are the most commonly used forms of the MMPI. When hand-scoring the MMPI, the scorer should first inspect the answer sheet for omissions, double-marked answers, and erasures. Erasures usually contraindicate random responses because subjects are demonstrating by their modified response a careful reading of the item content. Omitted and double-marked items are scored on the cannot say (?) scale. Double-marked items (items marked both true and false) will be scored as a deviant response, so a line should be drawn through the item so it is not counted when the template is placed over the answer sheet. Plastic templates for scoring are available from National Computer Systems in Minneapolis, as are the answer and profile sheets. There are different plastic scoring templates available for the Form *R* and Group Booklet Form. They are not interchangeable; the item sequence is different on the two forms, and the item layout differs somewhat between the two forms. The Group Booklet Form presents the items in a reusable booklet. The first 366 items in the Group Booklet Form, plus an additional 33 items (listed in chapter 1), contain the necessary items for scoring the basic clinical and validity scales. The first 399 items on Form *R* are sufficient for scoring the basic validity and clinical scales. Many of the items not scored on the standard clinical and validity scales are scored on different supplemental scales that were developed after the MMPI was published. However, the purpose of retaining the nonscored items on the test, that is, the items that are not scored on the standard clinical and validity scales, was so that later improvements could be made with those items. There are 167 separate items that are not scored on any standard clinical or validity scale. The scoring keys for the Group Booklet Form contain two templates for five of the scales (scales *K, Pa, Pt, Sc,* and *Si*), as scored responses occur on both sides of the answer sheet. The templates indicate whether the front or back side of the answer sheet is to be scored. Form *R* uses one template per scale, because all of the items are contained on one side of the answer sheet. The scoring templates for the Group Form do not contain a key for scoring scale *L*. However, the 15 items on scale *L* are easily scored by counting the number of false responses for items: 15, 30, 45, 60, 75, 90, 105, 120, 135, 150, 165, 195, 225, 255, and 285. The layout sequence for these 15 *L* items is positioned in an easy-to-remember pattern on the first side of the answer sheet. There is a template for scoring scale *L* on Form *R*.

To score the Form *R* and the Group Booklet, an answer key is lined up over the answer sheet revealing the darkened answers appearing through the transparent boxes. These marks are counted and represent the raw score on each scale (after the front and back are counted on the Group Form). For the Group Form, the answers from the back and front of the answer sheet are summed to produce a total raw score for those five scales with front and back answers. There are separate scale 5 (*Mf*) keys for males and females on both forms of the MMPI. Because there are differences in *T*-scores by sex for the clinical scales (not the validity scales), it is necessary to enter the raw scores of the subject on the side of the profile sheet appropriate to the sex of the subject. One word of caution to test-users employing the plastic templates is to keep them away from excessive heat so they do not expand and become improperly fitting. The test-user wishing to hand-score special scales for which there are no preexisting templates or profile sheet conversion tables is advised to consult *An MMPI Handbook, Volume I* (Dahlstrom, Welsh, & Dahlstrom, 1972). The test publisher provides additional scoring templates for some commonly used supplemental scales (scales *A, R, Es,* and *Mac*), which are scored in the same manner as the standard scales.

The Card Form, a less frequently employed format of the test, requires three basic steps for scoring. First, the cards that contain a significant deviant response must be sorted or identified. These responses are then entered on a recording sheet. Finally, answer templates are applied to the recording sheet so that a profile can be constructed from the scored responses.

The cannot say or unanswered items should be recorded first. This is accomplished by drawing a heavy black diagonal line (or question mark) in the appropriate block indicated by letter and number on the recording sheet. These marks (or question marks) are counted and recorded in the space labeled "?" on the answer sheet.

When subjects take the Card Form, they are instructed to sort the cards into true, false, or cannot say piles. Afterwards, the examiner separates the true and false deviant responses from the nonscorable responses. For the true responses, this is done by counting the number of items classified as true with the lower right-hand corners cut off. Likewise, the scorable false responses will be those with the lower left-hand corners clipped. Each item in the true category with lower right-hand corners clipped should be recorded by marking an "X" in the appropriate space on the answer sheet identified by code letter (A–J) and number (1–55). The same is done with the significant false items with lower left-hand corners clipped. After the recording is completed, the scoring keys are placed over the answer sheets so raw scores can be counted and converted to T-scores. The L items are the last 15 items on the record form and are counted by tallying the Xs among these items (J41–J55). After this scoring process is completed, the cards are prepared for the next subject by shuffling them. A few easy, nonthreatening items should be placed at the front of the box so the subject is not disturbed by the first four items. The *MMPI Manual* (Hathaway & McKinley, 1983) should be consulted for more detailed scoring instructions.

SELECTION AND USE OF NORMS

When individuals take the MMPI, their scores are reflecting how they compare to the original Minnesota standardization group. After the original work in norming the MMPI was completed, Hathaway and Briggs (1957) reexamined the original Minnesota sample and eliminated subjects with incomplete backgrounds or test data. This purified the sample and was eventually incorporated into the T-scores printed on the standard profile sheet. Appendix C contains the T-score conversions of raw scores on each validity and clinical scale. T-scores derived from norms in *An MMPI Handbook* (Dahlstrom, Welsh, & Dahlstrom, 1972, 1975) and other MMPI reference works do not necessarily match precisely with the T-scores on the standard profile sheet because of the purified sample (Greene, 1980).

A recently published large-scale normative project was conducted by Colligan, Osborne, Swenson, and Offord (1983) at the Mayo Clinic in Rochester, Minnesota. Colligan et al. tested a contemporary sample of normal individuals in rural Minnesota in order to compare the results of the original standardization group. Greene (1985) noted in an excellent critique of their work that there are important differences between the mean scores on the standard MMPI scales for the contemporary and original samples generally ranging from one to six T-score points ($\frac{1}{3}$ to $\frac{1}{2}$ standard deviation). He also pointed out that they employed normalized T-scores versus linear T-scores, which are used with the traditional profile sheet. Colligan et al. used normalized T-scores, because the original norm T-score distributions of most MMPI scales have varying degrees of positive skew, making it difficult to accurately compare T-scores across scales (Colligan, Osborne, & Offord, 1980; Miller & Streiner, 1986). Normalized T-scores *are* comparable across scales. However, the Colligan et al. norms need to be further researched before employing them for routine clinical use. Miller and Streiner (1986) found an absence of correspondence between code-types when using the original and new norms based on linear transformations and normalized *T*-scores, respectively. They recommended that Colligan's et al. norms be used only in conjunction with the original norms until the clinical relevance of the differences are determined.

Recently, Pancoast and Archer (1989) reviewed findings from 21 studies of normal adults, comparing obtained MMPI scale values to the standard norms. They concluded that the original MMPI adult norms seemed to have been based on an atypical sample and did not represent an accurate fit to the population mean values at the time they were collected. That the Minnesota normals were probably a biased sample is supported by Dahlstrom, Welsh, and Dahlstrom's (1975) observation that most samples of normal adults have consistently shown slightly higher mean values on the MMPI than the original normative sample. Also, Pancoast and Archer (1989) pointed out that later samples of normals omit fewer items than did the original sample (14 items for males and 15 items for females). The effects of these omitted items would be to lower the mean scores for the Minnesota normal group.

Despite the problems with the original norms, we recommend that MMPI users continue to employ the original norms until the necessary validity studies indicate otherwise. Contemporary interpretation of code-types is based on an extensive literature. As Butcher and Owen (1978) pointed out, "if modifications [in the MMPI] are too drastic, the instrument may be unacceptable to present users . . . they may continue to use the present MMPI because it is a known entity (p. 507). Pancoast and Archer (1989) stated that "changes in MMPI norms could create an essentially new test instrument that would require the development of a new correlate literature to justify clinical use" (p. 391). However, the degree to which there is some loss of applicability in our accumulated base is an empirical issue as of yet undetermined.

Perhaps the most important and ambitious project since the birth of the MMPI has recently been completed. A discussion about the restandardization of the MMPI and its implications is presented in chapter 9.

PLOTTING THE PROFILE

After the answer sheet has been scored, raw scores must be carefully transferred to the profile sheet and converted to *T*-scores. After raw scores are recorded under each scale, a different proportion of *K* is added to the appropriate scales. The fraction of *K* to be added is easily computed by consulting a table listed on the profile sheet showing all the raw-score values of *K* with different proportions of those values (see Table 2.1). The scorer should draw a line under the raw-score value of *K* so that the appropriate fractions can be added to the clinical

TABLE 2.1
Fractions of K*

K	.5	.4	.2
30	15	12	6
29	15	12	6
28	14	11	6
27	14	11	5
26	13	10	5
25	13	10	5
24	12	10	5
23	12	9	5
22	11	9	4
21	11	8	4
20	10	8	4
19	10	8	4
18	9	7	4
17	9	7	3
16	8	6	3
15	8	6	3
14	7	6	3
13	7	5	3
12	6	5	2
11	6	4	2
10	5	4	2
9	5	4	2
8	4	3	2
7	4	3	1
6	3	2	1
5	3	2	1
4	2	2	1
3	2	2	1
2	1	1	0
1	1	0	0
0	0	0	0

**Source:* Minnesota Multiphasic Personality Inventory (MMPI) Copyright © The University of Minnesota 1943, renewed 1970. Reproduced by permission.

scales. The raw score plus K is then plotted onto the profile sheet (see appendix D). If a test-user does not wish to employ the K correction, he or she can consult appendix C in order to convert the non-K-corrected raw scores into appropriate T-scores. Simply omitting K and directly plotting the value(s) onto the profile sheet will result in an incorrect conversion. Because the standard profile sheet is based on adult norms with the K-correction factor, special conversion tables for adolescent profiles (ages 12 through 17) should be consulted (Marks, Seeman, & Haller, 1974). The most frequently used adolescent reference for the MMPI (Marks, Seeman, and Haller, 1974) does not employ K corrections, so a user wishing to compare their adolescent profile to the Marks, Seeman, and Haller (1974) system would need to plot non-K-corrected profiles with the appropriate age conversions for the raw scores (Archer, 1987). Special tables are separately provided for different age categories of boys and girls with different raw scores and their corresponding non-K-corrected T-scores in appendix E.

The test-user should indicate on the profile sheet whether adult or adolescent norms are being used. It is recommended that both adolescent and adult norms be plotted for 17- and 18-year-olds, so that they can both be examined and compared. It is also recommended that adolescent norms be solely used for plotting 12- to 16-year-old subjects. Special profile forms are available from Psychological Assessment Resources, Inc. in Odessa, Florida that allow the MMPI-user to directly plot the non-K-corrected adolescent scores and convert them to T-scores without the use of any special tables. Naturally when a computer scoring service or computer program is employed, the changes are more readily accomplished.

Within the profile matrix, the marks or dashes represent raw-score values (see appendix D). Each dash represents a raw-score value of one. Each scale except for scale 5 (female) shows an increasing T-score value for each raw-score point added. The final raw score is indicated on the profile sheet by plotting the raw-score placement on the appropriate scale. After all the scale scores are indicated in this fashion, a solid line is drawn between the clinical scales to connect them. Likewise, the validity scales are connected. The clinical and validity scales, however, have a partition between them and they are not connected (see appendix D). Similarly, the supplemental scales shown on the standard profile sheet are not connected to the clinical scales in the profile.

After the profile is drawn, the test-user is provided with a raw score and corresponding T-score for each scale. The T-score values are located at the extreme left and right columns of the profile matrix. T-scores have a mean of 50 and a standard deviation of 10. For example, if a subject obtains a raw score of 7 on scale F, this means their T-score is 60, one standard deviation above the mean. The profile sheet shows darkened lines at T-score values of 30 and 70 to indicate scores that are within two standard deviations of the mean. Scores above or below these ranges indicate a significant deviation from the original normal standardization group pattern of responding and are considered abnormal values. The *T*-score values were arbitrarily set for scales cannot say, *L,* and *F,* and there are no male/female differences between raw-score values and corresponding *T*-score values for any of the four validity scales. However, the standard clinical scales have different *T*-score values for males and females. This can be easily seen by observing the raw-score values at a *T*-score of 50 (mean) for males and females. Equation 1 shows how a *T*-score is derived. However, it is not necessary to use this formula, as the conversion from raw scores to *T*-scores is already provided on the printed profile sheet (see appendix D).

$$T = 50 + \frac{10\ (X\text{-}M)}{SD}$$

X = the subject's raw score
M = the mean score on the scale
SD = standard deviation

A *T*-score is basically a standard score or *z* score that has been restandardized by multiplying the *z* score by 10 and adding or subtracting it from 50 (Anastasi, 1982).

CODING THE PROFILE

Soon after the publication of the MMPI, two systems were developed to codify the information yielded by the scoring process. The first system was developed by Hathaway (1947), and a more comprehensive method followed, designed by Welsh (1948). The function of coding is to provide a convenient means of identifying some of the salient characteristics of the profile, especially with respect to its elevation and pattern. Although single-scale elevations are important to examine and interpret, the general emphasis in clinical use of the test has been to interpret profile patterns; a profile pattern is the configuration of scale scores relative to each other. By coding a profile, a test-user can organize the data into a simple-to-read summarization for clinical and research use.

One of the earliest uses of the Hathaway (1947) system was in the original *Atlas* (Hathaway & Meehl, 1951), a book of clinical case summaries grouped according to elevated scales or coded profile high points.

The first step in both coding systems substitutes numbers 1 through 0 for the 10 basic clinical scales, in order from left to right, in the standard profile arrangement, as shown by:

Hs-1	*Pa*-6
D-2	*Pt*-7
Hy-3	*Sc*-8
Pd-4	*Ma*-9
Mf-5	*Si*-0

The writing of the code begins by identifying the highest clinical scale T-score value and writing the number assigned to that scale (as in the foregoing list) as the first number of the code, with the remaining scale numbers following in descending order of magnitude. When two or more scales share the same elevation, they should be recorded in ordinal sequence from left (scale 1) to right (scale 0) in the profile. The next step is to indicate the relative magnitude of all scales in the profile.

In the Hathaway (1947) coding, all scale numbers precede a prime (') when the scale magnitudes are 70 or greater (T-scores). Scales with T-scores lower than 70 and higher than 54 appear to the right of the prime, and these are then followed by a dash (–). In Hathaway's coding system, no scale is coded that has a T-score within the range of 54 to 46. Following the dash, the code continues with the lowest scale in the profile that has a T-score less than 46. Some workers will deviate from the system by using double primes ('') to indicate scales with T-scores above 80 and three primes (''') for 90 and above. No number is recorded to the right of the dash if there is not a scale(s) with a T-score value of 46 or less. However, if there is a T-score less than 46, the scale with the lowest T-score in the profile is recorded followed by ascending values up to 46. When scales have the same elevation or are within one T-score point of each other, they should be underlined. The validity scales are coded to the right of the clinical scales in a way that obviously separates them. Rather than T-score values, raw-score values are recorded. The raw-score values for the validity scales are listed in the order of L, F, and K and are separated by colons (:). An X is written immediately after the code for the clinical scales to indicate profile invalidity if the raw score on L is equal to or greater than 10 or if the raw score of F is equal to or greater than 16. Following are two examples of the Hathaway (1947) code. Because the system records raw scores for the validity scales, no T-score values are reported for L, F, and K.

Example 1:
Raw Scores   T-scores
  L   F   K   1   2   3   4   5   6   7   8   9   0
  1   10   10   34 56 56 90 63 50 66 73 91 43
Hathaway Code: 948'7523 -1   1:10:10

Because scales 9, 4, and 8 exceed T-scores of 70, they are placed to the left of the prime sign. Scales to the right of the prime represent T-score values between 54 and 70. Scales 2 and 3 and 9 and 4 are underlined to indicate exact T-score values or scores that are within one T-score point of each other. Scale 1 is recorded to the right of the dash and represents the lowest scale on the profile, with a T-score value less than 46. Because no other scales fall below scale 1 in value, the coding for the clinical scales is complete. To the right of the clinical scales are recorded the raw-score values for L, F, and K.

Example 2:
  Raw Scores   *T-scores*
  L   F   K   1   2   3   4   5   6   7   8   9   0
  2   7   12   49 89 62 50 67 62 79 63 38 70
  Hathaway Code: 270'58<u>36</u> -9<u>14</u>   2 : 7 : 12

Because scales 2, 7, and 0 are equal to or exceed 70, they are placed to the left of the prime. The prime sign is always placed after the last number in the code, which represents a *T*-score of 70 or higher. Scales 5, 8, 3, and 6 are less than 70 and more than 54, so they are ranked in order of descending *T*-score values, to the right of the prime sign. The dash that follows scale 6 indicates that scale 9 is the lowest scale in the profile, and it is, therefore, listed as the first scale adjacent to the dash. Thereafter, scales are listed in ascending order up to *T*-score values of 46. Because scales 3, 6, and 8 are within one T-score point of each other, they are underlined. The numbers to the right of the clinical scales indicate the validity scales' raw-score values.

In contrast to the Hathaway (1947) method, the Welsh (1948) code records all scales in descending order of magnitude throughout the entire profile and omits none. The elevation symbols for this system are as follows:

T-score Values	*All Followed By*
90 and greater	*
80–89	''
70–79	'
60–69	–
50–59	/
40–49	:
30–39	#
29 and below	recorded to the right of #

In this coding system, an asterisk (*) follows all scales at 90 or above. Scales between 89 and 80 are coded to the left of a double prime (' '). To the left of the single prime (') appear all scales between 79 and 70. To the left of the dash (–) all scales between 69 and 60 are recorded. Scales between 59 and 50 are followed by a slash (/). Scales between 49 and 40 are coded to the left of a colon (:). Scales below 40 are coded to the left of a number symbol (#). As in the Hathaway (1947) method, an underlined scale indicates that adjacent scales are within one *T*-score point of each other. Following are the two examples used previously and are shown here using the Welsh (1948) system. Readers can contrast the differences between the two systems. Because the Welsh system codes the validity scales in order of highest to lowest *T*-score values, *T*-scores, rather than raw scores, are recorded. The validity scales are recorded to the right of the clinical scales, as is done with the Hathaway method.

Example 3:
Raw Scores   *T-scores*
 L   F   K   1   2   3   4   5   6   7   8   9   0
40   66   46   34 56 56 90 63 50 66 73 91 43
Welsh Code: 94*''8'75-23 6/0:1#   F-/KL:#

Example 4:
Raw Scores   *T-scores*
 L   F   K   1   2   3   4   5   6   7   8   9   0
44   60   49   49 89 62 50 67 62 79 63 38 70
Welsh Code: 2''70'5836-4/1:9*#   F-/KL:#

Even when there is no value in a specific *T*-score range, the appropriate symbol
should be recorded. That is why, in example 3, a double prime follows the
asterisk; no scale follows in the *T*-score range of 80 to 89. Marks, Seeman, and
Haller (1974) summarized Dahlstrom, Welsh, and Dahlstrom's (1972) comparison of the two coding systems by stating that

> The Hathaway code is a good deal more variable since it omits scales with certain
> magnitudes, as indicated above; . . . the code order changes in the Hathaway code
> but remains constant for the Welsh system; . . . the position of the highest scale is
> variable in the Hathaway system (e.g., it may be the last scale in a profile which
> has no elevations higher than 46), but constant in the Welsh system; and . . . the
> position of the lowest scale is comparably variable. (p. 9)

In actual practice, using the Welsh system appears more useful, but readers
examining research or clinical data organized with the Hathaway system should
familiarize themselves with that method.

The highest clinical scales represent what is called a *code-type*. Code-types
usually consist of the two or three highest clinical scales in a profile. Before a
code-type can be determined, the scales must be arranged in a hierarchical order.
Many clinicians do not use either coding system, because it is relatively easy to
code-type a profile simply by noting the high points. When two or more scales
are tied in *T*-score values, the ordinal position of the scales listed from left to
right takes precedence. Also, code-types are typically defined by the highest
scales in the clinical, not the validity, section of the profile.

3

Major Developments Subsequent to the Construction of the MMPI

INTRODUCTION

Since the creation of the original MMPI, many developments have reshaped how the clinician employs the test in actual practice. The large number and variety of MMPI items combined with the tradition of empirical scale construction have led to the development of numerous special scales and indices. Dahlstrom, Welsh, and Dahlstrom (1975) listed more than 450 scales that have been constructed for special purposes since the original clinical and validity scales were designed. Since 1975, scale construction has proceeded at a vigorous pace, and now the number of special scales for the MMPI exceeds the number of MMPI items (Butcher & Tellegen, 1978). However, the subsequent emergence of new scales does not follow any specific organization as did the original scales. The new or special scales, as they are often referred to, have basically followed the interests of the particular researcher and have involved a variety of construction approaches. A great many of these scales are not clinically useful, as they lack adequate validation or cross-validation (Clopton & Klein, 1978) and they are considered too limited or specialized for applied usage. For example, Archer (1987) indicated that few, if any, empirical investigations have been conducted examining the properties of special MMPI scales with adolescent respondents. Typically, adult norms for the special scales are applied to adolescents, and MMPI users should be cautious when interpreting the special scales in an adolescent population. Recent critiques of new MMPI scale construction have warned readers about the common methodological problems in MMPI research, and the reader is advised to consult these articles if doing similar work (Butcher & Tellegen, 1978; Clopton, 1978, 1982; Clopton & Klein, 1978).

As there are too many special scales to review here, we have selected the scales and indices that we have found to be the most useful or promising in clinical practice and/or the most often referenced. These scales represent a cross-section of different scale development strategies. The reader searching for special scales not described here is advised to consult the following sources: *An MMPI Handbook, Volume II* (Dahlstrom, Welsh, & Dahlstrom, 1975) lists hundreds of additional scales with their psychometric properties; *MMPI Supplemental Scale Manual* by Caldwell (1988) presents descriptive material about a number of useful scales with interpretation guidelines; and *The MMPI Interpretation Manual for Counselors and Clinicians* by Duckworth and Anderson (1986) also lists various scales with research references and suggestions for interpretation.

Early clinical users of the MMPI recognized that the rich content of the MMPI was specifically neglected or not efficiently utilized in interpretation. Efforts to improve interpretation evolved by developing special scales and indices from the original item pool. Although hundreds of scales and indices have been created, their development basically reflects three broad construction methods that parallel the designs used to assemble and create different types of other psychological tests as well. These three approaches are (a) the rational-theoretical approach, (b) the empirical method, and (c) the internal-consistency method.

The rational-theoretical approach involves a rational approach in selecting test items. That is, the items are assumed to bear a direct relationship to a particular domain of personality or behavior. The Woodworth Personal Data Sheet, described in chapter 1, serves as an example of a rationally derived instrument. The straightforward questions a clinician may ask a client about his or her tension, such as "Is it hard to relax?" are similar to a rationally derived test asking the same question (Lanyon & Goodstein, 1971). Lanyon and Goodstein (1971) defined a rational-theoretical continuum of tests with a priori inventories, such as the Woodworth Personal Data Sheet, falling toward the rational end of the continuum. Other tests that are congruent with a specific theoretical view of personality, such as the Thematic Apperception Test (Murray, 1943) or the Blacky Pictures Test (Blum, 1950), would fall nearer to the theoretical end.

The empirical strategy was the basic approach used to construct the MMPI scales as well as the California Psychological Inventory (Gough, 1987). Generally, items or scale scores are selected that reliably discriminate two groups, such as an abnormal from a normal group.

The internal-consistency strategy involves a statistical analysis of how item responses are intercorrelated and how these relationships are connected to a similar psychological construct. Factor analysis is the procedure usually identified with this approach, and tests derived from this method include the Eysenck Personality Questionnaire (Eysenck & Eysenck, 1975; Friedman, 1984; Friedman, Wakefield, Boblitt, & Surman, 1976; Wakefield & Goad, 1982) and the

Sixteen Personality Factor Questionnaire (Cattell, Eber, & Tatsuoka, 1970; Friedman, Sasek, & Wakefield, 1976), as well as many others.

As Lanyon and Goodstein (1971) pointed out, most sophisticated test developers employ a combination of all three strategies, as the approaches are not mutually exclusive. The MMPI, for example, although empirically derived, was developed from an item pool that was selected in a rational way. That is, the items were chosen on the basis of their having some perceived relevance to the goal of detecting psychopathology.

The following sections describe selected MMPI scales and indices, with the former categorized by the major test construction method employed.

RATIONAL-THEORETICAL APPROACHES

Harris-Lingoes Subscales

Originally devised in 1955 by Harris and Lingoes (1955; 1968) at the Langley Porter Institute in San Francisco, the Harris-Lingoes subscales continue to be used by some psychologists as adjunctive aids in improving clinical interpretation of MMPI profiles. The authors examined the item content of each clinical scale and grouped these items into categories that appeared homogeneous.[1] That is, items that appeared to reflect a single trait or attitude were grouped into new subscales, which Harris and Lingoes named on the basis of the item content. The basic need for these subscales existed because a particular scale elevation can reflect different item endorsement patterns for different individuals. For example, two individuals with the exact T-score elevation of 70 on scale 2 could have endorsed different content areas of depression items. One person may have endorsed many depression items related to psychomotor retardation, whereas the other person may have emphasized items related to mental dullness, both areas having different clinical implications for the treatment of depression. Dissimilar endorsement patterns of items within a scale are thought to be related to particular behavioral correlates.

Harris-Lingoes subscales were not developed for scales 1 and 7, as the items on these scales appear to be related to single constructs. Scale 1 content is obvious in nature and relates clearly to bodily concerns, whereas scale 7, also obvious in content, relates to anxiety, worry, and tension. Scales 5 and 0 are multidimensional in nature, but Harris and Lingoes (1955, 1968) chose not to

---

[1]There was at least one deviation from the method of regrouping items into categories from each clinical scale. Greene (1980) noted that Harris and Lingoes added to each subscale on scale 4 (but not any other clinical scale) two to six items not found on scale 4. Graham (1987) recommended retaining these items, as they have been included in the scoring of the subscales in past research and clinical usage. The items are identified in appendix F.

develop subscales for these scales, presumably because they were added later to the item pool and were not part of the original clinical scales. Scales 5 and 0 have been factor analyzed, and these results are presented later in this chapter. There are 31 subscales that Harris and Lingoes developed for scales 2, 3, 4, 6, 8, and 9. Three other subscales were developed by summing the scores on specific subscales but are not typically scored. The subscales are as follows in Table 3.1. The item content and direction of scoring for the Harris-Lingoes subscales is presented in appendix F. Norms were not originally reported by the authors, but they later made data available for psychiatric patients at the Langley Porter Clinic (Graham, 1987). Dahlstrom et al. (1972) developed tables for the Harris-Lingoes subscales from the original standardization group of normal males and females, and their data are reproduced in appendix G, Table one. These are recommended for usage in general clinical practice. Many computer scoring programs and interpretation services supply this information. The Archer (1987) *MMPI Adolescent Interpretative System,* published by Psychological Assessment Re-

TABLE 3.1
Harris and Lingoes Subscales

Subscales		*Number of items*
Scale 2—Depression		
D_1	Subjective depression	32
D_2	Psychomotor retardation	15
D_3	Physical malfunctioning	11
D_4	Mental dullness	15
D_5	Brooding	10
Scale 3—Hysteria		
Hy_1	Denial of social anxiety	6
Hy_2	Need for affection	12
Hy_3	Lassitude—malaise	15
Hy_4	Somatic complaints	17
Hy_5	Inhibition of aggression	7
Scale 4—Psychopathic deviate		
Pd_1	Familial discord	11
Pd_2	Authority problems	11
Pd_3	Social imperturbability	12
Pd_{4A}	Social alienation	18
Pd_{4B}	Self-alienation	15
Pd_4	Alienation	33

$(A + B$ yields this scale but is typically not scored. The name of this scale is alienation.)

Scale 6—Paranoia

Pa_1	Persecutory ideas	17
Pa_2	Poignancy	9
Pa_3	Naivete	9

Scale 8—Schizophrenia

Sc_{1A}	Social alienation	21
Sc_{1B}	Emotional alienation	11
Sc_1	Object loss	32
($A + B$ yields this scale but is typically not scored.)		
Sc_{2A}	Lack of ego-mastery/cognitive	10
Sc_{2B}	Lack of ego-mastery/conative	14
Sc_{2C}	Lack of ego-mastery/defective inhibition	11
Sc_2	Lack of ego-mastery/intrapsychic autonomy (this scale is a summation of Sc_{2A}, Sc_{2B}, and Sc_{2C})	35
Sc_3	Bizarre sensory experiences	20

Scale 9—Hypomania

Ma_1	Amorality	6
Ma_2	Psychomotor acceleration	11
Ma_3	Imperturbability	8
Ma_4	Ego inflation	9

Note: From Dahlstrom, Welsh, and Dahlstrom (1972. Copyright © 1960, 1972 by the University of Minnesota. Reproduced with permission).

sources, Inc. of Odessa, Florida, uses Harris-Lingoes subscales based on adolescent normative data derived from research conducted at the Mayo Clinic. For readers interested in constructing their own templates for hand-scoring the Harris-Lingoes subscales, the information in appendix F is sufficient.

By inspecting the T-score elevations on the different subscales, one can form impressions and interpretative hypotheses about the test-taker. The beginning MMPI clinician is advised to use the same general cut-offs as are used in interpreting the clinical profile. That is, T-scores above 70 and those in the 30 to 40 range may indicate important concerns. Graham (1987) offered some preliminary interpretative hypotheses for high and low scores but cautioned the user that the subscales should be used to supplement the standard scales and not to replace them.

There are several concerns about the reliability and validity of the subscales. The most important problems are related to the construction methodology of the subscales. The rational method of forming the subscales by clustering items into content areas is a highly subjective process. However, Harris and Lingoes made no attempt to cross-validate their subscales nor to relate them to external criteria.

This type of research is greatly needed. The one recent attempt to link behavioral correlates to the subscales failed (Calvin, 1975). A recent attempt (Miller & Streiner, 1985) to reproduce the actual subscales, by clinicians who were asked to rationally group the items, failed to duplicate more than about one third of the actual subscales. This suggests that the subscales reliability is poor and that the interpretation of the subscales may be as subjective as their development.

Another recent investigation (Foerstner, 1986) of the factor structure of various MMPI scales (including but not limited to the Harris-Lingoes subscales) showed that 10 factors accounted for the majority of variance. The first factor was named depression. The two highest factor loadings on depression were D_1 (subjective depression) and D_4 (mental dullness), with D_5 (brooding) having a near similar loading. However, subscales D_2 (psychomotor retardation) and D_3 (physical malfunctioning) did not load at all on the first factor. This suggests that these subscales may not be related to the construct of depression in the specific way Harris and Lingoes (1955; 1968) assumed. Likewise, the study shows other subscales failing to appear as significant factor loadings as would be expected from their subscale groupings. Therefore, this and other studies suggest that the subscales may not be as construct-related as necessary for practical application.

Because Harris and Lingoes grouped items that appeared to "hang together" it is likely these items are mostly obvious versus subtle in nature, making them susceptible to response sets (fake good and fake bad). Moreover, they made no efforts to eliminate item overlap. Therefore, it is reasonable to assume that the high intercorrelations among the subscales are a result of this structural redundancy. Harris and Lingoes (1968) presented their intercorrelations in mimeographed materials, and their results are summarized in Graham (1987).

Finally, more diverse norms in different settings are conspicuously absent and are needed to aid the interpretation process. However, until reliability and validity studies more clearly support the use of the subscales, the clinician is urged to be cautious about the practical applications of the Harris-Lingoes subscales.

Wiggins Content Scales

Like Harris and Lingoes, another investigator had interest in the content dimensions of the MMPI. Wiggins (1966) recognized that the empirical nature of the MMPI scales discriminated normals from abnormals, and that elevated scores increased the probability of a subject resembling the criterion group subjects. However, the standard profile does not offer information about the client's responses to the content of specific MMPI items. Wiggins set out to classify the items into content categories. He recognized, as did Harris and Lingoes, the heterogeneity of scale content in the MMPI standard scales. Wiggins (1969) described how two individuals can obtain similar MMPI scores yet achieve dissimilar scores on his content scales. The content scales can be used to further examine an individual's self-report and expand the interpretation of the standard MMPI profiles. They are not intended to supplant the use of the standard clinical profile. The 13 content scales are: Social maladjustment (*SOC*), Depression (*DEP*), Feminine interests (*FEM*), Poor morale (*MOR*), Religious fundamentalism (*REL*), Authority conflict (*AUT*), Psychoticism (*PSY*), Organic symptoms (*ORG*), Family problems (*FAM*), Manifest hostility (*HOS*), Phobias (*PHO*), Hypomania (*HYP*), and Poor health (*HEA*). A description of the MMPI content scales appears in Table 3.2. The items in the Wiggins scales with the keyed responses are provided in appendix F.

Wiggins began his scale development by considering each of the 26 content categories that Hathaway and McKinley (1940) suggested constituted the MMPI item pool. He treated each category as a scale. The items in each of the original 26 categories were keyed by noting the infrequent response of the Minnesota normal group. Wiggins used a normal college student sample to determine the internal consistency of the scales. He psychometrically refined the scales by combining different categories into single scales, rearranging items from one content category to another, and creating new categories. The final adoption of 13 scales represented a combination of rational and psychometric efforts, with each content scale being internally consistent, moderately independent, and reflective of the general substantive clusters in the total MMPI item pool (Wiggins, 1969). The 13 scales had internal consistency coefficients ranging from .505 to .872. The majority of coefficients were above .70.

The content scales were validated on additional normal populations and psychiatric samples (Greene, 1980). Wiggins assembled tables for using his content scales based on a university sample and for a Minnesota normative group. Graham (1977) recommended using the latter group, as it is similar to the one employed for presenting different research scales of the MMPI and is similar to the normative base used in determining norms for the standard scales in the MMPI. The tables Wiggins presented for transforming raw scores into *T*-scores, based on the revised Minnesota adult normal sample (Hathaway & Briggs, 1957) and university students, are contained in appendix G, Tables 2 through 5. The reader interested in using the Wiggins content scales should consult a recent article by Colligan and Offord (1988). Colligan et al. (1983; 1984) reexamined the MMPI responses of normal adults using a contemporary sample. The MMPI responses for a contemporary-census-matched sample were very different from the original normative group on all of the basic MMPI clinical scales. Numerous changes are also apparent for the Wiggins content scales, and thus Colligan and Offord (1988) warned Wiggins content scale users that if they are applying the original normative data they may be overinterpreting psychopathology in their patients. They suggested that clinicians use a more conservative approach in interpreting the content scales and "supplement the Wiggins profile with a

TABLE 3.2
Description of Wiggins Content Scales

SOC Social maladjustment: High *SOC* is socially bashful, shy, embarrassed, reticent, self-conscious, and extremely reserved. Low *SOC* is gregarious, confident, assertive, relates quickly and easily to others, is fun loving, the life of a party, a joiner who experiences no difficulty in speaking before a group. This scale would correspond roughly with the popular concept of introversion-extraversion.

DEP Depression: High *DEP* experiences guilt, regret, worry, unhappiness, and a feeling that life has lost its zest; experiences difficulty in concentrating and has little motivation to pursue things; self-esteem is low; is anxious and apprehensive about the future; is sensitive to slight, feels misunderstood, and is convinced that he or she is unworthy and deserves punishment. In short, he or she is classically depressed.

FEM Feminine interests: High *FEM* admits to liking feminine games, hobbies, and vocations; denies liking masculine games, hobbies, and vocations. Here there is almost complete contamination of content and form, which has been noted in other contexts by several writers. Individuals may score high on this scale by presenting themselves as liking many things, because this item stem is present in almost all items. They may also score high by endorsing interests that, although possibly feminine, are also socially desirable, such as an interest in poetry, dramatics, news of the theatre, and artistic pursuits. This has been noted in the case of Wiggins' *Sd* scale. Finally, of course, individuals with a genuine preference for activities that are conceived by our culture as feminine will achieve high scores on this scale.

MOR Poor morale: High MOR is lacking in self-confidence; feels that he or she has failed in life; is given to despair and a tendency to give up hope; is extremely sensitive to the feelings and reactions of others and feels misunderstood by them while at the same time being concerned about offending them; feels useless and is socially suggestible. There is a substantive overlap here between the Depression and Social maladjustment scales and the Poor morale scale. The Social maladjustment scale seems to emphasize a lack of social ascendance and poise, the Depression scale feelings of guilt and apprehension, whereas the present scale seems to emphasize a lack of self-confidence and hypersensitivity.

REL Religious fundamentalism: High scorers on this scale see themselves as religious, church-going people who accept as true a number of fundamentalist religious convictions. They also tend to view their faith as the true one.

AUT Authority conflict: High *AUT* sees life as a jungle and is convinced that others are unscrupulous, dishonest, hypocritical, and motivated only by personal profit. He or she distrusts others, has little respect for experts, is competitive, and believes that everyone should get away with whatever they can.

PSY Psychoticism: High *PSY* admits to a number of classic psychotic symptoms of a primarily paranoid nature. He or she admits to hallucinations, strange experiences, loss of control, classic paranoid delusions of grandeur and persecution, feelings of unreality, daydreaming, and a sense that things are wrong, while feeling misunderstood by others.

ORG Organic symptoms: High *ORG* admits to symptoms that are often indicative of organic involvement. These include headaches, nausea, dizziness, loss of motility and coordination, loss of consciousness, poor concentration and memory, speaking and reading difficulty, lack of muscular control, skin sensations, difficulty with hearing and smell.

FAM Family problems: High *FAM* feels that he or she had an unpleasant home life characterized by a lack of love in the family and parents who were unnecessarily critical, nervous, quarrelsome, and quick tempered. Although some items are ambiguous, most are phrased with reference to the parental home rather than the individual's current home.

HOS Manifest hostility: High *HOS* admits to sadistic impulses and a tendency to be cross, grouchy, competitive, argumentative, uncooperative, and retaliatory in his or her interpersonal relationships. He or she is often competitive and socially aggressive.

PHO Phobias: High *PHO* has admitted to a number of fears, many of them of the classically phobic variety such as heights, dark, closed spaces, and so forth.

HYP Hypomania: High *HYP* is characterized by feelings of excitement, well-being, restlessness, and tension. He or she is enthusiastic, high-strung, cheerful, full of energy, and apt to be hotheaded. Has broad interests, seeks change, and is apt to take on more than he or she can handle.

HEA Poor health: High *HEA* is concerned about his or her health and has admitted to a variety of gastro-intestinal complaints centering around an upset stomach and difficulty in elimination.

Note: From Wiggins (1966. Copyright © 1966 by the American Psychological Association. Reprinted by permission).

second profile line for comparative purposes based on the data from this contemporary normal sample" (Colligan & Offord, 1988, p. 27). Descriptive statistics for each of the content scales based on this contemporary sample and the Hathaway-Briggs improved Minnesota normal sample arranged by raw scores for males and females are presented in Table 3.3.

Basically, Wiggins developed his content scales using a single college student sample, thus it was important to further examine psychometric scale characteristics with other samples. He used a sample of Air Force enlisted men to serve as a noncollege normal population sample and three other college samples from different geographical regions. The internal consistencies of the content scales were analyzed and shown to be acceptable. Wiggins (1969) examined various groups and reported that they differed on his content scales, indicating his scales can discriminate criterion groups much in the same fashion as the MMPI clinical scales. However, as Wiggins (1969) pointed out, the scales were not devised for group discrimination purposes. The groups were (a) 261 Air Force men, (b) 272 psychiatric inpatient men, (c) 192 psychiatric inpatient women, (d) 125 outpatient men, (e) 25 outpatient women, (f) 96 University of Minnesota college men, and (g) 125 University of Minnesota college women. Many differences were found among the groups on the content scales, with the largest differences existing between the college groups and the same-sex patient group (inpatient and outpatient). Other significant differences existed between Air Force men and college men.

Wiggins (1969) discussed how the 13 content scales diagnostically classified six groups of psychiatric patients. The classified groups were brain disorders,

TABLE 3.3

**Raw scores for the Wiggins Content Scales on the Hathaway-Briggs (H-B)
and Contemporary Census-matched Samples *(CMS)* of Normal Adults**

	Raw score[a]			
	Men		Women	
Scale	H-B[b]	CMS	H-B[b]	CMS
HEA Poor health	4.9 (3.0)	4.9 (3.3)	5.9 (3.9)	5.0 (3.7)**
DEP Depression	7.0 (5.1)	6.0 (4.5)*	8.7 (5.1)	7.0 (4.9)***
ORG Organic symptoms	5.3 (4.3)	5.4 (4.1)	6.9 (4.6)	5.2 (4.1)***
FAM Family problems	3.7 (2.3)	3.8 (2.4)	4.1 (2.5)	4.1 (2.4)
AUT Authority conflict	9.5 (4.0)	9.1 (3.9)	8.0 (3.7)	7.2 (3.5)**
FEM Feminine interests	9.1 (3.6)	9.3 (3.3)	19.8 (3.4)	20.3 (3.1)
REL Religious fundamental-ism	6.3 (3.0)	6.7 (3.0)	7.2 (2.7)	7.8 (2.6)**
HOS Manifest hostility	9.5 (4.9)	8.8 (4.3)	8.6 (4.6)	7.0 (4.0)***
MOR Poor morale	8.0 (4.9)	6.7 (4.8)**	9.8 (5.0)	8.4 (5.0)**
PHO Phobias	5.6 (3.8)	6.8 (3.6)***	9.0 (4.4)	9.8 (4.4)*
PSY Psychoticism	8.1 (5.8)	7.5 (4.5)	7.7 (5.1)	7.0 (4.3)
HYP Hypomania	11.9 (4.4)	12.8 (3.8)*	12.5 (4.2)	11.8 (3.4)*
SOC Social maladjustment	8.6 (4.8)	10.6 (5.6)***	10.2 (5.2)	10.8 (5.8)

Note: From Colligan and Offord (1988). Reprinted by permission.

[a]Scores are reported as mean (SD).

[b]H-B: Hathaway and Briggs (1957) Improved Minnesota Normal Sample.

*, **, and *** refer to the two-tailed p value from the test, for each sex, of the null hypothesis that the H-B and CMS means are equal using the two-sample t-test and are $*.01 < p \leq .05$, $**.001 < p \leq .01$, and $***p \leq .001$.

affective psychoses, schizophrenic psychoses, psychoneurotic disorders, personality disorders, and sociopathic disorders. Three discriminant functions accounted for the majority of variance in multiple discriminant analyses. Hostility, authority conflict, depression, poor morale, and psychoticism were the most important contributors to group discrimination, but family problems, organicity, and hypomania also contributed to the classification.

A number of studies support the validity and usefulness of the Wiggins content scales. For example, Peteroy, Pirrello, and Adams (1982) found the depression scale to be a good predictor of length of stay in a psychiatric unit. In general, it appears that content scale scores are related to significant extra-test behaviors for many different populations (Boerger, 1975; Hoffman & Jackson, 1976; Lachar & Alexander, 1978; Payne & Wiggins, 1972). Many of the content scales are similar to the parent MMPI scales, such as the poor health scale and scale 1 (hypochondriasis). These and others are correlated with the standard

MMPI scales, but as Graham (1987) pointed out, many of the correlations are low enough or moderate enough to be measuring unique as well as common features. Users of the scales should realize that the content scales are susceptible to response set biases given their obvious nature. Therefore, the validity of very high or low scores may be suspect, and careful attention to the other procedures designed to detect response sets is recommended. These other procedures are more fully discussed later in this chapter and in chapter 5. Generally, Wiggins' T-scores above 70 and those at 40 and below could be considered high and low scores. However, these T-scores should be examined, not in terms of absolute values, but rather by the relative level of one content score to another. For example, if depression is the most elevated score at T-60, the client is self-reporting more depression than any other characteristic, and this is noteworthy.

Although more research is needed to assess the extra-test correlates of the content scales, they do appear to be practically useful, valid, and reliable. However, as previously stated, they are intended to augment and not replace interpretation of the standard clinical scales.

Subtle-Obvious Items

Although the validity scales are used to detect different types of test-taking attitudes, portions of the MMPI item pool itself have been utilized to construct other content measures of faking good (underreporting) and faking bad (overreporting). Wiener and Harmon (1946) were the first investigators to develop subtle-obvious subscales for the MMPI. They rationally separated items into two groups; the first group consisted of obvious items, that is, items with high face validity related to psychological disturbance. The second group consisted of subtle items, items that are considered less revealing of psychological problems. Items were assigned to these two categories based on consensus. Although interrater reliability information is not provided, their method yielded subscales for the following five clinical scales: scales 2, 3, 4, 6, and 9. Scales 1, 7, and 8 consist of mostly obvious items, making it difficult to subdivide these scales. The subtle-obvious subscales do not contain an equal number of items, and no efforts were made to balance them. The scales contain 110 subtle items and 146 obvious items. Greene (1980) stated that "the empirically determined deviant response for 65 (59%) of these subtle items was in the opposite direction from what would be expected by merely inspecting item content, whereas only 8 (5%) of these obvious items were scored in the opposite direction" (p. 60). The Wiener–Harmon obvious-subtle subscales with their scoring direction are listed in appendix F. T-score conversions for these subscales are listed in appendix G. In general, significantly higher scores on the obvious versus the subtle subscales may indicate a faking-bad posture or an exaggeration of psychological problems. Higher subtle subscale scores suggest a faking-good test-taking attitude. Greene

(1980) suggested that clients achieving T-scores of 70 or higher on all five subtle subscales with T-scores close to 50 on all five obvious subscales may be faking good. He said the converse relationship would indicate the presence of a fake-bad approach to the test. Specific cutting scores were not provided by Wiener and Harmon but they are needed to help the clinician determine the meaning of scattered T-score elevations on the subtle-obvious subscales.

The subtle-obvious distinction pioneered by Wiener and Harmon (1946), motivated other researchers to investigate this distinction more fully. Different interpretations of the meaning of subtle and obvious have left inconsistencies in the way the terms are used. For example, Seeman (1952) defined subtlety as indicating that "meaning can or cannot be arbitrarily assigned in a priori fashion" (p. 278) by a psychologically trained individual. Obvious items, according to Seeman, are those items easily discernable as to their meaning. Christian, Burkhart, and Gynther (1978) defined subtle-obvious items by having college students rate all of the MMPI items as being very obvious, obvious, neither obvious nor subtle (neutral), subtle, or very subtle. The mean obviousness ratings for all of the MMPI scales showed that scale F had the highest rating, indicating its items are obvious in nature. Scale L had a subtle rating, which is surprising because the items are usually seen as obvious as the scale does not "trap" sophisticated individuals faking good (Greene, 1980). Scale 8 was given a subtle rating, which is also surprising because it is generally considered obvious in nature. Regardless of the methods used to assess the items, the practical results appear to be similar (Dubinsky, Gamble, & Rogers, 1985). Many different subtle-obvious distinctions have been made, and Dubinsky et al. (1985) provided a useful overview of the subtle-obvious literature. They stated that regardless of the item sets used, subjects instructed to manipulate their MMPI scores tend to increase or decrease their obvious item scores, but their scores "for subtle items tend to move in the opposite direction from that desired" (p. 67). In other words, it is easier for subjects to more effectively manipulate the obvious versus the subtle items. These reviewers also indicate that norms for different populations are needed for all of the obvious-subtle subscales, regardless of their authorship.

The obvious-subtle subscales do not appear to be equally valid for all of the clinical scales. Validity studies examining subtle-obvious subscale correlations with different populations and different demand characteristics produced inconsistent results (Dubinsky et al. 1985), although some specific findings appear to be more consistent than others. For example, Hovanitz and Jordan-Brown (1986) assessed the validity of certain clinical scales with and without subtle items in a psychiatric patient population. The subtle-obvious items used in their study were derived from the Christian et al. (1978) study described earlier in this section. One of their findings was that the subtle subscale on depression did not contribute to a significant correlation found between the Beck Depression Inventory and the MMPI depression scale. Dubinsky et al. (1985) also observed that the MMPI depression scale correlates higher with the Beck Depression

Inventory when the subtle items are removed. They found that the obvious subscales related significantly to all of the questionnaire criteria in their study, whereas the subtle subscales showed significantly greater relationships to the diagnostic and drug classification measures used. The researchers interpreted their results as arguing strongly for the retention of subtle items within the MMPI. Hovanitz and Jordan-Brown (1986) pointed out that a series of different studies investigating the validity of the subtle items found that item validity depended on the specific scale that was employed. Using college students as subjects, Burkhart, Gynther, and Fromuth (1980) found that in scale 2 (depression) and scale 3 (hysteria), the obvious items were more predictive of criteria than the subtle items. Gynther, Burkhart, and Hovanitz (1979) found that the obvious items in scale 4 (psychopathic deviate) were more significantly related to the criterion than the subtle items.

Although more research is needed on the extra-test correlates of subtle-obvious scores, the Wiener–Harmon (1946) subscales do appear useful in helping the clinician further assess the validity of individual MMPI profiles. Greene (1988) used the Wiener–Harmon (1946) subscales in a study to determine the relative efficacy of various validity indices (e.g., F-K index) to identify subgroups of clients within three frequently occurring profile code types in a community outpatient mental health clinic. He found that clients who over-reported psychopathology (as measured by the differences between the T-scores and the five pairs of Wiener and Harmon subscales) stayed in treatment less time relative to clients who underreported psychopathology or did not distort their responses to the MMPI items. He concluded that the obvious and subtle subscales were effective in identifying clients who minimized and overclaimed psychopathology within three code-types (2–7/7–2; 7–8/8–7; spike 4 profiles) and recommended that these subscales be routinely scored to provide data that is not obtainable from validity scales L, F, and K.

The specific question of which subtle-obvious item sets are most valuable in clinical practice is as of yet undetermined. But as Greene (1980) pointed out, the Wiener–Harmon (1946) items do have the normative data necessary for interpretation that are not readily available for the other critical item lists. The different abilities of subtle-obvious items to predict various attributes raises again the issue of which approach (content versus empirical) is the most strategic in constructing personality scales.

EMPIRICAL APPROACH

MacAndrew Alcoholism Scale (MAC)

Probably the most frequently cited and used MMPI scale for detecting alcoholism or addiction proneness is the MacAndrew alcoholism scale (MAC) (Mac-Andrew, 1965). MacAndrew constructed his scale by comparing the MMPI responses of 300 outpatient alcoholics with 300 nonalcoholic psychiatric out-patients and retained the items that significantly differentiated the two groups. He originally identified 51 items, but because 2 items were obviously related to alcohol use, 49 items constituted the final scale.[2] Appendix F contains the *MAC* scale items with their keyed responses. Appendix G presents *T*-score conversions for the scale. The sample MacAndrew used to construct his scale consisted of all males, most of whom were white. Despite the parameters in MacAndrew's sample, Greene's (1980) review of the scale shows it to consistently distinguish alcoholic from nonalcoholic patients in different psychiatric settings "with the percentage of patients correctly classified ranging from 61.5% to 76%" (p. 194). Clearly, however, more studies with females and minorities are needed.

Colligan and Offord (1987a) suggested that some of the differences in data among *MAC* scale researchers may be due to unavailable performance standards among normal subjects. Using a new normal adult reference sample (Colligan, Osborne, Swenson, & Offord, 1984) that was comparable to the original Minnesota normative group (see chapter 2), these researchers presented a table of descriptive statistics and percentile ranks for raw scores from the *MAC* scale (males and females). They pointed out that MacAndrew's original cutting score (which many have continued to use without considering their specific population) of 24 or more as reflective of alcoholism is too low for a contemporary normal sample. Specifically, according to Colligan and Offord (1987b):

> a raw score of 24 is higher than 60% of the men in the new normal reference sample; thus, 40% of these men are identified as alcoholic. Although the *MAC* Scale was developed and cross-validated entirely on a sample of men, it probably has been applied with equal frequency to samples of women. A raw score of 24 is higher than 82% of the normal women in the sample; thus, 18% are classified as alcoholic. (p. 293)

They recommend that users of the *MAC* scale adopt a more conservative approach in using the scale for alcoholism screening purposes.

The use of the *MAC* scale in differentiating alcoholic patients from non-alcoholic psychiatric patients is generally well-accepted (Greene & Garvin, 1988). However, researchers have been concerned about the scale's capacity to detect alcoholism that coexists with a psychiatric diagnosis (Apfeldorf & Hunley, 1981; MacAndrew, 1981; Preng & Clopton, 1986). Preng and Clopton (1986) reported a lack of research in this area and investigated the scale's ability to detect alcoholism among patients with neurotic disorders and personality disorders. Their subjects were 140 male VA patients from an alcohol treatment ward and a psychiatric ward. Their ages ranged from 19 to 67, with a mean age

---

[2]Greene (1980) pointed out that these two deleted items are Group Booklet Form Items 215 and 460. Furthermore, he noted that Dahlstrom (1979) indicated that item 356 (false) on the *MAC* was listed incorrectly as item 357 (false) in Dahlstrom et al. (1975).

of 41.7 years. Drug abusers were eliminated from the study. Five diagnostic groups with 28 patients in each group were identified. The five groups were: (a) alcoholics, (b) nonalcoholic patients with neurotic disorders, (c) nonalcoholic patients with personality disorders, (d) alcoholics with a neurotic disorder, and (e) alcoholics with personality disorders. Diagnoses were made using *DSM-III* criteria. Because the DSM-III does not contain a distinct neurotic category, a patient's DSM-III diagnosis was categorized as neurotic if its equivalent DSM-II diagnosis was a neurotic diagnosis. As expected, the *MAC* scale scores of the alcoholic group were higher than the MAC scale scores of the nonalcoholic psychiatric patients. The optimal cutting score for correctly classifying alcoholic and nonalcoholic psychiatric patients was 29, which is considerably higher than that which is often suggested as the optimal cut-off score of 24. A score of 29 correctly classified 65.4% of the subjects. The most important comparisons, however, failed to show the *MAC* scale able to detect alcoholism among patients with either personality or neurotic disorders. Although the study did suggest that neurotic disorders (primarily dysthymic diagnoses) seemed to be linked with lower *MAC* scale scores for alcoholics compared to personality disorders (which do not appear to have much affect on alcoholics' *MAC* scale scores), significant differences failed to appear between the groups. According to the authors, these results imply that clinicians should consider alternative measures to the *MAC* scale when screening for alcoholism among patients with dsythymia and personality disorders. The *MAC* scale clearly needs further investigation before it can be considered useful in screening for alcoholism among psychiatric patients.

The *MAC* scale has been shown to be sensitive to problem behaviors other than alcoholism. Rathus, Fox, and Ortins (1980) used an abbreviated *MAC* scale (the first 20 items) in conjunction with the MMPI-168 (an abbreviated MMPI) to show that among 1,672 high school students, *MAC* scale scores are related to crimes against property and person and to marijuana usage. Other studies have suggested that the *MAC* scale is sensitive to substance abuse in general, as alcoholics, heroin addicts, and polysubstance abusers all score similarly (Kranitz, 1972; Lachar, Berman, Grisel, & Schoof, 1976). Although the literature is limited regarding the application of the *MAC* scale to adolescents, the scale appears to be generally useful in adolescent populations (Archer, 1987). Although Archer (1987) pointed out that cut-offs for identifying substance abusing adolescents are unclear, the general recommendations range from scores of 24 to 28.

High scorers on the *MAC* scale are described as being vulnerable to abusing drugs if they are not actually abusive at the time of testing (Greene, 1980; Hoffman, Loper, & Kammeier, 1974). *MAC* scale scores tend to remain stable despite treatment intervention, suggesting the scale is measuring a fundamental dimension of personality (Huber & Dahahy, 1975; Sherer, Haygood, & Alfano, 1984). Rebelliousness, resentment of authority, and impulsiveness are associated personality characteristics (Finney, Smith, Skeeters, & Auvenshine, 1971).

Scale 4 (*Pd*) is known to be associated with impulsiveness and substance abuse, and high *MAC* scores are often seen in conjunction with elevations on this scale (Pfost, Kunce, & Stevens, 1984). MacAndrew (1981) suggested that the *MAC* scale is a bipolar measure of differential sensitivity to reward and punishment, with high *MAC* scorers having a reward-seeking orientation and low scorers striving to avoid punishment. This rationale is consistent with another body of research conducted by Eysenck and Eysenck (1985) and Gray (1972), who have linked extroversion and introversion with similar descriptors.

Meyer (1983) offered a general cut-off score for using the *MAC* scale, with raw scores of 27 or higher being strongly suggestive of an addiction of some type. This text's authors have found the following general guidelines useful in their private psychotherapy outpatient population. The reader should be reminded that these are simply guidelines without any empirical derivation and should be cautiously used if at all.

Recommended Guidelines

1. Raw scores of 27 or higher are associated either with alcoholism or substance abuse, recovery from alcoholism or substance abuse, or an individual strongly opposed to the use of alcohol or other substances because of past experience (e.g., a family member who has been identified as alcoholic).

2. When an individual obtains a raw score of 24 or higher on the *MAC* scale and has also endorsed the item "I have used alcohol excessively" (Group Booklet Item 215) as true, the *MAC* score is a more powerful indicator of substance abuse than if the item was endorsed false.

3. When the neurotic triad (scales 1, 2, and 3) is elevated and the *MAC* score is elevated above a raw score of 24 without evidence of alcohol abuse, food abuse may be indicated.

4. Some code-types are frequently associated with alcoholism, but the *MAC* scale is not always elevated. These include the 2–6 profile, the 2–4 profile, 2–7 profile, and the 2–4–7–8 profile.

False positives are often obtained when the *MAC* scale is used in some populations (Uecker, 1970). Pfost, Kunce, and Stevens (1984) suggested that the *MAC*'s classification accuracy eventually might be improved by developing differential cut-off points for individuals with different personality profiles. It is important for clinicians to ascertain the characteristics of their patient population and use norms that are appropriate to their specific setting. Studies have clearly shown that the *MAC* scale can grossly misclassify Black subjects and male VA patients, so caution should be exercised in the use of the scale in these populations (Graham, 1985; Holmes, Dungan, & McLaughlin, 1982). Greene and Garvin (1988) stated that "no study has reported the correlates of the *MAC* for samples of women or men from any minority group" (p. 182). They warned

MAC scale users to be cautious in generalizing correlates derived from white male alcoholics to other groups and offered the reminder that "MacAndrew (1965; 1981) designed and discussed the use of the *MAC* only with men" (p. 182). Readers interested in a more in-depth summarization of the *MAC* literature should consult Greene and Garvin's (1988) recent chapter on substance abuse.

Overcontrolled Hostility (*O-H*) Scale

Megargee, Cook, and Mendelsohn (1967) developed the overcontrolled-hostility *(O-H)* scale by administering the MMPI to male inmates classified as extremely assaultive, moderately assaultive, inmates convicted of nonviolent crimes, and a group of 46 normals (men who had not been convicted of any crime). Using the empirical criterion approach, the researchers identified 55 items that differentiated the assaultive from the nonassaultive inmates and cross-validated these items in a new but similar sample. Item analyses resulted in a 31-item scale referred to as the *O-H* scale. Appendix F contains a listing of the items with their scoring direction, and appendix G presents *T*-score conversions for raw scores. The higher the raw score on the scale, the more the individual is said to resemble the assaultive inmate. The rationale for developing the scale is based on Megargee et al.'s (1967) concept that two types of individuals commit aggressive acts: (a) undercontrolled individuals with poorly developed inhibitions to frustration, and (b) overcontrolled individuals who manifest rigid inhibitions or defenses against the expression of aggressive impulses. The overcontrolled individual is vulnerable to "blowing up" or acting out in hostile, destructive ways when the provocation reaches some specific level against which they can no longer defend or tolerate. According to Graham (1987), "Megargee and his associates believe that the most aggressive acts typically are committed by the overcontrolled rather than the undercontrolled person" (p. 183). Graham (1987) stated that there is little data to support the use of the *O-H* scale in groups other than inmates, but other studies have replicated the correlates of elevated *O-H* scores in samples of forensic psychiatric inpatients (Lane & Kling, 1979) and psychiatric outpatients (Walters, Greene, & Solomon, 1982). Megargee et al. (1967) did not provide specific cutting scores for users of the scale. They suggested that users determine the most appropriate scores for minimizing false positives and false negatives in their particular clinical environment.

Graham (1987) pointed out that although in correctional settings high *O-H* scores tend to be associated with aggressive and violent acts, it is difficult, at best, to predict specific acts of violence from *O-H* scores. Graham (1987) said the "*O-H* scale has some potential use in other settings because it tells clinicians something about how subjects typically respond to provocation" (p. 184). The typical way high *O-H* scorers respond to provocation or frustration is by inhibiting their hostile impulses and denying any frustration. White (1975) provided support for the construct validity of the *O-H* scale by showing that subjects with

low *O-H* scores gave significantly more extrapunitive responses to the Rosenz-
weig Picture-Frustration Study, whereas subjects with high *O-H* scale scores
responded with more impunitive responses. It appears that *O-H* scores are
associated with an individual's characteristic way of coping with hostility
(White, 1975). Through a factor analysis of 200 male inmates, Walters and
Greene (1983) revealed the presence of five major factors measured by the *O-H*
scale. The first factor was named "absence of manifest symptomatology" and
significantly correlated with Welsh's (1956) repression factor and Harris and
Lingoes (1955, 1968) subscale Hy_1 (denial of social anxiety). Walters and
Greene (1983) concluded that a "denial of symptomatology, particularly social
anxiety, appears to be an important aspect of the personality pattern measured by
the *O-H* scale" (p. 562).

The *O-H* scale has been linked to the 4–3 MMPI code-type by several
researchers (Gearing, 1979; Persons & Marks, 1971; Walters, Solomon, &
Greene, 1982). High scores on scale 4 of the MMPI are positively correlated
with delinquency and criminal behaviors (Walters, 1985), and Greene (1980)
described the relationship of scale 3 to scale 4 as being an important determinant
of controlled behavior. Individuals with significantly higher scale 4 elevations
over scale 3 in a 4–3 profile are more likely to have difficulty inhibiting their
impulses. Greene (1980) suggested that high *O-H* scorers may share common
characteristics with the 4–3 high-point code-type, and he actually co-investigated
the relationship between *O-H* scorers and this code type (Walters, Solomon, &
Greene, 1982). Using a sample of 200 male inmates, 500 psychiatric outpatients,
and 102 psychiatric inpatients, Walters, Solomon, and Greene (1982) concluded
that the *O-H* scale and the 4–3 high-point pair are correlated and appear to be
measuring similar behaviors. They recommended that clinicians encountering
elevated *O-H* scores in a 4–3 code-type be aware of the potential for assaultive
behaviors. They did not comment on the meaning of subjects obtaining elevated
4–3 code-types without a correspondingly high *O-H* scale score. They did point
out that there is minimal item overlap between scales 4 and 3 and the *O-H* scale,
so it is unlikely that the correlation is due to an overlap artifact. Scales 4 and 3
have only four items in common with the *O-H* scale.

It is important not to assume that the 4–3 profile type can be interpreted
interchangeably with the *O-H* scale. Buck and Graham (1978) did not find
support for a relationship between the 4–3 profile type and violent behavior in a
male inmate population, and warned that caution "be exercised in generalizing to
populations that differ from those in which the 4–3 profile type is established" (p.
344). Clearly, there are inconsistencies in the research findings, and readers
should carefully assess the appropriateness of applying research findings to their
own tested population.

The meaning of low scores is uncertain on the *O-H* scale, although Graham
(1987) stated that low scores may be indicative of chronically aggressive individuals or persons who appropriately express their anger. High scorers are

reluctant to verbalize their anger, frustration, and psychological symptoms and are rigidly overcontrolled individuals without manifest anxiety.

The user of the *O-H* scale should be aware that approximately two thirds of the items on the scale are scored in the false direction. Therefore, an individual responding to the test items with a false response set is likely to elevate the score on this particular scale.

In the clinical experience of this text's authors, it appears important to observe *O-H* scale scores in relationship to the obtained code-type. For example, private outpatient psychotherapy patients with 4–9 code-types and low *O-H* scores (raw score less than 10) tend to express their frustrations as they are felt more often than other code types. High *O-H* scores occurring in 4–9 profiles tend to manifest more episodic outbursts, especially when consuming alcohol. Low scorers on *O-H* within a 4–3 code-type are seen as shouters; that is, they are individuals who are constantly angry and irritable, with a propensity to shout at people in their social environment. High *O-H* scorers with the 4–3 profile have been observed to manifest imperturbability but periodically "blow up" at specific persons in their environment whom they may perceive as nonretaliatory. Although these are clinical examples, it is important for researchers to further investigate the relationship of specific *O-H* scores to code-types.

Ego Strength (*ES*) Scale

Barron's (1953) ego strength *(ES)* scale is a commonly scored supplemental scale despite controversy over its usefulness (Clayton & Graham, 1979; Graham, 1987; Greene, 1980) and has been considered a prognostic index of treatment or a general index of personality assets (Dahlstrom, Welsh, & Dahlstrom, 1975). Specifically, MMPI responses were obtained from 33 neurotic patients; 12 men and 21 women composed the sample and ranged in age from 20 to 24 years with a strong majority of the sample having completed high school. Above average IQ scores were obtained for the sample, and socioeconomic status was considered to be lower middle class. The patients had voluntarily entered psychotherapy at the Langley Porter Clinic in San Francisco and were treated by psychiatric residents with little psychiatric experience. After 6 months of psychotherapy (when the resident's rotation through the outpatient service was completed) the 33 patients were divided by two independent raters into a group of 17 improved patients and 16 patients evaluated as unimproved. Improvement meant that a patient's self-report of well-being changed in relationship to his or her report prior to treatment, there was a lessening of different physical symptoms such as headaches, and there was improvement in certain cases of interpersonal relationships. The MMPI responses of the subjects given prior to treatment were then empirically identified to differentiate the two groups. The 68 items so identified became the ego strength scale and can be found in appendix F. Raw-score conversions to *T*-scores can be found in appendix G. Barron (1953) cross-validated the scale on three additional samples from the Langley Porter Clinic all receiving brief psychoanalytically oriented psychotherapy. The scale correlated positively with therapy outcomes, and Barron believed that high ego strength scores measured latent ego-strength and the capacity for personality integration. However, as Graham (1987) pointed out in his review of the *ES* scale, subsequent attempts to cross-validate the scale as a predictor of psychotherapy response have produced inconsistent results. Duckworth (1979) and Graham (1987) suggested that many of the failures to replicate Barron's finding that the *ES* scale was related to change in psychotherapy are because hospitalization, rather than psychotherapy, has been used as the change agent. Among the many contradictory results regarding *ES* scale emotional and behavioral correlates is a study by Crumpton, Cantor, and Bastiste (1960). Their findings suggest that the scale appears to be measuring an absence of particular ego deficits rather than the presence of ego strength. A factor analysis conducted by Stein and Chu (1967) yielded similar results. Greene (1980) more forcefully stated that "the plethora of studies reporting negative relationships between the *ES* scale and psychotherapy outcome indicates that the *ES* scale is of little usefulness in routinely predicting the response of a given client to psychotherapy" (p. 192).

Dahlstrom, Welsh, and Dahlstrom (1975) in a comprehensive review of the *ES* scale literature, stated that Barron's original findings are confusing, as patients assumed to be most in need of help (low scorers on *ES*) appear to benefit from it least, whereas those needing the least help (high scorers on *ES*) benefit the most. They pointed out that if a patient elevates the *ES* scale yet produces an unelevated MMPI profile, they are most likely denying their psychological problems. If the patient's MMPI displays evidence of a significant problem and the *ES* scale is near the general mean, their problems may be more situational versus chronic in nature. Caldwell (1988) attempted to summarize the issue of what high and low *ES* scale scores meant by stating the following:

> The prognostic implication of ES seems to be ironic: the more "together" the person is at the beginning of therapy, the more able the person is to utilize therapy and the more rapidly he or she is likely to get better. Conversely, the more disorganized the person is, the more treatments it will take to get better and the slower it goes. In this way, *E.S.* is more primarily a predictor of the rate of response and more indirectly a predictor of the long term potential for improvement. (p. 38)

Duckworth (1979) suggested that scores above a *T*-score of 55 are related to abilities to deal effectively with others and a likelihood of benefiting from psychotherapy. In general, high scorers on the *ES* scale are described as having resiliency, that is, they appear to "bounce back" from problems without becoming overwhelmed by them. Scores that are below a *T*-score of 45 indicate that the individual may feel in need of help and does not feel he or she has the personal resources to adequately cope with his or her problems, but in fact may be able to. Such individuals may be seriously maladjusted psychologically (Graham, 1987).

These descriptions are strikingly similar to the correlates for scale K. Clinical lore has it that the two scales are measuring similar constructs. However, Caldwell (1988) reported that although the K scale is in fact moderately correlated (.30) with the ES scale, readers should be aware of T-score differences of 10 or more between the two scales. He provided the following illustration:

> For example, if K is T-53 but ES is only T-37, then this may represent a very tenuous and precarious level of functioning. Conversely, a moderately disturbed profile with K at T-45 but $E.S.$ at T-60 may be associated with an impressive productivity or with managing many ongoing responsibilities, despite extensive frustrations and occasions of acute subjective distress. Thus, high K inflates the $E.S.$ Scale, and low K may lead to a significant underestimation of the current level of organization of the person's functioning. (Caldwell, 1988, p. 38)

The clinician wishing to use the ES scale should consult a recent article by Colligan and Offord (1987b), as they presented new normative tables for the ES scale based on a contemporary census-matched sample of normal adults. Hathaway and Briggs (1957) reported mean raw scores and standard deviations for the ES scale in their refined subsample of Minnesota normal adults, but the Colligan-Offord (1987b) table is a more current representation of response patterns among normal people.

INTERNAL CONSISTENCY APPROACH

Welsh's Anxiety (A) and Repression (R) Scales

Numerous investigations into the factor structure of the MMPI have been conducted in order to delineate the major sources of variance in the test. Although some factor analytic researchers have claimed to reduce the major sources of personality variance in the MMPI to two or three factors, Dahlstrom, Welsh, and Dahlstrom (1975) stated that this is an oversimplified and premature conclusion. However, two dimensions of personality do appear to have consistently emerged in the factor analytic literature. Welsh (1956) developed the anxiety (A) and repression (R) scales to measure the common dimensions of personality inherent in the MMPI. The first dimension, A, is conceptualized as reflecting anxiety although some experts interpret it more broadly as indicating general maladjustment or a lack of ego resiliency (Block, 1965). The second dimension, R, is referred to as repression and is also seen as indicating a generalized inhibition about expressing psychopathology. Welsh (1956) identified two other dimensions (psychoticism and control over unacceptable impulses), but more subsequent research has focused on his A and R dimensions (Dahlstrom, Welsh, & Dahlstrom, 1975). A major controversy existed among researchers as to whether the Welsh dimensions were valid measures of the primary personality dimensions in the test or more reflective of a response bias factor. Block (1965) conducted several factor analytic investigations and concluded that the anxiety and repression dimensions were in fact the two primary factors in the MMPI. The reader interested in this controversy should consult Block (1965) and Dahlstrom, Welsh, and Dahlstrom (1975) for more information.

Welsh (1956) constructed his scales using male VA patients. Early versions of each scale were administered to patients who were then classified into the upper and lower 10th percentile rank. These two groups were then contrasted in their item responses to the entire MMPI item pool. The items that discriminated the two contrasting extreme groups (upper and lower scores on the preliminary scales) were retained for inclusion on the final scales. The A and R scales consist of 39 and 40 items, respectively. The items with direction of scoring are provided in appendix F. T-score conversions for the scales are provided in appendix G. The predominant scoring direction for the A scale is true, with only one item scored in the false direction. The items on the R scale are all keyed in the false direction. Clearly a true or false response set bias will influence the scores on these scales (Greene, 1980). The A scale items are obvious in nature, evidenced by the fact that when subjects are instructed to fake good, they are able to appreciably lower their scores on scale A (Parsons, Yourshaw, & Borstelmann, 1968).

Welsh (1956) found that the A dimension has positive loadings on scales 7 and 8 with negative loadings on the K scale. The second factor, or dimension R, has positive loadings on scales 2, 3, 5, and 6 with a negative loading on scale 9.

The validity of the Welsh R scale has been most recently investigated by Watson et al. (1987). Watson et al. examined the validities of six MMPI repression scales using each scale and a projective repression instrument as criteria. The MMPI and projective instrument were administered to 190 male VA psychiatric patients with varied diagnoses. The Welsh R scale and Eichman (1962) repression factor (which was also developed in a similar manner to the Welsh R scale) were correlated highly with each other but neither showed a specific correlation with the other repression scales in the study. Watson et al. (1987) interpret their data as raising doubts about the usefulness of the Welsh R scale and the Eichman repression factor scale. The reader wishing a concise review of reliability studies on the A and R scales is directed to Graham (1987).

High scorers on scale A are described as anxious, unhappy, inhibited, self-doubting, submissive, lacking energy, and having difficulty concentrating (Duckworth, 1979; Graham, 1987; Greene, 1980). Low scorers are seen as outgoing, confident, clear thinking, and sometimes impulsive. Generally, the higher scale A is in relationship to scale R, the more likely it is that overt psychopathology will be expressed. Duckworth (1979) suggested scale A was more sensitive to situational anxiety and distress than MMPI scale 7, which is more representative of long-term characterological (trait) anxiety.

High scorers on scale R are described as unwilling to present their concerns, as denying angry feelings, conventional, unexcitable, and lacking insight about themselves. Low scorers are described as able and willing to discuss their problems, excitable, dominant, and impulsive.

Often, clinicians interpret scales A and R conjointly. Welsh (1956, 1965) suggested examining the elevations on the scales by three levels: low, medium, and high, which form nine categories or novants.[3] Table 3.4 provides the descriptors Welsh derived from a male VA patient population.

Gynther and Brilliant (1968) attempted to replicate the diagnostic classifications Welsh (1956) presented for conjoint use of his A- and R-scale scores. However, their major analysis failed to offer support for any of the diagnostic groupings that Welsh proposed, and the investigators concluded that the A-R categories may be invalid measures of "what they are supposed to measure" (Gynther & Brilliant, 1968, p. 574). These investigators were unable to determine the validity of the novant system, presumably due to the overlapping personality descriptors used to define the categories. This data and other studies lead us to agree with Welsh's (1965) caveat that his descriptions should be used only as hypotheses to be further assessed rather than as a firm basis from which to make personality inferences. Duckworth (1979) reported that only the high A-high R interpretation seemed valid in a college population, which suggests that users of the Welsh (1956) novant system be aware that his subjects consisted of white males in a VA hospital setting. Application of the Welsh descriptors to populations differing from the original sample characteristics should be used cautiously if at all.

The literature on interpreting scales A and R, like most other special scales, is based on adult norms and studies. Archer (1987) reproduced normative information provided by Gottesman and his colleagues for a sample of 15- and 18-year-old adolescents on special MMPI scales. Archer's (1987) review of the data indicates that the R scale is more affected by differences between adult- and adolescent-based T-score conversion values than is the A scale. However, because these data are derived from 15- and 18-year-old respondents, it is difficult to know how other age groupings would be affected. Archer (1987) issued a warning to clinicians interpreting adolescent A- and R-scale scores:

> It should be explicitly noted that A and R scale correlates have not been cross-validated within adolescent populations and, therefore, the attribution of these descriptors to adolescents is not supported by empirical data. Given the potential relevance of these dimensions to adolescent behavior, however, it is recommended that adolescent profiles be scored for the A and R scales and that impressions based on these special scales be cross-validated against other standard MMPI features as well as the adolescent's clinical history. (p. 125)

---

[3]The T-score cut-off value for low is 45 or less, 46 to 54 for medium, and 55 and above for high.

TABLE 3.4
Summary of Clinical Descriptors for Each
Novant in Welsh's *A* and *R* Scale Schema

I. High A–Low R

Subjects falling into this novant may be expected to be introspective, ruminative, and overideational, with complaints of worrying and nervousness. There may be chronic feelings of inadequacy, inferiority, and insecurity that are often accompanied by rich fantasies with sexual content. Emotional difficulties may interfere with judgment, so subjects are seen as lacking common sense. Patients in this novant do not use somatic defenses, and although they seem able to admit problems readily, the prognosis is poor.

II. High A–Medium R

Severe personality difficulties may be expected, with loss of efficiency in carrying out duties. There may be periods of confusion, inability to concentrate, and other evidence of psychological deficit. Symptoms of depression, anxiety, and agitation predominate, although hysterical disorders sometimes appear. Subjects are often described as unsociable.

III. High A–High R

Depression is often encountered with accompanying tenseness and nervousness as well as complaints of anxiety, insomnia, and undue sensitivity. Generalized neurasthenic features of fatigue, chronic tiredness, or exhaustion may be seen. These subjects are seen as rigid and worrying in a psychasthenic way and suffer from feelings of inadequacy and a brooding preoccupation with their personal difficulties.

IV, Medium A–Low R

This novant profile represents a heterogenous group of subjects, but often there are headaches and upper gastrointestinal tract symptoms following periods of tension and restlessness. Symptoms are often noted in response to frustration and situational difficulties, although subjects are reluctant to accept the psychogenic nature of their complaints. Patients tend to drop out of treatment quickly so that a superficial approach is frequently all that is possible. Ambition is often noted, but the level of adjustment may be poor with excessive use of alcohol.

V. Medium A–Medium R

Somatic symptomatology in this group tends to be specific rather than generalized, with epigastric and upper gastrointestinal pain predominating. In some cases there may be an active ulcer. Patients not showing somatic symptoms may complain of tension and depression. Frequently noted is the ability of these patients to tolerate discomfort rather than acting out.

VI. Medium A–High R

Subjects are often described as inadequate or immature and tend to use illness as an excuse for not accomplishing more. Lack of insight is often noted, with mechanisms of repression and denial prominent in adjustment attempts. Patients give a chronic hypochondriacal history with somatic overconcern particularly in the alimentary system; abdominal pain is common. Response to treatment is not often favorable, because they seem to have learned to use somatic complaints to solve emotional problems.

VII. Low A–Low R

Aggression and hostility may be noted in many subjects, and they are often described as arrogant, boastful, and self-centered; some are seen as dishonest and suspicious. Patients may show episodic attacks of acute distress in various organ systems, but these physical problems are not severe and generally yield to superficial treatment.

VIII. Low A–Medium R

Although subjects in this novant are characterized by attempts at self-enhancement, they are not viewed favorably by others; they tend to be seen as irritable, immature, and insecure. Under stress they are prone to develop symptoms that are usually localized rather than diffuse. Patients suffer from complaints arrived at after protracted periods of mild tension, but these are rarely incapacitating; there is an indifferent response to treatment and marginal adjustment is often noted.

IX. Low A–High R

Lack of self-criticism with impunitive behavior may be found in subjects in this novant, and they are often self-centered with many physical complaints. Occasionally there is mild anxiety and tension, but little depression occurs. Patients more often have pain in the extremities and the head rather than the trunk, but precordial and chest pain may be noted. They profit from reassurance, although insight is lacking into the nature of their symptoms.

Note: From Dahlstrom, Welsh, and Dahlstrom (1972. Adapted by permission).

Tryon, Stein, and Chu (*TSC*) Cluster Scales

The MMPI has been the target of many early factor analytic investigations at the scale rather than the item level. This was due to the fact that early computers could not handle the 550 separate MMPI items as variables in a factor analysis (Graham, 1977). It is more desirable to analyze individual items rather than scales, because the latter contain overlapping items that contribute to high scale intercorrelations, a factor compromising the necessary independent sources of variance. For example, the percentage of nonoverlapping items on the clinical scales ranges only from 17% to 33% (Stein, 1968). Tryon (1966) and his colleagues (Chu, 1966; Stein, 1968) developed procedures for cluster-analyzing large pools of items or variables and applied them to the MMPI. Specifically, they applied these procedures to the MMPI responses of 70 male VA hospital outpatient schizophrenics, 150 male VA hospital outpatient neurotics diagnosed as suffering from anxiety reaction, and 90 male military officers (considered the normal group). The patients and normals were matched for age and education, and the patient sample was intentionally selected to be mixed regarding emotional disturbance. Communality estimates for all 550 MMPI items were determined within the three samples, resulting in the elimination of 317 items for

> trivial communality and 57 for being rationally ambiguous in relation to the general content meaning of items within a cluster. This process resulted in clusters that are homogeneous both statistically and in content meaning. (Stein, 1968, p. 86)

Seven "pure" cluster scales with 192 items were derived, and each was named according to the rational content of the scales. Table 3.5 lists the names of the *TSC* cluster scales, and appendix F contains the items and scoring direction for each of the scales.

TABLE 3.5

TSC Cluster Scales

Cluster Scales	Scale Abbreviation	
1	(*I*)	Social introversion versus interpersonal poise and outgoing-ness (26 items)
2	(*B*)	Body symptoms versus lack of physical complaints (33 items)
3	(*S*)	Suspicion and mistrust versus absence of suspicion (25 items)
4	(*D*)	Depression and apathy versus positive and optimistic out-look (28 items)
5	(*R*)	Resentment and aggression versus lack of resentment and aggression (21 items)
6	(*A*)	Autism and disruptive thought versus absence of such dis-turbance (23 items)
7	(*T*)	Tension, worry, fears versus absence of such complaints (36 items)

Note: From K. B. Stein (1968. Adapted by permission).

High scores on these scales indicate the presence of traits or descriptors derived from the scale name, whereas low scores imply the absence of such traits or descriptors. Stein (1968) pointed out that clusters *I, B,* and *S* are the most independent clusters, with the highest correlation occurring between *I* and *B* (.33). The other four cluster scales are highly intercorrelated with all of the cluster scales. Stein (1968) reported normative data for 20 male and 13 female samples. The male–female comparisons revealed that cluster structures for males and females were similar. Internal consistency coefficients for the seven *TSC* scales are high, suggesting that internal consistency exists within the scales. Stein (1968) reported that Chu (1966) examined MMPI scale scores in relation to the cluster scales and found, for example, that MMPI scales 1 and 0 correlated, as expected, with *TSC* scales *B* and *I,* respectively. However, MMPI scale 6 had a low correlation (.16) with *TSC* scale *S.* Graham (1977) reported that some *TSC* cluster scales appear to be measuring features not reflected in the basic MMPI scales. Edwards, Klockars, and Abbott (1970) factor analyzed the MMPI records of 468 male college students that were scored for the TSC cluster scales and Welsh's (1956) *R* scale, Edwards' social desirability scale (Edwards, Diers, & Walker, 1966), and the MMPI *L* scale. They interpreted their results as indicat-ing that there is considerable redundancy in the seven *TSC* scales, with each scale keyed for socially undesirable responses or as loading on maladjustment. Stein (1970) objected to their conclusions on the grounds of methodological issues, stating that the social desirability scale items greatly overlap the *TSC* scales. He stated that this overlap, in part, confounded their results.

Although Stein (1968) reported that each of the *TSC* scales appears to show meaningful relationships to different measures (e.g., Edwards' personal preference schedule, Edwards, 1959), there is a paucity of research for the *TSC* scales. The scales are employed in applied settings, and some computer software programs provide scores on the supplemental scales. However, there are no commercially available scoring sheets for the *TSC* scales. The reader wishing to use the *TSC* scales can consult the data in Stein (1968) or Graham (1977) in order to convert raw scores on the cluster scales to *T*-scores. As there is so little research data regarding the interpretation of the *TSC* scales, the reader is advised to generally consider *T*-scores above 70 and below 40 as meaningful and consult Graham (1977) for high/low interpretative hypotheses for the scales. Clearly, more research is needed to evaluate the efficacy of continuing to use these scales in applied settings.

Serkownek Subscales for Scales 5 (*Mf*) and 0 (*Si*)

As mentioned earlier, Harris and Lingoes (1955) did not develop subscales for MMPI scales 5 and 0. Because scales 5 and 0 were added after the publication of the test, it took time for their assimilation into the mainstream of research and clinical practice. It was soon recognized that these scales represented important measures, and they came to be included in clinical interpretation and research. Research, however, on these scales has not received the same degree of effort that has been given to the other clinical scales.

Initial attempts were made to develop rationally constructed subscales for MMPI scale 5 by Pepper and Strong (1958), as cited in Dahlstrom et al. (1972). Pepper and Strong (1958) rationally identified and formed five subscales for scale 5 labeled (a) ego sensitivity; (b) sexual identification; (c) altruism; (d) endorsement of culturally feminine occupations; and (e) denial of culturally masculine occupations. However, MMPI users did not appear to adopt these subscales (Graham, 1987), and other efforts were made to develop useful subscales for scales 5 and 0.

Graham, Schroeder, and Lilly (1971) set the stage for the future development of subscales by factor analyzing the responses to scales 5 and 0 from 422 psychiatric inpatients and outpatients and normals. They identified at least 17 factors, with 7 factors considered to be psychologically interpretable for each scale. The 7 factors for scale 5 are (a) sensitivity-narcissism (sensitive to others reactions, lacking self-confidence); (b) feminine interests; (c) denial of masculine interests; (d) homosexual concerns; (e) denial of social extroversion; (f) denial of exhibitionism; and (g) demographic variables including educational level, marital status, and age. The first factor accounted for 21% of the variance, and taken together the 7 factors accounted for only 25% of the common variance (Wong, 1984). The 7 scale 0 factors that were identified are (a) inferiority-discomfort; (b) lack of affiliation; (c) low social excitement; (d) sensitivity; (e) interpersonal trust; (f) physical-somatic concern; and (g) demographic variables including educational level, marital status, and age. The first factor accounted for the most common variance.

Serkownek (1975) used the item factor loadings in the Graham et al. (1971) study to construct six subscales for scales 5 and 0. The demographic factors in the *Mf* and *Si* analyses were not used to form subscales. In order for an item to be retained for inclusion on a subscale, it had to have a factor loading of .30 or higher (Serkownek, 1975). Consistent with the format employed by Harris and Lingoes (1955), Serkownek noted the items with the highest factor loadings and named the subscales in accordance with their item content. The number of items on the Serkownek subscales range from a low of 4 on Mf_4 to a high of 27 for Si_1. The subscales are listed in Table 3.6, and the item composition with the direction of scoring is provided in appendix F. Norms derived from a sample of male clinic patients are provided in appendix G, Table 9.

K. Serkownek (personal communication, 1988) pointed out that although most of the items on the subscales are consistent with the scoring directions on the parent MMPI scale, there are 13 items from the subscales on scale 5 and 8 items on the scale 0 subscales that are scored in the opposite direction in order to remain consistent with their factor loadings. These items and their keyed responses are identified in appendix F.

TABLE 3.6
Serkownek Subscales for Scales 5 and 0

Abbreviation	Items	No. of Items
	Scale 5	
Mf_1	Narcissism-hypersensitivity	18
Mf_2	Stereotypic feminine interests	14
Mf_3	Denial of stereotypic masculine interests	8
Mf_4	Heterosexual discomfort-passivity	4
Mf_5	Introspective-critical	7
Mf_6	Socially retiring	9
	Scale 0	
Si_1	Inferiority-personal discomfort	27
Si_2	Discomfort with others	14
Si_3	Staid-personal rigidity	16
Si_4	Hypersensitivity	10
Si_5	Distrust	12
Si_6	Physical-somatic concerns	10

Limited reliability and validity data exist for the subscales on scales 5 and 0. Internal consistency is assumed for the subscales, given their empirical derivation. Graham (1987) reported test–retest reliability coefficients for males and females (over a 6-week interval) provided by Moreland (1985). For males, on all of the scale 0 (*Si*) subscales, the coefficients range from .68 to .89 with an average of .77. For females, the range is from .63 to .87 with an average of .76. For males on the scale 5 subscales, the range of test–retest reliability coefficients range from .67 to .83 with an average of .78. For females, it ranges from .69 to .83 with an average of .76. Williams (1983) reported 1-week test–retest reliabilities for scale 0 subscales averaging .84 for females and .68 for males.

In a large-scale study, Foerstner (1986) investigated the interrelationships among the 63 MMPI subscales developed by Serkownek (1975), Harris and Lingoes (1955), Wiggins (1966) and Wiener and Harmon (1946). The stability of the factor structure was also studied across different populations. Nine hundred MMPIs from male and female psychiatric inpatients, chemical dependent residents, and private practice outpatients were analyzed. Ten factors were identified that accounted for 75.5% of the total variance. The 10 factors were named: (a) depression (*D*); (b) agitated hostility (*AH*); (c) social introversion (*SI*); (d) cynical distrust (*CD*); (e) health concerns (*HC*); (f) ideas of reference (*IR*); (g) traditional feminine interests (*TFI*); (h) family conflict (*FC*); (i) innerdirectedness (*ID*); and (j) qvetch (*Q*)—vague dysphoria or hypersensitivity. Most of the factor structures were similar for the samples, although a difference existed between the factor structure of psychiatric inpatient samples and private practice outpatients. Of interest in this discussion about scales 5 and 0 is Foerstner's (1986) findings for the Serkownek (1975) subscales. Si_4 (hypersensitivity) loaded on the first factor *D* (.67) as did Si_1 (inferiority-personal discomfort) (.65) and Si_5 (distrust) (.44). Si_3 (staid-personal rigidity) loaded negatively on the second factor *SI* (.71). Si_1 also loaded on the third factor *AH* (.64). Si_5 loaded on the fourth factor *CD* (.63). Mf_1 (narcissism-hypersensitivity) loaded positively on the first depression factor (.57), with Mf_4 (heterosexual discomfort) loading negatively on the *Si* factor (−.50). Mf_2 (stereotypic feminine interests) loaded on the expected seventh factor named *TFI*.

It is clear from the data reported in Foerstner's (1986) study that scales 5 and 0 are multifactorial rather than measuring unique masculine-feminine or introversion factors. Also, it appears from Foerstner's data that depression is a major factor in scale 0.

The subscales for 5 and 0 are routinely scored by many computer scoring services, as clinicians often want the information contained in these subscales. Hand-scoring of the scales is possible by consulting appendix F in this book and constructing appropriate templates. Scales 5 and 0 are multidimensional in content, with any elevation (or declination) indicative of the respondent attributing to him- or herself any one of at least six factors individually or in interaction with each other (Wong, 1984). Schuerger, Foerstner, Serkownek, and Ritz

(1987) pointed out that the subscale correlates for scale 5 are generally nonpathological in nature. That is, the only subscale for scale 5 that suggests psychopathology is Mf_1 (hypersensitivity). On the other hand, the Si subscales, with the exception of Si_3 (rigidity), appear pathology-related. The reader interested in how the Serkownek subscales correlate with other special subscales is referred to Schuerger, Foerstner, Serkownek, and Ritz (1987).

CRITICAL ITEMS

Content scales and subscales are not the only way to derive meaningful adjunctive information from the standard MMPI profile. Examination of specific item responses can be another method of identifying important psychological problems or concerns. *Critical item* is a term used to imply that a certain item endorsement signals a response that may indicate a specific psychological concern or behavior problem. The first critical items appeared in the Woodworth Personal Data Sheet (1920) with 10 items marked as "neurotic tendency items" (Koss, 1979). Endorsement of any of these items suggested that an individual was neurotic, irrespective of the rest of his or her responses. Many automated scoring programs print out a list of critical item responses endorsed by the client. The listing of these items is intended to alert the clinician to specific behaviors, such as suicidal feelings, so that he or she may further investigate these concerns. It is difficult to know whether the generally face-valid critical items are directly related to the behavior in question.

At least five sets of critical items have been developed to date. The first critical item list was published by Grayson (1951), with Gravitz (1968) later publishing frequency data showing item endorsements by normal adults. Grayson's 38 items were rationally selected to reflect important psychopathology deemed relevant to a Veteran's Administration clinical setting. The items were not empirically validated to determine their relevance to an individual's behavior. Koss (1979) reported that 32 (85%) of the 38 Grayson items are scored on the Sc scale and/or the F scale, and that 16 items (40%) are scored exclusively on scale F. Koss pointed out that the considerable overlap with F (which measures a tendency to fake bad) creates concern as to whether the Grayson critical items are measuring anything independent of scale F. Furthermore, the deviant scoring direction of the majority (92%) of the items is true, thereby making the list vulnerable to an individual responding with a true response bias. Greene (1980) reported that a normal sample consisting of university students endorsed an average of 6 Grayson critical items, leaving him to question "how critical these items actually are" (p. 173). Greene (1980) concluded by stating, "Thus, there is little evidence that the Grayson critical items are useful either in identifying behaviors that need attention or in classifying clients as normal or pathological" (p. 173).

Caldwell (1969) developed a longer, more comprehensive critical list using a rational procedure similar to Grayson's. Caldwell broke his 69 items down into nine content areas, which included suicidal thoughts, somatic concerns, sexual difficulties, and peculiar experiences and hallucinations (see appendix H). Although the Caldwell items are more generally representative of the MMPI content than the Grayson items, the majority of items again overlap scales F and Sc, making the admonitions about the Grayson items also applicable here. The use of the Caldwell and Grayson items has "continued despite limited and, in some cases contradictory data with regard to their validity" (Evans, 1984a, p. 512). Koss, Butcher, and Hoffman (1976) stated that the Caldwell and Grayson items do not necessarily reflect the behavior of potential interest to the clinician. It should be noted, however, that Caldwell was the first to organize critical items by content categories, thereby facilitating their use. Recent efforts have been directed toward developing more valid critical item lists for the MMPI. Koss and Butcher (1973) and Lachar and Wroebel (1979), in independent projects, constructed item sets using an empirical rather than a rational item selection procedure.

Koss and Butcher (1973) and Koss, Butcher, and Hoffman (1976) developed a 67-item critical list using an empirical method to differentiate psychiatric patients admitted in crisis from psychiatric patients admitted but not in crisis. Six different crisis states were identified that became the content areas for the Koss and Butcher (1973) critical items. The critical content areas are: acute anxiety, depressed-suicidal ideas, threatened assault, situational stress due to alcoholism, mental confusion, and persecutory ideas. Most of the items in these content areas are obvious or face valid for the specific crisis areas, making it easy for the clinician to flag important areas needing further investigation. However, as Greene (1980) pointed out, normal individuals tend to endorse critical items, making it time-consuming and perhaps unnecessary to explore every critical item endorsement. Given the large number of items in some critical item lists, research is needed to specify when a clinician should further explore the meaning of critical item endorsements. Although means and standard deviations for different subject groups are provided by Koss and Butcher (1973) and Lachar and Wroebel (1979), cut-off scores are needed to further assist the clinician.

Lachar and Wroebel (1979) empirically developed critical items by first rationally identifying 14 content areas relevant to a clinical setting. Clinical psychologists then read the entire MMPI item pool and indicated the items relevant to each of the 14 categories. Items agreed on by at least 6 of the 14 psychologists, coupled with the Caldwell (1969) and Grayson (1951) critical item sets, were used to differentiate normals from psychiatric patients. A final list of 111 critical items was derived that was grouped into 11 content areas. These areas cover psychological discomfort, reality distortion, and characterological adjustment issues. As with any other face-valid critical item, clients wishing to conceal their concerns can easily do so. Therefore, the Lachar and Wroebel (1979) critical items are as vulnerable to response set distortions as other groups of critical items (or any face-valid item in general). Greene (1980) pointed out that the immense number of items in the Lachar and Wroebel (1979) list precludes efficient use of the items. A client for example, endorsing 30 items would need to be questioned about every item if the underlying assumption about critical items is correct; that is, that each item reflects a substantive psychological problem. Again, as with the other critical lists, researchers needed to establish cut-off scores.

A recent study (Evans, 1984a) addressed the normative aspects for the Koss and Butcher (1973) and Lachar and Wroebel (1979) critical item sets. Evans (1984a) provided normative data for several normal and patient groups consisting of male and female alcoholics and male and female general psychiatric patients. Form *R* was used in his evaluation of critical item endorsement patterns. The entire 556-item MMPI is necessary to completely score the Koss and Butcher and Lachar and Wroebel items, but in actual practice the abbreviated Form *R* is typically administered. Administration of the first 399 items on Form *R* can yield abbreviated critical item sets. Therefore, Evans' (1984a) study is most useful for Form *R* users. He provides means and standard deviations on each of the aforementioned groups. Although Evans' report does not suggest the cut-off scores a clinician can use, he does show that normals do, in fact, in support of Greene's (1980) contention, endorse a few critical items.

More recently, D. S. Nichols (personal communication, December 12, 1987) developed a critical items list in response to referrals from physicians dealing with patients with neurological and psychiatric complaints as well as patients seen in the course of psychiatric evaluations for disability as a consequence of work injuries. Nichols believed other somatic symptom categories, such as the Lachar and Wroebel (1979) somatic symptoms classification, to be redundant with raw *Hs* and Wiggins' (1966) *HEA* and *ORG* scales. He therefore organized the somatic items into more discrete groupings. He felt this regrouping would not only assist in the preparation of reports but also afford a basis for research inquiries. He devised a list containing 221 items spread over 22 categories, which he considered more as mini-scales rather than mere collections of critical items. The categories and items were rationally constructed from a series of factor analyses (on a large midwestern sample of psychiatric patients) as well as from an examination of item overlap with the Wiggins (1966) content scales and other lists such as the Lachar and Wroebel (1979), and Koss and Butcher (1973) and Caldwell (1969) lists. The somatic categories include complaints relevant to different body regions and systems including the following: upper and lower gastrointestinal, head complaints, cardiorespiratory, and genitourinary, pain and discomfort, and sleep disturbance. Sleep disturbance is an augmented version of the Lachar and Wroebel category of the same name. Nichols devised four additional miscellaneous categories named assaultive impulse, delinquency, substance abuse, and sexual problems. He reported that assaultive impulse is nearly identical to the Koss and Butcher threatened assault category and the Lachar and Wroebel category. The delinquency category was largely derived from the factor analytic work he and Roger Greene (Greene & Nichols, 1987) performed and emphasizes actual misbehavior rather than mere cynicism or antisocial attitudes. The sexual problems category is an augmented version of the Lachar and Wroebel category named sexual concern and deviation.

Unlike the Koss and Butcher and Lachar and Wroebel lists, the Nichols list contains overlapping items, especially within the first section named health/somatic/neurological. The actual categories, items, direction of scoring, and norms for the Nichols critical item list appear in appendix H. The norms that Nichols provided are based on the refined Minnesota normal adult standardization group (Hathaway & Briggs, 1957) and a general medical population. Readers interested in obtaining more information can write Dr. David S. Nichols at the Dammasch State Hospital, Psychology Department, P.O. Box 38, Wilsonville, OR 97070.

Further research is needed to define cutting scores for the various critical items lists. Because the items in most of the lists are all face-valid, research is needed to generate more subtle critical items. The reader should be aware that response sets can easily influence the number of critical items endorsed. The reader who is interested in the Koss and Butcher (1973) or Lachar and Wroebel (1979) critical items is advised to consult the Evans (1984a) article if using the 399-item abbreviated version of Form R. Shorter forms (e.g., Mini-Mult) of the MMPI would most likely reduce the content categories scored for various critical items. Psychometric and normative data are greatly needed for all of the aforementioned critical item sets.

The authors of this text recommend that critical items be used to "red flag" or alert the clinician to potentially important problem areas (e.g. suicide, alcoholism) and to help create a bridge between the assessment phase and treatment intervention. The items can be used to create a meaningful dialogue, which can result in further diagnostic clarity and improvement in the client's status. It is recommended that the least threatening or most vague items be discussed before exploring the other critical items.

OVERLAP ITEM CONTENT

The overlapping items within the MMPI have been a source of concern to clinicians and researchers alike. The empirical criterion approach to test construction allows the total item pool to be used repeatedly with different criterion groups. An item is retained for inclusion in a scale if it discriminates a criterion group from a normal group. The number of scales that can be derived from this method is only limited by the number of available criterion groups (Stein, 1968). However, a major difficulty emerged as a result of this test construction methodology. The resulting MMPI scales were capable of differentiating the normals from each of the psychiatric criterion groups. However, because the psychiatric criterion groups were not contrasted with each other, overlap in item content resulted between the criterion scales. An item is considered an overlap item if it appears on more than one standard scale. A nonoverlap item is defined as an item appearing on only 1 of the 13 standard scales. The structural redundancy of the test has led to high interscale correlations inconsistent with the goal of differential diagnosis (Maloney & Ward, 1976; Rosen, 1962). Structurally independent scales or scales that are not highly correlated may be necessary or desirable for purposes of separating criterion groups. Furthermore, as Rosen (1962) pointed out, it would have been more logical for purposes of differential diagnosis to have used a reference group of psychiatric patients in addition to the normals employed.

Description of Overlap Content

The degree of item overlap between scales is extensive. Adams and Horn (1965) recognized this fact and developed a set of operationally independent keys for the MMPI scales. Welsh (1956) also attempted to develop pure or nonoverlapping scales but failed because he retained items scored in opposite directions for two scales. Wheeler, Little, and Lehner (1951) presented a table indicating the degree of item overlap between scales and Dahlstrom, Welsh, and Dahlstrom (1972) modified this table to make it more accurate (See appendix B, Table 2). Based on this modified table it can be determined that scale 8 (*Sc*) has 62 overlapping items, the greatest amount for any of the scales, whereas scale *L* has the fewest with 6 overlap items. The traditional neurotic triad, consisting of scales 1, 2, and 3 has 25, 47, and 50 overlapping items respectively, leaving only 8, 13, and 10 items, respectively, that are unique to each of those scales. The traditional psychotic tetrad consisting of scales 6, 7, 8, and 9 has 33, 39, 62, and 31 overlapping items respectively and 7, 9, 16, and 15 nonoverlap items, respectively. There are many more overlap items than nonoverlap items on each scale, thus the shortened or nonoverlap scales must suffer from lowered reliability, which in turn affects the intercorrelations of scales. However, the degree to which this is the case is unknown (Stein, 1968).

There is considerable range in the amount of item overlap with various scales. Some items (booklet item numbers 8 and 32) overlap as many as five and six different scales, whereas other items overlap only two scales. The largest number of items shared by any two scales is between scales 1 and 3 with 20 common items. Scales 7 and 8 overlap almost as much with 17 items in common. Only seven pairs of scales have no common items. They are, respectively, scales *L*, and *Hs*, *Hs* and *K*, *Pd* and *L*, *Hs* and *Mf*, *Hs* and *Ma*, *L* and *Si*, and *F* and *Si* (Wheeler, Little, & Lehner, 1951; Dahlstrom, Welsh, & Dahlstrom, 1972). Based on this text's authors' perusal of the items belonging to the basic scales, it was determined that the traditional neurotic and psychotic scales share a considerable amount of item overlap. Thirty-three items appear on at least one psychotic scale and one neurotic scale. Within the neurotic triad there are 21 items overlapping at least two scales and in some instances all three (group booklet item numbers 2, 9, 23, 43, 51, 153, and 189). Within the psychotic tetrad of scales, there are 28 items shared by at least two scales and one item overlapping all four psychotic scales (group booklet item number 22).

Methodological Concerns About the Overlap Content

Stein (1968) pointed out that the occurrence of overlapping items could present problems to the researcher wishing to study the internal structure of the MMPI and cites Guilford (1952) as having similar concerns. Researchers sensitive to the psychometric composition of the test have imposed methodological controls for these items. For example, Mees (1959), in a careful examination of the factorial structure of the MMPI, used only nonoverlapping items in his factor analysis to obtain pure measures of the component scales. Welsh (1956) was also concerned about the effect the overlapping items had on the correlations between scales as well as on the factor analysis of these correlations. By factor analyzing the correlations between nonoverlapping or pure scales, he was able to conclude that the relationship between several of the MMPI scales was due to both their common factorial composition and their common item content. Shure and Rogers (1965) were also concerned about the status of the overlap items and mention Guilfords (1952) warning to avoid factoring test scales that contain overlapping items. They noted, however, that researchers have ignored his advice and continue to produce studies that do not adequately consider the issue of overlap items.

In addition to citing Guilfords' methodological warning about factoring nonindependent scales, Shure and Rogers (1965) also criticize the results of a study by Wheeler, Little, and Lehner (1951). Wheeler et al. defined a neurotic and psychotic factor for the MMPI based on the high-factor loadings on the neurotic and psychotic scales. They factored the 13 MMPI scales but did not separate the overlap and nonoverlap items in their analysis. Shure and Rogers suggested that the neurotic and psychotic factors extracted in the Wheeler et al. study were derived from the existence of a methodological artifact associated with item overlap. Because the scales are intercorrelated, Shure and Rogers (1965) stated:

> This built-in correlation might contribute to a built-in factor structure such that factor analyses of data from different populations would tend to exhibit this factor structure regardless of differences among the populations and thus give a false or exaggerated appearance of factorial invariance. (p. 15)

To test the notion that the neurotic (N) and psychotic (P) factors are methodological artifacts, Shure and Rogers factor analyzed the MMPI interscale common-element correlations produced solely by item overlap.[4] Three factors were extracted; two factors were said to be similar to the N and P factors found in the Wheeler et al. study. Furthermore, Shure and Rogers also refactored the intercorrelational data from two other studies and their results showed that:

1. The original scale intercorrelations, based on nonoverlap and overlap items, yield the N and P factors.
2. Overlap scale intercorrelations based only on overlap items also yield the N and P factors.
3. Truncated scale intercorrelations, based only on nonoverlap items do not yield the N and P factors.

Shure and Rogers concluded from the results that a methodological artifact (the overlap items) is responsible for the presence of the N and P personality dimensions reported in several studies.

Other researchers disagree with Shure and Rogers' conclusions about the invalidity of the P and N personality factors found in the MMPI factorial studies. Anderson and Bashaw (1966) examined Shure and Rogers' findings and disagreed with the notion that sheer item overlap accounts for the factor patterns obtained on scale-level analyses of the MMPI. They particularly responded to the following critical question posed by Shure and Rogers (1965): "Why would a chance configuration of overlapping items yield two factors which are so similar to clinically identified patterns?" (p. 17). Anderson and Bashaw responded to this question by stating that the items common to more than one scale reflect common factors in the criteria used to develop the scales. Items for each scale were selected because they discriminated between the normal and maladjusted groups and the items included on more than one scale validly measure common aspects of more than one criterion. Based on this rationale, the overlapping items are not members of various scales as a result of "chance configurations."

---

[4]The interscale common-element correlation matrix, analyzed by Shure and Rogers, consisted of a set of correlations among the basic scales based solely on the actual amount of item overlap. These correlation coefficients were computed by the formula

$$r = \frac{Nc}{\sqrt{Na + Nc}\ \sqrt{Nb + Nc}}$$

in which Na = number of items in scale A not in scale B; Nb = number of items in scale B not in scale A; and Nc = number of items in common between scale A and scale B. These correlations show the degree to which each of the scales will covary with the other basic scales as a result of the experimental dependence arising from shared items (taken from Dahlstrom, Welsh, & Dahlstrom, 1972). This 13 × 13 matrix was originally published by Wheeler, Little, & Lehner (1951) and reprinted and modified in Dahlstrom's and Welsh's (1960), *An MMPI Handbook*. It also appears in the revised edition of an *MMPI Handbook* (Volume I) by Dahlstrom, Welsh, and Dahlstrom (1972). Table 2 in appendix B presents the item overlap among the basic scales and the intercorrelations resulting from this overlap.

Anderson and Bashaw also pointed out that the first two results described by Shure and Rogers (described previously) are consistent with the rationale that the P and N factors represent valid variances despite Shure and Rogers' interpretation. They also agree with Shure and Rogers' statement that their third result, namely that the truncated scale intercorrelations do not yield the N and P factors, should be interpreted cautiously. The truncated scales must necessarily suffer from reduced variances and covariances across the scales because the nonoverlap item content is so short. (Anderson & Bashaw, 1966). The low reliability obtained may be an explanation for the absence of the N and P factors. Another explanation for the nonappearance of N and P factors may rest on a theoretical premise expounded by Wakefield, Bradley, Doughtie, and Kraft (1975). These authors theorized that the unique variance of each scale should be represented by the nonoverlapping items. If this is so, one would not expect to find general factors like P and N in nonoverlapping scales. Rather, one would expect to find more specific variations of the general factors (Beckwith, Hammond, & Campbell, 1983).

Another study regarding this issue deserves attention despite its confusing results. When Mees (1959) factored the nonoverlap MMPI scales, he took steps to maximize the length of the scales and this could, in part, explain why he found the elusive P and N factors that evaded Shure and Rogers. However, the way Mees increased the length of the nonoverlap scales was to include a few overlapping items on several of the scales (five MMPI scales have fewer than 10 nonoverlapping items) and this confuses the distinction between overlapping and nonoverlapping scales and the factors that should be expected to appear on the scales. By including overlapping items on his so-called nonoverlapping scales, it is uncertain how much variance he was introducing that may have been related to P and N.

In a manner differing from the aforementioned researchers, Wakefield, Bradley, Doughtie, and Kraft (1975) examined the influence of overlapping and nonoverlapping items on the theoretical interrelationships of MMPI scales. These investigators began with the following premise, which is in agreement with the rationale of the Wheeler et al. (1951) and the Anderson and Bashaw (1966) studies: "If the overlapping items represent valid variances, they must represent factors that the scales containing them share" (Wakefield et al., 1975, p. 852). Wakefield et al. also hypothesized that if the overlapping items represent valid factors then the unique variance of each scale should be represented by the nonoverlapping items. Wakefield et al. stated:

> By virtue of their appearing on only one scale, these items must not measure the shared aspects of the criteria employed to select items for the scale. For example, items that are scored for both the Hy and D scales measure some more general factor or trait that includes the criteria for both scales—that is neuroticism. Items that appear on only one of these scales do not measure neuroticism in general but rather a particular variation within the general trait. (p. 852)

In order to test these hypotheses, these investigators began with a theoretical
model of personality described in an earlier paper (Wakefield, Yom, Bradley,
Doughtie, Cox, & Kraft, 1974). Basically, they used Eysenck's three personality
dimensions of psychoticism *(P)*, neuroticism *(N)*, and extraversion *(E)* to
represent a three-dimentional model of personality. From their results they
claimed that 9 of the 10 MMPI clinical scales (*Mf* was omitted) conform to the *P*,
E, and *N* dimensions Eysenck developed. Having found the hypothesized theoretical fit between the MMPI scales and Eysenck's personality dimensions,
Wakefield et al. (1975) scored the MMPI scales for overlapping and
nonoverlapping items. They found that the correspondence of the scales composed of overlapping items conform closely to their theoretical structure. The
correspondence of the scales consisting of nonoverlapping items with the theoretical structure was insignificant and therefore supported their hypothesis that
common factors would be represented by overlapping rather than nonoverlapping
items. Wakefield et al. (1975) interpreted their results as meaning that the
psychoticism, neuroticism, and extraversion factors found in the MMPI are due
to overlapping items. Their conclusion is consistent with the statement made by
Shure and Rogers (1965) "that the overlap items are responsible for the presence
of the N-type [neurotic] and P-type [psychotic] factors found in the empirical
studies" (p. 17). However, like Anderson and Bashaw (1966), they disagreed
with Shure and Rogers' conclusion that the *P* and *N* factors are methodological
artifacts or invalid factors.

It appears that in several studies the overlap item content of the MMPI relates
to the personality dimensions of psychoticism and neuroticism. However, until
recently no researcher had employed clinical criterion groups to test the hypothesis that the overlapping items could differentiate psychotic and neurotic subjects
(Friedman, Gleser, Smeltzer, Wakefield, & Schwartz, 1983; Gentry, Wakefield,
& Friedman, 1985; Wiederstein, 1986). The implications of such a study
go beyond methodological interest. The MMPI has been considered by many
as generally unsuccessful in distinguishing between different categories
of abnormality beyond the grossest levels (Rodgers, 1972; Wheeler, Little,
& Lehner, 1951). Possibly, as Wakefield et al. (1975) suggested, the mixture of overlapping items measuring more general personality characteristics and nonoverlapping items purportedly measuring more specific traits within a type category, may impede the differential diagnostic effectiveness of the
test.

Following the suggestions made by Anderson and Bashaw (1966) and Wakefield et al. (1975) that items common to two or more scales measure common
dimensions, three new scales were developed by Friedman et al. (1983) for the
purpose of differentiating groups of neurotic, psychotic, and normal individuals.
These scales are collectively referred to as the Friedman Overlap Scales *(FOS)*.
The individual scales are named the psychotic overlap scale *(POS)*, the neurotic
overlap scale *(NOS)*, and the maladjustment overlap scale *(MOS)*. These scales
were derived in a rational manner. Items that are scored on the traditional

psychotic scales (scales *Pa*, *Sc*, and *Ma*) were counted as items on the POS if they occurred on at least two scales within the psychotic triad and did not occur on any of the neurotic scales (scales *Hs*, *D*, *Hy*, and *Pt*). This produced 18 items that are scored on the POS. Similarly, the NOS consists of items occurring on at least two scales within the traditional neurotic triad (scales *Hs*, *D*, *Hy*) plus scale *Pt* and on none of the psychotic scales. This produced 30 items that are scored on the NOS. A third scale, the maladjustment scale, was developed for purposes of discriminating normals from psychotic and neurotic patients. This consists of 35 items occurring on at least one neurotic and one psychotic scale. All 83 items on the overlap scales were scored in the standard critical direction and were included only if they were scored in the same direction on the relevant scales.

Scales *L*, *F*, *K*, *Si*, *Pd*, and *Mf* were excluded from consideration in the construction of these new scales. The items and keyed responses for the Friedman Overlap Scales appear in appendix F. Appendix G contains the *T*-score conversions for the FOS.

Friedman et al. (1983) hypothesized that the NOS and POS would discriminate normals from neurotics and psychotics, and neurotics and psychotics from each other. MMPI data from four groups of subjects were studied. Group I consisted of 101 patients hospitalized in the psychiatric unit at Ohio State University Hospital with functional psychotic diagnoses (45 males; 56 females). Group 2 consisted of 85 patients with neurotic diagnoses (30 males; 55 females) from the same patient population. Group 3 consisted of 76 outpatients receiving treatment at the Mayo Clinic in Rochester, Minnesota for strictly medical (nonpsychiatric) problems (37 males; 39 females). Group 4 consisted of 38 college students taking introductory psychology classes at a technical institute in a large midwestern city (12 males; 26 females).

Discriminant analyses of the criterion groups were performed separately for the MMPI and the *FOS*. The standard MMPI (566 items) correctly classified 62% of both the neurotic and psychotic subjects, whereas the shorter FOS (83 items) correctly classified 54% of the neurotics and 52% of the psychotics.

The MMPI and *FOS* were equally effective in correctly classifying 88% of normal controls. It appears that based on this study and others (Gentry, Wakefield, & Friedman, 1985; Wiederstein, 1986), the Friedman psychotic and neurotic overlap scales appear to measure the general constructs of psychoticism and neuroticism. However, further research in a clinical setting is needed before they can be considered useful for differential diagnosis.

The clinician should be cognizant that the overlap content appears to represent more than just a methodological artifact associated with the empirical criterion group construction strategy; rather the overlap items, especially as they pertain to the dimensions of psychoticism and neuroticism represent valid factors common to the scales.

Other indices and scales have been developed without special regard to item overlap but have gained some recognition or have been proven clinically useful. These indices and scales are described in the next section.

SPECIAL INDICES AND SCALES

Validity Measures

Subsequent to the proper scoring of the MMPI and plotting of the profile, the test-user must determine if respondents answered the items consistently and whether they were presenting themselves in a way that exaggerated or underestimated their problems. The actual strategies for determining profile validity are discussed in chapter 5, but the essential scales and indices commonly used in the process of ascertaining profile validity are presented here. There are a number of different strategies and techniques used to identify faking or distortion on the MMPI. Grow, McVaugh, and Eno (1980) identified at least four of the most common strategies: (a) the F raw score (see chapters 1 and 5); (b) Dissimulation scale (presented later in this chapter); (c) Wiener's (1948) subtle and obvious items (presented earlier in this chapter and (d) F-K raw score difference (Gough, 1950) (presented in this chapter). Two other measures commonly used to assess inaccurate and inconsistent responding on the MMPI are the carelessness scale (Greene, 1978) and the TR index (Buechley & Ball, 1952). These measures are also discussed in this chapter.

F-K Index

Gough (1947, 1950) recognized that a fundamental problem in the use of any personality inventory was the possibility of "faking" responses. Although he acknowledged that the separate validity scales were useful in detecting faking, he found that by combining raw scale score differences he could more accurately classify MMPI profiles as invalid. Specifically, the F-K index (the raw score of K is subtracted from the raw score on F) was a more efficient classifier of faked bad profiles than scales F or K used alone. In creating the index, Gough (1947) had a group of 11 clinical workers feign two psychiatric syndromes.

> The first syndrome was defined as "an acute, severe, anxiety neuroses which would lead to separation from the service, but not to commitment to a mental hospital," and the second as "a nondeteriorated, acute, paranoid schizophrenic psychosis." Skilled judges were able to identify eight of the eleven psychoneurotic patterns when intermixed with 68 authentic psychoneurotic records, and were able to identify all of the psychotic simulations when they were intercalated with 24 authentic profiles. At the same time, a simple combination of the F raw score minus the K raw score was able to pick out ten of the eleven simulated records in each of the two situations. The F-K cutting scores proposed at that time were plus 4 and over for neurotic profiles, and plus 16 and over for psychotic profiles. (p. 408)

Gough later suggested that F-K scores of more than 9 indicated a fake bad attitude, suggesting the subject attempted to present himself with serious psychopathology. Scores of less than 0 on *F-K* indicated a fake good profile whereby the subject attempted to deny the presence of any type of psychological disturbance. Gough (1950) stated that the *F-K* index was less efficient in detecting fake good profiles as compared to fake bad profiles. He pointed out that the problem in establishing an *F-K* cutting score is one of minimizing false positives and false negatives. Grow, McVaugh, and Eno (1980) found that an *F-K* score of 7 or more for detecting faking bad and *F-K* score of 11 or less for detecting faking good were optimal in a clinical population of psychiatric inpatients and outpatients. There is, however, a wide range of differences found in studies utilizing clinical and normal groups for the optimal cut-off scores in detecting faked profiles. Greene (1980) pointed out that most studies utilizing the *F-K* index for detecting fake bad profiles have employed normal individuals directed to simulate psychological problems. College students have constituted the majority of these subjects, and Dahlstrom et al. (1972) noted the differences in conducting faking studies with college students. For example, it is known that college students tend to score higher on scale *K* by almost one standard deviation. Therefore, their elevated *K* scores will tend to bias their *F-K* index scores in the fake good direction.

Greene (1980) pointed out in his brief literature review of the *F-K* index that it has been difficult to identify any specific *F-K* score for the detection of students instructed to fake good under usual administration instructions for the MMPI. Presumably, students who are for the most part free of psychopathology find it difficult to look even better than they already are when instructed to fake good. Greene (1980) acknowledged another problem in detecting fake good profiles in college students (or anyone else) because a person who is effectively handling his or her problems and who is well-adjusted would be expected to score low on scale *F* and high on scale *K* indicating an absence of distress. Therefore, Greene (1980) stated that "normal persons taking the MMPI often will be inappropriately classified as producing fake-good profiles" (p. 51).

Greene's (1980) review contains some important conclusions. He stated that the usefulness of the *F-K* index in detecting fake bad profiles may be more limited with actual clinical patients who exaggerate their problems than with students. He recommended interviewing those who obtain a high *F* score and hence a high *F-K* index, to determine if their self-report of distress is accurate or exaggerated. He also questioned the utility of the index in detecting fake-good profiles in psychiatric patients. He pointed out that psychiatric patients and inmates have difficulty producing normal appearing profiles when instructed to do so (Grayson & Olinger, 1957; Lawton & Kleban, 1965). The Marks et al. (1974) study of projected discharge profiles seems to support Greene's call for additional research to examine whether normal profiles produced by subjects instructed to fake good are generally positive prognostic signs.

Lastly, Archer (1987) made it clear in his review regarding the *F* scale that adolescent inpatient respondents score significantly higher on scale *F* than adult psychiatric inpatients and that outpatient adolescents score similarly to adult inpatients on scale F. Given the higher F scale values among teenagers, Archer cautioned that the F-K index criterion should be used very carefully with these respondents.

Gough Dissimulation Scale (Ds)

Following his investigation of how the F-K index served to assess invalid protocols, Gough (1954) turned his attention to the development of the Dissimulation scale (Ds). Specifically, he identified 74 MMPI items that empirically differentiated a group of patients classified as "psychoneurotic" from a group of test "normals" instructed to take the MMPI simulating the role of a neurotic patient. The items separating the dissemblers from the patients were further studied in a cross-validation procedure. Important findings emerged showing that the patients obtained scores very similar to the nonpatient subjects who took the MMPI without instructions to dissemble. This suggests that certain of the prevailing stereotypes about neuroticism (those embedded in the 74 items) are fallacious. Furthermore, both patients and the control samples scored appreciably lower than the subjects instructed to simulate a neurotic role (Gough, 1954).

The 74-item Ds scale was revised when Gough (1957) published the California Psychological Inventory (CPI). Gough included the Ds scale on the CPI (approximately 200 items on the CPI were taken from the MMPI), but eventually shortened the scale to 44 items for use on both the MMPI and CPI. The rationale for reducing the scale length was that the original scale was considered to be too long, and it contained too many items with extreme declarations of psychopathology (Gough, 1987). Gough, however, reversed the direction of scoring for the scale on the CPI and renamed it the well-being (WB) scale. The WB scale was eventually reduced to 38 items for the current revision of the CPI (Gough, 1987). The Ds scale as described in Dahlstrom and Welsh's (1960) An MMPI Handbook (p. 53), is described as having 74 items with a revised Ds scale (the Ds-r) containing 40 items. The change from 44 to 40 items is due to modifications in the MMPI items when they were included in the CPI booklet. Four of the WB items were modified from the MMPI wording, which means that the Ds-r is in effect only 40 items long (Gough, 1988; personal communication). The items and their keyed responses for the Ds and Ds-r scales are presented in appendix F. T-score conversions for both scales can be found in appendix G, Tables 7 and 8.

Recent research appears to support the use of the Ds or Ds-r scale. Anthony (1971) instructed 40 nonpsychotic U.S. Air Force male clients, after taking the MMPI under usual administration conditions, to exaggerate the troubles that had brought them to treatment so that their readministered MMPI would reflect a more severe condition than they were actually experiencing. They were also asked to exaggerate in a way that was not clearly obvious. The 74-item Ds scale was scored, and the results showed an optimum hit rate of 86% in identifying exaggerated MMPI profiles. This hit rate was higher than the F-K (81%) and F raw-score (81%) hit rates. The findings support the utility of the Ds scale in discriminating exaggerated MMPI's from authentically produced deviant profiles. In support of Anthony's findings, Greene (1980) stated that the Ds scale appears useful in identifying fake bad profiles.

Walters, White, and Greene (1988) found some support for use of the Ds-r scale in an inmate population for identifying genuinely disturbed inmates. In the first part of a two-phase study, the investigators were interested in how the standard validity and clinical scales fared against the Ds-r (and other indices). The subjects were 72 male inmates with maximum security status at a U.S. penitentiary. A structured psychiatric interview was administered to the inmates generally within 1 day of an administered MMPI. A four-point rating scale was created to evaluate an inmate's proneness to exaggerate psychiatric symptomatology. The ratings were made by two psychologists familiar with both the inmates and their contact with others (e.g., work supervisors). The average length of time between the psychiatric interview and the rating assignment was 7.6 months. A rating of 1 on the scale reflected malingering, whereas a rating of 4 indicated no malingering or embellishment of symptomatology. The base rate estimate for psychopathology in this setting was estimated to be 60%. An abbreviated MMPI was scored (first 400 items of Form R), so only 28 rather than 40 Ds-r items could be scored. Therefore, prorated T-scores were calculated for the Ds-r scale. The results showed that the MMPI validity and clinical scales (with the exception of scale 1) could not accurately discriminate the malingerers from the nonmalingerers. Although the Ds-r scale failed to improve on the base rate criterion in the study without the assistance of an indeterminate category, it could differentiate malingering from genuine psychopathology. Low scores on the Ds-r scale were predictive of authentic pathology but high scores failed to correlate with malingering (Walters, White, & Greene, 1988). These findings, if extrapolated to other populations, make Greene's (1980) recommendation to MMPI users that they interpret Ds or Ds-r T-scores over 70 as indicating simulated or exaggerated pathology as possibly outdated advice. It is important that more research be conducted with the Ds-r scale in settings where external ratings (such as was done in the aforementioned study) are used as a validity criterion. The Ds-r scale appears to add information that the traditional MMPI validity scales fail to provide.

Carelessness Scale

Inconsistent responding to the MMPI has long been recognized as a source of profile invalidity. Whereas the 16 repeated items on the MMPI have been used to identify inconsistent responding, items that are psychologically opposite in content may be more sensitive detectors of uncooperative or inconsistent respondents on the MMPI. Haertzen and Hill (1963) found that a carelessness scale consisting of psychologically opposite items was more useful in identifying uncooperative subjects than repeated items in the Addiction Research Center Inventory.

Greene (1978) developed a carelessness scale for the MMPI designed to determine "whether the client is willing or able to complete the MMPI in an appropriate manner" (p. 410). The carelessness scale consists of 12 pairs of psychologically opposite items selected on an empirical basis. The items for the scale were chosen by examining the responses of 150 subjects to the 566 items on the MMPI. The responses of 50 Veteran's Administration (VA) patients, 50 clients at a university psychology clinic, and 50 introductory psychology college students were all placed in a 566×566 matrix. According to Greene (1979), a computer program

> selected all possible nonredundant pairs of items that were answered in a consistent direction more than 90% of the time. That is, a pair of items was selected if 46 out of the 50 individuals within a group answered the first item of the pair either true or false and the other item reached the same criterion with either the same or opposite answer as the first item of the pair. This procedure resulted in a selection of 271 pairs of items in the VA sample, 643 pairs of items in the psychology clinic sample, and 140 pairs of items in the college student sample. (p. 407)

Pairs of items overlapping with scales *L* or *K* were excluded, whereas pairs of items overlapping with scale *F* were only excluded when the content was evaluated to be deviant or bizarre. The empirical selection of the items thus far was based on their being answered in a consistent direction. The next step was to select pairs of these items that were psychological opposites. Two graduate students in clinical psychology and Greene separately selected pairs of items judged to be opposite and that had been selected empirically in at least two of the three samples. Pairs of items were retained for the carelessness scale only if all three judges agreed the pairs were psychologically opposite. Twelve pairs of items were identified, and the item numbers with directions of scoring are presented in Table 3.7.

The maximum score persons can receive on the carelessness scale is 12 if they answer all 12 pairs inconsistently. Greene (1980) suggested a cutting score of four or more inconsistent responses for identifying invalid profiles.

Greene pointed out that his cutting score is not based on any external criteria to validate the score. However, a cutting score of four or more corresponding to a *T*-score of 70, classified from 10% to 18% of the profiles in his sample as being of "questionable validity." He does provide the mean scores or number of inconsistent responses by each of the four samples used in the study. These were as follows: VA psychiatric patients—1.76 ($SD=1.45$), psychology clinic clients—2.20 ($SD=1.28$), and university students—1.48 ($SD=1.34$).

TABLE 3.7
Group Booklet Item Numbers and Statements for the Carelessness Scale

Pair No.	Item No.		Careless Answer
1.	10	There seems to be a lump in my throat much of the time.	Same
	405	I have no trouble swallowing.	
2.	17	My father was a good man.	Different
	65	I loved my father	
3.	18	I am very seldom troubled by constipation.	Different
	63	I have had no difficulty in starting or holding my bowel movement.	
4.	49	It would be better if almost all laws were thrown away.	Same
	113	I believe in law enforcement.	
5.	76	Most of the time I feel blue.	Same
	107	I am happy most of the time.	
6.	88	I usually feel that life is worthwhile.	Same
	526	The future seems hopeless to me.	
7.	137	I believe that my home life is as pleasant as that of most people I know.	Same
	216	There is very little love and companionship in my family as compared to other homes.	
8.	177	My mother was a good woman.	Different
	220	I loved my mother.	
9.	178	My memory seems to be alright.	Same
	342	I forget right away what people say to me.	
10.	286	I am never happier than when alone.	Different
	312	I dislike having people around me.	
11.	329	I almost never dream.	Same
	425	I dream frequently.	
12.	388	I am afraid to be alone in the dark.	Different
	480	I am often afraid of the dark.	

Note: From Greene (1980).

Greene (1980) pointed out that the carelessness scale has utility in detecting all false and all true response biases. Specifically, either response pattern would yield a score of seven deviant responses on the carelessness scale. Greene (1980) stated that the carelessness scale should help the clinician to recognize deception in a respondent who is too sophisticated to be detected by the obvious 16 repeated items in the test. Greene (1978) showed a positive correlation between the Test-Retest (TR) index (the 16 repeated items that are presented in the next section of this chapter) and his carelessness scale suggesting that the two scales may be measuring related behaviors. Bond (1986; 1987) suggested that the implicit assumption underlying an elevated score on the TR index and the carelessness scale is that a respondent answered carelessly; that is, a person failed to read the item content carefully thereby resulting in a failure to answer repeated items consistently and/or to endorse psychologically opposite items in similar directions. However, Bond (1986) pointed out that it may indeed be possible to carefully and consistently respond false to both items in some of the psychologically opposite pairs without it necessarily indicating that respondents contradicted themselves. Greene (1980) did suggest that confusion could account for a high score on his scale, but Bond elaborated on other explanations for high scores in the carelessness scale and the *TR* index, both presumably measures of careless inattention to the items.

In many cases individuals with higher inconsistency scores tend to endorse more maladjustment items; that is, they view themselves as having a range of psychological problems (Bond, 1986, 1987). Another way of viewing inconsistent responding involves indecision (Bond, 1987; Fulkerson & Willage, 1980). If an item is clearly applicable or inapplicable to an individual, it will be relatively easy to respond with certainty and consistency. However, an item with ambiguous application to the person involves a complex judgment process that can change on a repeated presentation of an item. Bond (1986, 1987) studied the MMPI responses of college students and found that indecision rather than carelessness may be a more important determinant of inconsistency on repeated items. Bond (1987) offered three possible reasons for which items may elicit indecision: (a) the degree of ambiguity in an item perceived by the respondent, (b) the perceived degree of relevance an item has to the respondent, and (c) the degree of conflict aroused in a respondent by an item that is applicable but of an undesirable nature. Whereas carelessness may be one factor for elevated scores in the *TR* index and the carelessness scale, other factors such as indecision and maladjustment could be important contributing determinants.

It appears that the carelessness scale (Greene, 1978) is misnamed and would be better labelled something less misleading as it appears to be measuring inconsistent responding due to several possible sources. The issue of how individuals respond to items is clearly an important area that deserves more research.

Test–Retest Index (*TR*)

Many MMPI users employ the Test-Retest index (*TR*) to further assess the test-taking attitude of the respondent on the MMPI. The *TR* index consists of the total number of items answered oppositely when the 16 repeated items are presented (Buechley & Ball, 1952; Dahlstrom, Welsh, & Dahlstrom, 1972). The 16 repeated items are drawn from scales 6, 7, 8, and 0 and were added to the Group Booklet Form to assist in the mechanical scoring of the inventory. The 16 items are actually scored only once in the test. The *TR* index can be scored on both the Group Booklet Form and abbreviated version of Form *R* as the latter contains all of the necessary items for scoring the clinical and validity scales within the first 399 items. The 16 items for the *TR* index are listed in Table 3.8.

TABLE 3.8
Group Booklet Item Numbers for the *TR* Index

Pair No.	Item Nos.	Items
1.	8–318	My daily life is full of things that keep me interested.
2.	13–290	I work under a great deal of tension.
3.	15–314	Once in a while I think of things too bad to talk about.
4.	16–315	I am sure I get a raw deal from life.
5.	20–310	My sex life is satisfactory.
6.	21–308	At times I have very much wanted to leave home.
7.	22–326	At times I have fits of laughing and crying that I cannot control.
8.	23–288	I am troubled by attacks of nausea and vomiting.
9.	24–333	No one seems to understand me.
10.	32–328	I find it hard to keep my mind on a task or job.
11.	33–323	I have had very peculiar and strange experiences.
12.	35–331	If people had not had it in for me I would have been much more successful.
13.	37–302	I have never been in trouble because of my sex behavior.
14.	38–311	During one period when I was a youngster, I engaged in petty thievery.
15.	305–366	Even when I am with people I feel lonely much of the time.
16.	317–362	I am more sensitive than most other people.

The original authors of the *TR* index (Buechley & Ball, 1952) investigated adolescent profiles but used only 14 of the 16 items due to the ease of scoring these items with a template (Greene, 1979). Currently, most users score all 16 items to derive an index score.

The *TR* index is a measure of response consistency, not response accuracy. A respondent may answer the MMPI items consistently (low *TR* score) but exaggerate or under-report symptoms or problems. Dahlstrom and Welsh (1960) reported that a raw score of 4 or more on the *TR* index is suggestive of an inconsistently answered test.

Greene (1979) investigated the response patterns of four different populations in order to provide normative data for the *TR* index and an optimal cutting score. Fifty subjects were included in each of the following groups: psychiatric patients at a Veterans' Administration (VA) hospital; clients at a university psychology clinic; young adolescents evaluated at a juvenile probation office; and university students enrolled in introductory psychology. The VA patients, psychology clinic clients, college students, and juvenile probation adolescents endorsed a mean number of inconsistent responses of 1.86 ($SD=1.97$), 1.90 ($SD=1.71$), 1.86 ($SD=1.97$), and 4.14 ($SD=2.84$), respectively. Greene (1979) stated that the higher *TR* index scores for the juvenile probation adolescents probably reflects a lack of cooperation and poor motivation on their part. A positive correlation was found for all groups between the raw score on scale *F* and the *TR* index. Greene (1979) stated:

Approximately 4–14% of the profiles that would be ruled invalid by the sole criterion of an F score greater than a T score of 80 were valid according to the TR index using a cutting score of 4 or more consistent responses. More importantly, 8–16% of the profiles that would be considered valid because of a T score less than 71 on the F scale were invalid according to the TR index. (p. 70)

Greene (1979, 1980) reported that the consistency of three of his groups (excluding the juvenile sample) to specific items and in the distribution of scores suggests that the *TR* index is unrelated to type or degree of psychopathology. The study also provides support for the notion that elevated *F* scale scores do not necessarily indicate that the subject answered inconsistently. If a subject answered consistently (low *TR* score), an elevated *F* score could be reflecting realistic distress. Greene (1979) suggested that a *TR* index cutting score of 4 be used for optimal identification of inconsistent responders.

Evans and Dinning (1983) also investigated the relationship between *F* scale scores and the *TR* index. They hypothesized that psychiatric inpatients who obtained low *TR* scores (responded consistently) and have elevated *F* scale scores "would produce profiles more indicative of conscious exaggeration of psychopathology than would inconsistent responders with similarly elevated F scale scores" (p. 246). From a large pool of MMPI profiles, 200 were selected for study and scored for the *TR* index and other validity determiners. Of the 200 scored profiles, 51 patients had MMPI's with *F* scores exceeding a *T*-score value of 90. Subjects were then classified into one of two groups. If their *TR* index score was 4 or more, they were classified as inconsistent responders. If they scored below 4, they were classified as consistent responders. Investigation showed that the consistent responders endorsed the clinical scales in a more pathological direction, obtained lower *L* and *K* scale scores, and endorsed more obvious vs. subtle subscales. They concluded that the consistent responders were exaggerating already significant levels of psychopathology. The inconsistent responders who scored highly on scale *F* were thought to have responded randomly to the MMPI either due to poor comprehension or a refusal to cooperate. Their results can help the MMPI user to distinguish between high *F* scores due to haphazard responding versus a "cry for help" by overclaiming symptomatology. It should be noted that a completely random response pattern would yield a score of 8 on the *TR* index (50% of 16 items).

Evans (1984b) sought to more extensively evaluate some of the features of high versus low *TR* MMPI respondents. To further understand the specific differences between the two *TR* groups in the Evans and Dinning (1983) study, Evans selected a similar sample of male psychiatric inpatients with very high *F* scale scores (*T*-90) and designated them as either inconsistent or consistent responders. He included additional measures that could be used to assess group differences. These included observations of test-taking behavior, medication records, the Whitaker Index of Schizophrenic Thinking Form *A* and the Shipley-

Hartford Vocabulary and Abstraction Scales. Reading levels, medication history, and test-taking behavior did not distinguish the two groups. Group differences emerged in two areas. High *TR* responders scored higher on the schizophrenic measure indicating thought disorder of psychotic proportion. The Shipley abstraction mean score for this group was equivalent to a subaverage Wais score of 80. The low *TR* group means were in the normal range for both these variables and Evans (1984b) suggested that the results indicate that high *TR* respondents are probably in a confused, psychotic state that produces erratic, random responding to the MMPI.

Rogers, Dolmetsch, and Cavanaugh (1983) sought to examine the usefulness of the *TR* index and carelessness scale (Greene, 1978) in discriminating random responders from malingerers and psychiatrically disturbed individuals. Forty randomly generated MMPI (20 male, 20 female) protocols were scored with 40 additional individuals (32 male, 8 female) selected as a consecutive sample from an outpatient forensic evaluation program. The latter clinical group was selected for comparison to the randomly generated MMPI group. The investigators believed that the forensic evaluation group would not be inclined to randomly respond to the MMPI because of the important consequences of their evaluations (insanity, competence to stand trial, civil commitment, etc.). Their results indicated that except for scales *K* and *Si,* the randomly generated profiles were significantly more elevated with a mean elevation (*T*-scores) of 76.0 for the clinical scales as compared to 65.3 for the clinical sample. Applying combined clinical decision rules ($F > 80$ and *TR* index > 4) to classify random responders, 97.5% of the random responders and 95.0% of the nonrandom responders were correctly classified. The authors recommend that if the *TR* index is not routinely scored, it should be scored and examined when the *F* scale exceeds a *T*-score of 80.

It is the opinion of this text's authors that routinely scoring the MMPI for the *TR* index and carelessness scale can increase the ability of the clinician to determine profile invalidity. Therefore, it is recommended that these measures be scored in addition to the traditional validity scales.

Neurotic/Psychotic Measures

The MMPI is routinely used to make diagnostic decisions about a wide range of patients. However, many of the decisions are difficult to make because the data are either incomplete and/or complex. Researchers have recognized that clinicians are limited in their capacity to interpret the MMPI without the aid of objective decision rules. As a result they have suggested that the adoption of such rules facilitates the effectiveness of the diagnostic process. In fact, some literature suggests that when very specific diagnostic decisions are required more reliance should be placed on data provided by objective decision rules (Dahlstrom, Welsh, & Dahlstrom, 1975; Goldberg, 1965; Goodson & King, 1976;

Meehl, 1973). The reader is referred to chapter 4 for a discussion of the clinical vs. actuarial issues.

Various decision rules have been developed to improve identification of clinical features not adequately reflected in single scales or in the standard MMPI profile pattern. Of interest here are the methods for discriminating psychotics from neurotics. Of the many attempts to develop indices for purposes of classifying MMPI profiles as psychotic or neurotic, a few seem to be most noteworthy based on their user acceptance and high reference rate in the literature. Goldberg's (1965, 1969) approach favors the use of simple, linear rules, whereas Taulbee and Sisson (1957), Peterson (1954), and Meehl and Dahlstrom (1960) favor the configural approach.

Peterson (1954) specified six psychotic profile signs that discriminated patients who later became schizophrenic. These signs were adapted from a study made by Meehl (1946) in which some features were identified that discriminated psychotic as opposed to neurotic MMPI patterns. These signs are: (a) T-scores on four or more clinical scales greater than 70; (b) F greater than 65; (c) Sc greater than $Pt;$ (d) Pa or Ma greater than 70; (e) $Pa, Sc,$ or Ma greater than $Hs, D,$ and $Hy;$ and (f) D greater than both Hs and Hy. The presence of three or more of these signs suggests a psychotic profile configuration. Of the major indices used to make a psychotic vs. nonpsychotic distinction, the Peterson signs are considered to be the most replicable and useful of the various configural approaches (Walters, 1988).

Taulbee and Sisson (1957) used a configurational analysis technique to obtain 16 pairs of scales for purposes of differentiating neurotic and psychotic patients. They found that their signs exceeded the judgment of experienced clinicians in differentiating neurotic from schizophrenic patients. To use their method, it is necessary to compare scale elevations and then count the number of scale pairs that agree with the identified signs. (Please see Table 3.9 for the scale pair signs.) Signs are scored as present or absent. If six or less signs are present, a schizophrenic profile is suggested; the presence of 13 or more signs is indicative of a neurotic profile. A score falling within the 7 to 12 range is considered an indeterminant score.

Walters (1988) stated "the Taulbee-Sisson (1957) signs are probably not a practical alternative to the Peterson signs due to the fact that the derivation sample was inadequately defined and that very little data are available on its predictive validity" (p. 63).

Meehl and Dahlstrom (1960) developed an elaborate set of 16 sequential rules for discriminating the profiles of psychotics or neurotics. The rules were developed using white male psychiatric cases but have been applied to profiles from female patients (Dahlstrom, Welsh, & Dahlstrom, 1972). To use the Meehl-Dahlstrom (M-D) rules, one must first plot the standard scale scores (T-scores) to obtain the MMPI profile. The profile then must be coded (the Hathaway or Welsh code is sufficient) and various ratios are computed according

TABLE 3.9
Taulbee-Sisson Signs (Scale Pairs) for Differentiating
Neurotic and Schizophrenic Groups

Hs(1) > Hy(3)	D(2) > Pa(6)
Hs(1) > Pd(4)	Hy(3) > Pd(4)
Hs(1) > Mf(5)	Hy(3) > Mf(5)
Hs(1) > Pa(6)	Hy(3) > Pa(6)
Hs(1) > Pt(7)	Hy(3) > Ma(9)
Hs(1) > Sc(8)	Pt(7) > Mf(5)
Hs(1) > Ma(8)	Pt(7) > Pa(6)
D(2) > Pd(4)	Pt(7) > Sc(8)

Note: Taulbee and Sisson (1957).

to specific formulas. The M-D rules are applied in order until a decision is reached that labels the MMPI pattern as neurotic, psychotic, or indeterminant. The last category reflects the fact that the MMPI pattern does not contain sufficient information to arrive at either of the first two diagnostic decisions. Another category, character disorders/behavior disorders was later added to the diagnosis function by expanding the rules (Henrichs, 1964, 1966). However, Henrichs (1966) reported relatively low hit rates in his cross validation samples indicating that his modified rules may not be of practical usefulness to the clinician.

The *M-D* rules represent a configural approach and have as a basic underlying assumption the belief that the information required to make differentiations resides primarily in nonlinear relationships among MMPI scales (Giannetti, Johnson, Klingler, & Williams, 1978). As the *M-D* rules were derived from a sample of white male psychiatric cases, Gynther (1972) stated that the rules' generalizability is limited. He showed that if one attempts to apply the *M-D* rules for discriminating psychotic from neurotic profiles to the incoming patients of a typical urban mental health center, "only about 10 to 15% are even potentially suitable for analysis and only about half of that percentage are actually available" (p. 104). Apparently, the rules do not apply to Blacks, organic patients, and others with high validity scale scores. Pancoast, Archer, and Gordon (1988) reminded MMPI users of the mixed results obtained by investigators studying the accuracy of the *M-D* rules. Goldberg (1965), Giannetti, Johnson, Klinger, and Williams (1978), and Gynther (1963) reported hit rates of 66%, 47%, and 38% respectively for the *M-D* rules. Gynther (1963) stated that the *M-D* rules appeared impractical for clinical use.

Goldberg (1965, 1969) challenged the assumption that the configural approach is best suited for discrimination purposes. He compared a number of techniques for discriminating psychotic from neurotic profiles and concluded that a simple linear combination of five single scales $(L+Pa+Sc-Hy-Pt)$ that are K-corrected T-scores outperformed even the most complex configural rules.

Goldberg statistically analyzed the Meehl-Dahlstrom (1960) data used to derive the *M-D* rules, as well as a subset of group profiles derived from Lanyon (1968). Through a series of sequential stepwise multiple linear regression analyses, he derived three linear indices each consisting of *K*-corrected *T*-scores with cutting scores for determining specific classifications (more specific information about the derivation of the Goldberg rules, the actual formulae and their clinical applications is presented in chapter 7). The three Goldberg rules or indices are intended to be applied sequentially to MMPI profiles. The first rule classifies a profile as normal versus deviant. The second rule classifies the profile as psychotic versus sociopathic, and the third rule yields a classification of psychotic versus neurotic. Cut-off scores for these rules vary. For example, Goldberg (1965) showed that the validity of the psychotic versus neurotic index is greater when the *T*-score on the *K* scale is 48 or lower, and is less accurate when *K* is 49 or greater. Webb, McNamara and Rogers (1986) pointed out that for outpatients it may be more accurate to use the cut-off points of below 40 and above 60, because the hypothetical normal person (i.e., who obtains *T*-scores of 50 on all scales) would receive a Goldberg index score of 50. The reader should note that the Goldberg formulae are based on *K*-corrected *T*-scores (Webb, McNamara, & Rogers, 1986).

As the Goldberg rules were derived from psychiatric samples, applying the rules to other types of patient populations or normal populations may lead to the misclassification of individuals. For example, O'Leary, Chaney, Brown, and Schuckit (1978) investigated the clinical utility and validity of the Goldberg indices with Veteran Administration alcoholic patients. They hypothesized that there would be differences between the life history responses of subjects who were classified using the Goldberg rules as sociopathic and those characterized as normal, neurotic, or psychotic. However, the analysis did not reveal significant differences between the groups suggesting that caution be exercised when applying the Goldberg rules to patients with a primary diagnosis of alcoholism. Goodson and King (1976) studied the efficacy of the Goldberg index ($L+Pa+Sc-Hy-Pt$) and *M-D* rules in a college population. Using two experienced PhD clinical psychologists as judges to determine a validity criterion, they compared the *GI* and *M-D* rules to classifications ratings made by these two psychologist judges. The judges independently sorted 131 MMPI profiles into five categories including psychoses, neuroses, personality disorder, normal, and invalid profiles. The *GI* correctly identified 63.4% of the psychotic profiles classified by the judges. The hit rates for the neurotic and personality categories were 44.4% and 24.3%, respectively, with the *M-D* rules showing a hit rate of 73.1% for psychoses and a 95.5% hit rate for nonpsychoses. However, Goodson and King (1976) pointed out that these percentages are misleading as the *GI* misclassified a high percentage of false negatives and false positives. In fact, 63% to 75% of the profiles were incorrectly classified. The *M-D* rules by comparison fared much better with an average hit rate of 85% for all categories compared to an average of 44% for the *GI*. The *M-D* rules had only a 12% false positive rate for psychoses compared to 50% for the *GI*. The judges' ratings agreed with the *M-D* rules more significantly than with the *GI* adding construct validity to both (Goodson & King, 1976). Researchers concluded that the *GI* is inflexible; that is, because the index forces a score into a psychotic, neurotic, or sociopathic category, invalid profiles will tend to be classified incorrectly regardless of their validity status. In addition, they found that the *M-D* rules outperformed the *GI* and that the *GI* may be inappropriate to use with a college population.

Researchers and clinicians both appear to apply the *GI* separately rather than using the three-stage formula that seems to improve the incremental validity of the rules (Nichols, 1974). Roy (1984) investigated the utility of the *GI* (neurotic vs. psychotic rule) to accurately diagnose psychiatric inpatients with a 2-7-8 code-type, one of the most common code-types in that population. The sample consisted of 111 male psychiatric inpatients at a midwestern VA hospital whose MMPI profiles consisted of a 2-7-8 high-point triad. Patients were classified as either schizophrenic or nonschizophrenic on the basis of their physician's discharge summaries. The GI was computed for each patient with the resultant classification of psychotic if the *K*-corrected *T*-score was 45 or more and nonpsychotic if the score was less than 45. The relationship between the discharge diagnoses and the Goldberg prediction was analyzed using a series of multiple discriminant analyses. Most important, according to Roy (1984), the application of the GI to all of the 2-7-8 profiles did not "improve the accuracy of diagnosis over base rate prediction alone" (p. 399). Scores below 40 or 99 did show a significant relationship with the discharge diagnoses, whereas the range between these two scores showed a random distribution. Roy (1984) stated that by adjusting the cutting scores, the *GI* could be clinically useful with the population being studied. However, although adjusting the cutting score may be useful, it is impractical to do so in most clinical situations. Goodson and King (1976) made this clear in the following quotation:

> An inflexible cutting score is not advised for a psychometric device, and some authors, including Goldberg, have suggested shifting the cutting score to fit the particular clinical setting. This would result in a time-consuming process that would require shifting the cutting score for each clinical setting, each population sample, and even for different individuals within the sample, and then comparing this new cutting score with some established measure of profile classification. It seems that a better solution for increasing the construct validity of the GI would be to increase the formula's validity rather than to shift the cutting scores. (p. 334)

Pancoast, Archer, and Gordon (1988) studied the congruence rate between clinical-discharge diagnoses rendered by a psychiatrist and MMPI derived discharge diagnoses from four MMPI diagnostic classification systems. The systems investigated relevant to this discussion were the Henrichs (1964, 1966) revision of the *M-D* rules and the Goldberg equations. The subjects consisted of

150 psychiatric inpatients who completed admission and discharge MMPI's. Psychiatrists assigned discharge diagnoses to patients independent of the MMPI. The discharge and admission MMPI profiles were classified into either psychotic, neurotic, personality disorder, or indeterminant categories based on the application of the four classification systems being examined (the other two systems included a simple high-point code based on the highest scale elevation and a system offered by Lachar, 1974). The results showed that the four different systems were similar in their ability to correspond to discharge diagnoses. Pancoast, Archer, and Gordon reported that all the systems were poor at identifying neurotic diagnoses. The Henrichs' system identified a high number of true positive classifications for psychosis while also yielding a high rate of false positives. Likewise, the Goldberg rules identified high true and high false positive rates for the character disorder diagnosis. The very modest hit rates across the systems lead them to conclude that diagnoses based exclusively on the MMPI are more likely to be incorrect than correct in terms of agreeing with psychiatric discharge diagnoses. The authors recommend that diagnoses not be made exclusively with the MMPI. Rather, other data sources such as patient and symptom history should be considered.

This text's authors are in agreement with the necessity of using other non-MMPI data for determining diagnoses. The reader interested in using the *GI* in clinical and or research settings is advised to carefully read the caveats offered by David S. Nichols in chapter 7 of this text (see Table 7.1).

Although various neurotic vs. psychotic or schizophrenic vs. nonschizophrenic indices have sparked clinical and research interest, Walters (1988) concluded that there is little basis for adopting special MMPI scales or indices in identifying schizophrenic profiles as the standard MMPI scales, particularly scale 8 (*Sc*), have strong construct validity support.

4

Approach to Interpretation

CLINICAL AND ACTUARIAL ISSUES

Although specific approaches to interpretation of MMPI profiles (including a practical outline of steps) is discussed in detail in subsequent sections, it is necessary to have a basic understanding of actuarial and clinical approaches to interpretation of tests such as the MMPI. To not understand the differences in these two approaches will doubtless cause the professional to make numerous clinical errors. Most mental health professionals continue to rely almost exclusively on clinical approaches, even though the power of actuarial methods in psychological assessment has been repeatedly and convincingly demonstrated (Marks, Seeman, & Haller, 1974; Meehl, 1970). Clinical approaches to interpretations are those that come from a professional's personal and professional experience. Actuarial intepretations are those derived directly by applying a formula to previously specified empirical rules.

In mental health fields, clinical judgment has long been considered to be a skill of central importance. It was developed as a professional accrued experience with clinical data such as presenting symptoms, life situation, and past history. This clinical judgment rested heavily on the internal norms about clientele (and indeed, people in general) that the practitioner developed. Years and varieties of experience were prized, because only then, it was believed, could one develop the depth of knowledge necessary to successfully consider all of the complex nuances. Personality was felt to be too complex to be represented adequately and accurately by test scores. Furthermore, results from psychological tests, though helpful adjuncts, were characteristically treated as clearly

111

secondary in importance as compared with an experienced clinician's judgments. In terms of persuasiveness, test data yielded to clinical impressions.

In the face of such a long-standing tradition, it is impressive that the MMPI was developed largely as an empirical answer to the very questions raised (in 1939 and 1940) by the apparent unreliability of clinicians' judgments. The need for an objective and more reliable measure of personality—independent of clinicians' personal impressions—was clear. The "dustbowl empiricists" of Minnesota used empirical procedures to develop objective alternatives to the subjective approaches of clinical interview, and indeed to the commonly used projective assessment approaches.

As use of the MMPI increased, however, clinicians often noted that certain scale values and/or configurations of scales were associated with personality characteristics over and above those previously empirically demonstrated. Sometimes these new observations or "insights" were empirically tested; sometimes they were not. Particularly, they were not tested for configurations that occurred infrequently.

Similarly, empirical conclusions commonly were derived and validated for one population of subjects (e.g., psychiatric inpatients) but were not similarly validated for other populations (e.g., outpatients, adolescents, marriage counselees, etc.). Generalizations from one population to another were often made, even though empirical support for such generalization typically had not been demonstrated.

Thus, although the MMPI has had a remarkably strong empirical base, substantial and extensive personality interpretations from the MMPI have been added based on clinical experience and judgment. This addition of clinical lore increased particularly as the units of analysis for the MMPI became more complex. Although the original empirical derivation focused on the individual item, interpretations by practitioners initially emphasized the analysis of each scale in isolation, then the intepretations of combinations of scales, and finally numerous complex configurations of scale combinations. Although the additional information from these clinical interpretations clearly has added a remarkable richness and breadth to the use of the MMPI, more recently questions have arisen as to whether they may have added substantial error variance at the same time.

In 1954, Meehl recognized that in the training of clinician's judgment, there were clear and definable rules that could be explicitly delineated. Furthermore, he discovered numerous studies showing that following objective, specifiable rules produced diagnostic judgments that apparently were superior in most instances to those of the clinicians. The result was his exciting publication entitled "Wanted: A Good Cookbook" (Meehl, 1956). In this publication, Meehl espoused that an actuarial, rather than a clinical, approach should be used wherever possible. Subsequent research has vigorously and repeatedly supported this view (e.g., Marks, Seeman, & Haller, 1974, Meehl, 1970).

Although the term *actuary* is more often heard in the context of the insurance business, it is every bit as relevant to psychology, particularly to assessment. In the insurance industry, certain definable and measurable factors are statistically associated with risks or the lack of risks. For example, age, smoking, longevity of parents, and occupation are all associated with risks of mortality, and that risk can be expressed in terms of a probability statement through using direct mathematical relationships. Note that there is no judgment involved. Insurance businesses have found that when judgment is added (e.g., "But he seems to be particularly healthy"), the accuracy of predictions generally becomes worse.

The same findings have occurred in psychology (e.g., Goldberg, 1965; Meehl, 1954; Sawyer, 1966). Despite the long-standing emphasis on pro-·fessional judgment, clinicians repeatedly have fared worse than the actuarial rules. In a meta-analysis of 20 studies of prediction using clinical and actuarial means, Meehl (1954) found that, "In about half of the studies, the two methods were equal; in the other half, the clinician is definitely inferior. No . . . fully acceptable study puts him clearly ahead" (p. 119). Similarly, Sawyer (1966) analyzed 45 studies, and substantiated Meehl's findings that the actuarial approaches showed clear and repeated superiority over clinical judgment in numerous situations with diverse types of data. Clearly the actuary is of greater assistance to the clinician than the clinician is to the actuary—at least in day-to-day clinical practice. In a more recent review, Meehl (1970) frankly stated that

> *it is difficult to come up with so much as one single research study in which the clinician's predictions are better that the statistical table or formula; in most studies the clinician is significantly worse.* There are few domains of social science in which so sizeable a body of evidence is so consistently in the same direction. (p. 9, italics added)

Even so, it is important to note that these studies deal primarily with prediction of measurable behaviors, and only occasionally with personality description. Although prediction and description certainly are both appropriate domains of clinical practice, they are clearly different tasks because not only are personality descriptions more difficult to validate, but they also may be inherently more complex. Nevertheless, actuarial approaches to personality description using the MMPI have shown a superiority over clinical judgments ranging from a 19% to 38% improvement in accuracy (Marks, Seeman, & Haller, 1974).

To understand (and use) actuarial approaches in prediction, personality description, psychological test interpretation, and diagnosis, one must first understand the terms *actuarial* and *base rates,* and clearly distinguish them conceptually from *cookbook* or *automated interpretation* approaches. Cookbook approaches are those that describe a systematic approach (or recipe) for arriving at some diagnostic conclusion or personality formulation. Some of these cook-book approaches have been automated, such that the decision-logic resembles an "automated clinician." Whether automated or not, such approaches may—or may not—have actuarial bases that are used in generating their descriptions and predictions. In many cookbook systems, the recipes for diagnosis and description are based solely on clinical lore; in other systems, actuarial and clinical approaches are mixed in unspecified ways.

Overall, the cookbook descriptions contained in the following chapters are actuarially based (where empirical data have been found to exist), but are enhanced by the addition of information based on clinical judgment. The reader should note that in the interest of comprehensiveness and clinical utility, in-terpretations of some scale configurations are based solely on combined clinical judgment, apparent consensus, and on survey of whatever research studies could be found that appeared (in the authors' judgment) to be helpful. The reader may wish to consult the purer actuarial approaches to personality description and prediction, such as Marks, Seeman, and Haller (1974), even though only about 20 or so two-point codes (out of a possible total of 45 two-point codes) in such systems have actuarial descriptions associated with them.

Thus, this book's approach to MMPI intepretation is similar to various automated or computerized interpretation systems that have been developed for the MMPI (described in Dahlstrom, Welsh, & Dahlstrom, 1972; Graham, 1987), although we feel our system is more detailed and allows more comprehensive consideration of alternatives by clinicians in interpreting MMPI profiles than is typical in current automated or other cookbook approaches. It is important to point out, as has been cogently noted by Marks, Seeman, and Haller (1974), that computerized interpretations need not be actuarially based. In fact, some (e.g., Fowler, 1969) are more aptly described as computerized imitations of a clinician whose memory is able to reliably recall prior interpretive guidelines, predictions, and conclusions. These guidelines, however, are often without actuarial basis, and instead stem from "clinical lore" or are "logical derivatives" from actuarial findings. For those profile configurations that occur only rarely, such depen-dence on clinical (rather than actuarial) bases for interpretations is heightened, and thus must be treated with particular caution given the research on actuarial vs. clinical accuracy.

The core conception of actuarial description has been well described by Marks, Seeman, and Haller (1974); "Actuarial descriptions consist of a set of descriptive attributes . . . assigned to individuals on the basis of . . . explicit . . . rules derived from experimentally-statistically demonstrated associations be-tween data (e.g., MMPI profiles) and the descriptive statements." This experi-ence table of the demonstrated associations between a set of data and certain descriptions, however, implies some comparison. That is, a given data score is associated particularly with that description or behavior, but compared to what? The comparison must be to the *base rate*.

Base rates refer to the frequency with which a behavior or characteristic exists within a given population. Some behaviors have such a high base rate that they are not likely to distinguish among people in meaningful ways, even though they may be true. These have sometimes been referred to as "Aunt Fanny" statements; that is, they are true about you, about me, and about my Aunt Fanny (Tallent, 1983). An example would be, "Sometimes I do not say all that is on my mind," or "My moods may change depending on what is happening in my life." Meehl (1973) also labeled this phenomenon the "Barnum effect" because many professionals apparently attempt to raise their credibility through overuse of such high base rate statements.

More meaningful are those base rates that are less common, or even comparatively rare, and thus allow for distinguishing between individuals or groups of individuals. Sometimes the base rates are so extreme that one can "play the base rates" in arriving at a professional judgment or conclusion, and have virtual certainty of being correct. For example, the incidence (i.e., base rate) of suicide among 5-year-old girls attending public school kindergarten is virtually nil—certainly less than one per thousand. Knowing nothing else about the person other than age, gender, and enrollment in public school, one could confidently predict an absence of suicidal risk with an accuracy rate of 99.999% or better—a rate that could hardly be improved upon by the addition of any psychological test data. (It is interesting to realize that psychological test data have the greatest potential for improving accuracy over the base rate predictions when the base rate is not extreme in either direction, but closer to 50/50).

However, base rates change with different groupings and for different populations. For example, the base rate of suicide increases with age; with reported depression; loss of social support. relative, or job; history of recent suicide attempts; etc. Or as another example, diagnosing brain damage is extremely hazardous among executive candidates for senior job opportunities in business, simply because of the rarity. To do so in such a setting would require virtually overwhelmingly clear and convincing evidence toward CNS dysfunction. The same diagnosis would be considered with far greater ease when working with patients on a neurology inpatient ward simply because you are not "fighting the base rate" in your search for accuracy of diagnosis.

The point to be realized, then, is that base rates differ across different groups, and thereby directly affect the prediction and description process. Thus, actuarial tables derived for one group with great accuracy (e.g., adults) may show far less accuracy with other groups (e.g., adolescents). The professional must know that to date, the actuarial research on the MMPI (or other psychological tests) has not identified nor systematically included comprehensive consideration of many major groups or demographic variables that clearly influence interpretation of tests such as the MMPI.

It is for these reasons that slavish and unthinking utilization of actuarial (or other nonactuarial cookbook) interpretations of the MMPI must be avoided.

Particular attention must be paid to recognizing when a given client differs from those upon whom the actuarial interpretations were derived (Ehrenworth & Archer, 1985). Naive applications of any system otherwise can result in situations such as a 24-year-old inpatient being diagnosed as suffering involutional depression because his MMPI profile configuration suggested it.

Despite the power of the actuarial approach, it is still a "work in progress" that is clearly outstanding as far as it has been developed—but it is in need of further expansion. The actuarial approach to MMPI interpretation is indeed most powerful, but only where the actuary is able to have access to relevant data about the client. Until that time, professionals using the MMPI have no choice but to use their comparatively unreliable internal clinical norms and professional memory.

For these reasons, using a cookbook or computerized interpretation system, though helpful, is not sufficient. The MMPI user must gain understanding of the personality dimensions (as well as the pathology dimensions) measured by various scales and configurations of the MMPI. Likewise, the MMPI user should be particularly alert to the need to modify MMPI clinical interpretations due to a person's age, intelligence, social or ethnic class, educational level, marital status, health status, medication influences, prior life traumas, and current situational difficulties. These factors clearly modify many of the interpretations made of MMPI profile configurations (Pancoast, Archer, & Gordon, 1988).

In the following chapters on MMPI interpretation, attempts have been made to highlight the most salient of these moderating variables. Others, however, may well exist, and the user's alertness to this fact is encouraged. Similarly, caution should be exercised when using MMPI (or other test data) in extremely high or low base rate situations, where the likelihood of improving on the base rate prediction is slim. Even so, generally the interpretations will have wide applicability because the actuarial base of these interpretations was derived from the most frequently occurring profile types.

PROCEDURES FOR PROFILE INTERPRETATION

Before interpreting the actual MMPI profile, the clinician needs to consider a number of basic questions that set the stage. There are a series of steps that will help organize the MMPI interpretations in a coherent and valid fashion.

The Referral Question

The MMPI, by itself, should be used to generate hypotheses about a client, rather than providing definitive statements, because very few clients will fit neatly into the rules needed to use only a cookbook description. The more background information available about a client, the more accurate and relevant the inferences drawn from the MMPI data.

It is always important to know why the client is being referred because the referral question and background information provide the framework that allows the MMPI interpretations to be most useful and valid. For example, a referring colleague sometimes requests an assessment because of a general concern, such as having difficulty "getting a handle" on the client's dynamics. On the other hand, sometimes the concern is specific, such as a suicidal, psychotic, or neurotic client. Using the aforementioned example, if a "difficult to get to know" client's profile emerges with a very high K, the assessment psychologist's report could serve as a validation of the referring colleague's difficulty (i.e., the client is difficult to get to know as evidenced by the high K), as well as providing a source of possible therapeutic strategies to unblock the over-control.

In a few cases, such as computerized assessment, the interpretation will be "blind;" that is, the computer program does not typically consider information such as the referral question, marital status, recent life events, etc.—all of which the clinician optimally would use in formulating interpretations. Even so, because of the computer's reliability and memory, computerized reports can be very helpful. Examples of computerized reports are presented in chapter 8.

Due to concerns about validity, many psychologists "hedge their bets" by using too many modifiers or qualifiers in an attempt to avoid making errors. Ownby (1987), for example, quoted a typical hedged report, "It appears at least somewhat possible that the client may develop a potentially more serious disorder." This sort of vague statement may avoid making an error, but is not helpful to the person reading the assessment report. Knowing something about the client from the referral question and/or background history can greatly help the report writer in reducing this kind of hedging. Such an improvement in specificity and accuracy by considering additional information is often referred to as "incremental power" (Marks, Seeman, & Haller, 1974). For example, an educated or middle-class person obtaining a profile elevated on scales 4 and 9 may, in fact, be a psychologist or someone involved in law enforcement because the 49/94 profile code, in the moderate ranges, is the modal profile for both groups. However the 49/94 profile is also the modal code-type at higher elevations for antisocial personalities (Duckworth & Anderson, 1986). If the testing psychologist had no idea about the referral question, the past behaviors, or the socioeconomic and educational variables, then descriptors of antisocial behavior might be used that could be inaccurate for a person of higher education. Thus, the testing psychologist should make every effort to get at least a few lines of background information with a referral question, such as, "Please evaluate this profile of a 22-year-old, male, high school dropout, recently in trouble with the law and with a history of truancy and petty theft. What is the likelihood that he will continue to act out, and is there any evidence of underlying psychotic processes?" Such a short description, with a referral question, immediately makes interpretation of the 49/94 profile less ambiguous for the report writing clinician who can now consider more accurately the extent to which actuarial rules fit this particular client, as well as the base rate likelihood for various behaviors in people with these background characteristics. At the very least, the basic demographic and referral question information should be completed on the profile sheet so as to enable the MMPI user to have the basic moderator variable information.

Often the referring psychologist may not have a clearly thought out referral question. In such a case, the testing psychologist is advised to call and inquire about basic referral questions in order to make the test report more useful.

Yet another reason to have a referral question and background data is because people sometimes obtain a profile that, at first sight, appears pathological, but when understood against the client's current situation, becomes less so. For example, a client obtaining a profile elevated on scales 2 and 7 may show a chronic life history of compulsive, anxious, and depressed behaviors, or they may be acutely responding to a recent, unpredictable loss. Similarly, an adolescent with high elevations on scales 8 and 9 may be showing a severe identity type of panic, or may, in fact, be responding to a drug overdose. Whereas a report written using only a cookbook approach could describe the client accurately regarding current functioning and behaviors, the diagnosis and therapeutic significance could be inaccurate. The referral question can hone the interpretation, the diagnosis, and the implications.

Demographic Variables

The next step, prior to analyzing MMPI data, is to ascertain the client's demographic parameters. No test should be interpreted without knowing the subject's age, sex, education, race, and occupation. Each of these variables influences how a particular set of scores is interpreted, as well as which norms are employed.

Age. One of the first large-scale studies (871 cases) on aging and the MMPI (Aaronson, 1958) found that peaks on scale 1 (*Hs*) and 2 (*D*) were relatively uncommon early in life, but became more common later. The reverse was true for scales 4 (*Pd*) and 8 (*Sc*). He interpreted these base rate shifts as reflecting the normal process of concern with physical health that is associated with aging, and with the common problems of impulse control and identity concerns affecting younger populations.

These findings have been replicated in normal adult samples reported by Dahlstrom, Lachar, and Dahlstrom (1986), who examined four age levels (18–24, 25–34, 35–49, ≥ 50). For white males, scales *F*, 4 (*Pd*), 8 (*Sc*), and 9 (*Ma*) significantly decreased in mean value as age increased. For white females, scales *L* and 0 (*Si*) increased in similar linear fashion across the four age levels, whereas scale *K* increased until age 50, and then declined. For Black males, scales *F* and 4 (*Pd*) decreased steadily as age increased; however scales 8 (*Sc*) and 9 (*Ma*) significantly decreased until age 50, at which time they increased slightly. For Black females, scale *L* increased as these normal subjects became older, and scales 4 (*Pd*), 8 (*Sc*), and 9 (*Ma*) steadily decreased. It is noteworthy that although highly significant differences between Black and white subjects existed at the lower age levels, these differences were significantly attenuated as age increased. Clearly what are normal MMPI scale values at one age differs from those values for other ages.

The most striking age-related differences in MMPI scale values of normal persons appear to occur when adolescents are compared with adults. In samples of adolescents, several studies (e.g., Archer, 1987; Ball, 1962; Marks, Seeman, & Haller, 1974) have indicated that scales 4 (*Pd*), 8 (*Sc*), 9 (*Ma*) and *F* are often elevated in normal adolescents by 10 or more *T*-score points—at least when adult norms are used.

Two-point code type frequencies likewise vary according to age. Webb's (1970) analysis of over 12,000 patients showed that clients above age 27 obtained the following code-types significantly more frequently than younger patients: 02/20, 12/21, 13/31, 23/32, 27/72, 34/43, and 36/63. Patients below age 27 obtained the following code-types more frequently: 47/74, 48/84, 49/94, 68/86, 78/87, and 89/98. Although Webb's analysis has limited generalizability due to his use of a median split resulting in a cut-off at age 27, the point he makes is valid; age is an important moderator variable.

Gynther (1979b) similarly stated that "younger patients in normal samples obtain more peaks and high scores on scales measuring nonconformity, rebelliousness, alienation, and energy level. Older patients in normal samples obtain more peaks and high scores on scales measuring concern with health, introversion, and to a lesser extent, scales involving depression." A profile with moderate elevations on the depression or hypochondriasis scales from a person over age 70 should be interpreted less pathologically than the same profile from a young adult.

Sex. Early in the development of the MMPI there was clear recognition of the need to have different norms for males and females because of the different patterns of endorsement of items for the two sexes. Thus, the raw score to *T*-score conversions were different for the two sexes. Subsequently it became evident that MMPI scale elevations had different correlates for the two sexes (Dahlstrom, Welsh, & Dahlstrom, 1972). That is, elevations on scale 6 did not necessarily mean the same for males as for females. In addition, scales 3 (*Hy*) and 6 (*Pa*) were more often high-point elevations for females, whereas scales 1 (*Hs*) and 7 (*Pt*) were more often highest for males (Webb, 1971).

Generally, these sex differences have been incorporated in the code-type interpretations that follow. What has not yet been adequately considered in interpreting MMPI patterns are the gender-related specific situations that may need to be considered in understanding the clinical significance of an MMPI profile. For example, spouse abuse is disproportionately an occurrence with wives, and the knowledge that a woman is being abused would make the anger reflected in an MMPI pattern more understandable. Similarly, the frustrations of a competent, independent woman in the business world would likely be reflected in portions of the MMPI profile, and reflect the situation, rather than enduring pathology. The clinician must be sensitive to such gender issues in order to adequately interpret many MMPI code-types.

Education. Beyond the matter of basic comprehension of the MMPI items, education is associated with MMPI scale elevations. As education increases, scales F and 0 (*Si*) decrease, and scale *K* increases. Likewise, men with higher education show fairly strong elevations on scale 5 (*Mf*) (Gulas, 1973), and women with similarly high education show moderately low scores on scale 5 (Dahlstrom, Lachar, & Dahlstrom, 1986, Graham & Tisdale, 1983). These patterns are likewise associated with increased intelligence test scores, and generally these findings are consistent regardless of age or ethnic group membership (Dahlstrom, Lachar, & Dahlstrom, 1986). As Dahlstrom et al. noted, "In general, then, all subjects who report some education beyond the level of high school graduation are more likely to answer the MMPI in less deviant ways. Their scores are consistent with greater personal effectiveness, fewer interpersonal and emotional difficulties, and better morale."

Race. Numerous studies reviewing the MMPI have shown significant differences between scores of Blacks and whites on the MMPI. Most often these differences have found scales *F*, 8 (*Sc*) and 9 (*Ma*) to be significantly higher, with other studies also showing scales *K* and 5 (*Mf*) to be lower. More recent evidence (Dahlstrom, Lachar, & Dahlstrom, 1986) however, strongly suggests that these apparent differences have been the result of influences of other variables, such as education, age, and rural/urban residence. At higher levels of socioeconomic status, racial differences virtually disappeared. Within racial groups, however, scale score differences between higher and lower socioeconomic groups were much greater than any differences between racial groups.

Even so, it is important to remember that Blacks, whether young or old, male or female, normal or institutionalized, generally obtain higher scores than whites on scales *F*, 8 (*Sc*), and 9 (*Ma*). Gynther (1979) suggested that these results appear to reflect differences in values and perceptions, rather than differences in psychological adjustment. Many studies, according to Gynther, revealed that the principal factor distinguishing between Blacks and whites was estrangement and mistrust of society, which was reflected on scales 4 and 8. Indeed, Dahlstrom, Lachar, and Dahlstrom (1986) noted that "by no means (are) all deviations (as reflected in elevated MMPI scores or in similar measures) evidence for dis-

order." Even so, these elevations and profile configurations are extremely valuable. As Dahlstrom et al. concluded, "the MMPI may be useful in the task of
characterizing the various coping and defense mechanisms to which minority
individuals may resort in their efforts to deal with the special circumstances that
they all too often encounter in America today."

Comparisons with Hispanics and other minority groups also suggest some
differences in average MMPI scores. In reviewing these studies, Greene (1980)
was not able, however, to discern any clear pattern of differences on the clinical
scales, although some validity scale differences appeared on scales L and K. His
review suggests that the differences between Hispanic populations and whites
were less than the differences between Blacks and whites on the MMPI. Dahlstrom, Lachar, and Dahlstrom (1986) made similar observations, and additionally noted that acculturation generally reduced the differences between the MMPI
scores of Hispanic and white populations.

It is important to note that caution should be used when interpreting MMPI
profiles from ethnic groups. Even so, in a comprehensive review regarding
ethnicity and the MMPI, Greene (1987) suggested that too much has been made
of average differences between ethnic groups' MMPI scores. His review suggests a "failure to find a consistent pattern of scale differences between any two
ethnic groups in any population." Instead, he pointed out, "It appears that
moderator variables such as socioeconomic status, education, and intelligence,
as well as profile validity are more important determinants of MMPI performance than ethnic status." As Greene (1987) and Dahlstrom, Lachar and Dahlstrom (1986) both noted, researchers should focus on the empirical correlates
associated with specific patterns and elevations on the MMPI for various ethnic
subpopulations, rather than reporting small mean differences between various
poorly defined ethnic groups.

Socioeconomic Variables

The major dimensions that define socioeconomic status (SES) in white subjects
can be matched only roughly to similar dimensions for subjects who are Black or
are from other ethnic groups, thus it is hazardous to make generalizations
concerning MMPI patterns that might be associated with socioeconomic variables (Dahlstrom, Lachar, & Dahlstrom, 1986). Even so, some patterns seem
sufficiently consistent to warrant specific mention.

Normal subjects from low socioeconomic groups, regardless of race or gender, tend to score higher on the F scale and on scale 0 (Si), whereas subjects from
higher socioeconomic backgrounds tend to score higher on the K scale (Dahlstrom, Lachar, & Dahlstrom, 1986; Duckworth & Anderson, 1986). For males,
scale 8 (Sc) decreases as socioeconomic status increases, whereas for women
scales 2 (D) and 5 (Mf) decrease as socioeconomic status increases.

Socioeconomic status is fundamentally comprised of and confounded with such preceeding dimensions as education, age, gender, and ethnicity, thus it is no surprise that socioeconomic status must provide a basic life pattern within which to interpret the MMPI. Certainly socioeconomic status influences the way adults present themselves on such tests as the MMPI, and appears to be more influential on the test results than the component demographic dimensions (Dahlstrom, Lachar, & Dahlstrom, 1986).

SPECIFIC STEPS FOR INTERPRETATION OF PROFILES

After you have assessed the basic demographic data, the profile can be examined.

Step 1. Note the Test-Taking Time

A person of average intelligence without significant reading, concentration, or decision-making problems usually takes 1 to 2 hours to complete the MMPI. If the test-taking time is shorter, suspect that the person may be impulsive and/or gave insufficient consideration to the items. Also be aware of the possibility of random responding (see chapter 5). If the test-taking time is longer than 2 hours, suspect psychological difficulties such as obsessive indecision, severe depression, guardedness, or intrusive thoughts that interfere with concentration. Certainly, however, the test-taking time is usually longer in persons with reading problems (broken or lost glasses, marginal literacy) or who have below average intelligence.

Step 2. Examine the Answer Sheet for Erasures

Examine the answer sheet for erasures, double-marked answers, omissions, and hesitation pencil point marks. Random responders generally do not erase. However, clients giving thoughtful consideration to their answers, or clients who are consciously concerned about how their responses will be received, often will erase, reflecting their change of mind.

Step 3. Plot the Profile Sheet

On the profile sheet, it is desirable to plot the MMPI using the appropriate norms for the group against which the individual is being compared. For example, an adolescent profile may be plotted using adolescent norms (Archer, 1987), or a general hospital patient against medical patient norms (Swenson, Pearson, & Osborne, 1973). In some cases it is helpful to plot the profile using two (or sometimes more) sets of norms. For example, a 17-year-old adolescent living away from home may be plotted according to both adolescent and adult norms. Multiple plotting on the same profile allows visual comparison of the differences allowing, for example, adolescent norms to be superimposed on adult norms to see the contrasts. Caution: Some norms, such as the adolescent norms provided by Marks et al. [1974], do not use K-corrections for raw score to T-score conversions. It should further be noted that special norms, such as adolescent norms, for converting raw scores to T-scores must be obtained from tables such as those listed in appendix E, because the typical profile sheet contains raw-score marks appropriate only for adults in general. The interpretation of any profile, however, should be based primarily on the norms appropriate for the age and the setting.

Step 4. Examine for Scoring Errors

After plotting the profile, it should be examined for obvious errors and incongruities that would suggest incorrect scoring, or all true or all false responding. Examine the answer sheet once again to make sure that double-endorsed items were not scored, and count the number of items (if any) that have been omitted. Though this requirement may seem obvious, persons hand-scoring MMPI answer sheets make errors that then effect all of the remaining interpretations.

With experience, you will come to recognize profiles that give you a funny feeling because they have been misscored or they are the classic all deviant or all nondeviant response set. For example, most profiles fall into one of the commonly occurring two- or three-point profile types (see chapter 6). Thus, for example, a profile with elevations on scales 9 and 0 and a very high F scale may indicate a scoring error because such a combination is so unusual. Initially, double-check your scoring. To catch your mistakes early in the process helps to delineate where the scoring errors are made, as well as reinforcing caution.

The Lie scale is one that requires particular care in scoring when the Group Booklet form is used, because it is scored without a template. Usually high scores on the L scale (for example above a raw score of 7) should always raise the possibility that this scale could have been incorrectly scored (Greene, 1980).

Another rule of thumb concerns scale F, which has 64 items many of which overlap with the so-called "psychotic scales" (scales 6, 7, 8, and 9). Consequently, a profile in which F is high but there are not significant elevations on scales 6, 7, 8, or 9 may have been misscored. Also, if F is low, but the profile is significantly elevated on the psychotic side, check to ascertain whether the F scale or the clinical scales may have been incorrectly scored. In other words, a high score on the psychotic scales should also be accompanied by at least a relatively high score on scale F.

Step 5. Welsh Code the Profile for Each of the Norms Used

The Welsh code is a commonly used shorthand way to describe the profile (see chapter 2). The numbers representing each scale (e.g., D = scale 2) are placed in rank order, with the first being that scale with the highest T-score, and the last having the lowest T-score. The rest of the scale numbers are distributed in order of declining T-score values.

Symbols are then interspersed within this rank order of scales to indicate the T-score elevations. The asterisk (*) is placed after those scales that have T-scores of 90 or more; quotation marks (") are placed after those with T-scores of 80 to 89; an apostrophe (') after those with T-scores of 70 to 79; a dash (-) after scales with T-scores of 60 to 69; a slant (/) after scales with T-scores of 50 to 59; a colon (:) after T-scores of 40 to 49; and the numeric sign (#) after scales with T-scores of 30 to 40. Profiles thus may be represented briefly, but with reasonable accuracy, in clinical or research reports. Although the Welsh code is universally used to portray the clinical scales, some experts use the same symbol system to code the validity scales, whereas other experts simply report the raw scores for the validity scales. This book uses the latter approach because questions have been raised about the appropriateness of the raw score to T-score conversions for these validity scales.

Step 6. Examine the Validity Scales

Initially these scales are interpreted individually, but they are also interpreted based on their relationships with each other. These interpretations can be obtained from chapter 6. Again it must be emphasized that the validity scale indices must be considered in light of the referral question, the current situation, and demographic variables as noted previously, otherwise the remainder of the clinical profile cannot adequately be interpreted.

Step 7. Identify the Code-Type at or Above $T=70$

Using the clinical scales in the Welsh code, identify a multiple code-type or a spike, and obtain interpretive information associated with that code-type through using the "look-up" table listed just after the table of contents.

A spike code occurs when only one scale is elevated at or above $T = 70$, or a single scale is "spiked" with no other scales within 20 T-score points. Multiple code-types are defined by the highest scales in the Welsh code at or above $T = 70$ in the rank order that they appear.

A two-point code-type is identified when 2 out of the 10 clinical scales are at or above $T = 70$, and are higher than all other scales. A three-point code-type is identified when 3 clinical scales are all at or above $T = 70$, and higher than the other 7. A four-point code-type is identified by the 4 highest clinical scales that are elevated at or above $T = 70$. For example, a patient with elevations on scales 2, 4, 6, and 8 (the so-called "saw-tooth" profile) is a four-point code type.

By custom, two-point codes are typically combined with their mirror image in a joint fashion. Thus, a two-point code-type of 49 will be combined with the two-point code-type of 94, and will be referred to as the 49/94 code-type. There are occasions, though, where research has shown that such a combination is inappropriate, because each has unique descriptive properties of persons. For example, the two-point code 36 is not customarily combined with the two-point code of 63 unless the T-score values of 6 and 3 are virtually the same. These exceptions are noted in chapter 6.

Sometimes questions arise concerning whether the third or fourth digit in a three- or four-point code might also be interchangeable. This interchanging generally is done only if the two digits are within three T-score points of each other. That is, a code-type of *1243" could also be considered as a code-type of *1234" if scales 3 and 4 are within three T-score points of each other.

Clinicians in private practice settings may often encounter profiles within the normal range; that is, the T-scores range only between 40 and 70. Such normal range profiles are particularly common for adolescents when adolescent norms are used, so much so that a T-score of 65 may be a more appropriate cutoff than a T-score of 70 (Archer, 1987). These elevations in the normal range are also classifiable using the Welsh code, and are still referred to as their two highest scales, though with some qualifications. For example, an adult client obtaining an elevation on scale 4 of 65, and an elevation on scale 9 of 65, with all the other clinical scales below a T-score of 65 could still be referred to by a 49/94 profile type, though the term "49/94, sub 70" would likely be used. In such situations, descriptions usually can be interpreted only as tendencies, and more emphasis should be placed on the less pathological descriptors associated with that particular code-type. Generally speaking, the more elevated a code-type is beyond $T = 70$, the more distinctive and the more pathological the descriptions associated with that code-type.

Scale 5 and scale 0 require special mention. Many, perhaps most, MMPI experts use all 10 clinical scales in their coding and interpretive process (Marks, personal communication, 1988; Webb, McNamara, & Rodgers, 1986, 1981). Thus a client with a T-score of 80 on scale 5, a T-score of 75 on scale 3, and a T-score of 70 on scale 9 would be interpreted as a 35/53 code-type, with scale 9 scored and interpreted separately as a single-scale elevation. This is the method used in chapter 6.

Some MMPI experts, however, choose not to use scales 5 and 0 in considering two- or three-point code-types (Briggs, personal communication, 1988), in the belief that scales 5 and 0 sometimes obscure clinical aspects of the profile. Instead, these professionals initially disregard elevations on scales 5 and 0 in their initial profile interpretation, but then add scale 5 and 0 correlates after the profile has been interpreted based on a two-point, three-point, or spike code analysis. Thus, these experts would interpret the previous example as a 39/93 code-type, with an additional high scale 5.

Because empirical evidence is lacking to demonstrate the superiority of one approach over the other, the reader is encouraged to consider both approaches as acceptable, and on occasion may wish to use both. As is noted in chapter 6, this procedure is specifically recommended for several code-types.

Step 8. Examine the Profile for Other Specific Interpretable Configurations

These are described in the relevant portions of chapters 6 and 8, but for clarity are also listed here. These configurations are patterns among the scales that are interpreted in addition to the code-type descriptions, and are generally considered to possess a similar level of descriptive accuracy. These interpretations allow one to add to or refine the interpretations already obtained from the two-, three-, or four-point codes. As with the code-types, the more these configurations deviate from $T = 50$, the more likely will these patterns accurately describe the person. Although the configurations listed are the most commonly recognized, certainly others exist that could be used by sophisticated MMPI users (see Dahlstrom, Welsh, & Dahlstrom, 1972).

- Conversion V (scales 1 and 3 greater than scale 2 by 10 or more T-score points).
- Paranoid Valley (scales 6 and 8 greater than scale 7 by 10 or more T-score points).
- Passive-Aggressive V (Female with scales 4 and 6 above $T = 70$, and scale 5 below $T = 40$).
- "Gull-Wing" profile (scales 1,2,3 and 4 above $T = 70$, scale 5 below $T = 50$, and scales 6,7,8, and 9 above $T = 70$).
- Angry Sexual Identity (scale 4 above $T = 70$, scale 5 below $T = 40$).
- Overly Energized (scale 9 above $T = 70$, scale 2 below $T = 40$).

Step 9. Examine Other Scales Greater Than or Equal to 70

The basic framework of interpretations from the MMPI profile should come from interpretation of the validity scales, the two- or three-point code, and the particular configurations in steps 5, 6, 7, and 8. By definition, those configurations examine scale elevations concurrently and in relation to each other, so they simultaneously consider the complex interactions of the traits and characteristics of the component scale elevations. Because of this advantage, descriptions derived from configurations are of particular importance and validity, and should be given primary consideration, with information from single-scale examination generally being secondary.

Even so, additional information to round out interpretation of the profile should be obtained by adding the information that can be derived by individually examining the scales having T-scores of 70 and above that were not ones that comprise the two- or three-point codes. The additional information obtained in this fashion typically is interpreted within the matrix of information already formulated from steps 5, 6, 7, and 8. Interpretive information about these individual scales is presented in chapter 6.

Step 10. Examine Scales Having Low Scores

Scales having T-scores at or below $T = 40$ are typically considered as being low scores. In general, less is known about the significance of low scores as compared with high scores on the MMPI. Even so, often low scores will significantly modify the clinical significance of elevated configurations, and should be examined for the contributions they provide. Descriptions of these are likewise presented in chapter 6.

Step 11. Score Critical Items, Special Scales and Indexes

Critical item lists, such as those developed by Grayson (1951), Caldwell (1969), Lachar and Wrobel (1979) and others are extremely helpful in further understanding why certain scale elevations have occurred. In addition, many of these "red flag" items need prompt follow-up in a clinical interview because they can reflect serious problems requiring immediate attention. Such follow-up allows confirmation that the person did indeed intend to mark those items (rather than having marked them in error). Certainly this should be done if there is any doubt that the person understood the items. The clinician may also wish to ask the person to elaborate on what he had in mind concerning the various items, an approach that can also serve as a helpful bridge into a therapeutic relationship.

Special scales, such as *Es, O-H, MAC*. etc. provide additional information to the basic matrix already formulated. Descriptions and interpretive information for over 100 such supplemental scales have been summarized by Caldwell (1988). Some of the frequently used supplemental scales are presented in this book, and conversion of raw scores to T-scores for these scales is done using the tables in appendix F. The T-scores for these scales are then typically plotted directly on the side of the basic profile sheet.

Similarly, the Goldberg Index, Taulbee-Sisson Index, or other such indices are examined. Depending on the setting in which they are used, these indices may provide more valid diagnostic information than simply using the code-type information.

Further information on strategies for integrating and interpreting MMPI profiles is contained in chapter 7, along with examples. The next two chapters, however, contain the basic information needed for routine clinical use of the MMPI.

5

Interpreting the Basic Validity Scales

Four standard MMPI validity scales provide the clinician with a frame of reference for interpreting the clinical scales. They give some indications of (a) whether the client read and understood the items, (b) the extent to which the person indicates unusual experiences, behaviors, or ideas, and (c) the extent to which the client might be trying to give a particularly favorable or particularly unfavorable self-portrayal. Clearly these factors must be taken into consideration in interpreting the overall profile.

However, in practice, the validity scales also have psychological correlates no less important than those of the clinical scales, and their original function as validation devices has been all but overshadowed by their utility in providing clinical information. The interpretations that follow, then, focus both on the validity and clinical information.

THE ? (CANNOT SAY) SCALE

As indicated in previous chapters, this scale consists of the number of unscorable (e.g., double-marked) items, or those items omitted. No significance is attached to the omission of 10 or fewer items, although in individual cases it is sometimes instructive to examine those omitted items to determine if a pattern emerges. If more than 10 items are omitted, however, the overall elevation of the clinical profile is likely to be lowered (except for scale 5 for women), reducing the probability of obtaining an accurate picture of the person's unique personality characteristics. Thus the client should be encouraged to try again to complete more items, if this is feasible. Even so, it is possible to interpret profiles with reasonable accuracy when as many as 60 items are omitted, though the attenuating effect on the profile clearly must be considered, as well as undertaking attempts to discover the reasons for the individuals' cannot say propensity.

It is important to remember that the conversion procedure of raw score to T-score indicated on the standard profile sheet is overly liberal in that a T-score of 50 on the ? scale is obtained when subjects have omitted or double-marked 30 items (Hathaway & McKinley, 1967). More recent studies (see Greene, 1980) suggest that no more than 5% of persons taking the MMPI leave more than 30 items blank. Consequently, interpretations of the Cannot Say scale are ordinarily based on raw-score cut-offs, rather than T-scores.

If reading or comprehension difficulties can be ruled out, moderate elevations (raw scores of 20 to 30) generally indicate highly idiosyncratic and contentious interpretation of items, and/or obsessional indecision, often with extreme intellectualization. This process may be seen in the legalistic overcautiousness of some paranoid patients who, if permitted, would leave a majority of items unanswered. In other persons, such moderate elevations reflect a reticence to respond openly to test items that clearly probe personal experiences or private feelings in particularly sensitive areas for that person.

Markedly elevated ? scores (raw score above 30) are not uncommon among severely emotionally impaired persons, who are unable to perform the decision-making task due to profound depression, intrusive thoughts, etc. The possibility should be considered, however, that such a high score may also indicate a highly resistive, uncooperative person.

If more than 30 items have been omitted and the profile cannot be returned for completion, two solutions still may be possible (Greene, 1980): (a) first score all omitted or doubly marked items in the pathological direction, and plot the profile; or (b) plot the profile with the items omitted. Once this has been done, compare both profiles and write a report discussing the two profiles and the nature of the omitted items. The report will be speculative, but valuable nonetheless. If there is some consistency (e.g., all religious items are omitted), the test interpreter can speculate in light of the two obtained profiles regarding some possible explanations.

THE L (LIE) SCALE

This 15-item scale, when elevated, reflects naive or even obvious attempts by a person to look unusually virtuous, culturally conservative, overly conscientous, or even self-righteous. Because frank, self-aware persons so rarely endorse such statements, L scale scores above T-score of 50 (raw score = 4) are unusual, except in persons who have cultural backgrounds that require strict cultural conformity, who are in occupations (e.g., clergy) that stress culturally acceptable personal and professional virtues, or who are in situations (e.g., job interviews) that prompt one to present oneself in a particularly positive light.

Education and age must be considered. Persons of less than average in-telligence, or less than high school education tend to score slightly (about 5 *T*-score points) higher. Persons above age 50 likewise endorse more *L* scale items, apparently associated with age-related increases in conservative attitudes.

Although the *L* scale clearly reflects test-taking attitudes, this scale is less adept at measuring conscious distortion. Psychologically sophisticated in-dividuals (particularly persons with college educations) are often able to see through the items on this scale, and yet may still attempt to portray themselves as unusually virtuous on other portions of the test. High *L* scale scores in persons with broadly educated backgrounds may be associated with judgment deficien-cies and underachievement, in addition to the characteristics noted later.

Raw scores of 5 to 7 suggest excessive concern and rigidity over matters of self-control and moral values, as well as overly conforming and conventional behaviors. Such preoccupation with high moral standards usually is attached to a fear of being found unacceptable by others unless the person scrupulously adheres to rules. Often such persons are unaware that others might view them in this way, and the defense mechanism of denial may be broadly characteristic of these individuals. Persons with education beyond high school particularly show lack of personal insight when these *L* scale elevations are present.

Raw scores above 7 are so uncommon that—assuming scoring errors or systematic response sets have been ruled out—the person is denying even the most common human faults. Such persons have pathologically intense needs to present a good front, and do so with ridigity, repression, and denial. Moral issues as well as their own integrity and concern with scruples permeate their daily lives to the point that they are typically seen as self-centered, self-righteous, and uncompromising. Their self-perception and life-style are unusually con-ventional. Nevertheless, such persons tend to be insecure and naively defensive, as though worried that their "life rules" might not be sufficient. They deny or gloss over unfavorable traits in themselves, repress foibles or unacceptable urges, and have little insight into their motives or behaviors. Unless the elevated *L* scale score can be accounted for on the basis of extreme naivete from a culturally restricted environment, or perhaps from conscious attempts to distort the MMPI profile, such persons typically make poor candidates for insight-oriented psychotherapy. Strategic or directive approaches are likely to work better.

Raw Scores above 10 are rare, and indicate an excessively introspective and ruminative person with episodic depression and anxiety who is likely to be seen as tense, insecure, passive, aloof, and wary. These persons typically have difficulty making friends quickly, and are usually unaware of how others view them. They have been described as slow and unoriginal in responses to situa-tions—even stereotypic in their overly conventional approaches. Neurotic pro-files on the MMPI clinical scales often accompany such elevated *L* scales, particularly scales 1 and 3. Rarely, high *L* scale scores are associated with either sociopathic lying or the sweeping naivete of manic clinical syndromes.

THE F (FREQUENCY) SCALE

The 64 items on this scale reflect the degree to which thoughts, attitudes, and experiences reported by a person are different from those of the general population. That is, persons who randomly marked items, who could not comprehend item content, or who were attempting to consciously portray a negative distortion of themselves endorse F scale items to a higher degree than the general population. Similarly, adolescents, as a group, obtain substantially higher F scale scores than adults (Archer, 1987; Marks, Seeman, & Haller, 1974), a finding that may reflect the unusual thoughts and feelings adolescents often report, and/or negative distortion of their self-image and of their social relations with others.

However, it is also likely that persons who truly have different thoughts (e.g., psychotic individuals) would also score high on the F scale, as would persons with unusual attitudes (e.g., juvenile delinquents) or alienating experiences (e.g., minority populations). It is not surprising, then, that fully one-third of the F scale items overlap with the clinical scales 6, 7, 8, and 9, and that elevations on scale F are often accompanied by elevations on these scales, particularly 6 and 8.

The T-scores on this scale were arbitrarily assigned to raw scores by Hathaway and McKinley (1967), but more recent experience (Greene, 1980) has suggested that these T-scores are inappropriate. Thus, raw scores provide a better basis for interpretating the F Scale.

Raw scores of 5 or less on the F scale suggest a person who is conventional, moderate, and in no particular distress at that time. Such persons also are generally seen as calm, dependable, sincere, unpretentious, and honest. For some individuals however, particularly those with scores of two or less, the possibility must be considered that they are denying or minimizing problems, and that they have systematically avoided admitting to distressing or unusual feelings or thoughts.

Raw scores of 6 to 10 indicate a willingness to acknowledge a number of unusual experiences or attitudes, and suggest independence of thought, and perhaps even willfulness. With adolescents, college populations, or creative people generally, such F scale elevations are typical. Similarly, when persons become involved intensely in relogous, political, or social causes that are different from the mainstream, the scores on the F scale are slightly elevated. Occasionally, however, particularly in mental health settings, such scores will occur in persons with notable psychopathology, but who have adjusted to experiencing chronic problems and therefore are not in great distress.

Raw scores of 11 to 16 (11 to 20 for adolescents), assuming that reading difficulties have been ruled out, suggest increased distress, and indicate unusual or markedly unconventional thinking and attitudes. Identity and belongingness issues are indicated, and the person is likely to be described as moody, changeable, restless, unstable, dissatisfied, talkative, and opinionated but self-deprecating. Young people struggling with identity problems and a need to define themselves through nonconformity frequently score in this range on scale F, and such scores are not uncommon among adolescents. Likewise, persons above age 20 who are sullen and rebellious with more characterological disturbances of an antisocial or schizoid type obtain such scores.

Raw scores above 17 (above 20 for adolescents) suggest the following possibilities: error in scoring; failure of the client to understand the items; lack of cooperation, where the client purposely responded in a random or haphazard fashion; reporting of numerous F scale items due to delusional thinking, confusion or other psychotic processes; or distortion due to a wish to put oneself in a bad light through falsely claiming or exaggerating psychological symptoms. With scores this high, the examiner should entertain the hypothesis that the profile is invalid, and should check this by considering the characteristics of the remainder of the profile, the actual test-taking behavior, and through considering possible motivations for exaggeration that might derive from the client's current situation.

Formerly, profiles with elevated F scale scores were routinely considered invalid and uninterpretable. More recent studies (summarized in Greene, 1980) have shown that even profiles with F scale scores above 25 are often both interpretable and accurate.

In clinical populations, F appears to be positively correlated with the severity of illness, although sometimes it may be a "cry for help." A clinical interview usually reveals very atypical thought processes, poor judgment, and distortion of reality, often accompanied by frank confusion, withdrawal, and lack of cooperation.

THE K (CORRECTION OR COPING) SCALE

This 30-item scale, though primarily considered a validity scale, contains very substantial clinical information about ego strength, reality contact, and coping abilities, as well as about defensiveness, guardedness, and test-taking posture. Unlike the other validity scales, the K scale does not have arbitrarily established T-score values. Consequently, the K scale scores are usually described with T-scores rather than raw scores, with the exception of the F-K Gough Dissimulation Index.

The K scale is an empirically derived "correction" scale developed to sharpen the diagnostic accuracy of scales 1, 4, 7, 8, and 9 with adult inpatients, thus the scale items are not as obvious as the L scale items. (Note: K-corrections are not added to adolescents raw scores when using adolescent norms to compute T-scores). Despite the addition of the K-corrections to these clinical scales, high scores on K are usually associated with lower profiles, whereas low scores on K are more often associated with higher elevation clinical profiles. As a result, it is important for the clinician to examine the contribution of K to such clinical scales as 7 and 8. The individual who has an elevated scale 8 because of a high K score is different than a person whose scale 8 is similarly elevated, but with a lower K score. The high K person is likely to be more in control of whatever pathology exists.

K can be thought of as representing coping, and low scores ($T < 45$) suggest that the person's coping abilities are low. The person's defenses are down, emotional hurts are actively being felt, and emotional-behavioral controls are likely to be poor. Such persons are typically quite willing to admit to psychological problems. They tend to be self-critical, have a poor self-concept, and to feel that they lack the skills to deal with their problems.

Markedly low K scores ($T < 35$) portray a person who is extremely self-critical and so self-focused that he or she may be exaggerating personal faults or problems. Unless the person is in a clear state of panic with feelings of impending catastrophe and loss of control, the possibility should be strongly considered that this extremely low K score represents a plea for immediate help, or perhaps is deliberate malingering.

It should be noted that adolescents often score low on K at times when they are searching for personal identity because of the openness and self-criticism involved in scrutinizing themselves and their personal values. A similar phenomenon is sometimes evident in persons engaged in the self-examination involved in insight-oriented psychotherapy.

Average K elevations (T 45 to 60) indicates a person who has an appropriate balance between self-disclosure and self-protection, and who generally feels in control of life situations. Even if clinical scales are elevated, such a K scale score suggests a reasonable coping ability such that psychological symptoms ascribed to clinical scale elevations are likely to be less florid and less evident to others.

Moderate K elevations (T 60 to 70) are found in people generally described as independent, enterprising, ingenious, resourceful, enthusiastic with wide interests, and a variety of interpersonal relationships. Their lives are generally well-managed and they feel in control. K scores in the average or moderately elevated range generally contraindicate loss of control or acting out, and are associated with low delinquency in adolescents, especially females. Prognosis for psychological assistance is generally better when K is average or moderate, than when K is below 45 or above 70.

High K scores ($T > 70$) reflect people who are particularly defensive and cannot tolerate suggestions that they might have problems with themselves or in controlling their life situations. Although they may see others as having psychological problems, they view emotional problems as weaknesses that they, themselves, do not have. They tend to be intolerant and unaccepting of un-conventional or noncomformist behavior in others, and are often judgmental. Although markedly concerned with being proper in the eyes of others, paradoxically they nevertheless are generally unaware and relatively insightless concerning their effect on others.

For women, these interpretations may be somewhat attenuated. Particularly for professional women or those older than 35, *K* scores in this range more often represent effectiveness and emphasis on control, with somewhat less defensiveness or lack of tolerance for others.

In clinical situations, persons with *K* scores above $T = 70$ show strong reluctance to be seen as patients, and reject suggestions that they might need assistance in understanding or managing their feelings or behaviors. They generally avoid examining problem areas because they view themselves as rational and normal, and often will go to great lengths in attempts to obtain approval from the therapist.

Test–Retest Index (*TR*) and Carelessness Scale (*CS*)

Although there is some disagreement on the usefulness of these indices for determining validity (see chapter 3), it is generally agreed that a raw score greater than 5 on either index indicates a careless, ambivalent, or confused response to the MMPI questions. In such cases, the profile should be interpreted as follows: (a) If the rules for validity using only *?*, *L*, *F*, and *K* scales indicate validity, but the *TR* and/or *CS* indexes are over 5, then interpret the obtained profile, but stress the possibility that the responder's confusion or ambivalence could be interfering with obtaining an accurate appraisal; (b) If the *?*, *L*, *F*, and *K* rules for validity are doubtful, and either *TR* and/or *CS* are over a raw score of 4, consider the profile invalid. In writing a report, state that confusion and/or malingering apparently has interfered with a valid appraisal; and (c) If the *CS* raw score is 7, and the *?*, *L*, *F*, and *K* rules for validity indicate a valid profile, interpret the profile, but caution the reader about the likelihood of malingering and/or confusion leading to a possible reduction in the validity of the profile.

Dissimulation Scale.   Some disagreement exists about the exact meaning of this scale (see chapter 3), but if it is elevated above $T = 70$ and the *?*, *L*, *F* and *K* rules for validity indicate a valid profile, interpret the profile—but with caution. The possibility exists that the client may be motivated to present a picture of being disturbed. In the presence of doubtful validity based on *?*, *L*, *F*, and *K* scale scores, and where the Dissimulation scale is above 70, consider the profile invalid with the client attempting to fake bad by exaggerating psychopathology.

VALIDITY SCALE CONFIGURATIONS

Random, All True or All False Responses

An important validity consideration is whether a client simply marked the items at random, marked all of them as being true, or all as being false. Early in MMPI development, these scenarios were examined, if for no other reason than to see how effective the validity scales truly were in detecting such test-taking behaviors. The configurations of the *L*, *F*, and *K* validity scales show distinctive configurations for each situation, although, as seen in Fig. 5.1, some actual clinical situations result in somewhat similar validity scale configurations.

Random marking results in a pattern shown in Fig. 5.1. Scales *L* and *K* are both above *T* = 55, and scale *F* is at or above *T* = 105. In addition, at least six of the clinical scales are additionally elevated at or above *T* = 70. Although the elevated clinical scales and the high *F* scale look similar to the "most open"

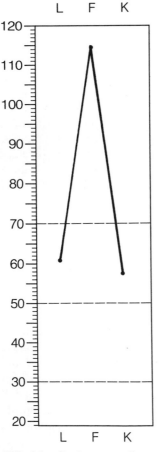

The validity configuration resulting from a random response set of an adult client shows the *F* scale greater than 100, the *L* scale slightly above 60, and the *K* scale around 55. The clinical scales (not shown here) are characterized by a generally elevated profile (six or more clinical scales above *T* = 70) and a psychotic slope, usually with a spike on scale 8 and a subspike on scale 6. A person responding in a random manner may adopt an idiosyncratic response pattern such as marking a block of four or five items as true followed by another block of four items as false, or they may mark true, false randomly. There is little that one can say about this configuration.

Report Language:

The profile appears to be invalid because the respondent answered the items in a random manner. The respondent may have done this out of confusion, and/or anger, and/or resistance to the testing situation. After the clinician has determined the reasons for this response pattern, the respondent should retake the test.

FIG. 5.1.   Random responding.

validity scale V pattern described later, it is important to note that scales L and K are far more elevated in the randomly marked profile.

All True marking causes an even higher elevation on scale F such that the T-score approximates 120, whereas scales L and K are at or below $T = 35$. In addition, the clinical scales show a distinctive elevation on scales 6, 7, 8, and 9 resulting in all four of those scales being elevated beyond $T = 90$. If this were a valid profile, such a person would clearly and floridly show agitated psychotic like behaviors with major disturbances in thought and behavior, and marked inability to cope with everyday life. Unless such a clinical picture is clearly evident, profiles showing a configuration such as shown in Fig. 5.2 should be considered as more likely due to a response set to answer all of the items as true. This calls for visual examination of the answer sheet.

All False endorsement results in a distinctive pattern of the validity scales. Scales $L,\ F,$ and K are all markedly elevated at or above $T = 80$ as shown in Fig. 5.3. In addition, scales 1, 2, 3, and 4 are elevated at or above T = 80.

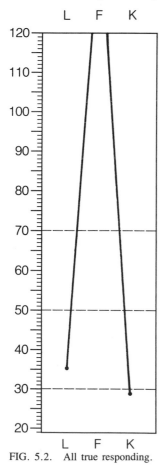

The discerning feature of this configuration is an extremely elevated F scale score, usually off the top of the profile sheet, and scales L and K are well below 50. On the clinical scales (not shown here) a psychotic slope typically occurs, with a spike on scale 8 and a subspike on scale 6.

Report Language:

The profile is invalid. The patient appears to have answered all the items in the true direction. The respondent may have done this out of confusion, and/or anger, and/or fear of the testing situation. After the clinician has determined the reasons for this response pattern, the respondent should retake the test.

FIG. 5.2. All true responding.

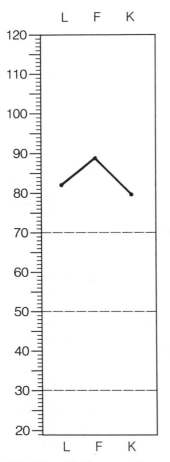

In an all false response set, the L, F, and K scales are all elevated above 80 and almost at the same level. This elevation on scale L is not surprising as L items are scored when marked false.

Report Language:

The profile appears to be invalid, because the respondent answered all the items in the false direction. The respondent may have done this out of confusion, and/or anger, and/or resistance to the testing situation. After the clinician has determined the reasons for this response pattern, the respondent should retake the test.

FIG. 5.3.   All false responding.

Common Validity Scale Patterns

The following descriptions and examples represent various L, F, and K configurations on the continuum from "most open" to "most closed" (see Fig. 5.4) in terms of admitting emotional and psychological difficulties and human vulnerabilities. The descriptions given apply both to males and females. There are no male or female differences in terms of validity scale norms. To make these validity examples more realistic, ages and educational levels have been added to each example. This also will remind the report writing clinician that demographic and education variables are important basic starting points for the interpretive process.

Four validity scale configurations are particularly important because they occur frequently and add substantially to the interpretations obtained through considering each validity scale separately. These four configurations are:

- Validity scale "V"
- Inverted "V"
- Ascending slope, and
- Descending slope.

Validity Scale "V" *("Most Closed")*.   This pattern, which is also called the "Most Closed Validity Configuration," occurs when scales L and K are above a T-score of 60, while scale F is at or below 50 (see Fig. 5.5). The more elevated are L and K, the more confidence can be put in the interpretation that this person was strongly attempting to present her- or himself in an extremely favorable light, and in doing so was minimizing or denying problems, unacceptable impulses, or feelings. This validity configuration occurs most often among job applicants or persons in other situations (e.g., child custody evaluations) where persons wish to appear particularly well-adjusted. Paradoxically, however, in inpatient settings this validity scale pattern is found frequently in psychotic patients, particularly those who are using much denial, repression, or continued attempts at control. Other diagnostic groups characterized by denial and lack of insight (such as hysterics, hypochondriacs, alcoholics, or other substance abusers) are also likely to show this pattern.

   This minimizing effect often influences the scores on the clinical scales, and such a factor should be taken into account when examining those scales. Clinical lore has it that it is often helpful, as a "rule of thumb," to "expand the clinical profile by 5 or even 10 T-score points to compensate for the effects of the "Validity V" configuration. That is, add 5 to 10 T-score points to each clinical

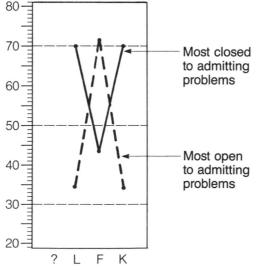

FIG. 5.4.   Most closed to most open configuration.

Education: High School   Age: 36
Marital Status: Single or Married   Sex: Male

Notes:

The *L* is high, suggesting a denial of basic human weaknesses, and black and white, moralistic, naive mode of thinking. The one item on *F* suggests a complete denial of any psychological pain or nonconformity. The high *K* suggests a sophisticated denial, adequate coping skills, and high ego strength. This is paradoxical in that the person is denying both in a naive and a sophisticated way. It is unlikely that this pattern reflects a personality style. Rather, it is more likely to reflect a response set unless it is from a postpsychotic reconstitution phase patient in which a person is frightened to explore any "shades of emotional gray" because of fear or confusion.

Most often this validity configuration is seen with people in custody evaluations or in response to job applications. It reflects a complete shutdown of openness and perhaps a panic around being evaluated. The panic is suggested because a sophisticated person, evidenced by the high *K*, is also approaching the test in a naive way, showing a failure of judgment in a person who "ought" to know better (i.e., high *K*).

Validity Scale—Report Language Suggestions:

The profile is borderline valid (if the *L* and *K* are at 75 or above, write "the profile is invalid"). It reveals someone who took the test in a very guarded and constricted way, putting their best foot forward and denying psychological problems or basic human weaknesses. This kind of validity configuration is usually seen in someone applying for a job or in a custody evaluation where the consequences of negative evaluations are high. These persons present themselves as psychologically healthy and above moral reproach. Although the profile has been corrected for defensiveness, it is unlikely to give a true personality picture.

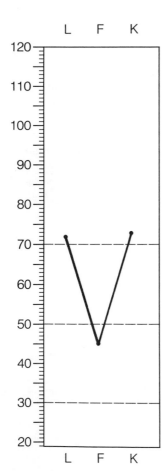

FIG. 5.5.   Most closed validity configuration.

scale above $T = 50$ in the profile. Such an approach to augmenting a profile often allows cautious interpretation of profiles that otherwise would have no interpretable clinical elevations.

Persons with this pattern seldom voluntarily seek treatment, and indeed most will have a reasonably adequate social adjustment, even though their behaviors and attitudes may cause substantial problems for those around them. To the extent that situational causes for this pattern (e.g., job application) can be ruled out, this pattern is associated with persons who are simplistic in their views, who cling to rules and regulations, and who see the world and the behaviors of others in terms of extremes of value judgments (i.e., good vs. bad).

Occasionally profiles will occur where K is markedly higher than F (20 or more T-score points). Such persons are extremely defensive and unwilling to reveal themselves psychologically. Because of their strong defensiveness, the validity of the test results must be carefully evaluated. This tendency to present a distorted image is likely to generalize to the treatment situation, and to interfere with the development of a therapeutic alliance. The reasons for presenting such an image can include: conscious attempts at deception, generalized negativism and refusal to cooperate, extreme rigidity and naivete, or inability to tolerate any suggestion of personal inadequacy.

Inverted "V". This configuration, also variously referred to as "Open and Candid," "In Pain," or "Plea for Help," occurs when scale F is above T-score of 65, and scales L and K are less than T of 50 (see Fig. 5.6). Such persons are openly admitting to personal-emotional difficulties, doubt their ability to handle the situation themselves, and generally are seeking assistance or are at least quite amenable to professional help. Thus this configuration is desirable in planning for psychotherapy or other professional intervention.

However, as F increases above a T-score of 80 and/or K decreases below 40, the person is likely to be experiencing very acute and pervasive distress, and to be lacking in coping abilities at that time. This may be to such a degree that the person is unable to respond to psychotherapeutic help until crisis intervention has been achieved, and some of the stress alleviated. With such a high F, however, the possibility should be considered that the person may be exaggerating conflicts, stress, and personal problems on the MMPI as a "cry for help" in order to obtain the most immediate attention, or may be attempting to simulate psychopathology. In such cases it is often wise to "mentally constrict" the clinical scale profile because the person's test-taking attitude has likely inflated the scores on those scales. This can be done by lowering elevated clinical scales by 5 to 10 T-score points.

Two subtypes of the "Inverted V" pattern have been noted by Greene (1980). In subtype 1, scales L and K are between 50 and 60, and scale F is greater than 70. This configuration could be referred to as "Experiencing Problems, but Coping Through Denial." These clients, though admitting problems, are trying

Education: High School   Age: 18
Marital Status: Single or Married   Sex: Female

Notes:

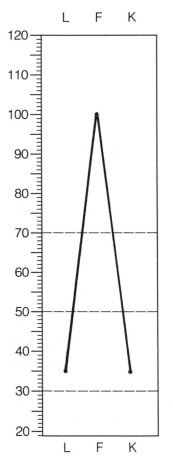

The profile is of questionable validity because of the high F and the low K. One rule of validity is the F minus K raw score (see chapter 3). In an adolescent, interpret this profile as valid but exaggerated, and probably not indicative of their true personality structure. This kind of validity configuration in either adolescents or adults is seen in someone pleading for help due to fear about what is happening to them. In some cases, it may be a malingering configuration. The absence of any L items suggests an openness to admitting human weaknesses, the high F score suggests an open endorsement of distress items, and the low K suggests a lack of guardedness, a low self-esteem, and low ego-strength.

Validity Scale—Report Language Suggestions:

The profile is borderline valid. It reflects someone who is emotionally hurting, pleading for help, and exaggerating her symptoms in a panic like fashion in order to draw attention to her plight. She feels unable to deal with her present predicament, and may well be exaggerating her symptoms in an attempt to obtain psychological support. Consequently, this person is likely to be open to psychological support. However, if there are any secondary gains from exhibiting severe psychopathology, the elevated profile could be due to malingering.

FIG. 5.6.   Panic or plea for help configuration.

to defend themselves by various coping mechanisms and perhaps somewhat by denying the effects their problems are having on their lives. Often the coping attempts of such persons are ineffectual, and they may be chronically and marginally maladjusted. Their life-styles tend to be quite stable over time.

Subtype 2 is sometimes referred to as "Good Ego Strength, Sophisticated, but Experiencing Problems." In this configuration, scale K is above 55, scale F is at least equal to scale K, while scale L is less than 50 (See Fig. 5.7). Persons with

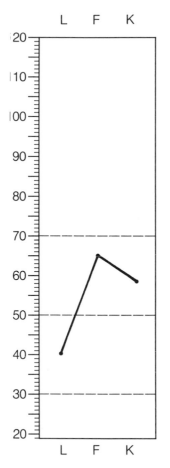

Education: College   Age: 40
Marital Status: Single or Married   Sex: Male

Notes:

The moderate *F* score suggests a moderate psychological disturbance. However, the client has good ego strength and coping ability as evidenced by his slightly above-average *K* score. This person is not psychologically naive, evidenced by his low L, and thus is willing to admit to basic human weaknesses. This could come from a college-educated person who is having some problems and is self-referred to a mental health professional, wanting help.

Validity Scale—Report Language Suggestions:

The profile appears to be valid. The client answered in a candid and open way, admitting some psychological difficulties at this time. He appears to be generally aware of personal or emotional difficulties, but does not appear to experience them as overwhelming.

FIG. 5.7.   Good ego strength, sophisticated, but experiencing problems.

this pattern typically cope well. Although they may have long-standing problems, they apparently have adjusted to them as a chronic life-style such that they create few feelings of distress. Even as scale *F* rises above 70, such persons typically feel good about their ability to cope, though simultaneously describing a variety of problems that may be severe. Such individuals usually wish only to receive help with current symptoms or problems, and are typically satisfied when current stress is reduced.

Ascending slope, sometimes called the "Sophisticated Defensive Profile," is characterized by validity configurations where the *T*-scores increase as one goes from *L* to *F* to *K*, thus making a linear trend upward (see Fig. 5.8). Generally the *L* scale *T*-score is about 40, the *F* scale *T*-score is about 50 to 55, and the *K* scale *T*-score is about 65 to 75.

Education: College   Age:
Marital Status: Single or Married   Sex: Female

Notes:

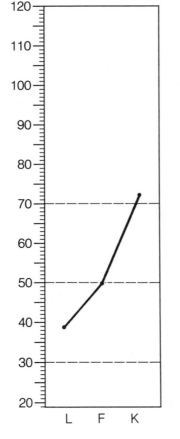

The low *L* suggests a lack of naive denial; the low *F* suggests conformity and an absence of psychological pain; and the high *K* indicates a "stiff upper lip" approach to psychological pain or stress. People with this profile are hard to interview because they resist engaging their feelings. They feel threatened by any loss of emotional control. It is important to determine if the high K is situation specific, occasioned by the demands of the testing situation, or if it is indicative of a trait in which emotionality has been constricted either due to social learning or personality style.

Validity Scale—Report Language Suggestions:

The profile is valid. However, it reveals a person who is emotionally constricted; uncomfortable expressing and feeling intense emotions. This emotional defensiveness could be due to the demands of the testing situation, or it could reflect a socially conditioned style of maintaining a "stiff upper lip" in the face of stress. In order to get a full sense of empathy for her, the therapist will have to multiply the intensity of what she is saying. For example, if she states that she is "frustrated," she may in fact be quite angry. If she states that she is "concerned," she may in fact be feeling quite worried. (Although several of the profile scales have been corrected for defensiveness through the addition of *K,* the clinical profile may still be somewhat of an underestimate.)

FIG. 5.8.   The sophisticated defensive configuration.

Persons with such patterns usually are not in distress, and have appropriate resources for dealing with their life situations. If they do have problems, they do not feel overwhelmed by them. College-educated or other widely experienced persons are somewhat more likely to show this pattern, and it reflects the array of their coping resources. Some job-applicants or normal persons in marital conflict

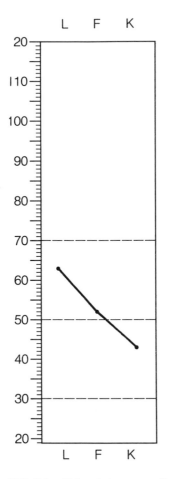

Education: High School   Age: 34
Marital Status: Single or Married   Sex: Male

Notes:

The high elevation on the L scale suggests naive psychological thinking, moralistic, and black and white views of the world. The low F suggests an absence of psychological pain, and the low K suggests openness, candor, and low self-esteem. People with this profile appear very open and nonguarded yet are psychologically naive and generally are unsophisticated. Often they are not well-educated.

Validity Scale—Report Language Suggestions:

The profile is valid. The client approached the test denying basic human weaknesses as if apprehensive about being judged or evaluated. His test suggests that he is psychologically naive and unsophisticated and that his values are inflexible, with little room for shades of gray. His approach to emotional and psychological problems will tend to be unsophisticated, and he may emotionally overreact to situations. He has low self-esteem, and probably sees himself as uncomplicated. Although he is open and candid, he may have difficulty with explorative psychotherapy because psychological concepts are likely to be unfamiliar and/or threatening to him.

FIG. 5.9.   Naive, but open, configuration (descending slope).

situations may also obtain this pattern, and in such cases this likely represents an attempt to portray themselves in a somewhat overly favorable light.

Descending slope, called "Naive but Open," is one where the T-scores decrease as one goes from L to F to K, resulting in a linear trend downward. Generally the L scale T-score is about 60, the F scale T-score is about 55, and the K scale T-score is about 45 (See Fig. 5.9).

Though such persons likely are having some life situational, emotional, or interpersonal difficulties, they are naively trying to make themselves look good, and are unlikely to admit problems or to want to come to grips with them.

Generally they are unsophisticated, have limited educational backgrounds, and lowered expectancies about the extent to which one can control or have an impact on one's own feelings, impulses, or life situations. They usually are poor candidates for insight-oriented psychotherapy.

The following validity configurations represent variants of the patterns described previously, and are provided to familiarize the reader with additional interpretations (see Figs. 5.10 through 5.13).

Education: 2 Years College   Age: 50
Marital Status: Single or Married   Sex: Female

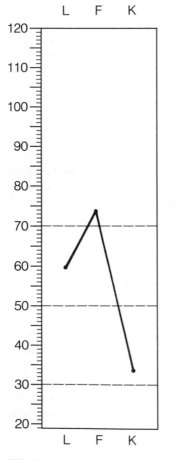

Notes:

This person has considerable elevation on F, suggestive of a moderate to severe disturbance. The moderate to high score on L suggests she views the world in rather simplistic, black and white, and moralistic terms, suggestive of a person who feels vulnerable to moral review. The low K suggests a lack of self-esteem, reduced coping resources at this time, and an openness and poignancy about the intensity of her feelings. However, her high L scores suggest that she is low in psychological sophistication and holds to traditional values in an unquestioning way.

Validity Scale—Report Language Suggestions:

The client answered candidly and self-critically, admitting to a number of psychological problems, unusual feelings and behaviors. She tests, however, as somewhat morally rigid and psychologically naive, tending to see the world in black and white, right and wrong terms, with little shades of gray. Her lack of defensiveness and her current psychological pain suggest she is having problems coping and is open to psychological intervention though her low self-esteem, her apprehensiveness about being morally judged, and her lack of psychological sophistication may hamper her in making rapid therapeutic progress.

FIG. 5.10.   Naive, open and disturbed configuration.

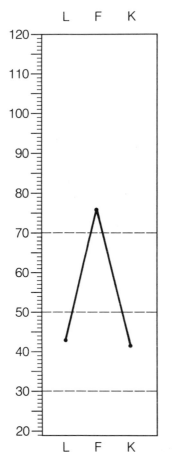

Education: College   Age: 38
Marital Status: Single or Married   Sex: Male

Notes:

This validity scale pattern is fairly common in many inpatient or private practices with disturbed populations. The client is reporting significant distress, evidenced by the high F. His low K suggests low self-esteem, low ego strength, emotional discomfort, difficulty coping, and an openness and willingness to admit to the numerous problems he is experiencing. This corresponds to the "most open" profile (Fig. 5.4).

Validity Scale—Report Language Suggestions:

The profile appears valid. The client answered candidly and openly, if somewhat self-critically, admitting to many psychological problems, anxieties, and unusual behaviors. He is reporting a severe amount of distress at this time, and he feels unable to handle his situation effectively. His self-image is low. He may be a good candidate for psychotherapy in that he is in a good deal of emotional pain and is willing to talk about it.

FIG. 5.11.   Distress in an open, candid, self-critical person.

Education: AA Degree   Age: 45
Marital Status: Single or Married   Sex: Female

<u>Notes:</u>

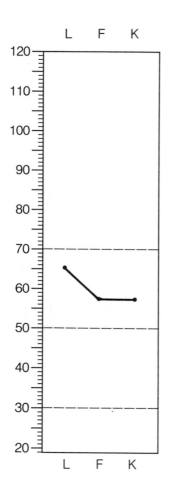

The *L* scale is elevated, suggesting a high degree of naive defensiveness and a moralistic black and white view of the world. At the same time, the moderate *F* score reveals that the person is experiencing some distress. The moderate *K* suggests some degree of ego strength and perhaps some defensiveness. This is paradoxical because the moderate *K* would suggest a fairly sophisticated psychological mindedness, but the high *L* suggests naive defensiveness. In this sense it is a peculiar validity configuration, and it may come from someone who is moderately psychologically sophisticated but very concerned about some kind of moral judgement, either around the testing itself or generally. Anticipate either unusual background experiences, alcoholism, or some atypical response set.

<u>Validity Scale—Report Language Suggestions:</u>

The profile appears valid. However, the client answered in a constricted and guarded way as if anticipating being judged or evaluated. She is denying basic human weakness, trying to put her best foot forward. Even though she is defensive and cautious about being evaluated, nevertheless she is reporting some distress which at this time she portrays as manageable. She is likely to be difficult to interview because of her defensiveness and her tendency toward naive and moralistic interpretations of psychological problems.

FIG. 5.12.   Unusual or paradoxical validity configuration.

Education: College   Age: 25
Marital Status: Single or Married   Sex: Male

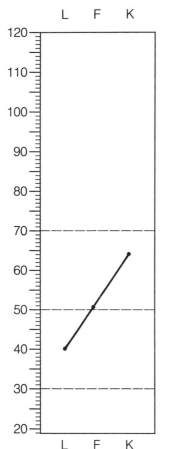

Notes:

In this profile the client shows a low *L* score, relatively low *F*, and moderate *K*. This profile is often
called the "college-educated" or "psychotherapist
configuration." This is because the person is reporting very few *L* items, suggesting psychological
sophistication; only a few *F* items, suggesting realistic reporting of breadth of experiences and mild (or at
least average) nonconformity; and a moderate *K*
showing above-average emotional control, coping resources, and high ego strength commensurate with
college graduates (or others having a history of coping and achieving in complex settings).

Validity Scale—Report Language Suggestions:

The profile appears valid. The person answered in a
manner that suggests above-average emotional and
intellectual sophistication consistent with a college
education. People with this kind of validity configuration see themselves as having few psychological problems and as adequately able to deal with
stresses. Should they seek therapy, their positive
self-concepts suggest a good therapeutic outcome.
Some of the profile scales have been corrected for his
defensiveness, but the interpretation may underestimate the full extent of the psychological difficulties because of his coping abilities at this time.

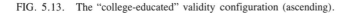

FIG. 5.13.   The "college-educated" validity configuration (ascending).

6

Interpretation of MMPI
Clinical Scales

INTRODUCTION

The following specific code-type and profile interpretations represent a mixture of actuarial and clinical information, and an integration of the recent information about adolescent and minority clients that seems most clinically relevant. The present authors have attempted to integrate these current sources so that the maximum number of diverse MMPI profiles can be intepreted. That is, actuarial data do not exist concerning all possible clinical configurations of the MMPI; however, clinical data based on observation and historical use do exist. By combining these two approaches (but using the actuarial knowledge as the basic matrix), it is feasible to interpret all possible two-point code-types, as well as some three- or even four-point codes, in addition to some other distinct configurations of MMPI scores.

Specific interpretations for these code-types and for other configural aspects of the MMPI are presented later in a convenient "look-up" fashion. Within this chaper, the code-types are presented in numeric order of the scales, or two-point codes, etc. In addition, there is a "Code-Type Look-up Table" immediately following the Table of Contents. Thus the user who has identified a specific scale, pattern or code-type on an MMPI profile can use the Code-Type Look-up Table to locate the pages containing interpretations associated with that pattern.

The primary sources for the current interpretations are (in alphabetical order) Archer (1987); Carkhuff, Barnett, and McCall (1965); Carson (1969); Duckworth and Anderson (1986); Dahlstrom, Welsh, and Dahlstrom (1972); Drake and Oetting (1959); Fowler (1966); Gilberstadt and Duker (1965); Greene (1980); Graham (1987); Hovey and Lewis (1967); Lachar (1974); Marks and

150

Seeman (1963); Marks, Seeman, and Haller (1974); Swenson, Pearson, and Osborne (1973); Van de Riet and Wolking (1969); Webb (1970); and Webb, McNamara, and Rodgers (1986, 1981). These are recommended as additional sources offering more depth and detail, as well as the documentation of the research bases for the various interpretations.

Generally MMPI interpretations have been developed on Caucasian subjects with an IQ of 80 or above and/or education above sixth grade, and mostly with adults. Recently, however, some researchers (e.g., Archer, 1987; Marks, Seeman, & Haller, 1974) have added substantially to the knowledge about clinical code-types of adolescents. Even so, the code-type interpretations provided in this chapter do not always contain information specific to adolescents, either because no difference was found between adults and adolescents for that particular profile, or because insufficient studies exist to allow differential comment. As was done with adolescents, Dahlstrom, Lachar, and Dahlstrom (1986) and others similarly have clarified many aspects that relate to interpretation of MMPI profiles of minority clients, aged clients, and other special populations. Modifications of interpretations based on the different characteristics and base rates of behaviors of these various groups is sometimes included in this chapter, and sometimes dealt with in the chapter on integration of test results. Even so, the reader is encouraged to become familiar with the *MMPI Patterns of American Minorities* (Dahlstrom, Lachar, and Dahlstrom, 1986).

THE CLINICAL SCALES

Scale 1 (Hs)

High scores ($T > 70$) occur in persons who are preoccupied with numerous physical complaints. They are generally lacking in joy, and see their bodies as a source of pain, fear, and discomfort, rather than as a source of pleasure. Often they are whiny, complaining, and narcissistically egocentric, and use their complaints to impose demands on others, or to control the behavior of others. Generally they handle their anger through making those around them miserable, and are typically viewed as stubborn, pessimistic, generally sour on life, unambitious, and lacking in drive.

Sometimes such high scores occur in persons with demonstrable physical illnesses, though more often such persons score in the moderately elevated range on this scale. In either case, they tend to be cynical or even defeatist about others' efforts to help them. Their symptoms and hypochondriacal patterns are typically long-standing, rather than a reaction to immediate stress, and are resistant to change. As patients, these people can be very frustrating or even infuriating in not following through with suggested treatments, and often shop from doctor to doctor.

Note that peaks on scale 1 are more frequent as age increases beyond 40, whereas peaks in college students or other younger populations is quite rare. When scale 1 is above $T = 85$, the somatic concerns are so great that somatic delusions should be suspected, perhaps associated with the beginnings of a schizophrenic episode. Schizophrenic patients may show such elevations on scale 1 early in their illness, even before gross clinical signs are evident in other test data or in their behaviors.

Moderately high ($T = 60-70$) scorers more often are reacting to physical disease, either in their current lives or in the past, and often have an accompanying elevation on scale 2. Their concern for health issues may simply be a constructive concern, or it may represent a hypersensitivity to health issues and an overconcern. Such persons tend to be pessimistic and constricted in their experiences.

Moderately low ($T = 40-50$) scores suggest a person who is not overly concerned with bodily function issues, and who is likely to generally be effective in daily living (unless scales 2, 6, 7, 8 or 0 are elevated beyond 70). Often such persons are described as capable, responsible, conscientous, alert, and with good judgment.

Very low ($T < 40$) scores are obtained by persons who (a) grew up in families where health was not an issue, (b) take pride in their health to the point of ignoring aches, pains, or illnesses until quite severe, or (c) were closely associated with family members who hypochondriacally used illesses in a manipulative way, and now are overreacting to this by rejecting even normal aches and pains. A particular pattern worth noting is where scales 2, 6, 7, 8, or 0 are above 75, because the low scale 1 in this configuration often reflects a disinterest in one's body to the point of not caring what happens, and/or feelings of inferiority concerning physical appearance in a sort of passive resignation.

Relations With Other Scales

High 1, Low 4 Code (Males), and High 1, Low 5 (Females).   This pattern is associated with home conflicts and unassertiveness in confronting problems. Not only do such persons have difficulty expressing angry feelings, but also tend to internalize such feelings and conflicts, often resulting in psychophysiological complaints. Pessimism, whining, and complaining are also typically found. This pattern is particularly distinctive where scale 1 is the highest elevated, but can also be interpreted as a secondary configuration even when other scales are more elevated.

12 Codes (See Also 21 Codes When Scales 1 and 2 Are Within 5 T-Score Points).   These persons exhibit physical symptoms and complaints, and show great concern over their physical functioning. Generally there is no demonstrable organic pathology, but even if real physical problems exist, they exaggerate their severity.

Within the numerous somatic complaints that they present, most often pain (such as headaches, stomach aches, and backaches), cardiac complaints, or gastrointestinal difficulties (such as anorexia, nausea, vomiting, or ulcers) are a primary focus. Fatigue, weakness, and dizziness often accompany, along with irritability and depression. Physical tension and anxiety may also occur, particularly if scales 7 or 9 are elevated.

Persons with this code-type are usually dependent and immature, but often are in conflict about assuming responsibilities. They tend to turn angry feelings inward rather than toward others, and excessive use of alcohol may be present. Feelings of depersonalization or suicidal impulses are not likely unless scale 8 is also elevated (see 128/218 codes). Repression and denial of emotional problems is characteristic; they lack insight and resist implications that symptoms are related to emotional causes or conflicts.

Medical patients with this pattern are difficult to treat because they often have learned to live with and to use their complaints. Although they may show good response to short-term treatment, the symptoms are likely to return. Traditional psychotherapy is likely to show meager results because these persons not only tolerate much discomfort, but also have difficulty accepting responsibility for their behaviors.

College students with 12/21 codes are generally shy, tense, introverted, unhappy, worried, insecure, and feel quite self-conscious, particularly in dealings with the opposite sex. Tension, insomnia, and social discomfort are usually more prominent than the bodily manifestations seen in older persons with this pattern. College women in particular tend to be indecisive, seek continued reassurance, and to "freeze up" on academic examinations. Headaches are particularly likely in these women when scale 5 is low.

Precollege adolescents show more marked emotional distress, where the shyness is accentuated by ruminations often to the point of obsessions or social isolation. Dependency and indecisions are marked, and these youngsters typically have few friends. Family history often reveals parental separations or divorce, and school phobias.

123 and 213 Codes (Also See 1234 and 1237 Codes; 213/231 Codes Where Scale 3 Is Within 5 T-score points of Scale 1). These persons show physical complaints particularly regarding abdominal-visceral pain, weakness and fatigue, and their history shows chronic long-standing hypochondriasis. Often their complaints are presented with some irritability, even though a passive-dependence is also evident. Confused or psychotic thinking, suicidal thoughts, obsessions, and compulsions are not likely. However, they are generally apathetic, depressed, lacking in assertiveness, unlikely to take risks, and may feel "over the hill" or in declining health.

Where scale 4 is the low point, this pattern suggests passivity, lack of heterosexual drive and sexual difficulties. With low point 9, it suggests a low energy level, a lack of vocational aggressiveness, and a strong tendency to "take to bed."

Women with low scale 5 are long-suffering in their assumption of duties, sacrifices, and unnecessary burdens to the point of masochism. If the L scale is also elevated, these women are particularly likely to have sexual or marital difficulties, and to complain of fatigue, lack of appreciation by others, and the need to be extremely conscientious at work.

1234 Codes (Also 2134 Codes if Scales 1 and 2 Are Within 5 Points of Each Other).   Typically these persons are heavy drinkers or alcoholics who are combative when drunk. Men with this profile show hostility toward women (often even physical beatings), particularly when their strong dependency needs are frustrated or not met. Poor work and marital adjustment are characteristic, accompanied by physical complaints (usually digestive difficulties such as ulcers, nausea, vomiting, or anorexia), hostility, depression, tension, and perhaps insomnia. In men, mother dependency yearnings appear to be in conflict with feelings of rejection by their mother. The most typical diagnoses are passive-aggressive personality, anxiety reaction, or psychophysiological reaction.

1237 Codes.   In addition to the 123 code-type features noted earlier (see 123 code interpretations), this group shows increased anxiety, tension, fearfulness, inability to be assertive, feelings of inadequacy, and dependent interpersonal relationships, usually in addition to psychophysiological ailments. Back and chest pains, and epigastric complaints are particularly common. These people are seen as weak, moody, fearful, highly inadequate, and unable to cope with everyday stress and responsibility (particularly if K is below 50). Such persons internalize conflict and anxiety. Males with this profile frequently marry a stronger woman, and in this relationship try to perpetuate a role of dependency. Chronic unemployment and alcohol dependency may occur.

128 and 218 Codes.   Often these are younger patients who are having bizarre complaints ranging over the entire upper body, and usually accompanied by fatigue, weakness, tension, and disturbances in thinking. Typically they show substantial mental distress and feelings of alienation from others, though their histories may also reveal notable dependency on others. Usually these persons are acutely prepsychotic or psychotic, and have somatic delusions.

129 and 219 Codes.   The concern about bodily functions and ailments is greatly distressing to such persons, who see them as virtual emergencies. Acute clinical distress, tension, agitation, and restlessness are prominent. Headaches, insomnia, and complaints such as spastic bowel are frequent. A neurological etiology for their problems must be considered, because this pattern has been associated with organic brain syndromes. However, it is at least as likely that the person is attempting to deny or mask depression, conflict, and/or passive-dependency in a hypomanic fashion.

120 and 210 Codes. Depression, withdrawal, indecisiveness, interpersonal avoidance, and feelings of inadequacy and guilt are accompanied by diverse somatic complaints and a defeatist attitude. Such persons are distinctly lacking in joy, and most often are seen as aloof, passive, and withdrawing in a misanthropic or schizoid fashion (particularly if scale 8 or 6 is also elevated).

13 and 31 Codes (Also See Conversion V.) These persons typically have symptoms involving eating, such as nausea or discomfort after eating, and sometimes show anorexia or bulimia. Their other major symptom is pain, which usually appears in the extremities (head, back, neck, arms, eyes, legs). Often fatigue, dizziness, numbness, and tremors are also found. If scales 2, 7, 8, or 9 are elevated, and/or K is low, then perplexity, anxiety, tension, and depression may also be significantly present.

Despite their problems, few of these persons are incapacitated by their symptoms, and continue functioning even though at a reduced level of efficiency. They present themselves as normal and responsible, and often will object to psychological examination or referral, and resent having their minds studied (particularly if L and K are elevated). As a result, they are difficult to engage in psychotherapy. They prefer medical examination for their problems, and lack insight into psychological factors that may underly or influence their problems. Some, particularly those older than 40, will have demonstrable physical pathology; even so, relevant psychological factors are typically present.

These persons show a strong need for attention, affection, and sympathy, and feel insecure without it. Often they will use their physical complaints for secondary gains whereby they can assure themselves of such attention. Other secondary gains may include avoiding responsibilities and duties and/or control of others through inducing sympathy from them. These people tend to be immature, egocentric, dependent, and selfish.

Although generally outgoing and sociable (particularly if scale 0 is below 50), their social relationships tend to be superficial and even manipulative. Generally they are optimistic (especially if scales 2 and 7 are within the normal range), and they make excessive use of repression, denial, rationalization, and projection wherein they blame others or situations for difficulties. Seldom do they express negative feelings such as anger in direct fashion; instead, they either avoid confronting those feelings or express them in passive-aggressive fashion. Establishing enduring, realistic relationships with members of the opposite sex is characteristically a problem, though typically such persons seek such relationships because such a relationship is socially proper.

Persons with a 13 code are more likely to have clear hypochondriacal features associated with complaining and pessimism. Persons with a 31 code will show more immaturity and dependency, with physical symptoms developing only when faced with stressful situations.

The 13/31 code is the second most common among both fathers and mothers of child psychotherapy patients. It is associated with mothers who are strongly protective of those close to them and who are extroverted and suggestible. When mothers have this code, it is associated with improvement both for the mother and the child. When fathers have this code, the prognosis is less favorable. Among fathers, this profile is associated with immature dependency, strong needs for acceptance, and the use of subtle and indirect strategies to gain affection and attention.

College women (5% of whom show this code) describe themselves as affectionate and thoughtful. Their peers, however, see them as selfish, self-centered, dependent, attention-seeking, irritable, emotional, high-strung, and with frequent physical complaints. Often there is a strong orientation toward marriage, but far less so toward academic concerns that often then emerge as problem areas.

College men likewise are seen as selfish, dependent, self-centered, and demanding. A primary complaint is that they do not get enough consideration from their families. Most appear socially at ease, fluent, expressive, and confident (particularly if K is high and 0 is low). In psychological settings, they often aggressively insist on knowing their test results, and on being given definite answers to their problems. Typically, however, they do not return for professional help after the first or second session. They rationalize, blame others, and generally avoid self-examination.

Conversion V.   Elevations on scales 1 and 3, with an intervening valley of 10 or more T points on scale 2, form what is called the Conversion V. This occurs most strikingly within 13/31 code-types (i.e., when scales 1 and 3 are the most elevated and are at 70 or above), but may also be interpreted secondarily even when other scales are the highest in the profile (except when scale 9 is distinctly elevated because scale 2 may then be reduced because of manic defenses being utilized).

Persons with Conversion V patterns show strong needs to interpret their psychological or interpersonal problems in living in ways that are socially acceptable. They deny troubles or inadequacies, and the anxiety-depression often found in 13/31 persons without a Conversion V pattern is typically absent (except in 137 or 138 persons). Many persons with Conversion V patterns develop somatic complaints or psychological symptoms of a highly reasonable and socially acceptable type that allow them to displace inadequacies or problems outside of themselves. They emphasize, but fail to show real concern about, their somatic symptoms, and the physical problems almost always are characterized by "secondary gains" wherein the person is able to avoid responsibilities and/or to manipulate situations or control the behaviors of others.

Normal profiles, with "Conversion V" patterns below 70, are typically obtained by socially outgoing people who are cheerfully optimistic. Because of their repressive tendencies, they frequently appear immature or even flighty. Under stress, they may develop psychophysiological complaints, but ordinarily they appear exceedingly normal, responsible, helpful, and sympathetic.

13/31, High K. Especially if scales 2, 7, and 8 are below 70, and F is below 50, these individuals are likely to be extremely concerned with presenting themselves as normal, responsible, helpful, and sympathetic. Often their lives are markedly organized around ideals of service to others and contribution to community. Such persons are very threatened by any suggestion that they might have psychological difficulties, which they see as weaknesses, or even that they have unconventional behaviors. They do not tolerate the role of patient well. Whatever physical symptoms might exist are unlikely to be debilitating. Although unlikely to profit from traditional psychotherapeutic interventions, these persons will likely benefit from professional reassurance. (See also Conversion V.)

132 and 312 Codes. In addition to the 13/31 code-type characteristics, these persons are particularly tense, distressed, and complain of weakness and fatigue (particularly if scale 9 is low). Their behaviors often indicate that they are depressed, although they may deny having feelings of depression. Such persons are typically conventional, conforming, and passive (especially if scale 4 is low), and are anxious to be liked by others (even more so if scale 0 is low).

134 and 314 Codes. Somatic complaints may be less prominent in such persons as compared with their behavior pattern that is opinionated, argumentative, snobbish, and even cocky or belligerent. Otherwise, the 13/31 characteristics are applicable. Conflicts between independence-anger vs. dependence-nurturance are likely, but such persons seldom have insight into why they alienate others. If the profile fits the Conversion V pattern, their somatic complaints are likely to stem from anger that is not openly expressed in a modulated fashion, but rather is expressed in episodic outbursts or indirectly through passive-aggressive means.

136 and 316 Codes. Although physical problems (particularly gastrointestinal problems or headaches) may develop during stressful situations, these persons are characteristically tense and hypersensitive to criticism or even to requests by others that could be construed as demands. Paradoxically, they tend to be rigid and stubborn themselves, and are often quite egocentric or even narcissistic. Often such persons (particularly males with this profile) are highly competitive, suspicious, quick to anger, and seek to control others, but tend to egocentrically rationalize their behaviors and have little insight into how others might see them, even though they may have participated in ruthless power operations.

Where scale 6 is within 10 *T*-score points of scale 3, then suspiciousness and anger will be more marked, and the possibility of early paranoid schizophrenia must be suspected. Where scale 3 is higher than scale 6 by 10 or more *T*-score points, overt paranoid features are less likely, and physical complaints will be more prominent.

137 Codes.   Severe anxiety (often mixed with depression) and panic attacks are experienced, typically accompanied by cardiac complaints (such as tachycardia) or epigastric distress. This will be even more pronounced if scale 9 is also elevated, and/or if *K* is below 50. Although anxiety attacks are the most common, phobias about illnesses are also found.

Persons with this profile are rigid and adapt poorly to situational changes. Often they are unrealistic about work and finances, and depend on a dominant spouse to take responsibility for managing their lives and to discipline the children. Poor vocational adjustment due to underachievement is likely. In psychotherapy these patients can be demanding and clinging, and are unable to accept aggressiveness from others or in themselves (particularly if scale 4 is also low).

138 and 318 Codes (See Also 1382 Codes).   These persons tend to have strange ideas and beliefs, particularly about religious and sexual topics, along with numerous vague somatic complaints. Occasionally major conversion reactions and hypochondriacal concerns exist, and appear to prevent more florid schizophrenic reactions. Religiosity and even religous delusions may be present, although the person may also be quite changeable both in mood and in beliefs. Many would be considered as borderline personalities, and their childhood histories often show a family background of psychosis and/or emotional deprivation. In males, fears regarding homosexuality are common, even though traditionally masculine occupations are usually chosen. These persons function much better when receiving structure in situations, and their bizarre symptoms may occur only when such structure is absent.

1382 Codes.   In addition to the 138 interpretation, notable depression, confused thinking, heavy drinking, and suicidal preoccupation are likely. Such persons are usually single or have poor marital adjustment. Typically they float from one job to another.

139 Codes.   Numerous somatic complaints are present (for example headaches, hearing and visual complaints, tremor, coordination difficulties) about which the person is quite upset. These persons have a low frustration tolerance, are irritable, and show temper outbursts, often becoming combative or destructive (particularly if scale 4 is also elevated, and/or if *K* is low). Interpersonal relationships are stormy, and divorces are frequent. Often these persons have histories of demanding perfection, and show little affection for their families. Often hostility may be shown directly, particularly following ingestion of alcohol. Most often this code is associated with personality disorders or with chronic brain syndromes associated with trauma. Sometimes, though less often, they are associated with anxiety reaction diagnoses.

14 and 41 Codes. This infrequent code (particularly rare among females) is associated with persons who show histories of inadequacies in meeting the demands and restrictions of groups or social regulations generally. They are bitter, cynical, pessimistic, negative, and become upset or even defiant at rules and regulations in a querulous, complaining, and self-pitying fashion. Their self-centered and demanding style is usually accompanied by physical complaints, particularly nonspecific headaches. They often have a pattern of socially unacceptable behavior and inadequacy in meeting the usual stresses and responsibilities of life. Excessive alcohol use is usually also present. In school or on the job, they show a history of indecision and poorly defined goals, and have difficulties in establishing enduring relations with members of the opposite sex. Although they may show reasonably good response to short-term symptomatic treatment, they will probably be quite unlikely to remain in treatment long enough to make real gains because they become quite concerned about any demands made of them by the therapist. The most common three-point codes are 143/413 and 142/412. Where scale 3 is also elevated, family and marital problems are suggested, centering around feelings of anger and intermingled with feelings of social inadequacy and conflicts over dependence and independence.

15 and 51 Codes. This is an uncommon code for males, and extremely rare for females. Most commonly, scales 3, 4, and 2 are the third highest scale for males.

Adult males tend to be fussy, complaining, cynical, and have a basically passive life-style. Somatic difficulties are frequently the focus of their complaints. Overt acting out is generally contraindicated, and seldom do they engage in open conflict or disagreement. Usually they are of above-average intelligence, and their socioeconomic status is middle or upper class.

Teenagers with this profile typically have difficulty expressing and discussing problems or conflicts they are having. Often they present themselves as being physically ill, and indeed have a history of serious physical illnesses as children. Teenage males are often described as effeminate and passive.

In females this code is uncommon, and must be interpeted differently depending on the person's social class background. In an urban, middle-class, relatively educated women, a 15/51 code suggests a pessimistic, complaining, immature woman who nevertheless is interpersonally competitive, aggressive, and perhaps dominating in her relations with men. In rural, lower-class, relatively uneducated women, the pessimism, complaining, and immaturity are present, but the aggressiveness may not be. Even so, such women typically have traditionally masculine interests and occupational expectancies (e.g., tractor driving).

In interpreting 15/51 codes, it is necessary to use the aforementioned interpretations, but then to examine the third highest scale in combination with scales 1 and 5 (that is, as though a two-point code). Thus, a 153 code would be examined first as a 15 code, then as a 13 code, and perhaps as a 53 code.

16 and 61 Codes.   These persons are rigid, grouchy, stubborn, hypersensitive to criticism, and overly quick to place blame onto others. They resent requests that others make of them, and feel put upon. They are evasive, defensive, and fearful of emotional involvement. Characteristically, they rely heavily on rationalization or projection to explain their irritability. Although most often overcontrolled, these persons (particularly adolescents) occasionally show violent outbursts.

When scale 8 is also elevated, the possibility must be considered that unusual somatic preoccupations exist, perhaps even somatic delusions. In some persons this seems to be an attempt to ward off a psychotic episode by "holding oneself together" through bodily preoccupations.

Profiles with 16/61 two-point codes are extremely rare both for males and females. Where they occur, the most common third highest scales for males are scales 2 and 4; for females they are scales 3 and 8.

17 and 71 Codes.   Chronically tense and anxious, such persons manifest many tension-related complaints. Obsessive overconcern with body functions and disorders, along with intellectualization, is common. Underlying feelings of guilt, inferiority, pessimism, and difficulties in being assertive are common. Though such persons often insist on continued health care, their behavior patterns are resistant to change. This code is more commonly obtained by males rather than females. For both sexes the most common three-point codes are 172/712 and 173/713.

18 and 81 Codes.   Poor social adjustment characterizes these persons, particularly with members of the opposite sex. They lack trust in others, feel alienated from others, keep others at a distance, and generally feel isolated (even more so when scale 0 is likewise elevated). Particularly when under stress, these persons are distractable and confused in their thinking, and periods of confusion or disorientation are possible. Emotionally, they are typically constricted or even bottled up, though this may alternate with episodes of sudden belligerence. Home life may have been severely disrupted by their emotional style. They do not appear to have learned ways of expressing feelings in a modulated fashion— particularly angry or assertive feelings. Often these persons show a variety of vague and medically atypical physical complaints. For some, these somatic preoccupations seem to represent an attempt to ward off a break with reality. In treatment, these patients show little response to simple reassurance, and are unlikely to attain much insight into personality difficulties. The most common three-point codes are 182/812, 183/813, and 187/817.

Adolescents with this code type are particularly distractable, forgetful, underachieving in school, and show somatic concerns such as headaches and insomnia. They have few friends, and their social adjustment is poor both in and outside of schools. Drug use history, and suicide attempts are likely, as is intense family conflict including overt conflict and fighting with parents. Two-thirds come from families whose parents are divorced.

19 and 91 Codes (See 129 and 139 Codes if Scales 2 and 3 Are Within 5 T-score Points of Scale 9. This rarely occurring code is associated with tense and restless persons in acute mental distress. They show clear overconcern with bodily functions and possible disabilities, even though this overconcern may be expressed in the form of verbal denial or attempts to conceal (or avoid confronting) physical dysfunctions. This pattern may reflect central nervous system or endocrine dysfunction expressed in the form of a high energy level (perhaps agitation) combined with numerous physical complaints. Where physical etiology has been ruled out, consideration should be given to the hypothesis that the person is attempting to mask an underlying depression (particularly if scale 2 is below 45), and that the distress stems from strong dependency needs that the person finds intolerable. Such persons, on the surface, appear extroverted and aggressive, but underneath are usually passive and dependent. Although they appear to be ambitious, they characteristically lack definite goals, or jump from goal to goal. Most commonly, scale 3 or 4 is the third highest scale.

10 and 01 Codes. Extremely rare, this code is associated with persons who are socially uncomfortable and withdrawn, aloof, cynically distrustful, passive, and unassertive. Usually, somatic complaints also are present. When scale 8 is also elevated as the third highest scale, schizoid withdrawal and social inadequacies are strongly suggested, usually combined with numerous somatic complaints. Most often scale 2 is the third highest scale, and when elevated above $T = 70$, the person is likely to show marked depression, accompanied by a distinct lack of social support systems.

Scale 2

Scale 2 is one of the most frequently elevated scales in clinical populations, but it is seldom elevated alone. In addition, scale 2 can be highly sensitive to both current mood and mood changes. Thus, interpretation of scale 2 elevations depends on the configuration of the rest of the profile. Most often, scales 7, 1, 8, or 0 are elevated along with 2, with scale 7 suggesting added anxiety, scale 1 a somatic component, scale 8 feelings of alienation and aloneness, and scale 0 indicating social withdrawal. Scale 2 does increase with age, which perhaps reflects an increased seriousness about life matters.

High scores ($T > 70$) reflect people who are anxious, worried, feeling low in self-esteem and pessimistic in their general outlook at this time. Typically they show a narrowing of interests, low frustration tolerance, poor morale, and generally feel discouraged, useless, and pessimistic. Elevations between 70 and 85 typically indicate good prognosis for therapy because the person is likely to be quite motivated to seek relief. The higher above 70, the more depressed and self-deprecating the person is likely to be. Scores above 80 suggest persons who feel so dejected that they are unable to concentrate or think clearly.

Moderately high ($T = 60$ to 70) scores suggest persons who are inhibited, serious, and self-evaluative, perhaps even lacking self-confidence. If no situational pressures currently exist, such persons are likely to characteristically think in terms of good and bad or right and wrong, particularly if L is also elevated.

Low scores ($T < 45$) are obtained by people who are alert, cheerful, active, self-confident, and who are likely to have a keen sense of humor and to be seen by others as enthusiastic and socially outgoing (particularly if scale 0 is low also). In some persons, however, there is a lack of inhibitions and a self-focus or even self-display, particularly if K and 9 are high. Low scores on scale 2 are often found in younger persons.

It should be noted that T-scores below 40, however, may indicate a denial of depression in a cyclothymic, labile person, particularly if scale 9 is also high. Some caution should therefore be exercised before dismissing a low scale 2 as insignificant.

Spike 2 occurs where 2 is the only scale elevated beyond 70 and the person is likely to be experiencing a reactive depression. Typically the person feels inadequate, lacking in self-confidence, is overly anxious and self-critical in an attempt to expiate guilt feelings by self-punishment as though that will atone for the misdeed or for not being able to influence or control the situation at hand in the proper way. Surprisingly, some persons will deny feeling depressed, though this mood may be apparent to others. Psychotherapy prognosis generally is quite good within a short time, and such patients often respond well to a directive-confrontive approach regarding why they are punishing themselves so harshly through their depression and self-criticism.

In college students, peak 2 profiles are clinically generally less significant, and more often reflect concern over situational problems (usually relations with opposite sex, studying, or vocational choices). Peak 2 college students typically resist efforts to probe deeply into the origins of their problems and instead seek to get advice from a parent-surrogate.

Relations with Other Scales

Spike 2, Low 9.   Depression is likely to be at least moderate to severe, and concerns typically center around fatigue and energy. Often such persons find it hard to arise in the mornings, and postpone responsibilities due to feeling tired and unable to cope. Symptomatic treatment and firm reassurance typically bring good results, as does a directive-confrontive approach. In older persons, however, this lack of stamina may be more associated with normal aging, rather than depression, per se.

21 Codes (See also 12 Codes; Also 123/213 Codes, if Scale 3 is Within 5 T-score Points of Scale 1).   The interpretation is similar to that of the 12 code, except that depression and tension-anxiety are more prominent features. The depression is usually of a restless, rather than apathetic nature. As with 12 codes, acting out is contraindicated (except for 1234/2134 codes). In spite of the obvious distress, such persons are often poorly motivated for psychotherapy. This code occurs more frequently as age increases, and is more common among males than females. Most often scales 3 and 7 are the third highest elevation.

213 and 231 Codes (See Also 123 Codes).   The interpretation is basically similar to that of the 21 code, although repression is a more evident part of the picture. These patients manifest depression and hypochondriacal concerns such as headaches, chest pain, or nausea and vomiting. Their depression, however, may be a smiling depression where they smile while they cry, but do not know why. They deny anger, are inhibited, and have an exaggerated need for affection. Typically they feel they received little nurturance from their father, and a significant proportion have a history of having lost one of their parents when they were young. They show conflicts over emotional dependency. Even though they often demand sympathy and get secondary gains from their symptoms, they feel dissatisfied, and worry over becoming too dependent. When scale 7 is also elevated, worry is a particular part of the clinical picture.

23 Codes (Also See 213/231 Codes if Appropriate; See 32 Codes if Scale 3 is Within 5 T-score Points of Scale 2).   Major characteristics associated with this code are overcontrol, depression, and fatigue. These persons feel bottled up, filled with self-doubts, lack interest or involvement in their surroundings, and generally keep their feelings inside except to express a general dissatisfaction. They find it quite difficult to express feelings more specifically. Marked episodes of anxiety are infrequent. Often (particularly with low 9) they feel week, fatigued, or exhausted, and their depression is typically long-standing. They tolerate unhappiness, and have accepted that they will function at a low level of efficiency where they may be unable to start tasks or to complete them when started. The most frequent three-point codes are 231/321, 234/324, and 237/327.

Paradoxically, men with 23 codes are superficially very achievement-oriented, but often complain of a lack of recognition on their jobs. Though they may seek added responsibilities, they also dread them because what they really want is the recognition. Some such men (particularly those with 237 or 239 codes) seem particularly serious, driven, industrious, or competitive, but also are both dependent and immature in their desire to be recognized.

Women with 23 codes (particularly with low 5 or low 9) show weakness, apathy, and prominent depression. Unhappiness and general inefficiency at work and home is typically chronic, with a long history of marital and family maladjustment (though divorce is not frequent). Despite their insecurity and distress, they show little sustained effort to seek help.

Although this code is more frequent among persons beyond age 25, it nonetheless occurs in adolescents and is associated with poor peer relationships. These adolescents are typically lonely individuals with few friends either inside or outside of school settings. Generally they are seen as passive, compliant, and obedient. Family patterns often show an underinvolved father in a professional occupation, and an overinvolved mother. Sexual acting out and drug abuse is not notably associated with this pattern for adolescents.

24 and 42 Codes. These persons have had difficulty maintaining control over their impulses, but currently are experiencing depression, remorse, or guilt. After acting out in a socially unacceptable manner, they feel distress. However, this may be the result of situational factors, such as being caught in socially unacceptable conduct or in a situation they cannot control, or the remorse may represent internalized guilt about their struggles to maintain control over unacceptable impulses. Though their apparent conscience pangs may be severe (even out of proportion to the event), their acting out behaviors are likely to recur in the future in a cyclic fashion. Home and family problems, loss of employment, and histories of social problems typically accompany this pattern. Heavy drinking, substance abuse, or alcoholism is frequent, as are legal difficulties. Most often, scales 7, 3, or 8 are the third highest scale.

Adolescents with this pattern show marked disregard for accepted social standards, are particularly resentful of authority figures, argumentative, afraid of involvement with others, blameful, and frequently involved with drugs. Legal violations (arrest, detention, conviction, probation) are common, as is running away from home or treatment centers. Most adolescents with this pattern feel alienated from other family members, and wish to escape from their intolerable and highly conflicted home situations. They perceive their parents as unaffectionate and inconsistent. Difficulties in school are common, and are usually related to difficulties in concentrating and truancy. This is a frequent profile pattern of unmarried mothers, and is associated with promiscuous sexual behavior.

At the time of testing, this person likely felt depressed, frustrated, dissatisfied, and restless. Pessimism about the future, low self-esteem, and distress about failures to achieve past goals are likely. Women particularly show crying episodes, depressed behavior, and perhaps suicidal ideation. Many show an inadequate and passive-dependent adjustment pattern. For persons beyond age 40, their failure to achieve accomplishments or satisfaction in life results either in self-blame and depression, or sometimes in projecting blame.

Although these persons may express firm intentions to change their behaviors, the pattern is persistent and the long-range prognosis is not encouraging. Although they may show rapid, temporary improvement, they are unable to remain in treatment long enough to make more than superficial changes. They are likely to be superficially deferential, but when confronted or pressured in therapy, these persons are likely to discontinue treatment, or even leave town or change jobs to avoid coming to grips with their problems. In general, they run from others' expectations of them. Even so, a combination of warm supports, firm limits, strategic therapy predictions, frequent contact, and environmental modifications may be significantly helpful.

243 and 423 Codes.   In addition to the characteristics described in the 24/42 code interpretations, it is likely that such persons are more intensely in conflict about maintaining emotional control of anger through repression and denial. Their anger is more likely to be expressed in passive-aggressive ways, or (if openly) in an unmodulated, rageful overreaction. Immaturity, egocentricity, and lack of insight into how others see them is common. These persons may establish relationships with marginally controlled, angry, acting out persons, thereby vicariously satisfying their own antisocial tendencies.

247, 427, 472, and 742 Codes (Also See 274 Code).   Family or marital problems are likely, centered around angry feelings that this person has, but is unable to express and feels intensely guilty about. Depression, tension, worry, and feelings of social inadequacy are usually present. Excessive alcohol use or episodic bouts of drinking are likely (even when the MAC scale is not elevated) in attempts to alleviate their depression. Frequently these persons underachieve, as though afraid to try because of possible failure. They are unlikely to be frank and open in discussing their problems despite their clear discomfort. Additionally, they typically overreact to minor problems, and react to them as though they were emergencies. Therapy prognosis is ofen poor, because of reluctance to endure the anxiety involved in treatment. Firm, directive, goal-oriented therapy, perhaps including assertiveness training, should be considered.

Males with this pattern are usually dependent and immature (particularly if scale 5 is also high), but verbally hostile. Marital discord is likely, and usually the wife is strong and dominating and/or minimally involved in a short-term marriage. These men often show a history of an extremely close relationship with their mother.

Females (particularly if scale 5 is low) present themselves as weak, inferior, guilty, and submissive. They virtually invite others to dominate them in a patronizing and deprecating way. Such relationships often appear to be masochistic ways of atoning for guilt, usually concerning unexpressed and unacceptable anger. Often their history shows a father who was hard-driving and successful.

248 Codes (Note: 284 and 482/842 Codes Have Different Interpretations).

Though depression, sullen anger, family and marital problems are most likely present, such persons are less likely to engage in overt angry acting out than is likely with 24/42 code types. Instead, they are more likely to withdraw into angry fantasy, feeling distrustful, alienated, and disaffiliated from others. Nevertheless, they fear loss of control over their impulses, and may be quite concerned over their unusual and disturbing thoughts. They are often seen by others as moody and unpredictable. Sexual difficulties of various sorts are quite likely. Suicidal ideation and multiple suicide attempts are frequently found. This code is a common one among mothers of child psychiatry patients.

25 and 52 Codes (See Also 275/725 Codes When Scale 7 Is Within 5 T-score Points of Scale 5).

Males with this code are inner-directed, unassertive, indecisive, idealistic persons who are depressed. They are relatively noncompetitive, perhaps to the point of passivity. Acting out is not likely, and conflicts tend to be handled internally though intellectualization. Often they are anxious and withdrawn, show a history of somatic complaints, and may complain of being unable to think clearly. Typically such persons are very self-aware to the point of being shy. They date infrequently, and generally show a relatively poor heterosexual adjustment. Most often this code is associated with scales 7, 3, 4, or 0 as the third highest scale for males.

Women very rarely obtain this code, and usually it is with Scales 0, 3, 1, 6, or 8 as the third highest scale. Although high 5 scores in women often reflect assertiveness, dominance, or aggressiveness, these third highest scales would suggest otherwise. Instead, it is more likely that women with 25/52 codes are depressed and inwardly focused, but attempt to be self-sufficient rather than depend on others.

Adolescents with this code usually are referred because of poor relationships with their siblings or friends, shyness, extreme negativism, or hypersensitivity. Interpersonally shy, passive, and unassertive, these adolescents often show overintellectualization combined with perfectionism and meticulous concerns. Anxiety, guilt, hypersensitivity, self-condemnation, depression, and social awkwardness are usually present. Others often see them as not particularly masculine, and they are frequently teased by their peers.

26 and 62 Codes.   Touchy, moody, depressed, and oversensitive to criticism, these persons have a strong underlying anger and most often a long history of interpersonal difficulties. Paranoid trends are usually evident. They read malevolent meaning into neutral situations, and jump to conclusions based on insufficient data. Resentfulness, agitation, fatigue, and aggressiveness are usually marked. Often these persons adopt a "chip on the shoulder" attitude in an attempt to reject others before they are rejected, or as a means to avoid becoming dependent. When scale 6 is markedly elevated and/or scales 4 and 8 are above a *T*-score of 70, the probability is increased that the person is in the early phases of psychosis.

27 and 72 Codes (See Also, As Appropriate, 273/723, 247/274, 275/ 725 for Males, 27/72 Low 5 for Females, and 278/728 Codes).   These codes are the most common among outpatients in mental health settings. Tension, depression, nervousness, anxiety, guilt, self-devaluation, excessive introspection, and nonproductive rumination are highly characteristic, usually accompanied by feelings of inadequacy, lack of self-confidence, reduced work efficiency, and insomnia. These persons focus on their personal deficiencies, even though their lives often show evidence of numerous personal achievements. Rigidity of attitudes, and strong concern over issues of right and wrong are often accompanied by sexual conflict. Often such persons are overcontrolled, and have difficulty expressing their feelings openly. In interpersonal relationships, they often show a pattern of dependency and lack of assertiveness. The most common three-point codes are 270/720, 278/728, 273/723, and 271/721.

Suicidal ideation is common, and attempts are a real possibility with 27/72 code types, particularly if scales 8 and 9 are elevated, and scale 1 and/or *K* are low. In such cases, careful evaluation of suicide potential is indicated.

Some elevation on scales 2 and 7 is considered desirable in candidates for psychotherapy because this usually indicates motivation for change from the internal distress, as well as a tendency toward introspection. Extreme elevations (e.g., above a *T*-score of 85), however, often mean that persons are so agitated and worried that they cannot focus sufficiently to profit from verbal psychotherapy, and other forms of intervention, such as psychotropic medications, may be necessary.

273 and 723 Codes.   These persons often accumulate significant stress, usually by setting high standards for themselves and by their apparent strivings. When their stress accumulates, they readily seek help from others, and in their depression and worry become markedly and clingingly dependent. Their apparent helplessness, docility and self-deprecating attitudes prompts others to want to save or protect them, and even experienced health care professionals must be careful not to get caught up in nonfunctional rescue behaviors. When scale 1 is also elevated, these persons are likely to not only have numerous anxiety- related somatic complaints, but also to have substantial self-pity, self-blame, and social withdrawal despite their desire to have others take care of them.

274 and 724 Codes (Also See 247 and 427 Code Interpretations If Scales 4 and 7 Are Within 5 T-Score Points of Each Other).

Anxiety, worry, and irritable depression are characteristic, and typically are combined with feelings of inadequacy and low self-confidence. Often such persons feel caught in situations over which they feel they have little control, and where they feel that it would be inappropriate for them to express their anger or resentment. These persons often nervously ruminate over their life situation, and may express their resentment toward others in passively aggressive ways.

Men with this profile often show histories of being emotionally rescued by their mothers, and often look to replicate this pattern later in their lives. Although seeking such dependent relationships, however, they nonetheless harbor resentment over the control that usually accompanies such relationships. When scale 3 is also elevated, the possibility of chronic alcoholism is quite likely, with the alcohol being used in an attempt to reduce the anxiety and cope with the depression.

Women with this profile often have been particular objects of attention and pride by their fathers. Usually they are self-effacing, and try to look weak and submissive (particularly if scale 5 is low). Their relationships with others may show recurring difficulties and they may have long affairs with married men.

275 and 725 Codes (Males); 27, Low 5 (Females).

In addition to the worry, depression, and excessive rumination, these persons show a particular submissiveness, almost as though inviting others to be patronizingly superior. They seem to have a chronic sense of failure, or at best an enduring ambivalence about their self-worth. Their self-presentation as inadequate, weak, inferior, guilty, and passive is most notable when scale 4 is also low. It is as though these persons are continually atoning in their depression by seeking relationships where others belittle them, and are most comfortable in such relationships. Heterosexual difficulties are also often present.

278 and 728 Codes (Note That 287 and 827 Codes Have a Different Interpretation).

Tense, anxious, depressed, extremely ruminative and filled with self-doubt, these persons are very likely to experience and to have suicidal thoughts. Obsessive thinking, fears, and phobias are common, along with a focus on their failures. These people are often meticulous, perfectionistic, set unreasonably high standards for themselves and others, and feel intensely guilty when they fail to meet these standards. Their excessive introspection and self-pressure often leads to difficulties in concentrating and reduced performance, which then leads to an increase in their depression and anxiety. Particular difficulty exists for them in making emotional commitments such as in establishing love relationships with the opposite sex. Often they will focus on the minute details of such relationships, attributing far more attention and worry than is warranted. Issues revolving around control, criticism, acceptance, and the expression of anger are common.

Suicide potential should be carefully evaluated with this code-type, particularly when scales K and 1 are below 50, and/or when scale 9 is also elevated. The elevation of scale 9 in this code suggests an agitated aspect to the depression. If scale 0 is elevated, the person's depression is more likely to be chronic, and accompanied by shyness, introversion, and feelings of physical inferiority. When scale 4 is low, passivity and submissiveness are also prominent, often accompanied by reduced sexual interests and sexual inadequacy.

Females with 278/728 codes who also score low on scale 5 are particularly likely to feel a need to atone for themselves, and may even provoke others to anger in this fashion. These women tend to berate themselves almost masochistically, and to show various physical complaints involving headaches, backaches, and sexual difficulties.

28 and 82 Codes (Also See 281/821, 284/824, and 287/827 Codes as Appropriate).

This code is associated with depression, agitation, social withdrawal, difficulty concentrating, and fear of losing control over one's impulses. Others see these persons as jumpy, keeping people at a distance, inefficient in making and carrying out plans, and somewhat peculiar in their thoughts and ideas. Adolescents in particular are highly emotional, and are unable to express their emotions in controlled and modulated fashion. If scales 2 and 8 are both highly elevated, the likelihood of serious psychological problems is quite high, and hallucinations or delusions may be present. Suicidal thoughts are likely, and should be carefully evaluated because persons with this code-type are more likely to have specific suicidal intentions.

Adults, and particularly adolescents, with this profile type show a fear of emotional involvement with others, and have conflicts about emotional dependency and sexuality. Their histories often show repeated hurts in childhood, and self-esteem and self-concept are unstable. Heterosexual relationships are usually minimal, or involve problems or behaviors that are unusual. Adolescents often show their emotions inappropriately, are truant, and have histories of drug abuse.

Establishing therapeutic relationships with such persons is difficult, and psychotherapy prognosis typically is poor. Chemotherapy may be more likely to be helpful, at least initially.

281 and 821 Codes.

In addition to the general characteristics associated with the 28/82 code, these persons show numerous somatic complaints. Usually these are vague or medically atypical, and may involve tremors, thinking difficulties, or even somatic delusions. This pattern may represent a self-focus that precedes a psychotic episode, and usually is associated with clear tension and intellectual confusion. In other persons, particularly when scale 3 is also elevated, these somatic complaints and related behaviors may prompt the therapist to attempt rescue behaviors, but these are then rebuffed by the person.

284 and 824 Codes.   In adults this code is often associated with schizoid or schizophrenic conditions, and scale *F* is usually also elevated. In addition to the 28/82 characteristics already noted, anger, rebellion, feelings of disaffiliation, and alienation from others are strong components. Fears of loss of impulse control are strong (particularly if scale 4 is above 80), and where acting out occurs, it is likely to be in strange and bizarre ways. Severe social and marital maladjustment is likely. (Where scale 4 is within 5 *T*-score points of scale 2 or 8, see the interpretation of the 482/842 codes).

   In adolescents, this code may not represent the enduring pathology indicated for adults. Instead, this code more likely reflects the sullen rebelliousness and alienation from social groups that is found in many adolescents. The poor impulse control is present, as are the unusual behaviors and mental inefficiency, but the underlying pathology is likely to be less severe.

287 and 827 Codes.   Persons with this code show depression and anxiety, tangential thought processes, feel alienated from people, are unduly sensitive to criticism, and are distrustful of people in general. They almost always show significant mental difficulties such as being unable to concentrate, episodes of dizziness, mental confusion, insomnia, and reduced ability to carry out duties and responsibilities. They may also show labile or inappropriate emotions, or even hallucinations or clear thought disorders. Characteristically, these persons avoid close interpersonal relationships and are afraid of emotional involvement, generally due to fears of becoming dependent. Conflicts over sexuality and self-assertion are often present.

   Suicidal thoughts, preoccupations, and threats are very likely, and should be evaluated carefully, particularly if scale *K* is below 50 and if 9 is above 70. Where suicides occur, they are often carried out in unusual or even bizarre ways.

29 and 92 Codes.   Most often scales 4 or 3 are the third highest elevation. Persons with 29/92 profile codes have a high energy level, but it is associated with depression or anxiety. The high energy level represents either an attempt at compensatory coping, or a loss of control. Three types of persons generally obtain this code.

   1. Persons with an agitated depression marked by overly expressive behaviors such as weeping and wailing, depressive rumination, and a self-absorption that borders on narcissism. As children, these persons may have had to be very emotional in order to get attention.

2. Persons who are trying to cope with underlying depression through using manic defenses. In some persons the grandiose thinking and denial may be sufficient to mask the depression. More commonly, however, these defenses are no longer effective. Often such persons then turn to heavy drinking.

3. Persons with organic brain dysfunction who are somewhat aware of their reduced functioning and abilities, and who are attempting to deny this to themselves and to hide this from others. Often these persons will show perplexity and agitation at their lack of abilities that previously were easily accomplished. They may attempt to regain control over their life environment through excessive structuring or systematizing, perhaps even to the point of appearing ritualistic.

20 and 02 Codes.   This code suggests a socially withdrawn and introverted person with a mild, but chronic and characterological depression. This depression often is related to poor interpersonal and social skills, combined with feelings of inferiority and shyness. Both adults and adolescents with this profile type feel nervous and inhibited, particularly in social gatherings, and have few friends. Many (particularly if scale 1 is low) also feel physically unattractive. Insomnia, guilt feelings, and worry are also often present. With this code-type, most often scale 7 or 4 is the third highest scale.

Common among mothers of children receiving psychological help, this code is often associated with only moderate improvement in treatment. Therapists see these mothers as in conflict about giving, and are often fearful of emotional involvement with others. They tend to keep others at a distance, keeping a rigid check on their own emotions to avoid having demands placed upon them or losing control of the situation (particularly if K is elevated also).

Scale 3 (HY)

High scores ($T > 70$) are obtained by persons who (a) are very much using repression and denial, (b) are quite conforming, naive, and childishly self-centered, (c) have anxiety-related somatic concerns, or all of these. They may be very demanding of affection, approval, and support, and have quite active (though superficial) social lives, but have extremely little insight into their behaviors. Some of these persons are blatantly exhibitionistic, and may act out sexually or aggressively, all the while using extreme denial and repression. Due to their strong need to be liked, their initial response to situations requiring commitment will usually be quite enthusiastic. Sooner or later, however, they become resentful of demands placed on them, and generally become passively resistive, whiningly complaining, or develop somatic problems that allow them to remove themselves from the situation.

Moderately high scores on scale 3 ($T = 60$ to 70) are obtained by persons who are generally optimistic and positive in their outlook on life. Often they are achievement-oriented, socially involved and outgoing.

Low scores (T < 45) generally reflect feelings that life is hard, and the person focuses on numerous personal and social problems. Repression and denial are greatly reduced, perhaps underutilized, and their interests often are substantially narrowed. Such people often are cynical, caustic, and misanthropic. When other scales in the profile are significantly elevated, such persons typically are extremely aware of their personal distress, and have trouble excluding disturbing thoughts and impulses from their consciousness.

With spike 3, no other clinical scale above $T = 70$, persons are over-conventional, and have a compelling need to be accepted and liked. They worry over possibilities of being unaccepted by their social group, and become very uncomfortable in handling confrontive situations that involve anger or self-assertiveness, and when dealing with authority figures or situations (such as academic settings) where they might be closely evaluated. In conversations, these people emphasize their optimism and good relations with others, and gloss over or minimize any unusual or deviant behaviors in themselves. Their backgrounds often show an unhappy home and/or marital life, primarily with a father whom they saw as overly evaluative and rejecting.

Women with peak 3, but with scale 5 below 40, are particularly likely to be socialized into the feminine role and to emphasize socially acceptable facades. Often they blatantly use feminine wiles to manipulate men or to be seductive, often without knowing it. Sexual problems, lack of assertiveness, and an inability to express anger openly are common. Where scale 0 is below T = 45, these women are typically quite extroverted and marriage-oriented, with many social skills.

Relations with Other Scales

Spike 3, High K. When scales 3 and K are both elevated, and particularly when scales F and 8 are low, the need to be liked, accepted, conventional, and to present oneself as having control of one's life is substantially exaggerated. Characteristically, these persons show an almost rigid optimism, and resolutely maintain that things are fine even when apparently surrounded by catastrophe and failure. These people emphasize good relations and harmony with others, and avoid (or become very uncomfortable in) situations where anger, disruptions or hurt feelings are involved, or where they must exercise independent decision or power.

31 Codes (See 13/31 Codes).

32 Codes (See Also 23 Codes if Scale 2 is Within 5 T-score Points of Scale 3).
In contrast to 23 code-types, these persons show more concern for their health and somewhat less overt depression. Fatigue, gastric complaints, headaches, dizziness, are common, although various other physical complaints may also be present. Usually these symptoms are rather mild, and clearly related to anxiety, depression, and attempts to overcontrol emotions.

Men with this profile pattern usually are in a clear state of anxiety (often mixed with depression) and may show an inability to concentrate in addition to physical symptoms. They are typically ambitious, conscientious, and serious about their responsibilities, and their concerns often center around business problems. They are concerned about appearing to be part of the mainstream, and deny unacceptable impulses or interpersonal difficulties. They resist psychological interpretations of their physical problems, and lack insight. Although reassurance about their physical condition is likely to be helpful, they are unlikely to seek continued psychological assistance. For men, scales 1, 8, and 9 are most often the third highest scale.

Women with 32 codes most often have a history of marital difficulties (though divorces are rare), frequently lack desire for sexual relations with their husbands, and report lack of sexual enjoyment. Typically they are depressed, and complain about the infidelity or drinking of their husbands. Extremely sensitive to criticism or rebuff, many of these women will tolerate chronic unhappiness. Commonly they feel inadequate, and have significant self-doubt. Even so, they keep their feelings bottled up and under tight control. They may complain of fatigue and exhaustion (particularly if scale 5 is also low), yet tend to be quite conscientious in their work. Physical symptoms of palpitation, sweating, insomnia, and vague fear are often reported. Sometimes this profile is associated with menopausal difficulties. For women, scale 1, 4, or 8 is most likely to be the third highest scale.

321 Code. In addition to the characteristics of persons with 32 codes, these people show numerous hypochondriacal complaints such as constipation, diarrhea, anorexia, insomnia, muscle tension, genital pain, palpitations, and exhaustion. Women with this profile frequently have recurring gynecological complaints and/or have had hysterectomies. Men more often show gastric distress or ulcers. In both sexes, marital problems are likely, as are emotional conflicts about sex. Depression and worry are related to feelings of inferiority or even hopelessness.

These people lack insight into themselves or others, and as a result often find themselves in uncomfortable interpersonal situations. They tend to react to such frustrating situations by becoming intropunitively depressed, often in ways that further hurt themselves. For example, they often overreact in ways that prompt criticism or rejection from others.

34 and 43 Codes. Although persons obtaining 34 codes often show clear differences from those obtaining 43 codes, the similarities warrant combined discussion. Both code-types are angry, immature, and egocentric. Marital disharmony, sexual promiscuity, divorce, alcoholism, and tenuous relationships with others are characteristic. They have not developed appropriate ways to express their anger in a modulated and timely fashion. However, the relative elevations of scales 3 and 4 serve as an indicator of the extent to which such persons will control and inhibit their anger and other impulses (if 3 is higher), or whether the emotions are more likely to be expressed (if 4 is higher). The 34/43 codes are quite common among mothers and fathers of youngsters with behavior problems. Frequently these parents subtly reinforce the acting out behavior of their children as an indirect way of expressing anger at their spouse. For males, scales 2, 5, and 6 are most often the third highest elevation. For females, the third highest scales most often are 2, 6, and 8.

Adolescents with 34/43 codes are seen professionally most often because of conflicts with parents and school authorities. Theft, drug use, school truancy, and running away from home are common, as are suicidal thoughts and sleep difficulties.

In 34 codes, where scale 3 is distinctly higher, the person is likely to express angry feelings indirectly, or to vicariously express anger and rebellion through becoming involved with acting-out individuals. Generally, though, the 34 code-type person appears quiet, and even conforming, though clearly self-centered. Seldom do they indicate that they are emotionally distressed unless situations do not go the way they want them to. Although marital and family problems are common, they lack insight as to their role in them. Because of their repression, denial, and overcontrol of anger, when outbursts occur, they are typically overaggressive, but subsequently well-rationalized.

Often these persons wish to be dependent, but also wish to be independent. They angrily vacillate between being called for too much and not being called for enough. That is, though they want to be dependent, they also find the expectancies and demands that accompany such a relationship to be very irritating. Women with this code often place great emphasis on superficial aspects of their life, are impatient, and demanding. They also often have mild episodic psychosomatic complaints, which are not incapacitating, but rather a focus of discussion and complaint.

In 43 codes, where 4 is distinctly higher than 3, the anger is dominant, though typically it is bottled up for long periods, and then expressed in rageful outbursts, sometimes even culminating in serious assault or murder. Many such persons appear to be quiet or even withdrawn for extended periods, and their outbursts are a great surprise, because the actual precipitating stress often is a quite small event. Their outbursts typically are not illogical or irrational (unless scale 6 or 8 is also significantly elevated), but rather the anger has built internal pressure gradually over a long period of time. In some such persons, the violent outbursts occur in a cyclic pattern that alternates with long periods of socially appropriate behavior, and is a pattern that is extremely difficult to change.

345, 435, and 534 Codes.   Men with this profile are notably immature in their relationships with others, and are generally sexually inadequate. They often feel a need for different or more than usual sexual stimulation. Frequently they have engaged in exhibitionism or voyeurism, and/or have fears of being homosexual. When scale 3 is higher than 4, there is less likelihood that the feelings and desires have been acted upon, particularly if K is greater than 50.

346 and 436 Codes (See Also 36/63 Codes if 6 Is Within 5 T-Score Points of 3).

Although outwardly these persons often appear to be conforming, they may have histories of episodic extreme acting out followed by long periods of apparently moderate behavior. Often such persons are hypersensitive to criticism, and are tense and anxious as a result of their angry feelings. Usually their anger is primarily at members of their family, but is highly rationalized and justified in their own minds. Often they rigidly feel that they are in the right and have little inclination to be forgiving. Many establish long-standing (but often turbulent) relationships with acting out individuals, thereby vicariously gratifying their own angry and rebellious impulses. Blame is a key part of their thinking style, and these persons seldom see a need to change or to introspect. Psychological treatment will likely be resisted.

35 and 53 Codes.

Males with this code tend to be passive and even somewhat withdrawn. They are more likely to contemplate than to act, and are seen as inhibited and insecure, although having strong needs for attention. Usually they are also shy, anxious, and socially uncomfortable (particularly if scale 0 is also elevated). Most show distinct moral and/or educational aspirations. Scale 4 or 6 is usually the third highest scale. This code is frequently seen in fathers of child psychiatry patients, and is associated with the use of denial, repression, and passivity as a defense. Though appearing concerned with the family situation, these fathers tend to let the family concerns take second place to their own self-concerns and needs.

In females this two-point code is rare. The most common third highest elevations are scales 4 or 1. Interpretation is best accomplished by initially ignoring the elevated scale 5 so as to treat the three-point code (e.g., code 354) as though it were a two-point code (e.g., code 34). Subsequently, the interpretations of the elevated scale 5 can be added.

36 and 63 Codes.

On the surface, these persons are hypersensitive to criticism, distrustful, tense, and even suspicious. Frequently they also have headaches or gastrointestinal complaints. Where problems exist, they are blamed on others or on situations. Under this surface lies pervasive and long-standing feelings of anger toward one's immediate family. Where the anger is recognized, it is well rationalized as justifiable resentment. In fact, most of these persons are difficult to get along with because of their self-focus and their guarded posture. This two-point code is substantially more common among females than among males, and most often the third highest elevation is scale 0 or 8.

Where scale 6 is higher than 3 by five or more *T*-score points, the person is likely to be angrily egocentric in striving for power and prestige, even to the point of ruthless manipulations. Typically such persons are quite rigid and defensive in their behaviors. Some may show marked paranoid features.

Where scale 3 is higher than 6, such persons are particularly unaware of their anger, though this may be quite evident to others. The self-focus and egocentricity is clearly present, usually along with the hurt feelings. However, the pattern is more one of martyred acceptance and resignation, rather than power struggles.

37 and 73 Codes.   Relatively uncommon, this code is associated with tension, anxiety, insomnia, chronic discomfort, and other psychosomatic complaints, as well as with academic underachievement. Unresolved dependency yearnings, combined with feelings of inadequacy, often underlie these symptoms. However, these persons use repression that significantly hinders insight, and will deny the existence of psychological problems. For both sexes, scales 2, 4, and 1 are most often the third highest scale.

38 and 83 Codes.   This code is an uncommon one, particularly among males. Scales 4, 1, 7, and 2 are most often the third highest elevation in the profiles of persons with this code-type.

These individuals are strange and peculiar both in thought and action, and have difficulties in concentrating, thinking, and remembering clearly, and in making even minor decisions. Though they feel alienated, these people have an exaggerated need for affection, but are afraid of getting involved in dependent relationships. When they do attempt to achieve affectionate responses from others, they typically do so in a childlike fashion that others find strange.

Their psychological turmoil may be so great as to represent major thought disorders such as autistic overideation or delusions, perhaps accompanied by behavioral regression. Feelings of unreality and emotional inappropriateness are usually accompanied by complaints of blurred vision, dizziness, numbness, and headaches. Some have brief, highly sexualized psychotic episodes, for which they have no memory later.

39 and 93 Codes.   Usually these persons are gregarious, outgoing, apparently self-assured individuals, though they may be quite superficial (particularly if scale 0 is below *T* of 40). Despite this, these persons are often described as verbally aggressive, as having dependence-independence conflicts, and as being particularly angry at a domineering mother. In clinical situations, they show histories of episodic attacks of anxiety and acute distress, often accompanied by palpitations, tachycardia, or symptoms in the lower gastrointestinal tract. Often these symptoms are medically unusual or impossible. Typically these somatic complaints respond well to symptomatic treatment combined with reassurance. The most common three-point code is 394/934.

30 and 03 Codes.   This rare code is associated with persons who are passive, dependent, and socially unassertive to the point of being withdrawn. Nevertheless, they appear to be relatively comfortable with this mode of adjustment, and prefer to avoid discomforting social situations, and to repress uncomfortable feelings. Reactions to stress may involve episodic psychosomatic complaints. Scales 1 and 2 are frequently the next most highly elevated.

Scale 4 (Pd)

High scorers ($T > 70$) are angry, rebellious, and find rules and regulations to be irritating. Their anger may be against their family, or authority and society in general, or both. Sometimes this anger may be a situational response (divorce, etc.), or adolescent rebellion, or may reflect the angry disaffiliation of being in a minority cultural group. When this is not the case, the pattern is likely to be long-standing and unlikely to change. However the way in which individuals handle the resentment and asocial impulses may differ greatly, depending on elevations of other aspects of the profile. In general, whether their anger is acted out behaviorally depends on whether scales 9 and/or 8 are elevated, and whether scale K is low. Generally, though, impulsiveness, poor interpersonal judgment, unpredictability, social alienation, and reduced sense of responsibility and morals are present, along with poor work and marital adjustment. They tend to sacrifice long-term goals for short-term desires, and seem limited in their capacity to anticipate consequences. Social relationships are typically shallow, and strong loyalties are rarely developed. Although these persons sometimes make a good first impression, their unreliability, self-orientation, manipulativeness, and resentment soon become apparent. Often these persons have come from homes where they felt uncared for, and subsequently focus on themselves as a defense against hurting.

In determining whether pathology exists, both the life situation and the person's age must be considered. High 4 profiles (using adult norms) are normal for adolescents, who characteristically are rebelling to break away from home and to establish their own sense of identity. Beyond the age of 25, however, a high 4 profile should be considered unusual. Beyond age 40, an elevated scale 4 most likely reflects long-standing interpersonal disaffiliation and antisocial behavior, whereas beyond age 60 such scores suggest alienation to the point of apathetic lack of involvement. Where there is no clear life event that would prompt such anger, the scale 4 characteristics are likely to be enduring and resistant to change.

Moderate elevations (T between 60 and 70) are associated with adventurousness, risk-taking, energy, sociability, and assertiveness. Generally these traits are positive ones associated with enterprising initiative, drive, and independence. When these people are frustrated, however, these characteristics can turn into clear irritation, aggression, and socially maladaptive behavior.

Low scorers ($T < 50$) tend to be conventional, stable, passive, and un-assertive. They are not adventurous, and often are dependent and even rigid in their adherence to socially conforming traditions. In counseling they are likely to seek reassurance concerning the attitudes that others have toward them. Although they may be quite affectionate, frequently they are not assertive in seeking sexual interactions.

Spike 4, also referred to as peak 4, occurs when scale 4 is the only scale above $T = 70$ (and to a lesser degree when scale 4 is 10 or more T-score points above all other scales). These persons are impulsive, resentful, rebellious, and in general have difficulty accepting rules, regulations, and authority. The likelihood of legal difficulties is high. Although they may be quite gregarious (particularly if scale 0 is low), their relationships with others are shallow, superficial, and brief. Long-lasting, intimate relationships are unlikely because these persons have difficulties with empathy, and with the responsibilities and demands that would accompany. They are unable to maintain organized behaviors toward long-term goals, and instead tend to focus on satisfying short-term desires. As scale 0 approaches a T-score of 30, these problems are likely to be more pervasive and severe, though the person may give an appearance of being suave and glib.

A low tolerance for frustration, an inability to delay gratification, and a generally hedonistic approach are often found, particularly if scale K is low. Self-control of angry feelings may be poor, and conflicts with parents, family members, and authorities are common. If scale K is above $T = 60$, and if the patient is of above-average intelligence and education, these behaviors are likely to be generally well-controlled. Legal difficulties for these persons are more likely to be of the white-collar variety.

Relations with Other Scales

High 4, Low 5 Codes (Also See Low 5 Code).   In males, the low 5 reflects a person's strong concerns about portraying himself as masculine, or even hypermasculine. Power, coarseness, and traditional masculine interests are emphasized. In persons of working-class backgrounds and education less than college, this may simply reflect traditional values of that group. In men of middle or upper social class with college education, this pattern more likely suggests a flamboyant facade to cover up feelings of inadequacy, particularly toward women. Often they repeatedly put women down in attempts to bolster their egos and to reassure themselves about power and control. In teenagers this pattern is associated with overt delinquency.

Women with this pattern are angry (often chronically so), but are unable to express these feelings directly. Their anger is directed particularly at men, and heterosexual problems are to be expected. Interestingly, these women are often superficial in their relationships, and frequently have identified with cultural stereotypes of women who are demure, yielding, and alluring, and seek to play such roles to satisfy their inordinate need for affection and attention. They usually are excessively demanding and dependent. Their anger toward men, however, prompts them to express their irritations in passively aggressive fashion, frequently through using sexual means to manipulate or control men. These women often provoke others to anger (particularly if scale 6 is also elevated) with such behaviors, but then pity themselves because they have been mistreated. Even so, they seem to derive pleasure from having precipitated a soap opera crisis. When scale 3 is also elevated, these women are particularly unaware of their impact on others, and deny hostile feelings. Not surprisingly, marital and family problems are likely, as are sexual dysfunctions and lack of sexual enjoyment. Headaches and backaches are also frequent.

41 Codes (See 14/41-Codes).

42 Codes (See 24-42 Codes).

43 Codes (See 34/43 Codes).

45 and 54 Codes.   This code-type can be adequately interpreted only by simultaneously considering the person's age, education, and gender. For adolescents, this code suggests persons who emotionally react vigorously, and who are prone to temper tantrums or even violent outbursts. They dislike rules, regulations and authority, and often show histories of truancy, school suspension, and failing academic grades. This is particularly so when scale 4 is higher than scale 5, and these persons have greater difficulty controlling their tempers. Drug usage, theft, and other risk-taking or antisocial behavior may also be present. However, these teenagers are also gregarious, extroverted, and generally well-liked by their peers. Despite their problems, in therapy they show good rapport and ego strength, and appear to have reasonably good prognoses.

Adults with this code who have less than 2 years of college most often are narcissistic, self-directed persons who seem to delight in defying social conventions in appearance and in behaviors. The openness and even flagrant nature of their defiance will increase as scales 4 and 9 become higher. Their interests are often unusual and varied, and they seem to delight in their nonconformity. In some persons this code is associated with homosexuality, and these persons are typically quite open about their sexual behaviors.

Adult men with college education or above are less likely to be narcissistically noncomformist, and instead are more likely to become involved in social protests, causes, or movements that have an antiestablishment element. Often these men are quite idealistic and self-aware, and are able to communicate their ideas clearly and effectively. Dominance and dependence are important issues for these persons. Although they engage in their nonconformist behaviors to reassure themselves of their independence and adequacy, nonetheless they wish to belong and to be dependent on others. Where scale 3 is the next highest scale, the person is likely to be more focused on overcontrol and to lean toward dependency or even passivity. (See 345/435/534 Codes). Where scale 9 is the next highest, the person is more likely to be emphasizing actions, dominance, and control of situations and people.

Women with 45 and 54 codes, most often have scales 9 and 8 as the third highest scale. Typically they have rejected or have never incorporated passivity as part of their feminine role and self-image. For some of these women, this constitutes an angry masculine protest and/or the adoption of a masculine like role in a lesbian relationship. In other women, particularly in rural areas, this profile for women only indicates a lifestyle that is not traditionally feminine, and instead focuses on practical, mechanical, or other work-oriented aspects of their subculture that requires self-assertiveness.

46 and 64 Codes.   This code is rare among adult normals though it is not uncommon among teenagers. This code is generally three times more common among female outpatients than among male outpatients, and suggests a somewhat less pathological picture when obtained by females. Most often scales 2, 3, and 8 are the third highest in such profiles.

Key features are anger, resentment, distrust, sullenness, irritability, hypersensitivity to criticism or to demands by others, and projection of blame onto others. These persons are quick to feel implied rejection or criticism, and they jump to conclusions based on inadequate data and little forethought. Their thinking typically focuses on how they have been hurt or neglected, how others are at fault, and how they can protect themselves or can get back at others. Their thinking is seldom oriented around their own role in creating difficult situations or problems. The histories of these people show severe social interaction problems, few close relationships, and often drug usage or alcoholism.

Teenagers with this code virtually always have continuing and severe conflicts with their parents, as well as with authority figures in general, who see them as bitter, hostile, and deceitful. Self-indulgent undercontrol of impulses is characteristic, accompanied by acting without sufficient forethought or deliberation. Defiance, disobedience, negativism, and argumentativeness are common. Often they are frankly provocative of others, but see no responsibility for their behaviors.

In adult men, the 46/64 code is often associated with psychotic or prepsychotic conditions (see 468/648 codes), or with borderline personalities (see 462/642 and 463/643 codes), all of which will show paranoid features of suspicion, distrust, and overgeneralization. When scale 4 is higher than scale 6, family and work difficulties are typical, along with anger being the predominant feature. When scale 6 is higher than scale 4, more blatantly paranoid features will predominate. Although these men generally control their anger and sullenly mull about it, episodically they may show vicious outbursts to the surprise of those around them.

In women, the 46/64 code may be associated with psychosis or prepsychosis (particularly if scale 8 is high and K is low), but more often appears to be associated with passive-aggressive personality styles, primarily associated with anger at men (see high 4, low 5). This is particularly so with 463/643 codes, where lack of insight, indirect instigation of problems, and blame of others is very likely to be present (see 463/643 codes).

462 and 642 Codes.   In addition to the anger and sensitivity associated with the 46/64 code, these persons usually are dramatically self-absorbed in agitated psychic distress, and complain of nervousness, anxiety, and depression. Often this is a manipulative demand for attention, sympathy, and control. Suicide threats are likely.

These people are mistrustful and skeptical of others, and are suspicious of their motivations. They are particularly resentful of, and have problems with, persons in authority, and often project the blame for their problems onto these authority figures. They rationalize their difficulties as due to matters beyond their control, or blame others. Sexual and marital maladjustment are likely.

Despite their discomfort with people in general, and their anger at authority, these people typically have an exaggerated need for affection and dependency (even more so if scale 3 is also elevated). It appears that much of their discomfort and criticism stems from fears of becoming overly dependent on (and therefore controlled by) others. Consequently, they may show a reduced sense of involvement with their families or co-workers.

463 and 643 Codes.   The inordinate demand for affection shown by these people is difficult to satisfy, particularly because of their sensitivity and quick irritability if their needs are not met. Usually their dependency needs are heterosexual, and are expressed in egocentrically demanding (even hostile) ways, sometimes involving blatant manipulation or provocation. This pattern is often self-defeating, however, because their partners feel taken advantage of, become irritated, and withdraw their affection. Often these persons similarly make excessive demands on therapists or others providing treatment, but simultaneously criticize and deprecate the treatment they are receiving. With their sensitivity to rejection, persons with this code type often feel chronically bitter, resentful and mistrustful, particularly of members of the opposite sex. Marital maladjustment is likely. Insight is lacking. In women who also have scale 5 below 40, a passivity, clinging dependency and self-pity is particularly likely (see high 4, and low 5). Physical complaints such as menstrual irregularities, sexual dysfunction, headaches, and backaches are also likely.

468 and 648 Codes.   This code suggests a severe, and probably chronic, emotional disorder, most likely paranoid schizophrenia if the person is a psychiatric inpatient. These persons are suspicious, angry, hypersensitive, blameful, and evasive. They are easily hurt by criticism, tend to read malevolent meaning into situations, and overgeneralize in their thinking. They tend to ruminate angrily about real or imagined injustices done to them, and may have delusions or ideas of reference. Their thinking may show tangential or loose associations, along with elements of grandiosity, at least in the form of egocentricity. These persons virtually always deny their anger (and other psychological problems), and instead attribute the anger to others, often through a rather transparent use of projection. Where they recognize their anger, it is well-rationalized and justified in their own minds.

Poor judgment, lack of insight, and impulsiveness often accompany the anger. Assault, drug abuse/addiction, and suicide attempts are all moderately frequent (and serious). Problems in interpersonal, marital, and sexual adjustment are typical. Reduced impulse control is more likely when scale K is below 50, scale 8 is within 5 T-score points of scales 4 and 6, and/or when scales 9 and 2 are also above 70.

47 and 74 Codes (Also See 247/427/274 Codes). Although anger is clearly a prominent feature with these people (both adolescents and adults), so is self-criticism and guilt. Behaviorally, their behavior typically shows a cyclical pattern. For a period they may act with little forethought or impulse control in a rather narcissistic and self-indulgent manner. During this time, they often trample unthinkingly on the wishes and feelings of others, often violating social or legal restrictions. Following their acting out episode (which typically involves sexual promiscuity and/or excessive alcohol use), they experience substantial remorse, shame, or guilt concerning the outcomes of their behaviors, perhaps even showing excessive self-pity. Though their conscience pangs may be exceedingly severe, the behavioral controls (usually an attempt at overcontrol) are temporary, and further acting out episodes are to be expected.

Underlying these behaviors, these persons appear to have substantial conflicts between dependence and independence. Despite their apparent behavioral social disregard, they are insecure and have strong needs for attention and reassurance. Many are ruminatively resentful, particularly concerning home conflicts where they often feel overly restricted or unappreciated by others. Their acting out may represent an immature expression of independence. Although characteristically these persons find rules and regulations imposed by others to be quite irritating, they are typically so concerned with their own feelings that they are markedly insensitive to the feelings and situations of others. The most common three-point codes are 478/748 and 472/742.

48 and 84 Codes (Also See 48 F, Low 2 Codes; 482/842 Codes, 486/846 Codes, 487/847 Codes and 489/849 Codes). Scales 7, 6, 2, and 9 are most often the third highest scale elevated with this code-type. For both adults and adolescents this code occurs in persons with marginal social adjustment, and who feel alienated from others. In adolescents, this code is fairly common, and reflects at least moderate and perhaps quite severe transient adjustment problems. In others it reflects a prepsychotic process. In any case, these adolescents are angry, peculiar, unhappy, show peculiar thought patterns, have ongoing interpersonal difficulties, and are impulsive in nonconforming ways. Typically they are academic underachievers, and often engage in delinquent behaviors. Anorexia, hyperkinesis, and histories of enuresis and encopresis are often present as well.

Adults and adolescents with this code-type have often experienced chaotic family lives characterized by intense home conflicts. Quite early in life, many of these persons learned to view others as untrustworthy, rejecting, hostile or dangerous, and established an enduring attitude of distrust and protective withdrawal toward the world. In addition, however, many also learn to protect themselves (and to alleviate their painful anticipations of rejection and hurt) by striking out first in anger and rebellion. Establishing a therapeutic alliance with such persons is difficult, and in therapy they are often evasive and/or deny that problems exist.

Adults with this code almost always show severe problems, usually as a major personality disorder or a psychotic process. Emotionally distant from others, these persons are peculiar in thought and action (particularly in sexual areas), show subtle communication problems, and are seen as unpredictable. Their poor social judgment, nonconformity, and impulsiveness lead to a high likelihood of acting out. Educational and occupational histories are marked by underachievement and marginal adjustment. Some of these persons become social isolates or nomads. Others involve themselves in the criminal fringes of society. Crimes committed by persons with this code (particularly if scales 6 and 9 are also elevated) are often senselessly brutal and savage, poorly planned or carried out, and involve sexual or homicidal attack. Men with this code are more likely to be involved in overtly criminal behavior. Older males may be sexual deviates. Often the acting out is conducted in ways that seem to ensure that they will get caught, and appears to be self-defeating behavior.

Women with 48/84 profiles often have had unwed pregnancies, and have histories of establishing relationships with men who are "social losers" and who often are less competent than they. These women have low self-concepts, and seem most comfortable with others who seem similarly less competent. They generally prefer to relate to others sexually, and appear to fear emotional involvement.

48 and 84 Codes with High F and Low 2.
These persons usually have become comfortable with their alienation from others, and treat others as objects. They are often aggressive, punitive, and seek to control others. If above average in intelligence, they may manipulate guilt and anxiety in others. Otherwise, their behaviors may range all the way from stern discipline to actual sadism. Some persons with this profile (particularly if K is also elevated) may enter occupations

emphasizing these characteristics, such as law enforcement, military specialties, etc. Others with his pattern are clearly diagnosable as sociopaths.

482, 842, and 824 Codes. In addition to the 48/84 descriptions given earlier, these people show depression, anxiety, tension, irritability, and generalized mental distress. Their emotions are highly variable, but generally revolve around feelings of guilt, inferiority, and hopelessness. Suicidal attempts are relatively common.

Enduring interpersonal relationships (particularly heterosexual ones) are unlikely. Often these persons are single, or have marriages filled with discord, and often have problems that revolve around sexual conflicts or difficulties. Although these persons have strong (often even exaggerated) needs for attention and affection, they are distrustful of others. Emotional involvement evokes fear, and these persons are overly sensitive to the slightest hints of emotional demands or expectancies.

486 and 846 Codes. In addition to the 48/84 characteristics, see the descriptions listed under the 468/648 code type.

489 and 849 Codes. Adding an elevated scale 9 to the 48/84 code interpretations increases the likelihood of behaviors being expressed through acting out in strange or even bizarre and unpredictable ways. This is particularly true if the *K* scale is less than 45. Often these persons show a history of repeated aggressive behaviors where others have gotten hurt. Behavioral agitation is often present, and assaultive, combative, or even frankly violent behaviors are a distinct possibility.

49 and 94 Codes. Both for adults and adolescents, this code is almost always associated with arousal seeking, self-indulgence, and a resentment of limits, rules, or regulations. Egocentric, narcissistic, and selfish, they are typically unwilling to accept responsibilities imposed on them, though they may expend significant energy to accomplish their own goals. Typically they focus much activity on seeking pleasure, excitement, and short-term goals. Social standards and values are of little importance to them, and they are likely to have markedly fluctuating values, or to construct their own values to conveniently fit themselves. The farther beyond age 20 the person is, the more enduring the pattern, and the more maladjustment is indicated.

In brief interpersonal contacts and social situations, these persons often create favorable impressions because they seem full of energy and confidence, and appear to have no insecurities or anxieties. Longer acquaintance, however, generally reveals them to be shallow and superficial in their commitments to others, and even irresponsible and untrustworthy, thus alienating others. Poor marital adjustment is likely, and many engage in extramarital relationships.

Adolescents with this code predictably have a low tolerance for frustration, repeated conflicts with their parents, truancy from school, and generally show impulsive, reckless, and provocative behaviors such as lying, cheating, or stealing. Drug and excessive alcohol use is common. These youngsters often repeatedly get into trouble legally or in social ways that damage their family's reputation.

Both for adolescents and adults, manifestly delinquent, hostile, or antisocial behavior is less likely to occur if scale K is above 50, and/or if scales 2, 5, 7, or 0 are the third highest scale above a T-score of 70. When scale 0 is below 50, the person typically will have a well-socialized veneer, although still possessing the 49/94 characteristics. Often these persons glibly manipulate others into antisocial behaviors, rather than overtly acting out the behaviors themselves. For males, scales 8, 5, and 3 are most often the third highest scale. For females, scales 8, 3, and 6 are most often the third highest.

Psychotherapy prognosis for these persons is generally quite poor, though maturity that comes with age may be helpful. Most seem to lack the ability to learn from past experiences, and lack the ability to delay gratification of their desires. Most terminate treatment early, and during treatment are generally irritable and hostile.

493 and 943 Codes.   In addition to the 49/94 features, these people are particularly self-centered and insightless concerning their stimulus value, their anger, and their effect on others. Their acting out is likely to be less frequent, and more often will be passive-aggressive and indirect. Where scale 3 is within 5 T-score points of scale 4, the characteristics of the 34/43 code-type may also be present (see 34/43 codes). Thus, some people with this code-type may store up their anger, only to unleash it in ragelike fashion, usually on a family member.

495 and 945 Codes.   The additional elevation of scale 5 is associated either with a person who is blatantly and defiantly adopting an unusual sexual orientation (usually homosexual), or more often with a person who is well-educated, broadly experienced, and whose impulsiveness and rebelliousness are thus tempered, more socialized, and better controlled. Sometimes these persons involve themselves in social causes that challenge existing traditions, particularly when scales 4 and 9 are only moderately elevated and when scale 7 is also at $T = 70$ or above. Even so, these persons dislike rules, regulations, or tight control by others, and value their autonomy and self-interests highly.

496 and 946 Codes.   These codes should raise serious concern about assaultive, destructive, and even homicidal behavior, particularly if scale 8 is also elevated. This pattern has often been noted in persons who suddenly become violent in bizarre ways, and who later indicate that they felt they were wronged or slighted. Their judgment is poor, as are their emotional controls (particularly if scale K is below 50).

498 and 948 Codes (See 489/849 Codes, and 496/946 Codes). In addition to the 49/94 features, the likelihood of strange, unusual, or even bizarre behavior is quite high. In persons over the age of 20, this code usually represents major and enduring psychopathology. In adolescents, this code is somewhat more often associated with situational difficulties and an intense adolescent rebellion, rather than incipient or overt psychosis that is more often found in older persons with this code. Nevertheless, both adults and adolescents show intense feelings of alienation from others, family conflicts, high energy levels, difficulties with authority, and rebellious behaviors.

40 and 04 Codes. This rare code most often has scales 2, 6, and 8 as the third highest scale. Persons with this code are both angry and interpersonally withdrawn. Typically they do not express their anger openly, have difficulty in being appropriately assertive, and tend to sullenly hold onto grudge feelings. Suspicious, resentful and shy, they tend to be passively resistant. Further intepretation depends on the three-point code or other configural analysis (e.g., high 4, low 5). It is often helpful to omit scale 0 in the three-point code, and to then obtain interpretations based on the remaining two-point code, subsequently adding information from the elevated scale 0.

Scale 5

High scores ($T > 70$) suggest men who are introspective, inner-directed, education-oriented, and who have a wide range of interests including aesthetic and contemplative preferences. Often these men are seen as idealistic and imaginative persons who are quite socially perceptive and interpersonally sensitive. In persons with broad educational and cultural background, these characteristics are to be expected. In some men, however, this pattern may reflect a rejection of the stereotypical masculine behaviors in favor of a relatively passive, noncompetitive style. Because scale 5 in men is strongly correlated with education, intelligence, and cultural breadth, interpretations should take this into account. This scale tends to be at least moderately elevated for well-adjusted members of various occupational groups such as social scientists, writers, artists, ministers, teachers, etc.

Elevation of scale 5 is never in itself sufficient to suggest homosexuality, either overt or latent. Homosexuals who wish to conceal their orientation can do so with relative ease on this scale. Even so, where scale 5 in males is above $T = 75$, and where education is less than 2 years of college or where there is restricted cultural exposure, these men are likely to not have a traditional masculine lifestyle. High scorers tend to be relatively passive men (particularly if scale 4 is low), and some are clearly effeminate in manner.

Females with elevated scale 5 tend to be assertive, competitive, tough-minded, and not particularly interested in appearing or behaving as other women do. Instead, they are more likely to be independent, self-confident, spontaneous, dominant, and even aggressive in thought and action. This may be expressed in pragmatic career and/or survival behaviors, in traditionally masculine sports or interest patterns, or in a dominant lesbian sexual orientation. Many of these women find it quite uncomfortable when they are in situations where they are not in control, particularly with members of the opposite sex. Among female adolescents, elevated scale 5 scores are associated with behavioral problems at home or school and/or problems with legal authorities.

Low scores ($T < 45$) are interpreted quite differently for males and females. Low scale 5 males show a traditionally masculine pattern of interests and behaviors, and often their interests are narrowed almost exclusively to those areas. They are adventurous, prefer action to contemplation, prefer outdoor activities, sports, competitive or mechanical activities, and often portray themselves as rugged and even coarse. Lower occupational achievement aspirations often accompany this pattern. In adolescent males, low scale 5 scores are associated with delinquency and school conduct problems.

Where scale 5 is extremely low ($T < 35$), these men appear to virtually have a compulsion to appear masculine, perhaps to the point of being a caricature, and repeatedly manufacture exhibitions of strength and endurance in a narcissistic fashion. Such an overconcern for demonstrating one's masculinity is usually associated with underlying self-doubts.

Low scale 5 females ($T < 40$) are generally sensitive people who are concerned about relationships, particularly with men. They tend to be nurturing and supportive, though this may also be accompanied by a submissiveness or even passivity to the desires of others. These women typically are concerned with presenting a neat, attractive, and feminine appearance in dress and demeanor, and often their interests are directed toward academic, home, or aesthetic areas. Most are attracted to sensitive men with whom they enjoy communicating. Professional and other college-educated women tend to obtain T-scores in the 40 to 50 range on this scale.

Extremely low scores ($T < 35$) on scale 5 usually reflect women who are emotionally constricted and bound by situations. They seem to need to reassure themselves of their self-worth through assuming numerous and frequent burdens, sometimes to an almost masochistic degree. If they are not sufficiently (in their own eyes) appreciated, they become filled with self-pity, and often then inspire guilt in others in a fault-finding fashion. Headaches, backaches, sexual dissatisfaction, and inability to enjoy sexual experiences are often found, and some of these women seem so caught up in a sense of duty that they are unable to allow themselves to enjoy pleasant experiences of any kind.

Relations with Other Scales

51 and 15 Codes (See 15/51 Codes).

52 and 25 Codes (See 25/52 Codes).

53 and 35 Codes (See 35/53 Codes).

54 and 45 Codes (See 45/54 Codes).

56 and 65 Codes.   Little is known about persons with this code-type. In general, they are sensitive to having their feelings hurt, and seem to be insecure and afraid of emotional involvement with others. When others place demands on them, these persons tend to become irritable. Many have high educational and career aspirations. Further information can be obtained if a third scale is elevated above $T = 70$ by temporarily disregarding scale 5, and interpreting the other two scales as though they were a two-point code (e.g., 564/654 code could be interpreted as a 46/64 code with an elevated scale 5).

57 and 75 Code.   Indecisive, worrying, introspective, tense, unhappy, and needing reassurance are terms that describe men with this code-type. Men with less than a college education are particularly likely to experience anxious or depressive episodes characterized by obsessive rumination over self-inadequacies and shortcomings. Frequently they feel inadequate in heterosexual relationships. Women rarely obtain this code, but when they do they are less aggressive and more self-analytical than would be expected just from a high scale 5 code. Even so, they are often intellectually competitive. For both sexes, the interpretations can be enhanced by considering the two-point code that results when scale 5 is omitted.

58 and 85 Codes.   Men with this code-type are quite inner-directed and spend much time in thought. Most complain of feeling confused, unhappy, alienated from others, and as having home conflicts. This interpretation should be enhanced by considering the two-point code that results when scale 5 is omitted.

59 and 95 Codes.   For males, the presence of the elevated scale 5 reduces the likelihood of overt acting out, apparently due to the increased use of intellectualization, denial, and rationalization. Indeed, most males with this code do at least reasonably well academically. Emotional dependency (particularly mother dependency), and lack of self-assertiveness are the most likely problem areas.

For females, the elevated scale 5 increases the likelihood of overt aggressiveness, though whether this aggressiveness would be expressed verbally or behaviorally will depend on other factors. These women are likely to be energetic, competitive (particularly with men), confident, unihibited, adventurous, though perhaps self-centered and irritable when their desires are thwarted or questioned.

For both sexes, further information can be derived by omitting scale 5 and examining the resulting two-point code-type information.

50 and 05 Codes. Males with this code are introverted, and generally retreat into personal or intellectual isolation rather than reaching out to others. They are cautious, inhibited, withdrawn, and anxious in contacts with others, and typically are overcontrolled and overideational. Socially they are awkward, have difficulty in being assertive, and many have doubts about their own adequacy. Difficulties and discomfort in heterosexual relationships are particularly common.

Females with this code typically are much less confident, spontaneous, vigorous, or assertive than would be ordinarily expected from the elevated scale 5. Often these women have less education or are from a working-class or rural social background.

For both sexes, further interpretation can be done by omitting scale 5, and examining the resulting two-point code.

Scale 6

High scores ($T > 80$) are virtually always persons who are suspicious, angry, broodingly resentful, and who clearly overinterpret situations as being directed at them. Most often these behaviors are clearly paranoid, with ideas of reference, projection as a primary defense mechanism, poor reality testing, and delusions of persecution and/or grandeur.

Moderately high scores (T between 70 and 80) occur in people who are clearly sensitive, both to the feelings of others as well as to getting their feelings hurt easily. Often this is associated with depression where the person takes too seriously the criticisms or remarks of others, and views criticisms of her or his ideas as criticisms of her- or himself as a person. These persons characteristically are somewhat guarded and distrustful in interpersonal relationships, as though they expect others to take advantage of them. They tend to be resentful because they see the smallest slight, and feel overly constrained or even controlled by expectations others may have of them on the job or at home.

Low scores ($T < 40$) are obtained by two widely divergent types of persons— those who lack personal sensitivity to others, and those who are so suspicious and wary that they have skillfully avoided endorsing the items on scale 6. The latter persons are essentially the same as those who score high on scale 6, though they may be somewhat brighter and more cunning. Most persons with such low scores, however, are conventional, trusting, interpersonally insensitive, naive, and gullible, and often have lower levels of intelligence and achievement.

Relations with Other Scales

61 and 16 Codes (See 16/61 Codes).

62 and 26 Codes (See 26/62 Codes).

63 and 36 Codes (See 36/62 Codes.

64 and 46 Codes (See 46/64 Codes, 462/642 Codes, 463/643 Codes, and 468/648 Codes).

65 and 56 Codes (See 56/65 Codes).

67 and 76 Codes.   This rather infrequent code most often has scales 2 or 8 as the third highest scale. Persons with this code are tense, anxious, hypersensitive, and often broodingly resentful. They often have a history of strained or disrupted interpersonal relationships where they have felt wronged (usually due to mis-interpretation on their part). Though they may feel quite inferior and/or guilty, they project these feelings onto others. When scale 6 is higher than scale 7, or even when the scores are virtually the same elevation, the possibility of de-compensation from obsessive-compulsive into a psychotic episode must be considered. For both sexes, most often scales 2 and 8 are the next highest scale.

68 and 86 Codes (Also See 468/648 Codes, 486/846 Codes, 489/849 Codes).   Most often scale 7 or 4 will be the next highest scale. Both for adolescents and adults the 68/86 code-type suggests serious psychopathology, and usually is accompanied by an elevation on the F scale, which reflects the large number of unusual experiences endorsed by the person. This is particularly so when a "paranoid valley" is present. The paranoid valley configuration occurs when scales 6 and 8 are both above $T = 70$, and both are at least 10 T-score points above scale 7. Even when several other scales are more elevated than scales 6 and 8, the possibility of paranoid schizophrenia must be considered when a paranoid valley exists.

Difficulties in thought processes are marked by overgeneralizations, mis-interpretations, and even frank delusions. Emotional inappropriateness, over-ideation, suspicion, distrust, difficulties in concentrating, poor reality contact, and disturbed interpersonal relations are present, perhaps accompanied by de-pression or fears and phobias. The thought content of these persons is almost always unusual, if not bizarre. Inner conflicts about sexuality are usually present. Typically they are socially withdrawn or isolated (most of these adults are single), and spend much time in self-absorbed fantasy. If married, their partner is likely to be emotionally deviant or alienated. Behaviorally, these people are unpredictable, particularly if scale 4 (see 468/648 codes) or scale 9 (see 689/986 codes) is also elevated.

Surprisingly, many adults with this profile show a history of being reasonably able to maintain employment, though episodes of fatigue, inefficiency, and difficulty concentrating may suddenly precede a psychotic episode that seems to occur without any clear precipitating event. Adolescents with this code often show violent tempers (particularly if scale K is below 50), have poor peer relations, spend much time in fantasy, do poorly academically, and show a family history of having received severe corporal punishment.

69 and 96 Codes (Also See 698/968 Codes).

This relatively uncommon code occurs more often among women. For both sexes scale 4 or 8 is most often the third highest scale. Persons with this code are tense, jumpy, and overreact to minor situations as though they were emergencies or dangerous personal threats to them. They tend to be loud, excitable, irritable, suspicious, and seem to have a need to continually explain (justify) why they are doing what they are doing. Family history may reveal an overly protective and affectionate mother who disciplined strictly, with a permissive but perhaps uninvolved father.

These persons seem to fear emotional involvement, and keep others at a distance. They are oversensitive to criticism, either open or implied, and seem to have a chronic mistrust. In seeming contradiction, often times many also have an exaggerated need for affection.

When these scales are elevated above $T = 80$, difficulties in thinking and concentrating occur, accompanied by perplexity and irritability. A grandiose, suspicious manic like panic may result, which can be accompanied by violence. This is even more likely if scale 8 is also elevated.

698 and 968 Codes.

In addition to the descriptions for persons with 69/96 codes, these persons are particularly likely to show mental perplexity, confusion, and difficulties in thinking and concentrating. Tangential or loose associations are common, as are delusions, paranoid suspiciousness, and hallucinations. Where scale 8 is within 5 T-score points of scale 6, see also 68/86 codes.

60 and 06 Codes.

This code is extremely rare for males, and uncommon for females. For females, it is more common in persons older than 30, and most frequently is associated with scale 2 or 4 as the third highest scale. Though little is known about this two-point code, persons obtaining it appear to be shy, withdrawn, socially uncomfortable, and tend to expect that others will not like or accept them. They are particularly sensitive to criticism, and appear to anticipate rejection because they already feel inferior (often regarding physical attractiveness). Generally these people are highly conforming and overcontrolled in their emotions.

Scale 7

High scores ($T > 70$) are obtained by persons who are tense, anxious, introspective, and who tend to be evaluative of themselves and others to such a degree that it leaves them with feelings of insecurity, inadequacy, inferiority, or guilt. Typically they are lacking in self-confidence, are indecisive, and uncomfortable with feelings. With higher scale 7 scores, the person is increasingly likely to be rigid, moralistic, perfectionistic, and to show obsessive or compulsive patterns.

Low scores ($T < 45$) are usually relaxed, comfortable, and without emotional distress. Most are self-confident and adaptable, and generally are efficient and capable, although others may see the person as unmotivated or lazy due to the lack of overt anxiety.

Relations with Other Scales

71 and 17 Codes (See 17/71 Codes).

72 and 27 Codes (See 27/72 Codes).

73 and 73 Codes (See 37/73 Codes).

74 and 47 Codes (See 47/74 Codes).

75 and 57 Codes (See 57/75 Codes).

76 and 67 Codes (See 67/76 Codes).

78 and 87 Codes.   This code is a frequent one among persons seeking psychological help, and scales 2 and 4 are most often the next highest scale. (See 278/728 and 478/748 when scale 2 or 4 is within 5 T-score points of scale 8). Persons with 78 and 87 codes are evenly divided between psychotic and neurotic diagnoses. In adults, when scale 8 is higher than scale 7, the likelihood of acute psychosis (particularly schizophrenia) is greater. This is apparently not true for adolescents where 78 codes appear to be as serious as 87 codes.

Persons with this code are filled with worry, anxiety, tension, and excessive rumination. They are unable to think or concentrate efficiently, and their distress is so great that insomnia and suicidal thoughts are quite likely. Suicidal potential should be carefully evaluated. When scale 8 is higher than scale 7, suicide attempts are often bizarre and involve self-mutilation. About half of persons with this code show hallucinations or delusions, flat affect, and clear difficulties in maintaining reality contact. The remainder show notable impairment of functioning, though not psychotic behaviors.

Lacking in confidence, they are shy and feel inadequate, particularly where heterosexual relations are concerned. Poor sexual performance often occurs due to the excessive anxiety. Though typically conscientious, their fears and excessive worry often lead them to have only mediocre or poor achievement. Many such persons drink excessively in order to relax.

79 and 97 Codes.   This relatively uncommon code most often has scale 8 or 4 as the next highest in the profile. These persons are anxious to the point of agitation. They are fearful, continually worried, overreact to events, and find it difficult to relax or to rid themselves of their almost constant rumination about their fears and inadequacies. Muscle spasms, backaches, and insomnia may also be present. Depression is usually present, particularly if scale 2 is also elevated, though some persons instead show an apparent manic pattern that may require pharmacological intervention. Adolescents with this code appear to have strong needs for attention, but fear losing control over themselves should they let go. Dependence-independence conflicts appear to be involved for these teenagers.

70 and 07 Codes.   An uncommon code, scales 2 and 8 are most often the third highest scale. Males with this code are shy, worried, tense, and feel inadequate regarding social skills and/or physical appearance. Many are introverted to the point of almost being nonverbal. Their lack of confidence and indecisiveness leaves them feeling confused, overcontrolled, and blaming themselves. Their ruminations result in insomnia. Many have strong home conflicts centering around assertiveness or dependence-independence issues particularly with their mothers.

Females with this code show the same pattern as for men only if scale 5 is below $T = 40$. Otherwise their problems are less severe, but nonetheless center around issues of lack of confidence, self-consciousness, feelings of physical unattractiveness or inferiority, social insecurity, and difficulties in establishing comfortable relations with members of the opposite sex.

Scale 8

Extremely high scores $(T > 80)$ are obtained by persons who clearly feel alienated and who are having difficulty in thinking clearly. They are unconventional in thought and action, perhaps even socially deviant, and are reluctant to become deeply involved in interpersonal relationships. They have basic and disturbing concerns about who they are and where they fit in the world, and basically feel that they do not belong. Many feel that they lack some fundamental part of humanness that others have that allows them to be so comfortable relating to others. Difficulties in communicating clearly are likely, and are due to their preoccupation with their own concerns and their intrusive or disorganized thoughts that interfere with clear and logical thinking. Although these people may give the appearance of being in reasonable reality contact, their conversations often have a quality of being just slightly off the mark.

Scale 8 scores above $T = 95$ more often reflect acute situational stress or severe identity crisis, instead of suggesting the more chronic thought disturbances (such as in schizophrenia) indicated by scores in the $T = 75$ to 95 range. The indecision and mental confusion in cases with such markedly elevated scale 8 is often dramatic, and requires providing clear structure and support for the person to reduce the confusion being experienced.

High scores ($T > 70$) indicate persons who feel somewhat cut-off and distant from others, and who feel uncomfortable with many interpersonal relationships. Often their thinking is unconventional, focused on abstract or theoretical issues (such as the "meaning" of some aspect of life), and contains elements of dissatisfaction with themselves, others and/or societal order.

Low scores ($T < 45$) are obtained by persons who are generally practical, conventional, and conservative in their behaviors and in their approach to life. Usually these persons are conforming (perhaps overly compliant to authority), responsible, dependable and cautious, but also may be unimaginative or even rigid.

Relations with Other Scales

81 and 18 Codes (See 18/81 Codes).

82 and 28 Codes (See 28/82 Codes).

83 and 38 Codes (See 38/83 Codes).

84 and 48 Codes (See 48/84 Codes).

85 and 58 Codes (See 58/85 Codes).

86 and 68 Codes (See 68/86 Codes).

87 and 78 Codes (See 78/87 Codes).

89 and 98 Codes.   This code type is associated with serious psychopathology for adolescents and particularly for adults (especially if scale F is also elevated). These persons are highly overideational, and spend a great deal of time in fantasy, daydreams, and rumination. Tension, agitation, and insomnia may be present. Increased speech, behavioral restlessness, emotional lability, and flight of ideas are likely. In interpersonal situations, such as therapy sessions, they are highly distractable, jumping from topic to topic. Therapeutic focusing is thus hindered because these persons seldom stay on a topic long enough to come to grips with it.

Discomfort in interpersonal relationships is typical, most often involving those of the opposite sex. Poor heterosexual adjustment is likely. Most of these persons are fearful of, and avoid, close interpersonal relationships, and distrust others' motives. Often these persons also show a history of high achievement aspirations, but mediocre achievement. They are particularly likely to become disorganized under stress. As this code becomes more elevated, the likelihood increases that delusions and hallucinations (particularly of a religious nature) will occur, and that a frankly psychotic picture will emerge. This code occurs more frequently in persons younger than age 27, and most often scale 4, 7, or 6 is the next highest scale.

80 and 08 Codes.   Scales 7 and 2 are most often the third highest scale elevations in this code-type. Markedly aloof and socially withdrawn, these persons are very uncomfortable in interpersonal relationships and avoid social interaction. They prefer to spend time in personal fantasy. Their social isolation tends to be so great that they often are alienated even from their own families. Typically they also feel worried, indecisive, anxious, depressed, and may feel misunderstood by others. They often feel confused about what is bothering them or what they want (or expect) from others, and are not only lacking in assertiveness with others but also with themselves. In counseling sessions they are likely to be largely nonverbal.

Scale 9

High scores ($T > 75$) are obtained by persons who are energetic, expansive, emotionally excitable, and who have high levels of both psychic energy and physical energy. Many of these people have an unusual capacity for sustained activity and effort, although as the scores go beyond $T = 80$ the efforts more often become fragmented and scattered, rather than organized. Along with their excess of energy, these people frequently take on more projects than they can complete. Generally they seem quite happy when they are so busy (sometimes euphoric), and may become depressed when their activities are constrained (particularly if scale 2 is below $T = 45$). In some persons, however, the energy is expressed more as tension, hyperactivity, self-centeredness, and irritability. In the extreme, these persons show clear verbosity, grandiosity, and difficulties in controlling or inhibiting their thoughts from becoming actions. This may represent efforts to ward off an impending depression.

Moderately high scores (T between 60 and 75) suggest an energetic, outgoing, and active person who likely is seen by others as pleasant and efficient. Scores in this range are typical for college or postgraduate students, because the energy level reflected in these scale scores is more commonly found among younger persons with high aspirations. Persons with scores in this range usually focus on their achievements to gain recognition and status, and tend to be rather independent in thought and action.

Low scores ($T < 45$) suggest a low energy level, lack of drive, listlessness, or even apathy. Although this may simply reflect temporary fatigue or illness, more often these low scores indicate a person who more chronically has low energy. Often these persons are lacking in self-confidence and have reduced goals for themselves. Many find it difficult to get out of bed in the morning or to expend extra effort on virtually any project. A very low score on scale 9 ($T < 40$) suggests notable depression even when scale 2 is not markedly elevated. It should be noted, however, that low scale 9 scores increase as persons get older, apparently reflecting normal aging processes. A low scale 9 in a person younger than age 45 is unusual, and should receive extra attention.

Relations with Other Scales

High 9, High K Code. When scale 9 and scale K are both above $T = 70$ (and particularly if scale 2 is below $T = 50$), these persons tend to be energetic, organized, managerial types, whose planning and organization prompt others to defer authority to them. Often these persons are excellent administrators, although some tend to be particularly autocratic or power-oriented such that ambiguity, indecision or uncertainty are virtually intolerable for them. These persons feel uncomfortable when they are not in control or in situations where they feel uninformed or where there is a lack of structure.

Many of these persons are highly competitive personalities. As scale K increases above $T = 70$, the likelihood increases that they feel driven to organize their lives and those around them, and that to appear dependent, submissive, emotional, or out of control of situations would be extremely threatening and uncomfortable for them. Many of these persons reassure themselves by overcontrol of others to such an extent that they require others to remain openly submissive and "in their place." Thus, fundamentally, these persons are basically insecure, and cling tenaciously to roles and appearances. In women, one may additionally see an almost exhibitionistic emphasis on physical attractiveness (particularly if scale 5 is below $T = 40$) as an attempt at self-reassurance and control over others.

91 and 19 Codes (See 19/91 Codes).

92 and 29 Codes (See 29/92 Codes).

93 and 39 Codes (See 39/93 Codes).

94 and 49 Codes (See 49/94 Codes).

95 and 59 Codes (See 59/95 Codes).

96 and 69 Codes (See 69/96 Codes).

97 and 79 Codes (See 79/97 Codes).

98 and 89 Codes (See 89/98 Codes).

90 and 09 Codes.   This code is rare, particularly among males, and little is known about it. Persons with this code, although likely to be energetic and perhaps even agitated, are also likely to be shy and withdrawn, perhaps even generally being loners. Often it is helpful with this code to initially ignore the elevated scale 0, and to examine the next two most elevated scales that comprise a two-point code, then using the elevated scale 0 to modify the interpretation as necessary.

Scale 0

High scores ($T > 70$) reflect one's preference for being alone rather than with others. Mild elevations may simply indicate a temperament style of being self-contained, autonomous, or even self-actualized (particularly if no other scale is elevated above $T = 70$), and can be quite adaptive in situations (e.g., college) requiring sustained periods of solitary activities. On the other hand, however, elevated scores (particularly above $T = 75$) suggest a person who is shy, interpersonally uncomfortable, insecure, introverted, and submissive. These characteristics are particularly striking with adolescents as they more often score low on scale 0. Scores above $T = 75$ generally suggest an absence of social supports, perhaps even an aloofness to a schizoid degree, and an enduring problem in establishing meaningful attachments with others. Elevations of scale 0 tend to reduce the likelihood of acting out indicated by other scale elevations (e.g., scales 4 and 9), but may indicate an increase in ruminations or self-absorption indicated by scales such as 2, 7, or 8.

Low scores ($T < 45$) are obtained by persons who generally prefer to be with others and not by themselves. Most often they are outgoing, gregarious, friendly, enthusiastic, and have strong needs for affiliation, social recognition, and status. Where the scores are below $T = 30$, their social aggressivness may prompt others to view them as opportunistic, manipulative, shallow, superficial, and even flighty. Impulse control problems may be present, although more often a low scale 0 suggests that the person may have socially acceptable outlets for behaviors that otherwise might be pathological.

Relations with Other Scales

01 and 10 Codes (See 10/01 Codes).

02 and 20 Codes (See 20/02 Codes).

03 and 30 Codes (See 30/03 Codes).

04 and 40 Codes (See 40/04 Codes).

05 and 50 Codes (See 50/05 Codes).

06 and 60 Codes (See 60/06 Codes).

07 and 70 Codes (See 70/07 Codes).

08 and 80 Codes (See 80/08 Codes).

09 and 90 Codes (See 90/09 Codes).

Normal Code, High K (K + Profile of Marks et al., 1974)

In clinical settings, when scale K is above $T=65$, and no clinical scale is above $T=70$, the following additional criteria must also be met. Scale F must be below $T=60$, scales L and K must be greater than scale F, six or more of the clinical scales must be below $T=60$, and K minus F must be equal to or greater than five T-score points.

This profile is often produced by persons who are highly defensive about admitting psychological problems, which they view as personal weaknesses. Usually they will avoid situations where their own performance might be compared unfavorably to others, and are generally cautious, anxious, or even inhibited. They are particularly influenced by others' evaluations of them, and as a result, are easily dominated, led, or controlled. Withdrawn from others, they are often seen as suspicious and fearful with a strong schizoid component to their personality.

7

Interpretation and Report Writing

Although preparing a written report is an important part of many psychologists' work, it is a procedure that has typically received insufficient emphasis, has been little researched, perceived as tedious to do, and often poorly done (Ownby, 1987). Although many factors account for this unfortunate situation, it is the initial learning experience with a test that often sets the stage for later difficulties in writing a test report.

Initially, most MMPI users have difficulty in integrating the vast array of data available from the MMPI. At times it can be daunting. Demographic and referral question variables are the backdrop against which 10 clinical and 4 validity scales covary across a wide possible range of T-scores. If special and research scales are added to the equation, often yielding information that appears contradictory or confusing, then it is little wonder that integrating the information in order to write an MMPI report is seen as a complex and tedious task.

This chapter is written with two purposes. First, a step-by-step elaboration of the approach to interpretation listed in chapter 4 is described, with strategies outlined for complex profiles. Second, some common pitfalls of report writing are discussed along with suggested remedies.

RECOGNIZING A CODE-TYPE

Before one has mastered the MMPI, it might seem difficult to recognize a code-type. Typically, however, the profile is easily recognizable. In other words one, two, three, or four of the clinical scales are clearly elevated above the rest, and are at more or less the same level above a T-score of 70. In this case, turn to chapter 7 and read the descriptors associated with a spike, two-, three-, or four-point code-type.

The more distinctive the code-type, the greater the confidence the clinician will have about the validity of the descriptive statements. Moreover, the higher the scales, the more confidence the clinician can have that the descriptive statements are both true and salient. Over the past 4 decades of MMPI use, a number of commonly occurring specific scale configurations have been described and have become part of the MMPI lexicon. These commonly occurring patterns (also described in chapter 4) are summarized here.

1. The Conversion "V" (See Fig. 7.1). The reader is reminded that the conversion V occurs when scales 1 and 3 are greater than scale 2 by 10 T-score points or more, and where 1 and 3 are at least T-score=70. In the classic conversion V, other scales may be elevated, but not as high as 1 and 3. The conversion V is a distinctive pattern with notable personality features.

2. The "Paranoid Valley" (See Fig. 7.2). This occurs when scales 6 and 8 are greater than scale 7 by 10 or more T-score points, and where 6 and 8 are equal to or above T-scores of 70.

3. "Spike 4" (See Fig. 7.3). Scale 4 over 70, and higher than all other scales by at least 10 T-score points.

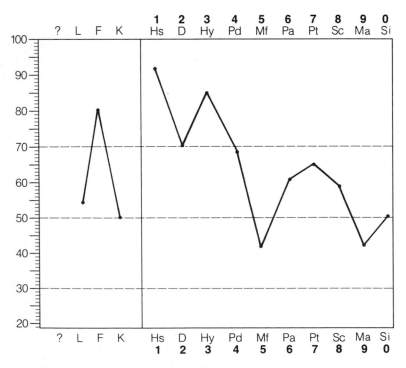

FIG. 7.1.   Conversion "V" or psychosomatic "V".

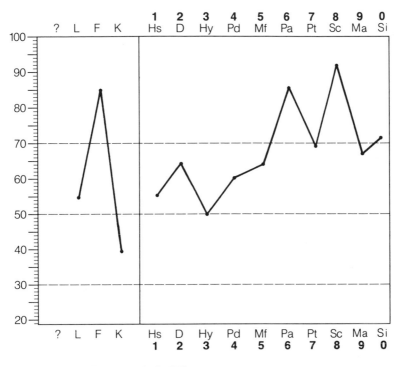

FIG. 7.2.   Paranoid valley or psychotic "V".

4. The "Gull Wing" Profile in Females (See Fig. 7.4). This occurs when the neurotic scales and scale 4 are all elevated; that is, scales 1, 2, 3, and 4, are all elevated at or over $T = 70$ and scale 5 in females is below $T = 50$. All the other scales on the psychotic side (i.e., scales 6, 7, 8, and 9) of the profile are also elevated at or above a T-score of 70. The shape of the profile looks like a gull wing; there are distinct symptoms, personality features, and traits associated with this profile.

5. The "Passive-Aggressive V" in Females (See Fig. 7.5). This occurs when scales 4 and 6 are elevated at or above $T = 70$ and scale 5 is below $T = 50$. Even though the other scales may also be elevated near or above a T-score of 70 with this particular configuration, the profile is often that of a passive-aggressive personality disorder. Due to its shape, it is often called the passive-aggressive "V." The lower scale 5 is, the more passively self-defeating is the female.

6.–7. The "Psychotic vs. Neurotic Slope" (see Figs. 7.6 and 7.7). A vertical line through scale 5 would divide the MMPI profile roughly between the neurotic left side of the profile and the psychotic right-hand side of the profile. A positive slope occurs when the psychotic scales are elevated above 70 and the neurotic scales are below 70. It is called a positive slope because a straight line drawn

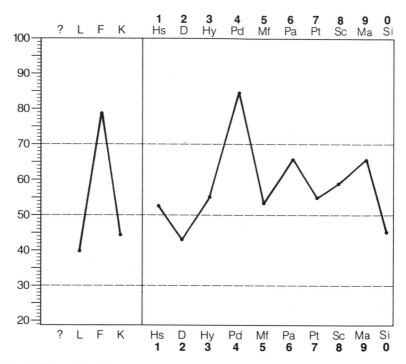

FIG. 7.3. "Spike 4" profile.

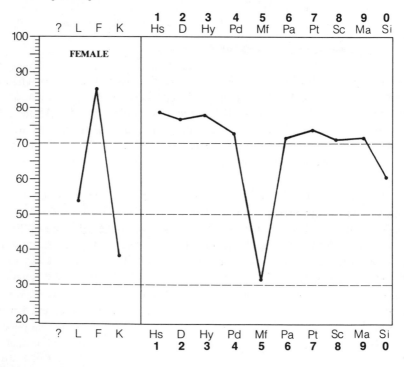

FIG. 7.4. "Gull-wing" profile.

202

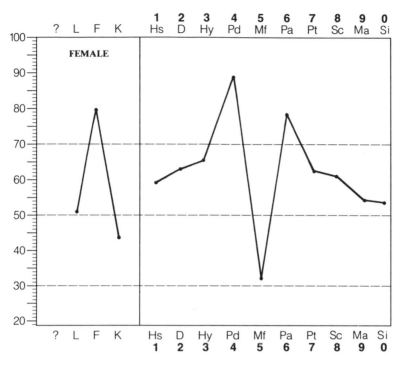

FIG. 7.5.   Passive-aggressive "V".

from the most elevated to the least elevated scales would be positive. This predicts a psychotic adjustment. A negative slope occurs when the left or neurotic side of the profile is elevated and the psychotic scales are relatively low. This generally predicts a neurotic adjustment.

No clinician, however, should assume that a profile indicates a psychotic adjustment only by the slope of the profile. The neurotic vs. psychotic slope concept is useful only as a starting point in a diagnostic decision process that asks the question, "Am I looking at a neurotic or a psychotic profile?" Determining psychotic vs. neurotic adjustment definitively is then accomplished by referring to the scale elevations, scale configurations, Goldberg Index, and the critical items, all being viewed within the context of the person's behavior and history.

8. The $K+$ Profile (See Fig. 7.8). In this configuration, no clinical scales are above a T-score of 70, and 6 or more clinical scales are below or equal to a T-score of 60. In the $K+$ profile, K and L are greater than F. Scale K is also higher than F by at least 5 T-score points, and is above a T-score of 60.

The $K+$ profile was identified by Marks et al. (1974) in an inpatient psychotic population only. In other words, this profile occurred in patients who were a false negative (test miss). The inpatient responder had gone through a minefield

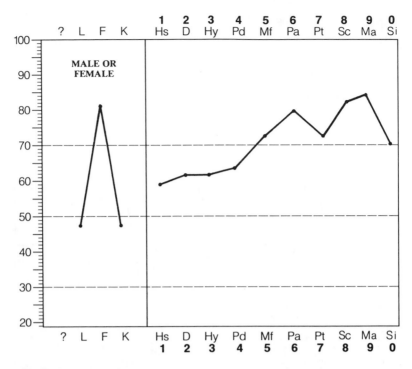

FIG. 7.6. Positive or psychotic slope.

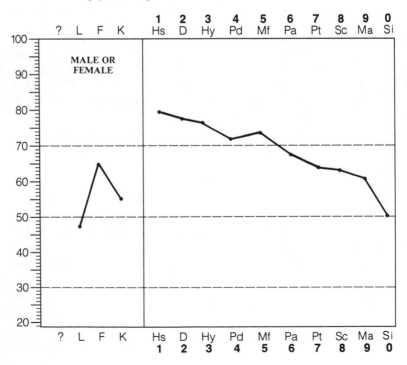

FIG. 7.7. Negative or neurotic slope.

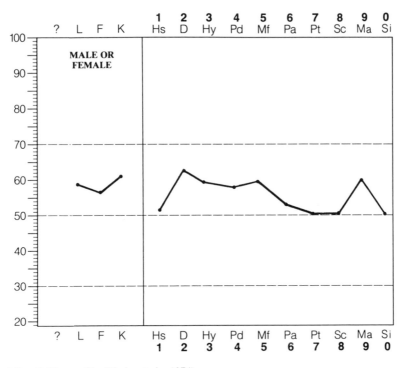

FIG. 7.8.   K Plus profile (Marks et al., 1974).

of test items, and somehow managed to survive without raising a red flag on any of the clinical scales. In an inpatient setting, Marks et al. (1974) found that 48% of these responders were psychotic. Thus, if a *K*+ profile is obtained by a person in an inpatient setting, describe the client's failure to report psychological pain and raise the distinct likelihood of a denial of problems. Integrate this information with what you know about the patient's history, behavioral observations, or other psychological test data. A possible way of dealing with the problem of a *K*+ profile is to ask the client to retake the test, answering the test from the perspective of how they feel at their worst. Psychologists are urged to remember that the *K*+ profile occurs in many different settings and in both sexes. The correlates were derived specifically within psychiatric inpatient settings, thus caution should be used in applying these correlates to populations other than psychiatric inpatients (Duckworth & Barley, 1988).

9. The "Floating" Profile (See Fig. 7.9). In this profile all scores on Scales 1 through 9 equal or exceed a *T*-score of 70 and are usually accompanied by an extreme elevation on scale F (Newmark, Chassin, Evans, & Gentry, 1984). Variability in configurations occur with this type of profile and no specific code-type is typically associated with it. It is likely that a significant portion of

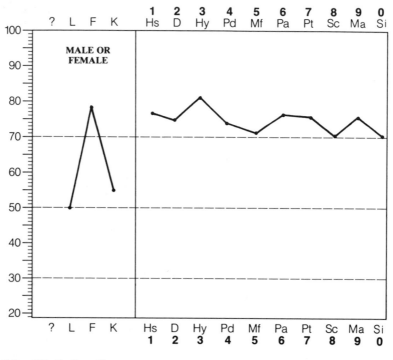

FIG. 7.9. "Floating" profile.

"floating" profiles are obtained by patients with borderline personality disorders as these patients tend to produce highly elevated profiles.

STRATEGIES FOR INTERPRETING PROFILES

Code-Type and Elevation

The code-type (e.g., 27, 49, etc.) defines a particular behavior, symptom, and experiential domain irrespective of elevation. For example, people scoring their highest scores on scales 4 and 9 will generally be alienated from society, impulsive, superficially charming but with a poor frustration tolerance. These characteristics will be fundamentally consistent across profile elevations, whether between T-scores 80 and 90, T-scores of 70 to 80, and even for T-score elevations 60–70. In other words, the symptom picture is basically similar for all 49s. However, the elevation of a profile predicts the intensity and severity of the symptom picture. The higher the profile, the more of a person's thoughts, feelings, and behaviors are likely to be dominated by the symptom picture predicted by a particular code-type.

Elevations between 60 and 70 T-scores predict a personality style rather than a symptom picture. For example, a 27 code above $T=80$ is quite likely to reflect a person who is experiencing a severe, agitated depression that thoroughly permeates daily life. Another person with a 27 profile at a T-score of 70 will likely show periods of despondency, agitation, and depression, followed by periods of feeling less depressed and anxious, or even without depression. Persons with a T-score elevation at 60 to 65 on scales 2 and 7 will generally show good adjustment with only occasional periods of agitation, anxiety and down moods. Their personality style will likely be that of a "prone to worry," responsible person.

In each case, the general symptoms are the same, although the elevation predicts their intensity, duration, and pervasiveness. A rule of thumb suggested by the authors for the description of a disorder as mild, marked, or severe, is as follows: a profile elevation between 70 and 75 predicts a mild disturbance, profiles between 76 and 90 predict a marked disturbance, and profiles over 90 predict a severe disturbance. When a profile is severely elevated above a T-score of 90, a code-type may be less important than just the elevation. For example, for someone who obtains a T-score of 100 on scale 2, a prediction of depression with all the classic symptoms of depression will fit regardless of whether the code-type is a 27, 29, or a 28. However, elevations on the other scales help greatly in defining the kind of depression (e.g., anxious depression—27/72, agitated depression—29/92, psychotic depression—28/82, etc.).

Interpretations in the normal range of 60 to 70 rely less on the elevation of any particular scale, but much more on the basis of code-type. For example, a 27 profile at T-score of 60 will predict a person who is prone to worry, experience anxiety over responsibility, be seen as responsible, and cautious about taking risks; however, a diagnosis of depression is unlikely. In other words, profiles in the normal range can be understood as identifying personality traits rather than psychopathology.

The caution of Duckworth and Barley (1988), however, is noteworthy. Although within normal limits profiles may often correctly identify a healthy person, such profiles can often generate false-negatives (i.e., overlook pathology), particularly within the following populations: (a) psychiatric inpatients where K is greater than $T = 70$; (b) adolescent inpatients; (c) prison populations, and (d) subjects with observed psychopathology, but who lack insight or accurate self-appraisal. As a result, profiles of persons in psychiatric settings often need to be exaggerated or overinterpreted, especially if the validity scales suggest a defensive response set. For example, a profile with scales 9 and 6 both elevated at a T-score of 65, with K and L near a T-score of 60, could be interpreted as indicating a controlled, rigid, tense, and brittle person who might become quite hostile, agitated, and even paranoid under stress. Butcher (1984) suggested that if all clinical scales are between T-scores of 60 to 64, content scales are better sources of personality descriptions than are the clinical scales.

STEP 1—ORGANIZING AND BEGINNING THE REPORT

In beginning to use the MMPI, most clinicians have difficulty integrating the personality descriptors into a consistent report. A common error is to list all the adjectives associated with elevations either on the single scales or the other recognizable code-types. Reports written in this manner present a string of disconnected adjectives and behaviors that often confuse the reader.

When writing a report, begin by summarizing the essence of the profile. The first step in interpretation is to understand what a profile is essentially about. Is it a situational, neurotic, psychotic, or character disorder profile? With what symptoms will the client present? Which symptoms or behaviors will be "glaring"? (For example, a profile with the highest elevation on scale 9 at a T-score of 90 will predict mania. The symptoms will likely be obvious.) Is this a profile that indicates primarily a depression? If so, what kind of depression? On the other hand, is it a profile of an acting-out, rebellious, angry person? If so, what kind of acting-out behaviors are suggested—sexual, passive-aggressive, self-defeating, etc.? Is it a profile of a confused paranoid person? If so, is it a transitory psychotic disturbance or a long-standing one? How will the person's conflicts or personality characteristics likely manifest themselves in various situations, such as on the job, with family, etc.? What is it about the person's characteristics that prevents that person from simply achieving a resolution of the problems?

The following section is meant as a guide to beginning a report, often the most difficult aspect for beginners. The statements are designed as "report openers" to set the stage for the rest of the descriptors. The first paragraph after the validity issues should generally describe the respondent's primary symptoms and complaints, or most central conflict. This approach likely ensures the report will validate or disconfirm the referring colleague's initial clinical impressions of their client, and sets the tone for the following sections. The following descriptions/symptoms have been written as though the profile was at least mildly elevated ($T \geq 70$). Modifications in some of the language would be needed if the profiles were more or less elevated, even though the basic characteristics would remain the same.

Guidelines for Beginning a Report

Scale		*Descriptors/Symptoms*
Scale 1 elevated above a T- score of 70, all other scales below Hs. (Spike 1)	1.	Fearful
	2.	Clinging
	3.	Immature
	4.	Passive
	5.	Psychologically unsophisticated
	6.	Somatizing

Scale	*Descriptors/Symptoms*

Report Opener:

"This is essentially a profile of a (severe, 91 plus;/ marked 76–90;/ mild 70–75 plus) somatizing disorder in a clinging, immature and passive individual with low psychological sophistication. Other symptoms often associated with the profile are: (list symptoms)."

Scale 1 highest; scale 2 added (12 profile)	1. Despondent
	2. Dependent
	3. Sad
	4. Passive
	5. Moody

Report Opener:

"Persons with profiles like this typically show a (severe/marked/mild) somatizing disorder in a depressed, dependent, and passive manner. This person will likely also show other symptoms such as: (list symptoms)."

Scale 1 highest; scale 3 added (13 code-type)	1. Hysterical/Somatizing
	2. Overcontrolled
	3. Psychologically naive
	4. Dependent

Report Opener:

"Profiles like this generally reflect a (severe/marked/mild) somatizing disorder in a neurotic, overcontrolled, psychologically naive, and dependent personality. Other symptoms frequently associated with this profile are: (list symptoms)."

Scale 1 highest; scale 4 added (14 code-type)	1. Dependent
	2. Manipulative
	3. Immature
	4. Impulsive
	5. Passive-aggressive

Report Opener:

"This person is quite likely to show a (severe/marked/mild) disorder in a somatizing, dependent, manipulative, immature, passive-aggressive manner. Other symptoms often associated with the profile are: (list symptoms)."

Scale 1 highest; scale 6 added (16 code-type)	1. Paranoid
	2. Suspicious
	3. Angry
	4. Blaming

Report Opener:

"This is essentially a (severe/marked/mild) somatizing disorder in a paranoid, suspicious, angry, and blaming individual. Such persons typically show other symptoms such as: (list symptoms)."

Scale 1 highest; scale 7 added (17 profile)	1. Anxious
	2. Tense
	3. Responsible
	4. Worried
	5. Obsessive/compulsive

Report Opener:

"The profile pattern indicates a (severe/marked/mild) somatizing disorder in an anxious, tense, worried, obsessive/compulsive individual. Other symptoms typically associated with such profiles are: (list symptoms)."

Guidelines for Beginning a Report (*Continued*)

Scale	*Descriptors/Symptoms*
Scale 1 highest; scale 8 added (18 code-type)	1. Confused 2. Schizoid 3. Immature 4. Alienated 5. Possibly psychotic

Report Opener:

"A (severe/marked/mild) somatizing disorder is likely to be present in a confused, immature, alienated, and schizoid personality. This person will likely show additional difficulties and symptoms such as: (list symptoms)."

Scale 1 highest; scale 9 added (19 profile)	1. Tense 2. Driven 3. Explosive

Report Opener:

"This profile pattern is one that occurs in (severe/marked/mild) somatizing disorders in persons who have a tense, driven and explosive personality. Other symptoms often associated with such profiles are: (list symptoms)."

Scale 2 highest above a *T*-score of 70, all other scales below *D* (Spike 2)	1. Vegetative symptoms, poor sleep, low sex drive, low energy. 2. Guilt 3. Anxiety 4. Low self-esteem

Report Opener:

"This is essentially a depression profile that is of (severe/marked/mild) proportions. Such persons most often also show symptoms of: (list symptoms)."

Scale 2 highest and over 70; scale 1 over 70 in second place (21 code-type)	1. Somatic symptoms 2. Anxiety 3. Low psychological mindedness 4. Immaturity 5. Dependency

Report Opener:

"This person appears to be experiencing depression combined with anxiety and somatic concerns. The profile suggests these problems are of (severe/marked/mild) proportions. Other symptoms typically associated with the profile are: (list symptoms)."

Scale 2 highest and over 70; scale 3 over 70 in second place (23 profile)	1. Somatic symptoms 2. Low psychological mindedness 3. Immaturity 4. Secondary gains 5. Self-sacrificing to gain emotional support

Report Opener:

"This is essentially a (severe/marked/mild) depression profile in a dependent, somatizing, self-sacrificing and immature individual. Typically such persons show other symptoms often associated with this profile such as: (list symptoms)."

210

Scale		Descriptors/Symptoms
Scale 2 highest and over 70; scale 4 over 70 in second place (24 code-type)	1. 2. 3. 4. 5.	Angry Self-defeating Suicidal Dependent Manipulative

Report Opener:

"This MMPI profile indicates a (severe/marked/mild) depression profile in an angry, self-defeating, dependent, and possibly suicidal, individual. Other symptoms often associated with the profile are: (list symptoms)."

Scale 2 highest and over 70; scale 5 over 70 (high in males, low in females) in second place (25 code-type)	1. 2.	Passive Dependent

Report Opener:

"A (severe/marked/mild) depression appears to be present in a passive, sensitive, creative individual. Other symptoms also likely are: (list symptoms)."

Scale 2 highest and over 70; scale 6 over 70 in second place (26 code-type)	1. 2. 3. 4. 5.	Bitter Blaming Paranoid Trapped Resentful

Report Opener:

"This person appears to be experiencing a (severe/marked/mild) depression, and is bitter, paranoid, and blaming. Persons such as this are additionally characterized as: (list symptoms)."

Scale 2 highest and over 70; Scale 8 over 70 in second place (28 code-type)	1. 2. 3. 4. 5.	Alienated Confused Withdrawn Schizoid Thought disturbance

Report Opener:

"Depression of (severe/marked/mild) proportions in a withdrawn, confused, schizoid individual is indicated by this profile. Other behaviors likely to be seen are: (list symptoms)."

Scale 2 highest and over 70; scale 9 over 70 in second place (29 code-type)	1. 2. 3. 4.	High-strung Explosive Driven Irritable

Report Opener:

"This person is essentially depressed to a (severe/marked/mild) degree, but is also a high-strung, driven, explosive and irritable individual. This pattern is likely to be expressed in behaviors such as: (list symptoms)."

Scale 3 above 70; all other scales under 70 (spike 3)	1. 2. 3. 4. 5.	Immature Psychologically naive Dependent Somatizing Obtaining secondary gains

Guidelines for Beginning a Report (*Continued*)

Scale	*Descriptors/Symptoms*

Report Opener:

"This is essentially a (severe/marked/mild) somatizing disorder in an immature, psychologically naive, dependent person. Other symptoms often associated with this pattern are: (list symptoms)."

Scale 3 highest and over 70; scale 1 over 70 in second place (31)	1. Somatizing
	2. Complaining
	3. Dependent
	4. Denying
	5. Secondary gains from illnesses or pain

Report Opener:

"This profile is of a person with a (severe/marked/mild) somatizing disorder, and who is immature, psychologically naive, dependent, and denying. Considerable secondary gains from physical symptoms are likely, along with masked depressive symptomatology. Other symptoms often associated with such profiles are: (list symptoms)."

Scale 3 highest and over 70; scale 4 over 70 in second place (34)	1. Overcontrolled
	2. Explosive
	3. Manipulative
	4. Role Playing

Report Opener:

"This is essentially a (severe/marked/mild) overcontrolled personality disorder profile from a person who is likely to present as conforming and cooperative, but will exhibit episodic, explosive, and impulsive behaviors. Other symptoms often associated with this profile are: (list symptoms)."

Scale 3 highest and over 70; scale 6 over 70 in second place (36)	1. Paranoid
	2. Controlled
	3. Conforming
	4. Projecting
	5. Denying

Report Opener:

"This profile is a (severe/marked/mild) one, and this person will likely show a paranoid pattern. Such persons are additionally typically over-controlled, inhibited, denying, and conforming individuals. Other symptoms often associated with this profile are: (list symptoms)".

Scale 3 highest over 70; scale 7 over 70 in second place (37)	1. Over-controlled
	2. Tense
	3. Anxious
	4. Passive
	5. Ingratiating
	6. Somatizing

Report Opener:

"This is essentially a (severe/marked/mild) profile of a denying, psychologically naive, anxious, and ingratiating individual, who is likely to develop hysterical symptomatology in response to psychological stress. Related characteristics often associated with this profile are: (list symptoms)."

212

Scale	Descriptors/Symptoms
Scale 3 highest over 70; scale 8 over 70 and in second place (38)	1. Confused 2. Sexually preoccupied 3. Possible hallucinations 4. Dissociative episodes

Report Opener:

"This is essentially an hysterical profile with psychotic features of mild, marked, or severe proportions. The patient is (very likely to/probably will/may) present as confused, sexually preoccupied, dissociative, and possibly experiencing psychotic episodes. Other symptoms often associated with this profile are: (list symptoms)."

Scale	Descriptors/Symptoms
Scale 3 highest over 70; scale 9 over 70 and in second place (39)	1. Overcontrolled 2. Explosive 3. Demanding 4. Manic 5. Approval seeking

Report Opener:

"This person appears to be overcontrolled, highly energized, and approval seeking to a (severe/marked/mild) degree. Such individuals are likely to exhibit explosive episodes whenever their goal-directed behavior is blocked. Other symptoms frequently associated with this profile are: (list symptoms)."

Scale	Descriptors/Symptoms
Scale 4 highest and over 70; no other scale elevated	1. Immature 2. Dependent 3. Passive aggressive 4. Manipulative 5. Hostile

Report Opener:

"This profile suggests a (severe/marked/mild) personality disorder in an immature, dependent, manipulative, and angry individual. Other patterns associated with this profile are: (list symptoms)."

Scale	Descriptors/Symptoms
Scale 4 highest and over 70; scale 5 over 70 in second place (45)	1. Passive 2. Dependent 3. Sexual problems 4. Manipulative

Report Opener:

"This person is likely to be immature, to have conflicts over dependency, and to exhibit relationship and sexual problems. These problems appear to be (severe/marked/mild), and the likelihood of a personality disorder should be considered. Other characteristics associated with this profile are: (list symptoms)."

Scale	Descriptors/Symptoms
Scale 4 highest over 70; scale 6 over 70 and in second place (46)	1. Angry 2. Passive aggressive 3. Suspicious 4. Victim—chip on the shoulder attitude

Report Opener:

"This person's profile is found in persons who are angry and suspicious to a (a severe/marked/mild) degree, and who adopt a "chip on the shoulder attitude." Such persons often see themselves as having been unfairly victimized. Other symptoms often associated with this profile are: (list symptoms)."

Guidelines for Beginning a Report (*Continued*)

Scale		*Descriptors/Symptoms*
Scale 4 highest over 70: scale 7 over 70 and in second place (47)	1.	Low frustration tolerance
	2.	Impulsive tension reduction
	3.	Anxiety that leads to acting out, which leads to anxiety

Report Opener:

"This profile suggests a person who is essentially (severely/markedly/mildly) anxious and dependent, whose poor controls lead him to act out impulsively whenever tension accumulates. These persons often show other symptoms associated with this profile such as: (list symptoms)."

Scale 4 highest over 70; scale 8 over 70 and in second place (48)	1.	Alienated from self and others
	2.	Angry
	3.	Lacking in empathy
	4.	Sexuality and aggression confusion
	5.	Acting-out behavior

Report Opener:

"This is essentially a (severe/marked/mild) profile of a distrusting, alienated, angry, acting-out individual. Other symptoms often associated with this profile are: (list symptoms)."

Scale 4 highest over 70; scale 9 over 70 and in second place (49)	1.	Impulsive
	2.	Superficially charming
	3.	Explosive
	4.	Acting out
	5.	Self-centered

Report Opener:

"This is essentially a (severe/marked/mild) acting-out profile in a person who is likely to be superficially charming, but essentially self-centered, and manipulative. In addition, this person could be described as: (list symptoms)."

Scale 6 highest above 70; no other scales over 70 (spike 6)	1.	Suspicious
	2.	Conforming
	3.	Projecting
	4.	Paranoid
	5.	Guarded

Report Opener:

"This profile suggests a (severely/markedly/mildly) paranoid individual who is likely to present as guarded, suspicious, argumentative, and vigilant for any implied or actual criticism. Other symptoms often associated with this profile are: (list symptoms)."

Scale 6 highest over 70; scale 7 over 70 and in second place (67)	1.	Tension
	2.	Argumentative
	3.	Controlling
	4.	Vigilant for criticism

Scale	*Descriptors/Symptoms*

Report Opener:

"Persons with profiles like this usually are tense, paranoid individuals who are constantly on guard against possible criticism, verbal or physical attack. The present profile would be characterized as (severe/marked/mild). Other symptoms often associated with this profile are: (list symptoms)."

Scale 6 highest over 70; scale 8 over 70 and	1.	Paranoid
in second place (68)	2.	Confused
	3.	Angry
	4.	Withdrawn
	5.	Possibly psychotic

Report Opener:

"This profile suggests a (severely/markedly/mildly) paranoid, confused, withdrawn and angry individual whose self-protective vigilance against attack may involve guns, knives, or other weapons. Such individuals also often show such characteristics as: (list symptoms)."

Scale 6 highest over 70; scale 9 over 70 and	1.	Tense
in second place (69)	2.	High-strung
	3.	Explosive
	4.	Possibly manic
	5.	Paranoid features

Report Opener:

"Profiles with this pattern are usually produced by persons with (severe/marked/mild) paranoid charactertics mixed with manic features. Such persons are usually tense, high-strung, explosive, agitated, and without adequate means of expressing strong emotions. Other symptoms often associated with this profile are: (list symptoms)."

Scale 7 highest over 70; no other scales over	1.	Tense
70 (spike 7)	2.	Worried
	3.	Poor self image
	4.	Guilty
	5.	Apprehensive
	6.	Compulsive
	7.	Possibly phobic

Report Opener:

"This (severely/markedly/mildly) elevated profile is essentially that of an anxious, tense, worried, guilty, dependent, and possibly phobic individual. Such persons are likely to complain of anxiety and tension, and may exhibit obsessive compulsive behaviors. Other symptoms may be present, such as: (list symptoms)."

Scale 7 highest over 70; scale 8 over 70 and	1.	Self-doubting
in second place (78)	2.	Profoundly low self-esteem
	3.	Worried
	4.	Tense
	5.	Anxious

Report Opener:

"Tense, anxious, and self-doubting to a (severe/marked/mild) degree, this individual likely suffers from profoundly low self-esteem. Persons such as this are typically characterized by: (list symptoms)."

Guidelines for Beginning a Report (*Continued*)

Scale		*Descriptors/Symptoms*
Scale 7 highest over 70; scale 9 over 70 and in second place (79)	1.	Agitated
	2.	Anxious
	3.	Preoccupied with fear of failure
	4.	Self-doubting
	5.	High-strung

Report Opener:

"This is essentially a (severe/marked/mild) profile of an anxious, self-doubting individual driven to succeed as a way of proving self worth. Other symptoms often associated with this profile are: (list symptoms)."

Scale 8 highest over 70; no other scales over 70 (spike 8)	1.	Confused
	2.	Low self-esteem
	3.	Ruminative
	4.	Lacking in empathy
	5.	Alienated

Report Opener:

"The MMPI profile suggests a withdrawn, schizoid individual of (severe/marked/mild) proportions, who is likely to show confusion, low self-image, self-doubt, and difficulties in interpersonal relationships. Other symptoms often found in such persons are: (list symptoms)."

Scale 8 highest over 70; scale 7 over 70 and in second place (87)	1.	Profound anxiety
	2.	Unrealistic self-deprecation
	3.	Confused
	4.	Sometimes psychotic
	5.	Inability to concentrate
	6.	Sexual inadequacy
	7.	Poor interpersonal relationships

Report Opener:

"This individual appears disturbed to a (severe/marked/mild) degree, associated with confusion, anxiety, and a distorted and negative self-image. Self-doubt, difficulties in problem solving and concentration are also likely to be present to a (severe/marked/mild) degree. Other symptoms include feelings of sexual inadequacy: (list symptoms)."

Scale 8 highest above 70; scale 9 above 70 and in second place (89)	1.	Tense
	2.	High-strung
	3.	Confused
	4.	Often psychotic

Report Opener:

"This is essentially a (severely/markedly/mildly) disturbed profile in a possibly psychotic, high-strung individual with manic features. Other symptoms often associated with this profile are: (list symptoms)."

Scale 9 highest above 70; no other scales above 70 (spike 9)	1.	Energetic
	2.	Unrealistically optimistic
	3.	Grandiose
	4.	Talkative
	5.	Possibly manic
	6.	Fears that slowing down may lead to depression

216

Scale	*Descriptors/Symptoms*

Report Opener:

"Persons with profiles such as this are typically manic (hypomanic if 9 is below 80), and are characterized primarily by being energetic, grandiose, unrealistically optimistic, irritable, and fearful of failure to a (severe/marked/mild) degree. Additionally, these persons are likely to be: (list symptoms)."

Scale 9 highest above 70; scale 2 over 70 and in second place (92)	1. Explosive
	2. Irritable
	3. Moody
	4. Possibly manic
	5. Tense

Report Opener:

"Both manic and depressive features are present to a (severe/marked/mild) degree in this profile. This person is likely to manifest irritability, explosiveness, and mood swings. Other likely symptoms are: (list symptoms)."

Scale 9 highest over 70; scale 8 over 70 and in second place (98)	1. Manic
	2. Psychotic
	3. Self-doubting
	4. Grandiose
	5. Confused

Report Opener:

"This profile suggests a (severe/marked/mild) manic disturbance with possible psychotic symptoms such as confusion, agitation, possible delusions and even periods of catatonia. These persons often show additional characteristics and symptoms such as: (list symptoms)."

STEP 2—LOOKING UP ADDITIONAL CORRELATES

You have now written an opening paragraph on the validity of the profile and the test-taking attitude of the respondent. You have begun the body of your report with a powerful opening statement. Your next statement should go on to list other likely complaints, symptoms, conflicts, etc. for that code-type obtained from chapter 6, and to integrate those findings within the contextual framework of the referral question, background and history, and current life situation of the person.

Once you have described the symptoms, behaviors, defenses, and other correlates of the primary elevated code-type, and for the specific configurations such as conversion V, look up the correlates for the next highest scale in the configuration (see chapter 6). Repeat this for all scales elevated above a T-score of 70 in descending order of elevation. Upon completion of this task, look up the correlates for any scale below a T-score of 50, if they are available. For example, look at Fig. 7.10. The profile is that of a 26/62 code-type. Look up the correlates for 26/62 code-type above $T = 70$ in chapter 6. The next highest scale is 7, which adds anxiety, self-doubt, guilt, and rumination to the symptom picture of a 26

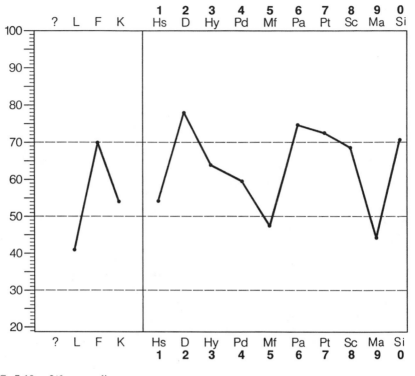

FIG. 7.10.   2/6 personality.

trapped, angry depression. The next highest scale is 0, which predicts introversion and social uneasiness and suggests a lack of social supports. There are no other scales above a *T*-score of 70 but scale 9 is below a *T*-score of 50. This indicates low energy and intensifies the low energy symptoms of depression, but somewhat reduces the likelihood of acting-out. Once a list of correlates from the basic scales has been generated, the next task is one of organizing the inferences.

Organization of Inferences

Reports should be organized into coherent paragraphs that flow logically. The opening paragraph should be conceptualized as though it had a separate heading such as *Validity* or *Test-Taking Attitude* (You may, or may not, wish to formally label such sections in your report; different settings encourage or discourage such separate labels). After you have written a brief description of the validity and test-taking attitude, begin the main body of the interpretation as a separate section such as *Personality Profile,* or *Symptoms, Behaviors, and Personality Traits.*

The following is one way of dividing a profile into entities that could form separate paragraphs of a report (e.g., Graham, 1977). It is best not to use separate headings for the paragraphs as it chops up the report and may distract the reader. In addition, you may wish to weave in examples from the person's behavior or background that particularly illustrate the characteristic being described, or that seem related to that symptom, conflict, etc.

1. Symptoms and complaints
2. Self-concept
3. Perception of the environment
4. Interpersonal relationships
5. Behaviors
6. Emotional control and response to stress
7. Psychological resources
8. Dynamics-etiology
9. Diagnostic impressions
10. Treatment implications

Symptoms and Complaints

After the opening statement, list the primary symptoms associated with the code-type and the secondary elevated scales. Remember that the client should be recognizable to the referring colleague from your first paragraph description.

Self-Concept

Once you have described the symptoms or complaints, describe the way the person sees him- or herself. In some cases, a few sentences will suffice because the disturbance is mainly characterized by acting-out behavior with little self-awareness and projection of blame onto others (e.g., 49/94 profile). In other cases, however, this will be a particularly important paragraph because the disturbance is primarily around self-image and self-dislike (e.g., 278/728, 86/68, 89/98 profiles). This paragraph could start with a sentence such as, "At the present time the patient sees himself as defective and alienated (high scores on 8), inadequate (high scores on scale 2), and vulnerable to criticism and humiliation (high scores on scale 8). On the other hand, a statement about self-concept with an acting-out profile (49/94 or 46/64) might start off as, "The client is unlikely to see himself as responsible for his present difficulties. He is likely to see his difficulties as due to other people, difficult situations, or "bad luck," and he will tend to project blame onto others."

Perception of the Environment

In this section describe how the person sees the outside world. For example, 68/86 persons see it as hostile, dangerous, and confusing. High scorers on scales 2 and 7 see the world in terms of their responsibility to it, so they strive to avoid failure. They see themselves as vulnerable to threat and loss of social approval. 48/84 persons see the world as hostile and uncaring, so they maintain a self-protective, angry stance. They have difficulty empathizing with others or reading other's responses to them. On the other hand, 46/64 code-type persons are vigilant for any demands being placed on them and they are likely to be guarded and protective of their autonomy, often feeling "cheated by life." As you read the descriptors in chapter 6, tease out the relevant sentences for each of your paragraphs.

Interpersonal Relationships

Given the previous perceptions of themselves and of others, describe how this effects their interpersonal relationships. Descriptions of interpersonal relationships also will vary in length depending on the code-type. For some profiles, a primary problem area will be interpersonal (e.g., in the 49/94 or 46/64 types), but for other profiles (e.g., 27/72) the problems are more of an intra-personal nature. A possible opening statement for this paragraph could be: "The client's interpersonal relationships are apt to be characterized by painful mis-understandings (as in 78/87 elevations), exaggerated demands for affection (as in 46/64 elevations), or explosive irritability (as in 49/94 elevations)."

Behaviors

People's behaviors flow from their self-concept, perceptions of the environment, and interpersonal relationships. In a sense, interpersonal relationships are manifested in behaviors, so you may have already covered some of this in the preceding paragraph. A good opening sentence for this section might start as: "Typical behaviors associated with this profile are: *(list items)*." For example, a person scoring high on scale 2, with complaints of fatigue, difficulties in concentration, guilt, anxieties, and difficulties in sleeping will show behaviors such as apathy, a general loss in alertness and drive, and a slowed down tempo. The behaviors you describe for a particular elevation ought to be linked in a meaningful way to the preceding symptoms, self-concept, and perception of the environment. Therefore a person elevated on scale 2 is likely to present with a slow interpersonal tempo, slow speech, and poor eye contact. Such a person would also likely withdraw from conflict and generally avoid assertive or goal-directed behavior. Using a different example involving a 4 spike elevation, you are unlikely to have a very long list of complaints because high scorers on 4 often do not have complaints as such (though others may have many complaints about them). Usually they are in therapy because of impulsive behavior that has led them into trouble. In this case, statements about their behaviors will predominate, so you might state, "They are likely to be in trouble because of sexual or other acting-out behavior problems. They are self-centered individuals who blame their problems on outside circumstances or difficult situations but rarely take responsibility for their behaviors. Typically they are alienated people who exhibit an adolescent type of rebellion and nonconformity to accepted social norms and values. Rarely loyal, they see the world as a dog-eat-dog place where they have to have the upper hand in order to avoid being exploited. Typical behaviors are lying, impulsivity, poor frustration tolerance, and poor long-term planning. Marital or relationship difficulties are suggested, along with difficulties in accepting routine and conforming to structured work situations."

To summarize, some code-types generate a longer list of symptoms than complaints. Other code-types generate longer lists of symptoms and complaints than descriptions of behaviors. It is useful to remember that clients present complaints and clinicians identify symptoms.

Emotional Control-Response To Stress

Whenever a person is stressed, their defensive behaviors increase and their symptoms generally worsen. The clinical and validity scales of the MMPI are reflective of defensive behaviors. Elevations of K and Es (ego strength) suggest better coping ability than lower scores on these scales. Lowered scale 0 scores generally indicate a broader array of social and interpersonal supports, as well as a history of more socialization.

Clinical scale configurations are often associated with varying amounts of emotional control or responses to stress. For some code-types, increases in stress can lead to dangerous behaviors. For example, 68/86 types can become combative under stress, or 24/42 persons who have been threatening suicide can actually attempt it. High 9 individuals can become increasingly manic or suddenly depressed under stress. In this section discuss what kind of stressors are most likely to lead to an increase in symptoms and maladaptive (or adaptive) defensive behaviors for the profile you are describing.

The following are some examples, drawn from the authors' experiences, of stressors associated with particular code-types:

Code-type	Stressors
27/72	Accumulation of responsibilities
28/82	Perceived withdrawal of emotional support from previously supportive person.
43/34	Rejection or being discounted.
46/64	Demands being placed on them.
49/94	The imposition of controls on their behavior.
93/39	Disapproval and/or being controlled.

Psychological Resources

Material for this section comes primarily from the code-type, and from scores on the Es scale and the elevations on the F and K scales (see chapter 6). High scores on the Es scale predict adequate psychological resources to deal with stress. For example, a person obtaining a 48/84 profile at an elevation of 75 with an ego strength T-score of 70, and a T-score of 70 on scale K, is probably coping with life better than a 48/84 profile alone would suggest. However, it is nonetheless likely they will be experiencing interpersonal conflicts, turmoil, and a lack of adequate emotional fulfillment in their interpersonal relationships. They are unlikely to be presenting as psychotic or acting-out in obvious antisocial ways because the K and Es scores predict control and ability to handle stress. As another example, the higher the F score in conjunction with a lower K score and lower Es score, the less psychological resources a person has available to deal with the stress exhibited in the clinical profile elevation. Conversely, the higher the K score and the higher the Es score, the more coping resources that are available to the person.

The relationship between K elevations and psychological resources is curvilinear. The lower the K score, the less ego strength and the lower the self-concept. In the midranges, where K is 60 to 70, a person has adequate psychological resources to deal with stress. At elevations over a T-score of 70, a person is likely to be rigid and out of touch with feelings, and therefore less flexible and less able to tolerate psychological self-exploration.

Dynamics—Etiology

Some report writers may divide their profile at this point with a heading such as *Dynamics—Etiology*. Such a section allows specific emphasis to be given to the manifestations of the subject's personality and/or pathology as it dynamically interacts with the person's background, history, current interpersonal relationships or life situation. Other report writers prefer to intersperse such information throughout the report to illustrate or amplify personality aspects. Some MMPI textbooks (e.g., Marks, Seeman, & Haller, 1974) describe typical background experiences associated with a particular code-type. If these are available, then begin this section with a statement such as (using a 49/94 code-type): "People with profiles such as this often come from backgrounds with authoritarian, demanding and punishing parents, such as seems to be the case with this person," or (using a 48/84 code-type), "Persons with this profile pattern are often described as coming from backgrounds in which there was deprivation, hostility, and sexual abuse, factors that clearly seem to exist in the present patient's background and history." Where there is documented evidence of relevant background experiences, include it.

Diagnostic Impressions

This is probably the most difficult part of report writing because the MMPI is neither diagnostically pure nor efficient. Through experience, however, the clinician will develop diagnostic expertise that will allow the current MMPI profile to be integrated with the relevant situational and background dimensions, thus allowing accurate diagnoses to be formulated. If one scale is particularly elevated over the others, then that scale usually determines or highly colors the diagnostic picture; even so, it is rare that one scale is uniquely more elevated than the others. Therefore a definite diagnosis of depression, paranoia, or personality disorder, etc., is not always possible using such an approach, because several elevated scales will need to be considered.

The following guidelines to diagnosis are offered:

1. The highest scale predicts the type of diagnosis (scale 2 = depression, scale 7 = anxiety, scale 9 = mania, etc.) when one scale is singularly elevated.

2. The slope of the profile suggests whether the diagnosis will fall in the neurotic or psychotic realm. Is it a neurotic slope (negative slope) or a psychotic slope (positive slope)?

3. Consider strongly those diagnoses actuarially associated most frequently with that two- or three-point code, or with that configuration (e.g., conversion V). Where evidence exists, these have been listed under each code-type in chapter 6.

4. Compute the Goldberg Index. Is it in the psychotic or the neurotic direction? The Goldberg Index is discussed in detail later. See Tables 7.1 and 7.2 for a description of how to properly employ the Goldberg Rules, as well as the typical Goldberg Index values associated with each code-type.

4. When writing a report, it is often advisable to give one or two alternative diagnoses depending on behavioral observations or history. For example, an adolescent 89/98 profile might be indicating a panic around a drug reaction, or it might indicate a severe identity disturbance. Schizophrenia could be a possible diagnosis, but tell the reader what to look for in the client's history. Using the 89/98 adolescent as an example, the diagnosis section could contain a statement such as: "A history of schizophrenia in the family of origin would make the prognosis more guarded. If the history does not suggest a chemically induced disturbance, this profile could reflect a schizophrenic disorder."

Treatment Implications

MMPI users will have to use their clinical experience and the treatment literature to write the last section of the MMPI report, although the MMPI can provide some clues as to the client's treatability, issues that are likely to arise in a

TABLE 7.1
Notes for the Clinical Use of the Goldberg Rules

The Goldberg Rules are a set of three linear indices, each of which employs a combination of K-corrected MMPI T-scores in an equation for which a sign value (cutting score) has been established.

All of the Goldberg Rules were developed using regression procedures on large data sets. Rules I and II were derived from 208 of the group profiles from Lanyon (1968) and Rule III (Index) emerged from the analysis of 861 individual male profiles collected from seven psychiatric centers (mostly VA and university hospital inpatients) previously used in Meehl and Dahlstrom's (1960) study of configural rules for discriminating psychotic from neurotic profiles. The methods and data on which these indices are based have immediate implications for their use in clinical practice. Several of these will be referred to in the discussion of each rule. The most important point is that the Goldberg Rules do not lend themselves to straightforward use in decisions involving the individual case. The differences in base rates between various kinds of settings (e.g., clinics, private practice, college counseling centers, VA hospitals, state mental hospitals, job screening, prisons, etc.) will have large effects on the rate of correct decisions if the cutting scores for the three rules are held constant. Another thing to bear in mind is that the Goldberg Rules show a different range of values for each of the common two- or three-point profile types (see the next table of index values for a sample of cases provided by Alex B. Caldwell, and corresponding values for profiles in the Marks and Seeman [1963] and Gilberstadt and Duker [1965] codebooks). Take Goldberg Rule III for example: Code-types 138 and 86 are both associated with a high frequency of psychosis, yet the ranges of values for Rule III are almost completely nonoverlapping. The typical range of values for 138 profiles for Rule III is from 35 to 55, whereas that for 86 profiles is 65 to 90. Thus, decisions based solely on the Rule III cutting score of 45 will result in too many 86 profiles being called psychotic, whereas too few of the patients with 138 profiles will be called psychotic. As a result of these problems, the Goldberg Rules are probably best thought of as a means of classifying large *groups* of patients or profile *types* rather than a way of classifying individual profiles one by one.

Let us now consider each rule separately:

Rule I: Normal vs. Deviant ($Hs + 2Pd- Ma$)

Scores above 123.5 are called deviant while scores below 123.5 are considered normal. This rule probably performs best in populations or settings with a high base rate (say, at least 30%) for psychological normality such as general medical patients, college counseling centers, police applicants, Peace Corps volunteers, etc. It should be applied with considerable caution to outpatients and should be avoided completely in inpatient psychiatric settings. Among the latter group, false negatives (patients erroneously classified as normal) occur at a particularly high rate among patients with code types in which scale 9 is one of the two high points or as scale 9 equals or exceeds T-65. This rule appears to work better in outpatient settings when applied only to those profiles which do not fulfill the inclusion criteria for the Normal $K+$ profile, have no more than two scales greater than T-70, and in which scale 9 is no greater than third highest. In inpatient settings, Rule I may be thought of as a Mania vs. Other indicator. Scores of 123 and below are obtained by patients with high activity levels who are less ambivalent, apathetic and depressed than patients in general, and who do not manifest a sense of inadequacy/inferiority (Lane and Lachar, 1979). Manic cases typically show Rule 1 below 123.5 and Rule III above 45.

Rule II: Psychiatric vs. Sociopathic, Personality Disordered ($2Pd-Hy-Sc$)

Scores above 11 are considered sociopathic while scores below 11 are called "psychiatric". This rule corresponds roughly to the DSM-III distinction between Axis I (Clinical Syndromes) and Axis II

(Personality Disorders). The assignment of separate axes to these two kinds of disorders by the American Psychiatric Association Task Force on Nomenclature and Statistics was decided upon for the explicit purpose of encouraging, where appropriate, simultaneous classification: "This separation (of clinical and personality conditions) ensures that consideration is given to the possible presence of disorders that are frequently overlooked when attention is directed to the usually more florid Axis I disorder" (American Psychiatric Association, 1980, p. 23). The implication for the practical utility of Rule II, then, is that values exceeding the cutting score should serve to alert the clinician to the likely presence of a personality disorder, rather than as a device to *classify* the individual patient.

Rule II is relatively more sensitive in detecting those personality disorders lying at the more unstable end of the overcontrol—undercontrol continuum, such as Antisocial and Narcisstic Personality Disorders, while being correspondingly less sensitive to those at the more constricted end of this continuum, such as Dependent or Obsessive-Compulsive Personality Disorders.

Classification accuracy is undoubtedly best for this rule in settings with high base rates for character pathology such as prisons, drug and alcohol treatment or rehabilitation programs, and so on. In clinic and psychiatric settings, this rule results in an intolerably high false negative rate for neurotic and especially for psychotic conditions. The problem is that as scale 4 reaches about T-80, the profile tends to be classified as sociopathic regardless of its total configuration. The 46/64 code-type is the outstanding miss for this rule but 48/84, 482/428, 274/742/472, 96/69, and 94 are also frequently misclassified as personality disordered.

Rule III: Neurotic vs. Psychotic $(L + Pa + Sc- Hy- Pt)$

Scores at 45 or above are considered psychotic while scores below 45 are called neurotic. This rule is commonly referred to as the Goldberg Index. Great caution should be exercised in applying this rule outside formal psychiatric settings. Because scores are obtained by subtracting the sum of two scales from the sum of three different scales, and because the average score for normals for each scale is near T-50, the majority of individuals in unselected samples will obtain scores on the Goldberg Index well within the psychotic range. It is therefore inappropriate to compute this index in presumptively normal samples such as applicants for employment, general medical patients, college counselees, and so forth. Rule III is unique among the three Goldberg indices in having some intelligible dynamic meaning in terms of the patient's psychological distance from others. High values are likely to reflect a marked distrust of others and strong needs for insulation, detachment and withdrawal in interpersonal relations. Low values suggest overattachment with dependency and clinging.

All of the profiles in the original data set were collected prior to 1960 and most prior to 1955, so it is very unlikely that affective disorders were fairly represented in the criterion diagnoses. Major depressions were almost certainly overrepresented in the neurotic group and underrepresented in the psychotic group at a period when schizophrenia was over-diagnosed in this country. As a consequence, Rule III will almost certainly show greater sensitivity and specificity for schizophrenia than for affective disorders. Frequent misclassifications occur with the 278, 29/92 and 78/87 profile codes. 278s are misclassified as psychotic and as neurotic with about equal frequency, while 29/92s are called neurotic too often and 78/87s are called psychotic too often. Elevations on L and endorsements of most of the dozen or so somatic items on scale 8 will result in some 13/31 profiles (especially those of female patients) being erroneously called psychotic. As suggested earlier, the 138 profile is the classic miss for Rule III with the majority of patients with this code misclassified as neurotic.

Note: These notes on using the Goldberg rules were written by David S. Nichols and were reproduced with his permission.

TABLE 7.2
Mean Goldberg (N–P) Index Values by Code-type

Code-type	Caldwell Report Index Values[1]	Gilberstadt & Duker (1965)[2]	Marks & Seeman (1963)[2]
123'[a]	34	18	
13' or 31'	32	24	40
231' or 213'	30	16[b]	30
26' or 62'	62		
27' or 72', basically 273' and not 274' or 278'	26	14	28
274', any order	36	26	36
278' any order	46	45	48
28' or 82'	58		58
29' or 92'	43		
321'	28		23
34' or 43'	40	33	
36' or 63'	53		
37', 73', 137' any order	25	19[c]	
38', 83' or 138' any order	44	36	53
39' or 93'	37	34[d]	
4' and (A–B)>10[e]	48	45	
46' or 64'	66		65[f]
48' or 84', not 489'	58	56[g]	56
49' or 94', not 489'	49	45	53
489', any order	60		
68' or 86'	77	99[i]	92[i]
69' or 96'	70		78
78' or 87'	49	42	
89' or 98'	62	71	68
9', B<70, 2<50[j]	54	55	

[1] These values were derived from a file sequential sampling of adult cases processed by the Caldwell Report. Cases included psychotherapy outpatients, psychiatric inpatients, workers' compensation and other forensic evaluations, parents in child custody cases, and a diversity of normals including police and other job applicants. For further information write Alex Caldwell, PhD, Caldwell Report, 1545 Sawtelle Blvd., Los Angeles, CA 90025.

[2] Goldberg index values were derived from each corresponding adult psychiatric mean profile by code-type.

[a] Primed codes were used; the mean N–P index values for unelevated profiles are usually quite similar with no consistent pattern of differences.

[b] Code-type 1237'/2137'

[c] Code-type 137' or 13'7.

[d] Code-type 139, 1 or 3 or 9>T–70.

[e] (A–B)> 10 indicates scale 4 minus the next highest of the eight clinical scales is more than 10 points. Gilberstadt and Duker specify 4>T–70 and no other scale >=T–70.

[f] 65 is the average of Code-type 4–6/6–4, mean N–P Index 78, plus Code-type 4–6–2/6–4–2, mean Index 52.

[g] Code-type 8–2–4(7).

[h] Code-type 4–8–2/8–4–2/8–2–4.

[i] High F scores were not excluded nor was the N–P Index adjusted for excessive F elevations.

[j] B<70 indicates the second highest of the eight clinical scales is below T-70, and scale 2 must be less than T-50.

clinical treatment setting, and types of therapeutic intervention that are more or less likely to be effective. The K scale is generally a good indicator of therapy suitability. Extremely low scores on K (below T-score of 40) suggest low self-esteem and low ego strength (and therefore psychological availability for treatment), but often poor prognosis because of a lack of psychological inner resources. T-scores in the range 50 to 70 typically predict a good therapeutic outcome, whereas T-scores above 70 predict emotional rigidity and constriction. Therefore a poor therapeutic outcome is often due to client difficulties in opening up.

Some code-types reflect behaviors that are more amenable to treatment than other scales. For example, 27/72 code persons are amenable to treatment because they tend to be conscientious, reasonable, and follow treatment suggestions. On the other hand, elevations on scale 4 predict a poor response to treatment whether it is pharmacological or psychotherapeutic. 48/84, 46/64, 43/34, 49/94, and spike 4 are all configurations that predict a relatively enduring personality picture that is unlikely to change significantly due to therapy. The exception to this is when elevations on scale 4 are the result of a recent let down or psychological trauma such as divorce or loss of job. In this case a history of good adjustment prior to the precipitating circumstance would suggest a good response to treatment. A lifelong history of passive/aggressive or acting-out behavior in the presence of elevations on scale 4, however, would suggest a poor treatment prognosis. For people with elevations on scale 4, psychotherapy should focus primarily on helping them learn how to postpone gratification, tolerate frustration, and deal with structured situations. For profiles with significant primary elevations on scale 2, psychopharmacological intervention should always be considered as one alternative. This is also true for profiles with high scores on psychotic scales 6, 8, and 9. Pain medication should be avoided or carefully considered for all code-types in which scales 1, 3, and 7 are highest, and if there is no clear organic cause for the pain. Beginning users of the MMPI who have limited clinical experience, should attempt to build a data base of treatment suggestions by reading standard books on personality and psychopathology, and associating them with basic configural code-types.

CODE-TYPE CLASSIFICATION AND INTERPRETATION OF "COMPLEX PROFILES"

Some profiles do not fit cleanly into a recognizable code-type. In this case, you need to divide the profile into manageable, recognizable entities, and then build a composite personality picture. The floating profile mentioned earlier (see Fig. 7.9) in which all clinical scales are elevated at more or less the same T-score level, is an example of such a complex code-type. It is used here as an example of how to break down a profile into entities. One strategy, adopted from Caldwell, is to divide the profile into high-point pairs in order to generate a set of descriptors for each pair. First write down, in order of elevations, all the elevated scales. Using the example in Fig. 7.9, the following list is generated: 3–1; 6–2; 7–4; 5–8; 0–9. Under each number write the corresponding letter of the alphabet as shown as far as the fourth highest elevation.

3–1 6–2 7–4 5–8 0–9

a   b   c   d

Then divide the profile and interpret in high-point pairs as follows: *a–b,* which is 3–1. Then interpret *a–c,* which is 3–6. Then interpret *b–c,* which is 1–6. After that, take the correlates for each of the scales in descending order. In this case the anchor for the interpretation is the 3–1 (i.e., 13/31 two-point) code-type. Looking up the 13/31 code-type in chapter 6 reveals such persons to be somatizing, dependent, psychologically naive, and immature individuals who have difficulty facing anger directly. Descriptors for elevations on 3 and 6 (see 36/63 code-type in chapter 6) reveal persons who are hypersensitive to criticism, distrustful, and occasionally suspicious with somatic symptoms. Looking up correlates for 1–6 (see 16/61 code-type in chapter 6) reveals them to be rigid, grouchy, stubborn, hypersensitive to criticism, and quick to place blame on others.

The profile that emerges so far is that of a hypersensitive, somatizing, tense, possibly suspicious individual. Next add the correlate for the single scales, starting with scale 2. Elevations at this *T*-score level suggest sadness, apathy, guilt, and depression. The anchor for the personality picture is the 13/31 profile, so the symptoms of depression will be manifested as somatic complaints and tension. The correlates for scale 7, the next highest scale, predict anxiety, tension, and guilt. Given the 13/31 backdrop, the person is unlikely to be aware of guilt and anxiety, but rather to experience it as tension and somatic symptoms whenever responsibilities accumulate. Correlates for the next highest scale, scale 4, suggest acting out and impulsivity, but against the backdrop of the 3-1, 3–6, and 1–6 configuration, suggest passive aggressiveness and dependency. This is because the primary elevations form the basis of the personality picture, and the other scales modify that base. The 3–1 pattern contraindicates aggression. Consequently, the acting out associated with scale 4 will be modified and expressed as passive resistance, self-defeating behavior, and dependency on others.

To begin the assimilation process, write all your descriptors on a blank sheet of paper. Attempt to group similar descriptors together. Eliminate descriptors that are contradictory to the primary code-type and secondary scale pairs. The primary three code-types become the context within which the fourth, fifth, and all other individual clinical scales (including special scales) are interpreted. Your purpose will be to make sense of the contradictions, and to add those symptoms and descriptions that confirm each other so that you can use them in the report with a higher degree of certainty.

Scale 5

Elevations on scale 5 will modify the profile interpretation. For men, elevations on scale 5 will mitigate against aggressive acting-out behaviors and will modify the scales that otherwise would predict such behaviors. Because elevated scores on this scale for men are associated with sensitivity and an interest in relationships, it acts as a suppressor variable for acting-out behaviors. For example, a male profile elevated on scales 4, 8, and 9, with scale 5 elevated, would predict a charismatic, but confused and angry person whose acting-out is likely to be in indirect antisocial ways, such as through white-collar types of crime or unusual sexual behaviors. Scale 5 correlates with education and intelligence, so elevations on that scale will modify the profile in the same way that these demographic variables would.

Low 5 scores in females (below a T-score of 35) suggest passivity, and would increase the likelihood of passive aggressiveness in profiles that would otherwise suggest direct anger. In females, the addition of low scale 5 to a 49/94 profile would suggest more sexual acting-out than antisocial acting-out behaviors.

Scale 0

Elevations on scale 0 (Si) represent social veneer and comfort, or lack thereof, and thus modify other aspects of profile interpretation. For example, some code-types (e.g., 68/86) indicate that interpersonal relationships are a problem; when scale 0 is additionally elevated, these interpersonal problems are even more striking. Conversely, the same 68/86 profile, but where scale 0 is at or below 50, would suggest a better prognosis because the person apparently has a history of social interactions that were satisfactory. Thus the person is more likely to have (or to be able to establish) an interpersonal support network. Another example is that of 49/94 code-types. When Scale 0 is additionally elevated, the person is less likely to blatantly act out in aggressive fashion, and is more likely simply to be sullenly asocial. If Scale 0 is low, the person would be more likely to act out, but in socially skillful ways that are quite effective in manipulating others.

Energizers and Suppressors

Some scales act as energizers or activator variables, whereas other scales act as suppressor factors. An energizer variable is one that increases the likelihood that the attributes of a particular code-type will be manifested behaviorally. For example, a 24/42 code-type with scale 9 coded third and above $T = 70$ would increase the likelihood of impulsive, self-destructive, or self-defeating behaviors. Similarly, elevations on scales 4 and 8 would predict an angry, alienated, and confused individual. Adding scale 9 coded third and above $T = 70$ would predict impulsive, antisocial, and bizarre acting-out behavior as the alienation and anger get energized by scale 9. Scales 9, 4, and 8 can be considered energizers. Scale 4 predicts poor impulse control, and thus increases the likelihood that behaviors will get acted out impulsively. Elevations on scale 8 also predict poor impulse control due to disordered thinking.

Suppressor variables are those that inhibit the likelihood of the attributes of a particular code being expressed in overt behaviors. Scales 2, 5, and 0 act as suppressor variables. For example, a 49/94 profile, with scales 5 and 0 coded third and fourth and above $T = 70$, would predict an angry person, but one who is not likely to act out. Rather, scales 5 and 0 would suggest a sensitive individual who tends toward introversion, and whose acting-out behavior would more likely manifest itself in some kind of intellectual rebelliousness, or perhaps in a circumscribed way, such as promiscuity.

Strategies for Providing Feedback to the Client

Consumer interests and society are placing demands on psychologists to reveal test results to clients. Learning how to give feedback can minimize client apprehension around the issue of testing and, if done well, can enhance therapeutic effectiveness. The language of psychopathology, which is the essence of the MMPI, is often judgmental and inappropriate for therapist/client sharing, and for building a therapeutic alliance. This is because the MMPI was conceived as a clinical instrument designed to identify problems. Most of the clinical scales were constructed with clinical groups to diagnose clinical problems characterized in clinical terms. The basic scales were developed originally not as measures of personality, but as measures of clinical and nonclinical problems. Their mainstream use continues to be in evaluating abnormal, maladaptive, or undesirable aspects of personality and behavioral functioning, rather than normal, adaptive, or desirable ones. Terms such as *hostile, dependent, secondary gain, demanding, manipulative, acting-out,* etc. are commonly used in reports, although some clinicians have voiced concern that they are antithetical to building a therapeutic relationship (Erdberg, 1979). Some colleagues have characterized psychological testing reports as generally being written such that they are little more than character assassinations. Reports cannot readily be shown to clients because they are often judgmental in content in ways that conflict with the client's self-perception at that time, and might even be harmful to the client's self-concept.

A therapeutic alliance is more likely to be forged if the client feels that the central thoughts, feelings, and concerns expressed are valid and empathically understood. This kind of understanding can develop through open, nonjudgmental discussion of test findings in which a client is part of the evaluation process, rather than simply part of an evaluation product.

A phenomenological approach has been developed by Lewak, Marks, and Nelson (1988) based on the largely unpublished formulations of Alex Caldwell. According to this approach, individuals are viewed as products of genetic and environmental factors. Maladaptive behavior is seen as a product of stress (fear) operating within an individual who has a diathesis (i.e., a predisposition or set of vulnerabilities) for the type of disorder that occurs. From their perspective, it is assumed that each person inherits a repertoire of available psychological defenses (antibodies) against stress. Under increased stress, those defenses that effectively reduce pressures become fixed and maintained in accordance with their reinforcing value. From the Lewak et al. perspective, any particular defense could then be understood in the context of the stress that initially induced it.

Take for example, scale 1 (*Hs*). Persons with elevations on this scale are typically described as immature, dependent, psychologically naive, and preoccupied with somatic concerns. In the Lewak et al. approach, the judgmental terms *immature, psychologically naive,* etc. make sense when seen from the perspective of a frustrated therapist whose task may be to rid the client of the habit of switching attention to physical health when other psychologically painful conflicts arise. Lewak et al. caution, however, that from the client's perspective, a concern about physical health may at one stage have been an adaptive response to a perceived overwhelming threat to his or her physical integrity. Staying in bed, worrying about deteriorating health and being preoccupied with the availability of medical health care makes sense from the perspective of the client who is terrified of bodily damage or death. These authors have developed a way of giving feedback based on Caldwell's belief that eight clinical scales each reflect different basic patterns of fear-conditioned (defensive) avoidant behaviors. Scales 5 and 0 do not represent conditioned fear-avoidance responses, but rather personality traits. The scales and their associated fears and defenses are summarized in Table 7.3.

As shown in Table 7.3, for example, clients who score high on scale 2 have at some stage in life likely experienced inordinate pain over some significant and irretrievable loss. They may have responded by blocking further needs or wants in order to avoid further loss. Similarly, according to this view, clients with a spike 9 profile fear deprivation or failure. Such spike 9 clients would respond by heightened activity in order to maintain a frequent reward schedule, and would constantly plan toward the future to avoid the onset of depression.

According to this perspective, the more elevated the scale, and the more scales elevated in the profile, the more of the client's life will be devoted to self-protection by engaging in defensive behaviors. The stressors identified by the scale elevation will usually determine the class of stress to which a client is

TABLE 7.3
MMPI Scales and Associated Fear-Conditioned Defensive Responses

Scale	Fear	Response
1	Death, physical attack, illness, or pain	Maintaining physical integrity by overprotecting the body.
2	Irretrievable and significant loss	Blocking wanting or needing in order to avoid further loss.
3	Emotional pain	Positivizing unpleasant experiences by selectively blocking inputs (blindness, numbness).
4	Rejection, being unwanted, or abandoned	"Numbing out" emotional responding, not allowing oneself to get emotionally involved to avoid letdown.
6	Humiliation, being criticized, evaluated	Maintaining constant vigilance against attack.
7	Shock, unexpected events	Thinking ahead and worrying to anticipate onset of shock.
8	Hostility, being disliked or despised by those on whom one depends.	"Shutting down" cognitive processing to avoid unbearable reality.
9	Deprivation or failure.	Increasing activity level in an attempt to maintain reward schedule.

most susceptible, and client history will usually reveal that early experiences have determined the situational events most likely to elicit the self-protective fear-responses.

Most clients want feedback because feeling understood by a trained therapist can, in itself, be of substantial value (Erdberg, 1979). The general approach to giving feedback should be empathic in nature. The client's behavior should be understood in terms of the fears and anxieties motivating the client to engage in defensive behaviors. Using the fear paradigm previously described can be a good way of making clients' present behaviors understandable to them.

Guidelines for Giving Feedback

The following general approach has been found useful in giving feedback to clients about their MMPI profiles:

1. After the client is comfortably seated, the scored MMPI profile is turned toward them, and they are told something like:

"You answered many questions, some of which I am sure seemed unusual or even peculiar to you. That is because the procedure was designed for a broad variety of persons. All of the questions were scored, and we divided your personality into ten dimensions as follows . . ." (The client observes as the clinician counts from scale 1 through scale 0. This allows the client to examine the shape of the graph.)

2. Next the client is told:

"Here on the left side (the clinician points to the validity scales) are some scores that tell me the way in which you answered the test. For example, were you self-critical, eager to tell me how you are feeling, or did you approach the test in a 'stiff upper lip' manner? Are you the kind of person that likes to handle their own problems?" And so on.

3. The client is then told that the lines at $T = 30$ and $T = 70$ represent statistical boundaries that define a range where most people score if they are not in any psychological pain or distress. Be careful to emphasize that an elevated profile indicates discomfort, pain, and distress, rather than deviance. (Note: Use discretion in sharing profile feedback, because many people misinterpret their results when they see an elevated profile. If a profile is grossly elevated, the actual profile graph does not have to be shared with the client. Rather, the clinician can verbally outline the test results for the client.)

4. Use everday language to describe the profile. Remember that many clients are cautious and defensive, anticipating being somehow judged. If they argue with you, then you have made them defensive, and you are defeating your own purpose. If at any stage the client disagrees with the feedback, see it as an opportunity to engage in a dialogue. For example, for someone with elevations on scale 9, you might have told them that they have a great deal of energy, ambition, and drive, only to have them interrupt you to argue by saying that those statements are not true. Rather than becoming defensive, you should "go with the resistance" and give a response such as, "Tell me about your energy level" or "I would appreciate your helping me understand better about your ambitions." Once they have clarified their understanding of these dimensions, proceed with the rest of the feedback. It is highly recommended that the feedback be woven into a dialogue, rather than having the client passively receive the information from the clinician! Some clients want to hear all the feedback issues before responding, perhaps to see how accurate the test is, or perhaps to see what they "need to defend themselves against." Encourage a dialogue. Give the feedback as questions much more often than as statements of fact.

5. Continue with the rest of your feedback, interspersed with dialogue and with the clinician asking questions such as, "Perhaps you can give me an example of your energy level" (or other characteristic). Be empathic and understanding, and try to help the client see how their pathological behavior makes sense when understood in light of their history and from their perspective. For

example, a person scoring high on scale 2 might be sad and despondent most of the time, and so it would be appropriate to inquire about any catastrophic losses that have left the client feeling hopeless about ever being happy. Watch for when the client shuts off and stops listening due to anxiety, or when they interrupt and divert their own attention or the conversation to another topic. Allow them to take a breather because their interruptions or distractions are cues that they have assimilated as much information right then as they are ready to process.

Try to organize your feedback by focusing periodically on a few anchor statements that you can explore as themes, and that can lead to other statements if all progresses well. For example, persons scoring high on scale 4 often respond to an initial feedback statement of, "Your profile suggests that you are a survivor and that right now you are being cautious about letting yourself get emotionally involved in case you are let down and disappointed." The clinician could then say, "Why are you being so cautious? What is going on?" After the client has responded to this, other feedback can be explored, but the clinician can return to this basic theme later as it relates to other issues being discussed during the session.

6. It is often useful at the end of the feedback session to ask the client to "Summarize what you have heard from me today." This could be done in the last 10 minutes so that any misunderstandings can be clarified.

Clinicians can modify their feedback depending on the purpose of the MMPI testing. In some cases it may be used as part of the diagnostic and treatment planning process. In other cases it may be used during the course of treatment. For example, a second MMPI given some time into therapy may reveal that a client is feeling more despondent and self-disliking than had been indicated on the previous MMPI. This, shared with the client, could then open up questions such as, "Is the client responding to reawakened, old memories brought alive by the therapy?" Based on the therapy, the dialogue could be used as a stimulus to refocus the therapy.

In brief treatment approaches, clients could be given feedback from the MMPI so that specific behavioral corrective measures could be employed to alleviate the present distress. For example, a client scoring high on scales 2 and 7 could be given specific behavioral techniques for working on lowering anxiety without further psychological intervention if that is not desirable or possible.

Evaluating Feedback

The feedback process is most useful when envisioned as a joint exploration (clinician and client) of the client's current emotional and psychological status. It is important for the client to be given some way of evaluating feedback so that its accuracy can be validated. Remember that it is the explorative dialogue that forges a stronger therapeutic alliance. Joint treatment planning is more likely to enhance the treatment process than an arbitrary treatment approach. Do not get defensive if a client disagrees. Instead you can ponder out loud as to, "I wonder why the test would have suggested that?" and go on to explore the client's perspective because it is particularly valuable clinical data.

The approaches to sharing feedback with clients already described can be used whether the MMPI has been administered and scored by you, or whether a computer-generated MMPI interpretive report (such as those presented in chapter 8) is used.

8

Computerized Interpretation of the MMPI

INTRODUCTION

Computer applications in psychology have grown remarkably over the last 2 decades. Initially used primarily for scoring test items on academic and psychological tests, computers have increasingly been used for more complex processes in ways that not only are more reliable than similar tasks done by humans, but also more cost-effective. At present, numerous computer-assisted psychological testing procedures are available, covering a number of psychological tests including the MMPI, Rorschach, and Halstead-Reitan. Despite some initial reluctance, the psychological community shows an increasing acceptance of such computer uses, and indeed this acceptance is reflected by society at large.

There are several advantages of computer-generated psychological reports (Butcher, 1987):

1. *Reliability:* The computer has far fewer bad days than humans, and the same input results in the same output.

2. *Memory:* The computer can store and more rapidly retrieve with accuracy far more detailed information than the human, at least if that human does not have ready access to a library.

3. *Objectivity:* Interpreter-bias is minimized in computer-generated reports. Once the interpretation rules are programmed, they are applied automatically and regularly to specified cases, regardless of extraneous circumstances.

4. *Rapidity:* The speed of computer processing and printing is extremely great. It is nothing for a computer to score, interpret and print psychological reports from several thousand MMPI tests in 1 day, a feat far beyond human capability.

236

5. *Cost-Efficiency:* Because of all the above factors, the computer-generated reports are clearly cost-efficient, and will undoubtedly become more so in the decades to come.

Of course there are disadvantages as well (Butcher, 1987).

1. *Excessive Generality:* Matarazzo (1986) pointed out that computer-generated reports rely on modal descriptions and do not do justice to the individual aspects of a person. However, as noted in chapter 4, the actuarial approach, based on just such descriptions, continues to regularly excel the skills of human clinicians. Even so, the relevant dimensions that modify interpretations of tests (e.g., socioeconomic status, education, recent job loss, etc.) are still not routinely included for consideration by most computerized interpretation programs.

2. *Algorithm Limitations:* A related criticism, then, is that the objectivity and accuracy of the computer is only as good as the objectivity and accuracy of the person who developed and programmed the computer.

3. *Potential for Misuse:* Because of the ease of use, and the apparent reliability, there is an added possibility for overreliance on the reports, and the possibility of unqualified users having access to the data.

4. *Confusing Abundance of Packages:* Because of the large number of computer-assisted test-interpretation packages, the clinician often has difficulty in selecting among the offerings. This is made even more difficult because most of these packages were developed in a proprietary, businesslike fashion, and (unlike data in the public domain) the algorithms used by the computer in scoring and interpretation are considered private, and not open to ordinary inspection.

Standards on the use of computers in psychological testing and assessment have been developed by the American Psychological Association, and the reader is encouraged to become familiar with these. They are entitled "American Psychological Association Guidelines for Computer-Based Tests and Interpretations" (1986), and are available directly from the American Psychological Association (also printed as appendix B in Butcher, 1987). In these standards the point is clearly made that the user of a computerized interpretation service remains just as professionally responsible as if that user had used that test without assistance from a computer.

THE MMPI

The MMPI was first computer-interpreted at the Mayo Clinic in Rochester, Minnesota (Rome et al., 1962) in what in retrospect was a fairly simple, scale-by-scale approach. At present, there are numerous sophisticated programs that interpet the MMPI in configural fashion. Several of these are presented later.

This presentation does not constitute an endorsement of these automated MMPI interpretation services; they are presented simply as examples of the current state of the art to apprise the reader. As is evident in chapter 9, the revision of the MMPI (known as MMPI-2) will have an unknown effect on the MMPI interpretations currently being offered by various companies. Most probably the effect will be to broaden the offerings.

All of the following computer-generated reports are included to familarize the reader with such reports. It must be remembered, however, that although these reports are reliable in that computers have better memories than people, they suffer from the disadvantages of not being capable of considering base-rate data about the clinician's unique practice, or about other aspects of a referral question. Furthermore, though most computer reports are somewhat actuarially based, they are only partially so, and their accuracy is only as good as the professional(s) who wrote the program.

CALDWELL REPORT
1545 SAWTELLE BOULEVARD
LOS ANGELES, CA 90025
(213) 478-3133

July 27, 1988

NAME: Sample Adult Profile

AGE: 40

SEX: Male

EDUCATION: 18 years

MARITAL STATUS: Separated

REFERRED BY: _____

DATE TESTED: April 9, 1988

TEST ADMINISTERED: Minnesota Multiphasic Personality Inventory (MMPI)

Test Taking Attitude

He was moderately self-favorable in responding to the MMPI. He tended to give socially correct answers and to minimize weaknesses. The interpretive statements appear valid.

The supplemental validity scales indicate that the self-favorableness reflected by the K scale was due to higher socioeconomic status attitudes. There does not appear to have been any conscious attempt to distort the test results.

Symptoms and Personality Characteristics

The profile indicates a mild to moderate level of depression and anxiety. Tension, worrying, and emotional overreactions to minor threats are suggested along with self-doubts, self-criticisms, and lack of self-confidence. Ambivalences, indecisiveness, and difficulties in sleeping would not be unusual with this profile. The profile suggests a below average level of energy and activity and a generally slow but effective pace and productive output. Overlearned self-restraints around expressing anger are suggested. He may complain of a lack of self-confidence and of difficulties in getting started on new tasks. Nevertheless, his ego strength tests as well above average which predicts organized functioning and immediate practical self-sufficiency in many areas.

He appears repressive and relatively lacking in insight. He may be seen as having somewhat Pollyana or wishful attitudes with a denial of bad intentions. He would strongly dislike aggression and violence. He is apt to be defensively narrow as to what symptoms he will admit as being "neurotic" or as showing emotional illness. Anxieties and guilt about sexual activities and urges are also common with this pattern. His dependency needs would interfere with self-assertiveness and give him difficulties in handling any acting out by family members.

He is apt to be conscientious about his responsibilities if not unduly self-blaming over minor deficiencies in his performances. Frustrations in his family relationships would relate to guilt over self-centered and occasionally manipulative actions. Others may see his moral values as inflexible if not as subtly punitive. This could be expressed through self-righteous judgments or emotional withholding. His overall balance of masculine and feminine interests tends mildly toward verbal or esthetic interests rather than mechanical and outdoor activities. He would orient toward the theoretical and abstract aspects of immediate problems much more than toward their practical and concrete consequences.

In many cases rejections and deprivations in the childhood family had forced the patients to take on responsibilities at a comparatively early age. They identified positively with their parents and expressed favorable feelings toward them. Their mothers were described as anxious, critical, and perfectionistic, and these patients were in turn critical of their wives by comparison to these perfectionistic ideals. Their close relationships were stable over extended periods of time, but they were hesitant to go against family members, so that their decisions were actively influenced by family judgments. In the absence of family support, their level of responsibility was uneven. They were vulnerable to becoming overwhelmed by an accumulation of stresses such as financial commitments and family illnesses. At this time their anxious clinging behaviors as well as their specific symptoms were seen as reflecting their incompletely resolved dependency strivings.

Diagnostic Impression

The profile has mainly been associated with diagnoses of depression. It should be re-emphasized, however, that his self-favorableness makes his profile somewhat more ambiguous than most.

Treatment Considerations

Tricyclic antidepressants have proven beneficial for many similar patients. The low level of drive and energy would particularly suggest the consideration of drugs with energizing effects. The use of such medications might have to be followed carefully, even if they were indicated for weight control as well as activity level. These patients were quick to discontinue such drugs because of their dislike of the increased irritability and the disturbance of their sense of psychological equilibrium. The profile suggests a fluctuating response to treatment; phases of covering over may alternate with a return of the symptoms. Later in treatment he could abruptly develop an eagerness to terminate. A careful review with the patient—or with family members or other informants if available—could help to search out any recent setbacks of personal goals or unexpected losses of pleasure and gratification that the patient might "pass over" as too painful to bring up. These may include potential misfortunes that might occur if he were to risk any real or substantial life changes as well as recent adversities and threatened setbacks. Interpersonal and career assertion may need initially gentle but steadily increasing encouragement.

The profile suggests that he would be guarded and defensive toward intensive interviewing about personal feelings and intimate reactions. Underneath this there may be a fear of moral judgment. This fear of being shamed and judged may have to be relieved before therapy can proceed in any other area. Any past inappropriate or "crazy" behaviors in public could well be a focus of unrelieved shame. At times his ways of reporting his emotional feelings could be rather narrow and carefully modulated, so that the therapist would need to "multiply" the intensity of such feelings in order to gain a full sense of empathy for him. For example, the report that he is feeling "a bit worse" may be a troubling upset and "a bit better" a noteworthy improvement. In general his emotional constrictions and his tendency to declare certain topics "off limits" could necessitate careful handling and patience in therapy.

Precipitating circumstances in similar cases have included emotional losses, a decline in dependency supports, and the breakdown of interpersonal roles so that resentments were increasingly turned inward. The ventilation of hurt feelings and of anger toward family members has been beneficial in similar cases. He may have been frustrated or disillusioned about the achievement of successes which he had hoped to gain for himself. The working through of his reactions to this could be quite helpful. It would be important not to lose sight of tangible action choices in favor of abstract, wishful thinking. The working through of his reactions to this could be quite helpful. Similar patients responded positively to reassurances that many others have experienced similar angry feelings and sexual urges. The ventilation and more ready acceptance of such impulses could lead to a relaxing of his relatively high and inflexible internalized standards and to increasingly positive expressions of these impulses.

Thank you for this referral.

   Alex B. Caldwell, Ph.D.
Diplomate in Clinical Psychology

ABC/cfh

CALDWELL REPORT
1545 SAWTELLE BOULEVARD
LOS ANGELES, CA 90025
(213) 478-3133

Name Sample Adult Profile

Date April 9, 1988

MMPI CRITICAL ITEMS

THE CIRCLED ITEMS WERE ANSWERED AS INDICATED
IN THE PARENTHESES

Distress and Depression

5. I am easily awakened by noise. (True)
27. Evil spirits possess me at times. (True)
86. I am certainly lacking in self-confidence. (True)
142. I certainly feel useless at times. (True)
152. Most nights I go to sleep without thoughts or ideas bothering me. (False)
158. I cry easily. (True)
168. There is something wrong with my mind. (True)
178. My memory seems to be all right. (False)
182. I am afraid of losing my mind. (True)
259. I have difficulty in starting to do things. (True)
337. I feel anxiety about something or someone almost all the time. (True)

Suicidal Thoughts

88. I usually feel that life is worthwhile. (False)
139. Sometimes I feel as if I must injure either myself or someone else. (True)
202. I believe I am a condemned person. (True)
209. I believe my sins are unpardonable. (True)
339. Most of the time I wish I were dead. (True)

Ideas of Reference, Persecution, and Delusions

35. and/or 331. If people had not had it in for me I would have been much more successful. (True)
110. Someone has it in for me. (True)
121. I believe I am being plotted against. (True)
123. I believe I am being followed. (True)
151. Someone has been trying to poison me. (True)
200. There are persons who are trying to steal my thoughts and ideas. (True)
275. Someone has control over my mind. (True)
293. Someone has been trying to influence my mind. (True)
347. I have no enemies who really wish to harm me. (False)
364. People say insulting and vulgar things about me. (True)

Peculiar Experiences and Hallucinations

33. and/or 323. I have had very peculiar and strange experiences. (True)
48. When I am with people I am bothered by hearing very queer things. (True)
66. I see things or animals or people around me that others do not see. (True)

184. I commonly hear voices without knowing where they come from. (True)
291. At one or more times in my life I felt that someone was making me do things by hypnotizing me. (True)
334. Peculiar odors come to me at times. (True)
345. I often feel as if things were not real. (True)
349. I have strange and peculiar thoughts. (True)
350. I hear strange things when I am alone. (True)

Sexual Difficulties

20. My sex life is satisfactory. (False)
37. and/or 302. I have never been in trouble because of my sex behavior. (False)
69. I am very strongly attracted by members of my own sex. (True)
74. I have often wished I were a girl. (or if you are a girl) I have never been sorry that I am a girl. (Male: True; Female: False)
133. I have never indulged in any unusual sex practices. (False)
179. I am worried about sex matters. (True)
297. I wish I were not bothered by thoughts about sex. (True)

Authority Problems

38. and/or 311. During one period when I was a youngster I engaged in petty thievery. (True)
59. I have often had to take orders from someone who did not know as much as I did. (True)

118. In school I was sometimes sent to the principal for cutting up. (True)
205. At times it has been impossible for me to keep from stealing or shoplifting something. (True)
294. I have never been in trouble with the law. (False)

Alcohol and Drugs

156. I have had periods in which I carried on activities without knowing later what I had been doing. (True)
215. I have used alcohol excessively. (True)
251. I have had blank spells in which my activities were interrupted and I did not know what was going on around me. (True)
460. I have used alcohol moderately (or not at all). (False)

Family Discord

21. and/or 308. At times I have very much wanted to leave home. (True)
96. I have very few quarrels with members of my family. (False)
137. I believe that my home life is as pleasant as that of most people I know. (False)
212. My people treat me more like a child than a grown-up. (True)
216. There is very little love and companionship in my family as compared to other homes. (True)
237. My relatives are nearly all in sympathy with me. (False)
245. My parents and family find more fault with me than they should. (True)

Somatic Concerns

2. I have a good appetite. (False)
9. I am about as able to work as I ever was. (False)
23. I am troubled by attacks of nausea and vomiting. (True)
55. I am almost never bothered by pains over the heart or in my chest. (False)
114. Often I feel as if there were a tight band about my head. (True)
125. I have a great deal of stomach trouble. (True)
153. During the past few years I have been well most of the time. (False)
175. I seldom or never have dizzy spells. (False)
189. I feel weak all over much of the time. (True)
243. I have few or no pains. (False)

Name: Sample Adult Profile
Referred by: _____
Date Tested: 4/9/88

2-D and Subscales

	RAW	T
D (full scale)	26	72
D-O	8	50
D-S	18	78
D1	8	53
D2	9	70
D3	3	49
D4	1	45
D5	2	49

3-Hy and Subscales

	RAW	T
Hy (full scale)	22	60
Hy-O	0	39
Hy-S	22	70

Hy1	4	53
Hy2	9	66
Hy3	1	45
Hy4	0	39
Hy5	6	75

4-Pd and Subscales

	RAW	T
Pd (full scale)	15	60
Pd-O	3	42
Pd-S	12	62
Pd1	1	45
Pd2	2	37
Pd3	7	48
Pd4a	4	45
Pd4b	1	39

5-Mf and Subscales

	RAW	T
Mf (full scale)	28	65
Mf1	8	67
Mf2	2	41
Mf3	4	58
Mf4	3	58
Mf5	5	64
Mf6	6	56

6-Pa and Subscales

	RAW	T
Pa (full scale)	10	56
Pa-O	1	44
Pa-S	9	63
Pa1	0	41
Pa2	2	49
Pa3	8	71

8-Sc and Subscales

	RAW	T
Sc (full scale)	4	55
Sc1a	1	39
Sc1b	0	31
Sc2a	0	41

	RAW	T
Sc2b	0	39
Sc2c	0	41
Sc3	1	44

9-Ma and Subscales

	RAW	T
Ma (full scale)	10	43
Ma-O	4	44
Ma-S	6	37
Ma1	1	45
Ma2	3	45
Ma3	3	47
Ma4	1	40

O-Si and Subscales

	RAW	T
Si (full scale)	29	54
Si1	7	44
Si2	6	62
Si3	11	61
Si4	3	50
Si5	1	26
Si6	3	62

Name: Sample Adult Profile
Referred by: _____
Date Tested: 4/9/88

Major Clinical Variables

	RAW	T
ES (Barron)	53	64
MAC (MacAndrew)	20	44
SAP (MacAndrew)	5	35
Mt (Kleinmuntz)	10	46
N-P INDEX (Goldberg)		45

Interpersonal Style Variables

	RAW	T
ER-S (Block)	27	59
EC-5 (Block)	13	44

		RAW	T
ORIG	(Welsh)	29	55
INT	(Welsh)	72	80
Do	(Gough et al.)	20	65
Dy	(Navran)	12	42
Pr	(Gough)	2	32
Re	(Gough et al.)	26	64
Et	(Altus and Tafejian)	4	30
St	(Gough)	24	64
R-S	(Byrne et al.)	25	44
Lbp	(Hanvik)	11	57
O-H	(Megargee et al.)	12	44
Ho	(Cook & Medley)	7	33
Ba	(LaPlace)	54	75

Distress-Control

		RAW	T
A	(Welsh)	5	41
R	(Welsh)	19	57
Ca	(Williams)	8	47
Cn	(Cuadra)	27	55
So-r	(Edwards and Fordyce)	36	66
Th-r	(Pearson et al.)	10	50
Wb-r	(Pearson et al.)	16	68

Validity & Stability

		RAW	T
T-R		0	
CS		2	
T-R + CS			2
Ds	(Gough)	2	37
Mp	(Cofer et al.)	13	52
Sd	(Wiggins)	14	47
Ss	(Nelson)	78	78
Rc	(Goldberg et al.)	31	64
Ic	(Pepper)	13	44
Tc	(Pepper)	9	45

Wiggins Scales

	RAW	T
HEA	2	42
DEP	3	42

			Tryon, Stein & Chu Factor Scales			
ORG	1	40				
FAM	5	56				RAW	T
AUT	4	36				
FEM	12	58	TSC	I-I	12	63
REL	3	39	TSC	II-B	1	43
HOS	6	43	TSC	III-S	4	43
MOR	4	42	TSC	IV-D	3	48
PHO	3	43	TSC	V-R	3	47
PSY	4	43	TSC	VI-A	2	42
HYP	10	46	TSC	VII-T	11	61
SOC	11	55				

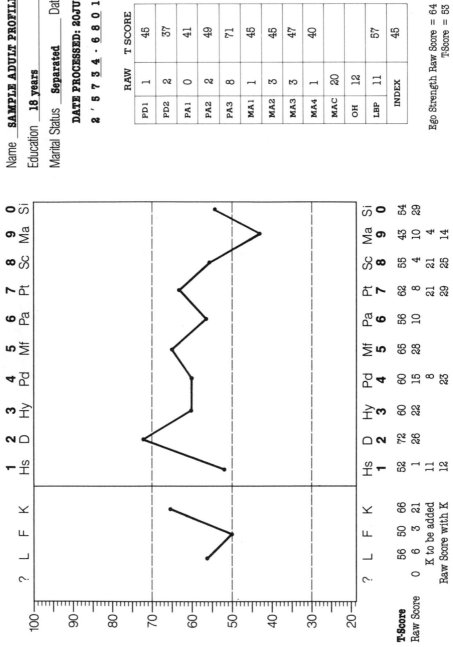

Name **SAMPLE ADULT PROFILE**

Education **18 years**   Age **40**

Marital Status **Separated**   Date Tested **4/9/88**

DATE PROCESSED: 20JUN1988

2 ' 5 7 3 4 - 6 8 0 1 / 9 :

	RAW	T SCORE
PD1	1	45
PD2	2	37
PA1	0	41
PA2	2	49
PA3	8	71
MA1	1	45
MA2	3	45
MA3	3	47
MA4	1	40
MAC	20	
OH	12	57
LBP	11	57
INDEX		45

Ego Strength Raw Score = 64
                T-Score = 53

	?	L	F	K	Hs 1	D 2	Hy 3	Pd 4	Mf 5	Pa 6	Pt 7	Sc 8	Ma 9	Si 0
T-Score														
Raw Score	0	56	50	66	52	72	60	60	65	56	62	55	43	54
		6	3	21	1	26	22	15	28	10	8	4	10	29
K to be added					11			8			21	21	4	
Raw Score with K					12			23			29	25	14	

248

CALDWELL REPORT
1545 SAWTELLE BOULEVARD
LOS ANGELES, CA 90025
(213) 478-3133

NAME OR CODE ___SAMPLE ADULT PROFILE___ REFERRED BY ___-------------___ DATE __4/9/88__

ABBREVIATIONS FOR RATINGS:
EXC = EXCESSIVE
BOR = BORDERLINE
M/O = MILD/OCCASIONAL

1. VALIDITY AND ACCEPTABILITY OF MMPI PROFILE

EXC	BOR	M/O	
		X	denied common, trivial moral faults
		X	excessively minimizing of psychological problems
		X	serious psychological problems may have been covered over
			too many atypical and rarely given responses

Acceptable   1 2 <u>3</u> 4 5 6 7 8 9 10   Not Acceptable

2. SERIOUS PSYCHOLOGICAL-EMOTIONAL PROBLEMS

EXC	BOR	M/O	
			overconcern about own health, potential medical absence and disability problems
			prone to pain and other body complaints without sufficient physical basis, overreactive to injuries
X			depressed, low morale would interfere with functioning
		X	slowed down pace, may not keep up
		X	lacks emotional stability and self-regulation
			could misinterpret the motives of others and act on wrong beliefs
	X		insecure, fearful, lacks mature identity
X			unable to handle hostility from others, may disorganize under intense hostility
			overexcitable and easily distracted
			unrealistic optimism, apt to get "carried-away"
			starter but non-finisher
			deficits of practical coping

Not indicated   1 2 3 4 5 <u>6</u> 7 8 9 10   Serious Disorder

3. STABILITY AND JUDGMENT

EXC	BOR	M/O	
		X	deficits of conscience and integrity
			potential for over-reactions and loss of judgment under stress
			potential antagonism to normal discipline
			impulsive, failures to anticipate consequences
		X	accident prone
			serious longterm risk of alcoholism and/or drug abuse

Good   1 <u>2</u> 3 4 5 6 7 8 9 10   Unacceptable

4. SELF-CONTROL AND ANGER CONTROL

EXC	BOR	M/O	
			undercontrolled aggression under stress
			could be dangerous to others
			irritable, hasty reactions
			"chip-on-the-shoulder" attitude
	X		could be self-righteous and punitive
			rigid and brittle controls; potentially explosive

Favorable   1 2 <u>3</u> 4 5 6 7 8 9 10   Poor risk

5. WORK FACTORS

EXC	BOR	M/O	
	X		risk of undue "time off sick"
	X		moodiness, could drag others down
X			inhibited, lacks needed assertiveness
	X		problems in handling criticism
		X	lacks flexibility, rule-bound
	X		potentially irritating or disturbing of staff morale
			lacks longterm persistence, vocational stability
			lacks warmth, sensitivity
			distant and slow to trust others
			rationalizer
		X	manipulative of others
	X		lacks realistic self-appraisal
			overly ambitious, unrealistic
			likely to seek responsibilities beyond training and experience
		X	low overall effectiveness

Favorable   1 2 3 4 <u>5</u> 6 7 8 9 10   Bad risk

OVERALL ACCEPTABILITY

	LEVEL 1 MOST ACCEPTABLE
	LEVEL 2
	LEVEL 3
X	LEVEL 4
	LEVEL 5 LEAST ACCEPTABLE
	NOT ACCEPTABLE

Name: John Q. Doe

Date of Birth: 4/23/43

Date of Testing: 07/26/87

Sex: M

Age: 44

Date of Report: 7/26/87

THE LEWAK–MARKS MMPI FEEDBACK REPORT

by
Richard Lewak, Ph.D.
Philip A. Marks, Ph.D.
Gerald Nelson, M.D.

This is a computer generated feedback interpretation of the Minnesota Multiphasic Personality Inventory (MMPI) developed by Richard Lewak, Ph.D., Philip A. Marks, Ph.D., and Gerald Nelson, M.D.

This report is derived from a feedback approach developed and used at the Del Mar Psychiatric Clinic in California. It is designed to provide clients or patients with an empathic and nontechnical understanding of their MMPI results. The material is best suited for use at the time of initial or pre-treatment testing, and should be appropriate for adults—age 18 and over—who are voluntarily seeking professional help for personal, marital and vocational counseling or treatment.

The report appears in four parts; and while the provider should use his or her professional judgment in deciding what part(s) to share with the client, the authors have found the following ways most useful:

Part I: Is designed for the therapist only. It briefly describes the patient's personality and offers treatment suggestions for the therapist.

PART II: May be given to the patient in its entirety, or may be shared issue by issue in session with the therapist. It is vital that the patient be encouraged to evaluate the accuracy of each issue using the scales provided in this part of the report.

PART III: Consists of hypothetical background experiences common among persons with the patient's test profile.

PART IV: Provides self-help suggestions which may or may not be shared or discussed with the patient, depending upon the therapist's own clinical judgment.

Produced and distributed exclusively by Applied Innovations, Inc., Wakefield, RI 02879, (401) 789-5081, (800) 272-2250

Name : John Q. Doe		Acct Code : 1234-
Age : 44 Sex: M		Birthdate : 04-23-43
Report Date : 07-26-87		Test Date : 07-26-87

MMPI Test Results:

T-Scores for Validity and Clinical Scales

L	66	1			(Pa)	59
F	56	2	(D)	58	7	(Pt)	58
K	68	3	(Hy)	73	8	(Sc)	70
		4	(Pd)	64	9	(Ma)	45
		5	(Mf)	61	0	(Si)	50

Validity

This is a clinically elevated profile of a patient who apparently was cooperative, understood the instructions, and answered the questions in a consistent and accurate manner. The profile is therefore valid.

Notes to the Therapist

This patient's clinical scale results correspond to the 1-3/3-1 profile type.

Clients or patients with this profile typically block the anger and sadness aspects of the mourning process. They often cry, but not about the painful losses. They also may get angry but not about the painful event, or the person involved or seen as responsible for the painful event. Their response to pain, psychological and physiological, typically, is to deny it, to look at the bright side and to develop increasingly severe physical symptoms in response to their tension.

Insight therapies might focus on the early frightening experiences as a way of getting the patient to work-through the mourning process. Assertiveness training is useful to help the patient deal with his or her difficulties with confrontation in the here and now.

Catharsis and systematic desensitization might help relieve the stored up feelings and guide the patient toward not being so frightened of engaging painful feelings, and relaxation techniques are very useful to help relieve some of the patient's physical symptoms.

Name	: John Q. Doe		Acct Code : 1234-
Age	: 44	Sex : M	Birthdate : 04-23-43
Report Date	: 07-26-87		Test Date : 07-26-87

Your Approach to the Test

John, "the way you approached the test suggests you were feeling vulnerable to being criticized and judged. You have very high standards so it's easy for you to feel that you could be open to some kind of moral review. Perhaps you were raised in a home with rigid values that you still impose upon yourself, or perhaps you felt that this test was going to expose you in some way, so you approached it very cautiously."

"Your profile suggests that you may be experiencing some psychological stress right now that is troubling but not unmanageable. You are facing it which is making it easier for you to deal with."

"Your results suggest that you are a person who is hard to "read" emotionally. Normally you are not strongly expressive emotionally so that people will have to multiply the intensity of what you are saying in order to get a full sense of empathy for you. If, for example, you say you are "somewhat" upset, you may in fact be quite angry or sad. Perhaps growing up you were discouraged from expressing your feelings so that now you are uncomfortable in doing so. Sometimes people may mistake your emotional reserve for 'aloofness' or even 'coldness' or disinterest."

Your Present Feelings, Behaviors and Concerns

John, your profile suggests the following issues that may be affecting your present feelings, behaviors and concerns. Please read each issue and then rate how closely or accurately that issue corresponds to how you feel about yourself. Use the rating scale provided after each issue to record your response by circling the number that best describes the accuracy of the statement for you. Then return these pages to the therapist or doctor who gave you the MMPI.

1. "Your profile indicates that you have grown accustomed to accepting a moderate amount of pain and discomfort."

1	2	3	4	5	?
Correct		Partially Correct		Incorrect	Uncertain

2. "You are probably in pain and misery most of the time but you value being cheerful and positive about things so you try to live with the pain and endure it."

1	2	3	4	5	?
Correct		Partially Correct		Incorrect	Uncertain

3. "You may experience a variety of physical symptoms such as headaches, backaches, stomach upsets, tingling in your extremities, numbness, and nausea."

1	2	3	4	5	?
Correct		Partially Correct		Incorrect	Uncertain

4. "Your physical symptoms very likely get worse under stress, especially if you are in a situation where you have to confront somebody or if somebody confronts or is angry with you."

1	2	3	4	5	?
Correct		Partially Correct		Incorrect	Uncertain

5. "Seeing physicians to help you deal with your health concerns is painful and frightening because you anticipate that they will become angry with you and not attend to the full extent of your physical concerns."

1	2	3	4	5	?
Correct		Partially Correct		Incorrect	Uncertain

6. "It also may be frightening to you because you are never sure whether the doctor will discover some new and frightening illness. At the same time, if the doctor doesn't find ways to help you, it leaves you feeling hopeless and frightened."

1	2	3	4	5	?
Correct		Partially Correct		Incorrect	Uncertain

7. "You may find yourself spending most of your time and energy worrying about what could possibly go wrong next physically, and have little energy or time left to think about anything that could give you pleasure or that could spark your interest other than your health concerns."

1	2	3	4	5	?
Correct		Partially Correct		Incorrect	Uncertain

8. "People with your profile often suffer from feelings of complete exhaustion."

1   2   3   4   5   ?
Correct   Partially Correct   Incorrect   Uncertain

9. "You probably find that you have to push yourself to accomplish even some basic things."

1   2   3   4   5   ?
Correct   Partially Correct   Incorrect   Uncertain

10. "You are a sensitive person, so that being hurt or rejected or having to perhaps hurt or reject anybody else is very difficult for you."

1   2   3   4   5   ?
Correct   Partially Correct   Incorrect   Uncertain

11. "You will spend a lot of energy trying to avoid these situations, sometimes to the point of wanting to deny unpleasant things and hope they go away."

1   2   3   4   5   ?
Correct   Partially Correct   Incorrect   Uncertain

1. "In addition, John, your profile indicates that you can be as comfortable in your relationships with men as in your relationships with women. You probably have no difficulty talking with men and with women you can enjoy talking about your relationship with them without needing constant "updates" or "feedback" on the status of the relationship or on how well you are doing."

1   2   3   4   5   ?
Correct   Partially Correct   Incorrect   Uncertain

2. "Men with your profile usually have a good balance between their 'masculine' and 'feminine' sides. You have some cultural, verbal and aesthetic interests but you also enjoy some traditionally masculine interests."

1   2   3   4   5   ?
Correct   Partially Correct   Incorrect   Uncertain

3. "Men with your profile will enjoy indoor as well as outdoor activities, both as a participant and as an observer. They like sports and the challenge of physical and competitive activities."

1	2	3	4	5	?
Correct		Partially Correct		Incorrect	Uncertain

4. "Issues of practicality do not weigh more heavily than issues of aesthetics for you. You try to balance how something looks and feels with what you think about it and how practical it may be."

1	2	3	4	5	?
Correct		Partially Correct		Incorrect	Uncertain

1. John, "in addition, your profile shows that you are a little shy, reserved and become somewhat uncomfortable with large groups of new people. With strangers you may feel self-conscious and periodically will be lost for words. If you have to relate to new people in a structured situation, such as in giving a prepared speech, then you may be quite comfortable. It is in unstructured situations with people you don't know that is likely to bother you."

1	2	3	4	5	?
Correct		Partially Correct		Incorrect	Uncertain

2. "It seems that right now you are feeling badly about yourself; feeling that you are not worth liking and afraid that if you let others get close they will undermine you, attack you, take advantage of you or make fun of you."

1	2	3	4	5	?
Correct		Partially Correct		Incorrect	Uncertain

3. "You may find yourself periodically experiencing dark moods which seem to well-up from nowhere and are not tied to any specific situation. It is these times when you feel most alone, disconnected and down."

1	2	3	4	5	?
Correct		Partially Correct		Incorrect	Uncertain

Your Possible Background Experiences

Growing up frequently was very difficult for people with this profile. Often they had an angry or explosive parent who frightened them to the point of being "afraid for their lives." Just as often they had experienced some frightening loss or losses of one kind or another and had nobody to turn to for comfort. They soon learned that they had to stay positive and cheerful and occasionally they "numbed" themselves to the pain to avoid feeling overwhelmed by it.

Sometimes people with your profile have difficulty remembering their childhoods, especially periods which could have been painful. Your tendency to deal with emotionally painful things by trying to look on the "nice" or positive side might hamper you in your relations with others. You will have some difficulty wanting to explore your problems because you don't like to deal with negativity and conflict.

1	2	3	4	5	?
Correct	Partially Correct			Incorrect	Uncertain

Self-Help Suggestions of Things You Can Do

1. When your physical symptoms seem to worsen, check and see if you are experiencing some anxiety over facing some conflict or being angry with somebody close to you.

2. Try and practice confronting others whenever you can, to learn to stand up for yourself. If you should feel a "little" upset you might, in fact, be quite angry. Practice telling others you are angry so that the anger doesn't build up inside of you as tension.

3. Work on giving yourself permission to do what you want sometimes and not be so concerned about what is "the right thing to do" socially or for others.

ADULT MMPI FEEDBACK REPORT
EVALUATION FORM

Date _____
Profile Code: _____ Patient's age ___ Sex ___ Race ___
Input/Output _____ ID _____
Rater's knowledge of pt: ___ Extensive, ___ Moderate, ___ Slight.
Hours of patient contact? ___

This form is designed for recording the accuracy of this report and will be used to upgrade and improve future versions. Please ask the patient to evaluate the feedback by circling, following each issue and background experience above, the number indicating the correctness of each and record these by circling the corresponding numbers appearing below. Please then complete a similar evaluation based upon your knowledge of the patient and record this also by circling the appropriate number below. Please also evaluate the usefulness of the other two aspects of this report, include any comments or suggestions, and return this page to Dr. Philip Marks, P.O. Box 2555, Del Mar, CA 92014. Thank you.

1 = Correct (Accurate in entirety, can be verified from what is known)
2 = Essentially Correct (Accurate in most respects, may have minor inaccuracies)

3 = <u>Partially Correct</u> (Partially accurate, partially inaccurate, or some-times either/both)

4 = <u>Generally Incorrect</u> (Incorrect in most respects, may have minor accuracies)

5 = <u>Incorrect</u> (Inaccurate, misleading or contradicts what is known)

Patient's/Client's Ratings

Issues	Correct		Partially Correct	Not or In-Correct		Uncertain
1	1	2	3	4	5	?
2	1	2	3	4	5	?
3	1	2	3	4	5	?
4	1	2	3	4	5	?
5	1	2	3	4	5	?
6	1	2	3	4	5	?
7	1	2	3	4	5	?
8	1	2	3	4	5	?
9	1	2	3	4	5	?
10	1	2	3	4	5	?
11	1	2	3	4	5	?
12	1	2	3	4	5	?
13	1	2	3	4	5	?
14	1	2	3	4	5	?
15	1	2	3	4	5	?

Therapist's Ratings

Issues	Correct		Partially Correct	Not or In-Correct		Uncertain
1	1	2	3	4	5	?
2	1	2	3	4	5	?
3	1	2	3	4	5	?
4	1	2	3	4	5	?
5	1	2	3	4	5	?
6	1	2	3	4	5	?
7	1	2	3	4	5	?
8	1	2	3	4	5	?
9	1	2	3	4	5	?
10	1	2	3	4	5	?
11	1	2	3	4	5	?
12	1	2	3	4	5	?
13	1	2	3	4	5	?
14	1	2	3	4	5	?
15	1	2	3	4	5	?

Background Experiences

		Partially		Not or In-		
Correct		Correct		Correct		Uncertain
1	2	3	4	5	?	

Therapist Notes

(Usefulness) Circle: Extremely / Very / Somewhat / Little / Not Useful

Self-Help Suggestions

(Usefulness) Circle: Extremely/Very/Somewhat/Little/Not Useful

OVERALL SATISFACTION

            Circle: Total/Considerable/Some/Little/None

Comments:

Return to: Dr. Philip Marks, P.O. Box 2555, Del Mar, CA 92014

MMPI ADOLESCENT INTERPRETIVE SYSTEM

developed by
Robert Archer, Ph.D. and PAR Staff
Copyright © 1987 by
Psychological Assessment Resources, Inc.
All rights reserved.

Client	: TEST REPORT	Age	: 15
Sex	: Male	Marital Status	: Single
Education	: 9 years	Date of Birth	: 04/01/72
Prepared for	: PAR on 01/10/88	File Name	: Report

The following adolescent MMPI interpretive information should be viewed as only one source of hypotheses about the adolescent being evaluated. No diagnostic or treatment decision should be based solely on these data. Instead, statements generated by this report should be integrated with other sources of information concerning this client, including additional psychometric test findings, mental status results, psychosocial history data, and individual and family interviews, to reach clinical decisions.

The information contained in this report represents combinations of MMPI actuarial data derived from major works in the adult and adolescent MMPI literatures. This report is confidential and intended for use by qualified professionals only. This report should not be released to the adolescent being evaluated or to his or her family members.

Welsh Code and Scale Elevations

Welsh Code: 49'62783/105: K/F:L#

Mean Clinical Scale Elevation = 58.2

This adolescent is reporting a moderate to high level of overall maladjustment and psychological disturbance.

Mean Excitatory Scale Elevation = 67.0

The Mean Excitatory Scale elevation is based upon the mean of T-score values for scales 4, 8, and 9. These scales serve as measures of moderator

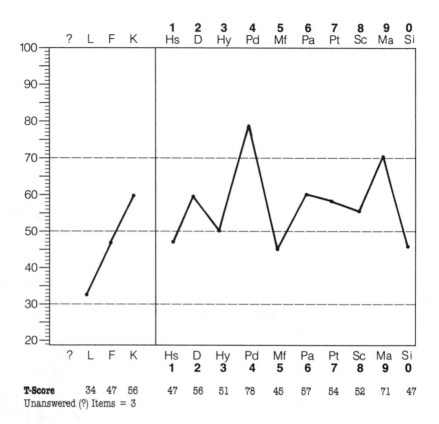

T-Score	?	L	F	K	Hs 1	D 2	Hy 3	Pd 4	Mf 5	Pa 6	Pt 7	Sc 8	Ma 9	Si 0
		34	47	56	47	56	51	78	45	57	54	52	71	47

Unanswered (?) Items = 3

variables which may act to increase the probability of delinquent or anti-social behaviors in adolescent populations. When the Mean Excitatory Scale score exceeds 65, particularly when accompanied by relatively lower scores on scales 2 and 0, the probability of impulsive acting-out or antisocial behaviors becomes pronounced.

Standard Validity Scales

Unanswered (?) Items = 3

There were a few items omitted in completing this MMPI. These omissions may represent areas of limitation in the adolescent's life experience which rendered certain items unanswerable. There is little probability of profile distortion as a result of these omissions.

L T = 34

Scores in this range are typically obtained by individuals who generally respond in an open and candid manner to test items. Low values on scale L are occasionally obtained by adolescents employing an "all true" or "fake bad" response set.

F T = 47

Scores in this range usually indicate that the respondent has answered the test items in a manner similar to most normal adolescents. While some clinical scale elevations may occur, this teenager has not reported signs of highly deviant psychopathology.

K T = 56

Scores in this range are moderately elevated and may reflect a self-reliant stance involving a reluctance to seek help from others. Among normal adolescents, scores in this range may also indicate defensiveness. In psychiatric settings such scores often reflect an unwillingness to admit psychological problems.

Validity Scale Configuration

This validity scale configuration is indicative of an adolescent who responded to the MMPI in a valid, accurate, and cooperative manner. The validity scale features produced by this teenager are characteristic of normal adolescents, and are unusual for teenagers evaluated in psychiatric settings.

Standard Clinical Scales

Hs (1) T = 47

The obtained score is within normal or expected ranges. This adolescent has not expressed a pattern of unusual concerns or preoccupations regarding physical health or functioning.

D (2) T = 56

The obtained score is within normal or expected ranges and depressive symptomatology was not reported as a problem area for this adolescent.

Hy (3) T = 51

The obtained score is within normal or expected ranges and this adolescent probably has the capacity to acknowledge unpleasant issues or negative feelings.

Pd (4) T = 78

Adolescents in psychiatric or criminal justice settings frequently produce substantial elevations on this scale. Scores in this range are typical for adolescents who are characterized as rebellious, hostile toward authority figures, and defiant. These adolescents often have histories of poor school adjustment and problems in school conduct. Higher scores on this scale present an increased probability of overtly delinquent behavior. These adolescents often show an inability to delay gratification and are described as being impulsive and having little tolerance for frustration and boredom. Primary defense mechanisms typically involve acting-out, and such behaviors may be unaccompanied by feelings of guilt or remorse. While these adolescents typically create a good first impression and maintain an extroverted and outgoing interpersonal style, their interpersonal relationships tend to be shallow and superficial. They are eventually viewed by others as selfish, self-centered, and egocentric.

Mf (5) T = 45

Males obtaining scores in this range often exhibit an exaggerated identification with the traditional masculine role which may place an overemphasis on strength and dominance. Such adolescents often have a higher frequency of delinquency, school conduct problems, and lower levels of academic achievement. They have a relatively narrow range of interests and higher frequency of dropping out of school.

Pa (6) T = 57

The obtained score is within normal or expected ranges and items related to paranoid ideation or excessive suspiciousness were not typically endorsed.

Pt (7) T = 54

The obtained score is within normal or expected ranges and this adolescent appears to be capable of meeting current life experiences without excessive worry or apprehension.

Sc (8) T = 52

The obtained score is within normal or expected ranges and suggests intact reality testing and coherent thought processes.

Ma (9) T = 71

Scores in this range are typically obtained by adolescents who are described as overactive, impulsive, and restless. They frequently prefer action to thought and reflection. They are often unrealistic and grandiose in terms of goal setting. These adolescents have a greater likelihood of school conduct problems and delinquent behaviors. They are perceived by others as insensitive, self-centered, egocentric, talkative, and energetic. At marked elevations, scores in this range may reflect a presence of symptoms related to mania such as flight of ideas, grandiose self-perceptions, and euphoric mood.

Si (0) T = 47

The obtained score is within normal or expected ranges and reflects a balance between social introversion and extroversion in terms of attitude and behavior patterns.

Clinical Scale Configural Interpretation

4-9/9-4

This MMPI profile is classified as a 4-9/9-4 codetype, which occurs more frequently among adolescents than adults. Specifically, this codetype is found among 5% to 7% of adults and 10% to 13% of adolescents in clinical settings.

Teenagers who obtain this profile type display a marked disregard for social standards and are likely to manifest difficulties in acting-out and impulsivity. They are described as egocentric, narcissistic, selfish, and self-indulgent, and are often unwilling to accept responsibility for their behaviors. In social situations, these teenagers are extroverted and appear to make an excellent first impression. Their egocentric and interpersonal style, however, typically results in chronic difficulties in establishing close and enduring relationships. They are usually referred for treatment because of defiance, disobedience, impulsivity, provocative behavior, and truancy in school. It is likely that teenagers with this codetype will develop a history of repeated legal violations and court actions.

Adolescents who produce this codetype frequently receive Personality Disorder diagnoses (301.XX) which involve antisocial and narcissistic features. Conduct Disorder diagnoses (312.XX) are also common. Their primary defense mechanism consists of acting-out, and these teenagers often enter treatment settings without evidence of substantial emotional distress such as anxiety or depression. Therapists perceive these adolescents as resentful of authority figures, narcissistic, egocentric, socially extroverted, self-centered, selfish, and demanding.

Adults with this codetype have a markedly poor prognosis for personality or behavior change as a result of psychotherapy. The prognosis for adolescents with this codetype probably is inversely related to the age at which psychotherapy is undertaken. The earlier the psychological intervention, the greater the probability of successful treatment. Effective treatment efforts might be focused upon maintaining clear contingencies between the adolescent's behavior and the environmental consequences; i.e., holding the adolescent consistently responsible for their behaviors and setting appropriate limits and consequences for irresponsible or antisocial behaviors. In this latter regard, the use of carefully structured legal restrictions, such as clearly defined probation contingencies, are often useful for teenagers who have manifested repeated legal violations.

Harris Lingoes Subscales

The following interpretations for the Harris-Lingoes Subscales are provided to generate hypotheses which may be useful in supplementing the interpretation of the standard validity and clinical scales. The clinical correlates employed in these descriptions are based entirely upon research from adult populations; accuracy with regard to adolescent populations is unknown. Hypotheses derived from these descriptions should be validated with independent data. Scores used in generating these interpretive comments are based on normative data collected at the Mayo Clinic and provided by Robert C. Colligan and Kenneth P. Offord.

Familial Discord (Pd1) Percentile = 98.6

High Pd1 scorers view their home situations as unpleasant and lacking in love, support, and understanding. They describe their families as rejecting, critical, and controlling.

Authority Problems (Pd2) Percentile = 99.0

High Pd2 scorers resent authority and societal demands, and they often have histories of academic and legal difficulties. They have definite opinions about what is right and wrong, and they stand up for their beliefs.

Social Imperturbability (Pd3) Percentile = 59.1

The obtained score is within normal or expected ranges.

Social Alienation (Pd4A) Percentile = 57.7

The obtained score is within normal or expected ranges.

Self-Alienation (Pd4B) Percentile = 63.1

The obtained score is within normal or expected ranges.

Frequently Scored Research Scales

The following interpretations for the Frequently Scored Research Scales are provided to generate hypotheses which may be useful in supplementing the interpretation of the standard validity and clinical scales. The clinical correlates employed in these descriptions are based entirely upon research from adult populations; accuracy with regard to adolescent populations is unknown. Hypotheses derived from these descriptions should be validated with independent data. Scores used in generating these interpretive comments are based on normative data collected at the Mayo Clinic and provided by Robert C. Colligan and Kenneth P. Offord.

(A) Percentile = 56.3

The obtained score is within normal or expected ranges and indicates unremarkable levels of anxiety and discomfort.

(R) Percentile = 42.9

The obtained score is within normal or expected ranges and this adolescent appears to be capable of expressing or discussing problem areas and negative feelings.

(Es) Percentile = 61.5

The obtained score is within normal or expected ranges and indicates an average capacity to respond to insight-oriented interventions.

MAC Raw = 28

High scores for adolescents have been related to an increased probability of alcohol and substance abuse. Behaviorally, these adolescents typically appear to be extroverted, sensation seeking, assertive, and impulsive. The high probability of alcohol and drug taking problems would strongly suggest that this teenager be evaluated in terms of the need for substance abuse prevention or treatment interventions. Caution should be exercised in interpreting high MAC scores for minority group adolescents. It is probable that a high rate of false positives may occur for non-white respondents.

END OF REPORT

Name   : Adolescent Teen   Acct Code : ZZZZ
Age   : 16   Sex: M   Birthdate
Report Date: 07-10-80   Test Date : 07-08-80

MARKS ADOLESCENT MMPI REPORT
Version 2.2
Copyright 1986 Dr. Philip A. Marks

This is a computer generated interpretation of the Minnesota Multiphasic Personality Inventory (MMPI) developed by Philip A. Marks, Ph.D.

The report is based on the author's own national study of emotionally disturbed adolescents in treatment and is supplemented by findings from studies involving both adolescents and adults. It is designed to provide an interpretation of MMPI scores, normed specifically for adolescents aged 12 to 18. Especially suited for 'initial' or pretreatment testing, it should be useful for patients seen in a variety of clinic, hospital and office settings. The report may not be appropriate for adolescents tested under different circumstances.

No section of the report is prescriptive or definitive. Rather, each is suggestive and tentative, and should be viewed as consisting of hypotheses which are essentially unverified outside of clinical work. The report should be considered in conjunction with information from interviews, observations, and other psychological tests supplemented by clinical judgement and knowledge of the individual patient. The information is confidential, and in its present form should not be given to patients, their parents or guardians, or those who are not health care professionals.

Produced and distributed exclusively by Applied Innovations, Inc., Wakefield, R.I., 02879, (401) 789-5081

THE MARKS ADOLESCENT MMPI REPORT

Name   : Adolescent Teen   Acct Code : ZZZZ
Age   : 16   Sex : M   Birthdate :
Report Date: 07-10-80   Test Date : 07-08-88

MMPI Test Results:

T-Scores for Validity and Clinical Scales

L	53	1	(Hs)	76	6	(Pa)	62
F	63	2	(D)	79	7	(Pt)	67
K	48	3	(Hy)	67	8	(Sc)	61
		4	(Pd)	49	9	(Ma)	45
		5	(Mf)	54	0	(Si)	56

VALIDITY

This is a clinically elevated profile of a youngster who was cooperative, understood the instructions, and answered the questions in a consistent and accurate manner. The profile is therefore valid.

Teens with similar F scores tend to be moody, dissatisfied and restless adolescents who may be experiencing periodic distress. They may also have some unusual thoughts or feelings, or some special health concerns. Youngsters with similar K scores are usually open, cooperative and self-disclosing adolescents who may have difficulty coping with new and stressful situations.

ACTUARIAL PROFILE INTERPRETATION

This patient's MMPI results correspond to the 1-2/2-1 profile type. This profile occurs among 2.8% of adolescents and 2.8% of adults.

Adolescents with this profile are most likely to be referred for treatment because they are shy, overly sensitive, and obsessed with specific topics. They are fearful, sometimes phobic and have difficulty relating to others. Adolescent patients with this profile tend to be personally isolated and have few if any friends. They are hesitant to make decisions and often express a sad mood. They are suggestible and overly responsive to others' evaluations of them, and see themselves as good-natured yet sulky. Although many are serious, ambitious, and achievement oriented, they worry about their ability to realize their goals. Their difficulty with school is due in part to difficulty in concentrating, and they view their lack of education as the biggest obstacle in life. Most are quite slow academically with frequent truancy, grade failures, and placement in "slow-learner" classes. Some, a minority, are diagnosed as "school phobic." They are frequently anxious and preoccupied, and many are compulsive, ruminative, obsessional, and over ideational. A number fear that they will be unsuccessful in life. Despite their dissatisfaction with some aspects of life, they tend to accept this stoically without blaming others.

These adolescents are, in general, relatively slow to move from a home-centered to a peer-centered orientation. They tend to relate relatively well to their parents and depend upon them to make their decisions. They seem to be fearful of being teased and making mistakes when they make their own decisions. Most have mothers who may be considered domineering, although as disciplinarians they tend to be lenient. Their fathers are seen as warm, sympathetic and somewhat passive. The majority of these adolescents comes from homes where their parents were either separated or divorced. In general, these patients seemed to be treated as if they were younger than their actual age, and their behavior is relatively immature.

Their psychotherapists often describe them as grossly depressed. They are quiet, insecure, tend to delay action, have difficulty committing themselves to any definite course, and seem to seek from their therapists the kind of attention and protection they received from their mothers. They are seen as moderately disturbed, their judgment is somewhat impaired, and their rate of speech is slow. They complain of weakness and becoming tired easily, particularly when they feel guilty. They are suggestible and overly responsive to others' evaluations rather than their own and are much more likely than most adolescents to deal with their problems internally or by talking with their parents or others as opposed to acting them out. They are perfectionistic and demanding toward themselves, and when they fail to perform according to their own and others' expectations their reaction is to give up and to ruminate passively rather than to compensate actively. Basically insecure, they possess a significant need for attention. Their therapists also see them as preoccupied and reflective. They are much less likely than other adolescents to smoke or drink, or have any other significant involvement with drugs.

Adolescents with a 2-1 pattern (in contrast to a 1-2 pattern) appear more self-assured and socially at ease. They have a greater capacity for forming close interpersonal relationships.

Adolescents with this level of scale 3 scores tend to be well-behaved, conforming, achievement oriented, socially involved and friendly. They have a need to be liked and accepted and their social relationships are usually superficial. Often they come from "middle" or "upper" class backgrounds and are seen as self-centered, immature and demanding. They typically display a pleasant and pollyannish attitude and rarely admit to having psychological difficulties. When threatened they blame others and deny that they might be angry, afraid or upset. Often under stress they develop physical symptoms to avoid school and other responsibilities which leads to "playing sick" as a way of manipulating their parents and teachers. Denial, conversion, undoing, repression and idealization are common mechanisms of defense.

Those with this level of scale 0 scores are likely to be somewhat shy, timid, lacking in self-confidence and feel especially uncomfortable in large groups or with new people. Around strangers they feel self-conscious and seem at time "lost for words." In social situations they may feel uneasy and plan ways to leave if the situations become too stressful. They rarely need new friends but can enjoy small groups of people or the few friends they know well. They tend to be reliable, dependable, sensitive, reserved and a little on guard in relations with peers. They are seen as modest, quiet, somewhat inhibited and "hard" to get to know. Confronting others and being assertive can be difficult. Elevated scores are associated with less impulsive and antisocial behaviors and with greater self-control.

Teens with this level of scale 5 scores tend to be interested in practical matters, physical and outdoor activities and in acquiring, building, and repairing things. They often are competitive, athletic, cheerful, thrill-seeking and adventurous boys with stereotypic male interests. They tend to enjoy cars, sports, hunting, body building, phsyical contact and talking to "guys" but care little for art, aesthetics, indoor activities or knowing gentle, sensitive or intelligent friends. Typically they find talking about problems and feelings less useful than attempting to do something about them, since actions usually "speak louder" than words. They are seen by others as cheerful, humorous and easy-going but also as reckless, aggressive, some-what narrow-minded and insightless and can be verbally coarse and crude. Problems of lower intelligence, delinquency, misconduct, confused gender identity and academic underachievement may be common. Frequently there is a close father-son relationship and a relationship with mother that is distant or limited. Idealization and displacement may be mechanisms of defense.

CLINICAL DIAGNOSTIC IMPRESSIONS

Among adolescents in treatment, the 1-2/2-1 profile and associated symptoms and complaints suggest an Overanxious Disorder (313.00), Dys-thymia (300.40), and a Specific Developmental Disorder Not Otherwise Specified (315.90). Unlike the same pattern for adults, the 1-2/2-1 profile for adolescents is not associated with alcohol use, substance abuse, somatic complaints or accompanying pain behaviors. However, a 1-2 code may occur for adolescents diagnosed with a variety of nonprogressive physical disorders.

CLINICAL TREATMENT CONSIDERATIONS

These adolescents experience considerable subjective distress in the form of anxiety and/or depression. There are accompanying features of passivity, dependency, compulsivity, and difficulties with their studies at school.

The prominence of anxiety suggests benefits from progressive relaxation followed by systematic desensitization through either imaginal presenta-tion of fear producing situations, in vivo exposure, modeling, or some combination. Where the anxiety is cognitively or perceptually mediated, cognitive restructuring is indicated. The repressed feelings often directed toward significant others can be aroused by monitoring of thoughts and fantasies, by encouraging abreaction and catharsis, and by providing assis-tance in working these through. Concomitant treatment aimed at skill training for deficits in self-expression (assertiveness) or maladaptive be-havior (dependency) can yield benefits with instruction in role playing, self-monitoring, covert modeling, and behavioral rehearsal.

In the absence of any physiological determinants, a non-agitated specific depression is often responsive to cognitive-behavioral therapy supplemented by rational-emotive procedures. From the outset, it is desirable to avoid reinforcing any depressive referents or verbalizations. Audio or video tapes can be used to record sessions and illustrate such usage. A contractual arrangement can follow to avoid negative self-statements and increase positive ones. Self-monitoring of both mood and actions will frequently lessen depressed mood and increase participation in selected activities. Covert negative reinforcement can be used by introducing highly negative or aversive images, which can be quickly terminated by imagining performance of positive or desired behavior. Coping-skill training, behavioral rehearsal, modeling, and prompting are useful to help overcome behavioral deficits and enable the adolescent to cope with the requirements at school. These can be augmented by contingency management techniques to help develop a better self-concept, and can be followed by an examination of the adolescent's beliefs through RET. Unrealistically high standards or self-expectations, which often derive from distorted perceptions of self-competence, can be alleviated by rational restructuring. Clinically it may be advisable to combine or integrate one or more of these procedures with traditional therapy, family therapy, group therapy or with medications.

There is no drug or class of drug specifically effective for adolescents with this profile, or for adolescents with any of the associated clinical diagnoses. Antihistamines, benzodiazepines, and low doses of phenothiazines are in clinical use for the treatment of anxiety, and the tricyclic antidepressants and ECT are often used against depression. The latter, however, may not be as appropriate for this code-type of depression as for the more severe depressions. Clomipramine is in clinical use for obsessive and compulsive symptoms.

SUMMARY EVALUATION
MMPI ADOLESCENT REPORT

Age: 16   Sex: M   Race:___ Marital Status:_____ID: ZZZZ
Education___(yrs) Occupation_____Inpatient/Outpatient___
Hours of client therapy/contact___Evaluation Date:_____
Rater's   knowledge   of   client: _____Extensive,___Moderate,_____
Slight,_____None
Reason for taking the MMPI:

Please complete the information above and evaluate this report by circling the number corresponding to the accuracy of each section. Only evaluative those sections for which information actually appears in the report. If a section is rated as 1 or 0, please indicate the nature of the inaccuracy. Simply skip sections where information is missing or not given in the report.

Also, please indicate your overall satisfaction with the report, write in any comments you may wish to make, and return this form to: Applied Innovations, Inc., South Kingstown Office Park, Wakefield, RI 02879 Thank you.

RATINGS
4 - Accurate (Correct in its entirety)
3 - Essentially Accurate (Having only minor inaccuracies)
2 - Partially Accurate (Correct in some respects, Incorrect in others)
1 - Generally Inaccurate (Having only minor accuracies)
0 - Inaccurate (Misleading or contradicts what is known)

SECTION

	Accurate		Partially		Inaccurate
Validity					
Profile	4	3	2	1	0
L Scale	4	3	2	1	0
F Scale	4	3	2	1	0
K Scale	4	3	2	1	0
Profile Interpretation					
Two-Point Code (1-2/2-1)	4	3	2	1	0
Referral	4	3	2	1	0
Family: Father	4	3	2	1	0
Mother	4	3	2	1	0
Siblings	4	3	2	1	0
School: Academic	4	3	2	1	0
Other	4	3	2	1	0
Peers/Friends	4	3	2	1	0
As sees self	4	3	2	1	0
As seen by others	4	3	2	1	0
As seen by therapist	4	3	2	1	0
Conflict/Defense	4	3	2	1	0
Emotional Tone/Mood	4	3	2	1	0
Control/Temper	4	3	2	1	0
Physical Health	4	3	2	1	0
Drugs Alcohol	4	3	2	1	0
Legal Problems	4	3	2	1	0
Scale 3	4	3	2	1	0
Scale 0	4	3	2	1	0
Scale 5	4	3	2	1	0
Diagnostic Impressions					
Axis I	4	3	2	1	0
Axis II	4	3	2	1	0

Treatment Considerations

Summary Statement	4	3	2	1	0
Pychotherapy Statement	4	3	2	1	0
Behavior Therapy	4	3	2	1	0
Pharmacotherapy	4	3	2	1	0

Overall Usefulness or Satisfaction
(Circle One:)   Total / Considerable / Some / Little / None

COMMENTS:

Name   : Adult Client   Acct Code : XXXXX
Age   : 39   Sex : M   Birthdate :
Report Date : 08-10-88   Test Date : 07-08-88

THE MARKS MMPI ADULT REPORT
Version 2.2

Copyright 1986
Donald S. Strassberg, Ph.D.
Leslie M. Cooper, Ph.D.
Philip A. Marks, Ph.D.

This is a computer generated interpretation of the Minnesota Multiphasic Personality Inventory (MMPI) developed by Donald S. Strassberg, Ph.D., Leslie M. Cooper, Ph.D. and Philip A. Marks, Ph.D.

The report is based on the authors' own research and clinical experience supplemented by the clinical and research findings of others (see documentation for specific references). It includes information derived from a variety of patient groups, and is designed to provide professionals with an interpretation of MMPI scores, normed for clients ages 18 and over. It should be useful for patients seen for psychological assessment or psychotherapy in a variety of clinic, hospital and office settings. The material may not be appropriate for adults tested under different circumstances.

No section of the report is prescriptive or definitive. Rather, each is suggestive and tentative, and should be treated as hypotheses which are essentially unverified outside of clinical work. The report should be considered in conjunction with information from interviews, observations, and other psychological tests supplemented by clinical judgment and knowledge of the individual patient. The information is confidential and should be considered as a consultation between professionals. In its present form, it should not be given to clients, their relatives or guardians, or others who are not mental health professionals.

Produced and distributed exclusively by Applied Innovations, Inc., Wakefield, R.I., 02879 Phone: (401) 789-5081.

Name   : Adult Client   Acct Code : XXXXX
Age   : 39   Sex : M   Birthdate :
Report Date : 08-10-88   Test Date : 07-08-88

MMPI Test Results:

T-Scores for Validity and Clinical Scales
L	53	1 (Hs)	68	6 (Pa) 69
F	55	2 (D)	76	7 (Pt) 70
K	52	3 (Hy)	65	8 (Sc) 58
		4 (Pd)	63	9 (Ma)48
		5 (Mf)	67	0 (Si) 75

VALIDITY

This is a clinically elevated profile of a client who was cooperative, understood the instructions, and answered the questions in an accurate manner. The profile is therefore valid.

Clients with similar K scores are usually candid and adaptable individuals with a resilient ego-defense system, but an uncertain self-concept and only partially effective coping mechanisms.

ACTUARIAL PROFILE INTERPRETATION

This client's clinical scale results correspond to the 2-0/0-2 two-point code type. This pattern occurs among 3.4% of adults receiving clinical evaluations.

Those with this pattern are shy, introverted, inhibited individuals with a life-long pattern of difficulty in forming and maintaining close relationships. They feel quite insecure in social relations, particularly those involving the opposite sex. They are distrustful and tend to maintain an emotional distance from others.

As infants, it is likely that they were rarely held, cuddled, kissed, hugged, or given other types of physical affection. As children, they were probably protected from emotional and physical experiences. Typically, they were raised to believe that one's feelings (both positive and negative) are private, and to express them would be a weakness that could lead only to shame and embarrassment. They now fear sharing of themselves with others, and will project a formal, rigid, detached, objective, or "professional" manner in interpersonal relations. Any appearance of warmth, friendliness, or tender concern is usually brief and superficial, and a transparent defense against their anxiety at the moment.

These individuals are worriers, many of whom have come to accept a mild amount of unhappiness as normal. Feelings of inadequacy are usually seen, and insomnia may be a problem. They may be seen by others as distant, aloof, unassuming, reliable, intellectual, and as living quiet and orderly lives. They rarely voluntarily seek professional help.

Scores in this scale 7 range are associated with individuals who are anxious, tense, ruminative, and self-doubting. Their anxiety and apprehension may interfere with their daily adjustment. They tend to feel guilty and indecisive. They are frequently described as conscientious, moralistic, perfectionistic, rigid, and dissatisfied with life. They tend to set unrealistically high standards for themselves and others, and become self-doubting and self-critical when they fall short of their own expectations. Explore for the possibility of phobias and obsessive-compulsive features.

In addition, men with similar scale 5 scores balance interests in sports, physical activity, and practical matters with art, music, literature, and science. They enjoy indoor as well as outdoor activities, both as a participant and as an observer. They are often sensitive, inquisitive, introspective, conversational and verbally expressive. College educated men frequently obtain similar scale 5 scores.

CLINICAL DIAGNOSTIC IMPRESSIONS

Among adults in treatment, the 2-0/0-2 profile is associated with the following DSM-III-R disorders:
Axis I: 309.00 Adjustment disorder, with depressed mood,
300.40 Dysthymia, 296.2x/3x Major depression.
Axis II: 301.82 Avoidant personality disorder;
301.20 Schizoid personality disorder.

TREATMENT CONSIDERATIONS

Fears of intimacy and trust are important issues for many of these patients, and the gaining of their confidence is essential toward developing a treatment relationship. Once trust is established, the reasons for their avoidance should be explored and addressed via a cognitive/behavioral approach, gestalt therapy, reality therapy, crisis therapy, or brief therapy. Progressive relaxation and desensitization, perhaps combined with stress inoculation or restructuring supplemented with assertion training, rehearsal, and self-management, can be helpful for avoidance behaviors and for reducing fears associated with the risks in forming relationships. Feelings of inadequacy and a poor self-concept can often be lessened with social skill training, cognitive restructuring, feedback and reassurance. Clinically it may be advisable to combine one or more of these procedures with couples therapy, marital therapy, or group therapy at some stage of treatment.

Anxiolytic drugs occasionally are helpful for patients whose anxiety is sufficiently great to impair their daily functioning, but the depression associated with this profile is often chronic or characterological in nature and therefore is not usually responsive to antidepressants. Patients with long histories of a psychological disorder or who appear to be decompensating are probably best treated with a nonsedating phenothiazine.

SUMMARY EVALUATION
MMPI ADULT REPORT

Age: 39   Sex: M   Race:___ Marital Status: ___ ID: XXXXX
Education ___(yrs) Occupation _____ Inpatient/Outpatient___
Hours of client therapy/contact___ Evaluation Date:_____
Rater's knowledge of client:___ Extensive, ___ Moderate, ___ Slight, ___ None
Reason for taking the MMPI:

Please complete the information above and evaluate this report by circling the number corresponding to the accuracy of each section. If a section is rated as 1 or 0, please indicate the nature of the inaccuracy. Also, please indicate your overall satisfaction with the report, write in any comments you may wish to make on the back of this sheet, and return it to: Applied Innovations, Inc., South Kingstown Office Park, Wakefield, RI 02879 Thank you.

RATINGS
4 - Accurate (Correct in its entirety)
3 - Essentially Accurate (Having only minor inaccuracies)
2 - Partially Accurate (Correct in some respects, Incorrect in others)
1 - Generally Inaccurate (Having only minor accuracies)
0 - Inaccurate (Misleading or contradicts what is known)

SECTION

	Accurate		Partially		Inaccurate
Validity					
Profile	4	3	2	1	0
L Scale	4	3	2	1	0
F Scale	4	3	2	1	0
K Scale	4	3	2	1	0
Actuarial Interpretation					
Two-Point Code (2-0/0-2).	4	3	2	1	0
Scale 7	4	3	2	1	0
Scale 5	4	3	2	1	0
Diagnostic Impressions					
Axis I	4	3	2	1	0
Axis II	4	3	2	1	0

Treatment Considerations
    Psycho-Behav. Therapy   4   3   2   1   0
Medications   4   3   2   1   0

Overall Usefulness or Satisfaction
(Circle One:) Total / Considerable / Some / Little / None

Sample Report I

THE MINNESOTA REPORT™*

for the Minnesota Multiphasic Personality Inventory™: Adult System
By James N. Butcher, Ph.D.

Client No. : 112279   Gender : Male
Setting : Mental Health Outpatient   Age : 34
Report Date : 82/11/10

PROFILE VALIDITY

This is a valid MMPI profile. The client has cooperated in the evaluation, admitting to a number of psychological problems in a frank and open way.

Individuals with this profile tend to be blunt and may openly complain to others about their psychological problems. The client tends to be quite self-critical and may appear to have low self-esteem and inadequate psychological defense mechanisms. He may be seeking psychological help at this time since he feels that things are out of control and unmanageable.

NOTE: This MMPI interpretation can serve as a useful source of hypotheses about clients. This report is based on objectively derived scale indexes and scale interpretations that have been developed in diverse groups of patients. The personality descriptions, inferences and recommendations contained herein need to be verified by other sources of clinical information since individual clients may not fully match the prototype. The information in this report should most appropriately be used by a trained, qualified test interpreter. The information contained in this report should be considered confidential.

SYMPTOMATIC PATTERN

Individuals with this MMPI profile usually are experiencing much psychological distress and personality deterioration. He is quite disturbed, hyperactive, and seems to have a great deal of difficulty with emotional control, all of which may threaten others. He may have quite unrealistic or bizarre plans, and he may have a loud and boastful manner.

Individuals with this profile are usually viewed as having a thought disorder. They are confused, disorganized, have a hard time concentrating, and tend to withdraw into fantasy and to manifest paranoid ideation.

There is a strong likelihood that the client is experiencing delusions or hallucinations, and he shows many other signs of serious disturbance, including autistic thinking and bizarre speech. Many individuals with this profile are unable to care for themselves and require supervision or a controlled environment.

He has diverse interests that include aesthetic and cultural activities. He is usually somewhat passive and compliant in interpersonal relationships, is generally self-controlled, and dislikes confrontation. He may have difficulty in expressing anger directly and may resort to indirect means.

INTERPERSONAL RELATIONS

He appears to have quite disturbed interpersonal relationships, and he is very unpredictable and demanding with others, becoming hostile when his needs are not met. He appears to have a poor sexual adjustment. Many individuals with this profile are quite uncomfortable in heterosexual relationships and tend to avoid marriage. He is probably behaving in unpredictable and erratic ways which may produce a great deal of marital strain.

The content of this client's MMPI responses suggests the following additional information concerning his interpersonal relations. He views his home situation as unpleasant and lacking in love and understanding. He feels intensely hostile and resentful of others, and would like to get back at them. He is competitive and uncooperative, tending to be very critical of others.

BEHAVIORAL STABILITY

His MMPI profile reflects a pattern of extreme personal instability. He is quite overactive and unstable and may behave in erratic and threatening ways.

DIAGNOSTIC CONSIDERATIONS

Individuals with this MMPI profile are usually quite disturbed. Although the most likely diagnosis for this profile type is Schizophrenic Disorder, a Major Affective Disorder (i.e., Manic) also needs to be considered. Some individuals diagnosed as having a Borderline Personality also produce this profile type.

The possibility of dangerous or self-destructive behavior needs to be evaluated. His extremely high score on the MacAndrew Addiction Scale suggests great proneness to the development of an addictive disorder.

Client No.: 112279
Setting: Mental Health Outpatient
Report Date: 82/11/10

Gender: Male
Age: 34

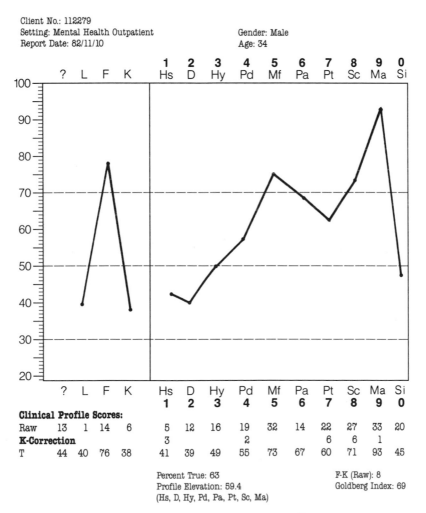

Clinical Profile Scores:

	?	L	F	K	Hs	D	Hy	Pd	Mf	Pa	Pt	Sc	Ma	Si
Raw	13	1	14	6	5	12	16	19	32	14	22	27	33	20
K-Correction					3			2			6	6	1	
T	44	40	76	38	41	39	49	55	73	67	60	71	93	45

Percent True: 63
Profile Elevation: 59.4
(Hs, D, Hy, Pd, Pa, Pt, Sc, Ma)

F-K (Raw): 8
Goldberg Index: 69

Welsh Code: 9*58"67-4/301:2#   F"?L:K

Client No.: 112279   Report Date: 82/11/10

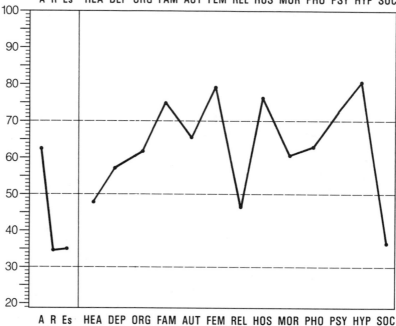

Supplemental Profile Scores:

	A	R	Es	HEA	DEP	ORG	FAM	AUT	FEM	REL	HOS	MOR	PHO	PSY	HYP	SOC
Raw	21	8	34	4	10	9	9	15	19	5	22	13	10	21	25	2
T		61	34	33	48	56	59	73	64	77	46	75	60	62	72	80	36

Further evaluation of substance use or abuse problems is strongly recommended.

TREATMENT CONSIDERATIONS

Individuals with this profile are treated primarily with psychotropic medications. They are probably not open to individual, insight-oriented psychotherapy, since they are having reality contact problems, suspicious mentation, and have great difficulty forming relationships. The client has a thought disorder and a concentration problem that prevent him from focusing upon issues in an interview.

EXTENDED SCORE REPORT

Supplementary Scales:	Raw Score	T Score
Dependency (DY)	29	61
Dominance (Do)	15	51

Responsibility (Re)	14	35
Control (Cn)	33	71
College Maladjustment (Mt)	19	58
Overcontrolled Hostility (O-H)	15	59
Prejudice (Pr)	16	58
Manifest Anxiety (MAS)	23	62
MacAndrew Addiction (MAC)	37	93
Social Status (St)	28	73
Depression Subscales (Harris-Lingoes):		
Subjective Depression (D1)	7	50
Psychomotor Retardation (D2)	2	32
Physical Malfunctioning (D3)	1	35
Mental Dullness (D4)	3	55
Brooding (D5)	4	60
Hysteria Subscales (Harris-Lingoes):		
Denial of Social Anxiety (Hy1)	5	59
Need for Affection (Hy2)	4	46
Lassitude-Malaise (Hy3)	2	49
Somatic Complaints (Hy4)	1	43
Inhibition of Aggression (Hy5)	2	46
Psychopathic Deviate Subscales (Harris-Lingoes):		
Familial Discord (Pd1)	3	57
Authority Problems (Pd2)	5	55
Social Imperturbability (Pd3)	9	56
Social Alienation (Pd4a)	10	66
Self Alienation (Pd4b)	8	66
Masculinity-Femininity Subscales (Serkownek):		
Narcissism-Hypersensitivity (Mf1)	7	61
Stereotypic Feminine Interests (Mf2)	7	74
Denial of Stereo. Maculine Interests (Mf3)	6	73
Heterosexual Discomfort-Passivity (Mf4)	1	33
Introspective-Critical (Mf5)	2	37
Socially Retiring (Mf6)	3	35
Paranoia Subscales (Harris-Lingoes):		
Persecutory Ideas (Pa1)	6	68
Poignancy (Pa2)	3	55
Naivete (Pa3)	2	41
Schizophrenia Subscales (Harris-Lingoes):		
Social Alienation (Sc1a)	6	60
Emotional Alienation (Sc1b)	2	48
Lack of Ego Mastery, Cognitive (Sc2a)	3	60
Lack of Ego Mastery, Conative (Sc2b)	3	55
Lack of Ego Mastery, Def. Inhib. (Sc2c)	6	80
Bizarre Sensory Experiences (Sc3)	10	81
Hypomania Subscales (Harris-Lingoes):		
Amorality (Ma1)	3	59
Psychomotor Acceleration (Ma2)	9	87

EXTENDED SCORE REPORT (*Continued*)

Supplementary Scales:	Raw Score	T Score
Imperturbability (Ma3)	5	59
Ego Inflation (Ma4)	8	83
Social Introversion Subscales (Serkownek):		
Inferiority-Personal Discomfort (Si1)	11	61
Discomfort with Others (Si2)	3	43
Staid-Personal Rigidity (Si3)	0	1
Hypersensitivity (Si4)	4	57
Distrust (Si5)	9	77
Physical-Somatic Concerns (Si6)	3	62

CRITICAL ITEM LISTING

The following critical items have been found to have possible significance in analyzing a client's problem situation. Although these items may serve as a source of hypotheses for further investigation, caution should be taken in interpreting individual items because they may have been inadvertently checked. Critical item numbers refer to the Group Form test booklet.

ACUTE ANXIETY STATE (Koss-Butcher Critical Items)
   5. I am easily awakened by noise. (T)
  13. I work under a great deal of tension. (T)
 238. I have periods of such great restlessness that I cannot sit long in a chair. (T)
 337. I feel anxiety about something or someone almost all the time. (T)
 506. I am a high-strung person. (T)
 555. I sometimes feel that I am about to go to pieces. (T)

DEPRESSED SUICIDAL IDEATION (Koss-Butcher Critical Items)
  41. I have had periods of days, weeks, or months when I couldn't take care of things because I couldn't "get going". (T)
 142. I certainly feel useless at times. (T)
 418. At times I think I am no good at all. (T)

THREATENED ASSAULT (Koss-Butcher Critical Items)
  39. At times I feel like smashing things. (T)
  97. At times I have a strong urge to do something harmful or shocking. (T)
 145. At times I feel like picking a fist fight with someone. (T)
 234. I get mad easily and then get over it soon. (T)
 381. I am often said to be hotheaded. (T)

MENTAL CONFUSION (Koss-Butcher Critical Items)
33. I have had very peculiar and strange experiences. (T)
50. My soul sometimes leaves my body. (T)
66. I see things or animals or people around me that others do not see. (T)
345. I often feel as if things were not real. (T)
349. I have strange and peculiar thoughts. (T)

PERSECUTORY IDEAS (Koss-Butcher Critical Items)
157. I feel that I have often been punished without cause. (T)
284. I am sure I am being talked about. (T)
293. Someone has been trying to influence my mind. (T)
347. I have no enemies who really wish to harm me. (F)
364. People say insulting and vulgar things about me. (T)

CHARACTEROLOGICAL ADJUSTMENT—ANTISOCIAL ATTITUDE
38. During one period when I was a youngster, I engaged in petty thievery. (T)
56. As a youngster I was suspended from school one or more times for cutting up. (T)
118. In school I was sometimes sent to the principal for cutting up. (T)
269. I can easily make other people afraid of me, and sometimes do for the fun of it. (T)
294. I have never been in trouble with the law. (F)

CHARACTEROLOGICAL ADJUSTMENT—FAMILY CONFLICT
21. At times I have very much wanted to leave home. (T)
245. My parents and family find more fault with me than they should. (T)

SEXUAL CONCERN AND DEVIATION (Lachar-Wrobel Critical Items)
69. I am very strongly attracted by members of my own sex. (T)

SOMATIC SYMPTOMS (Lachar-Wrobel Critical Items)
62. Parts of my body often have feelings like burning, tingling, crawling, or like "going to sleep." (T)
174. I have never had a fainting spell. (F)
194. I have had attacks in which I could not control my movements or speech but in which I knew what was going on around me. (T)

251. I have had blank spells in which my activities were interrupted and I did not know what was going on around me. (T)
281. I do not often notice my ears ringing or buzzing. (F)
544. I feel tired a good deal of the time. (T)

Case Summary

John C. is a 34-year-old marketing executive in a large corporation. Although he has had serious difficulties with some supervisors in the past, his talent and industriousness make him a valuable asset to his company, and management has been generally tolerant of his problem behavior. He has been quite successful and has advanced rapidly in spite of his "bad boy" image. John was recently encouraged to seek psychological help by his present supervisor following an incident in which he came to work drunk and became verbally abusive to several employees in his department.

John has recently been undergoing both family problems and increased job pressures. After seven years of marriage his wife, fearful of his abusive behavior toward her and the children, recently obtained a court order forcing him to move out of their home. She had been unsuccessful in getting him into treatment for his alcohol abuse. John was encountering numerous problems before the recent alcohol incidents at work. His department had been operating with reduced effectiveness for over a year—since shortly after John was promoted to department head. Employees complained of John's arbitrariness in making decisions, his increased absences, and his requirement that others work extra time (without pay, owing to the company's salary structure).

John missed the first two clinic appointments set for him. When he came for the third appointment, he was administered the MMPI and was interviewed. He stayed an extra half hour talking almost incessantly, despite his frequent reminders to himself that he was late and had to leave. He was quite verbal in the interview—leaving little opportunity for the psychologist to ask questions. He skipped around from topic to topic never going into much detail. He ignored efforts to focus on material relevant to the evaluation. When he was confronted with the question of alcohol abuse, he simply replied, "Well, doc, like everybody else, I take a drink now and then, but let me tell you about . . ." He later refused a referral to a chemical-abuse treatment program. However, he agreed to return for a second visit.

During the second session John talked more pointedly about the problems he was encountering and was more open to the recommendation that he be referred for a psychiatric evaluation for his mood problems. John had experienced additional difficulties between the two visits—he had been arrested for drunk driving. He was more willing to consider that he was abusing alcohol. During this session the MMPI findings were discussed with him. He was taken with the fact that his response to MMPI items had "predicted" his problems so clearly, even though he was not aware of them at the time he took the test.

John was scheduled for a chemical-dependency evaluation at an in-patient alcohol treatment facility. It was recommended that he be given an early appointment with the staff psychiatrist to evaluate the possibility of a mood disorder.

Sample Interpretive Report 2

THE MINNESOTA PERSONNEL INTERPRETIVE REPORT[TM]*
for the Minnesota Multiphasic Personality Inventory[TM]
By James N. Butcher, Ph.D.

Client No. : 222   Gender : Male
Report Date : 28-DEC-83   Age : 48
ISS Code Number : 111 3
Occupation : Flight Crew

PROFILE VALIDITY

This applicant's approach to the MMPI was open and cooperative. The resulting MMPI profile is valid and probably a good indication of his present level of personality functioning. This suggests that he is able to follow instructions and to respond appropriately to the task, and this may be viewed as a positive indication of his involvement with the evaluation.

PERSONAL ADJUSTMENT

The applicant is quite immature, self-oriented, and impulsive, and shows little regard for others. He may have a history of interpersonal and legal conflict, and may present a spotty achievement and work record. He may

---

NOTE: This MMPI interpretation can serve as a useful source of hypotheses about clients applying for positions in which stable psychological adjustment has been determined to be essential for success on the job. The MMPI was not originally developed for use in personnel selection, however, and contains a number of items that some people believe to be irrelevant or inappropriate for that purpose. This report is based upon empirical descriptions derived largely from clinical populations. Caution should be taken in applying these interpretations in a pre-employment screening situation. The MMPI should NOT be used as the SOLE means of determining a candidate's suitability for employment. The information in this report should be used by qualified test interpretation specialists only.

behave unreliably and carelessly, and may rebel against authority. Apparently unable to learn from past mistakes, he gets himself involved in the same problem situations over and over again. He seems to accept little responsibility for his shortcomings and tends to blame others for his difficulties. He may be hostile and aggressive toward others.

INTERPERSONAL RELATIONS

Although he is usually likeable and creates a good first impression, his relationships are typically superficial and he may frequently use other people for his own ends. He seems unable to develop stable, warm, and trusting personal relations, and he tends to have disrupted social and family relationships. He typically shows very little guilt over the interpersonal difficulties he creates.

He is generally comfortable in social relationships. He appears to meet and talk with other people easily and shows little anxiety about being in social situations.

The content of this applicant's MMPI responses suggests the following additional information concerning his interpersonal relations. He views his home situation as unpleasant and lacking in love and understanding. He feels like leaving home to escape a quarrelsome, critical situation, and to be free of family domination. He tends to be interpersonally dominant, asserting a high degree of self-confidence and forcefulness. He willingly expresses strong opinions.

BEHAVIORAL STABILITY

He is a rather unstable person who often becomes embroiled in difficulties as a result of his personality problems. His profile is quite stable, however, and not likely to change much over time.

POSSIBLE EMPLOYMENT PROBLEMS

Flight crew applicants with this MMPI profile should be carefully evaluated for the possibility of impulsive behavior or poor judgment. A history of nonconforming or acting-out behavior is somewhat likely with this profile.

This applicant tends to have difficulty avoiding trouble. He tends to get bored and frustrated and consequently may act impulsively or carelessly. Individuals with this profile often behave irresponsibly and unreliably, and may develop a cavalier attitude about standards or work regulations. In addition, they may create interpersonal problems on the job, causing tension among co-workers. Their rebellious attitude toward authority may make them difficult to supervise. Absenteeism and rule infractions at work are frequent problems among individuals of this personality type.

Client No.: 222   Gender: Male
Report Date: 28-DEC-83   Age: 48
Occupation: Flight Crew

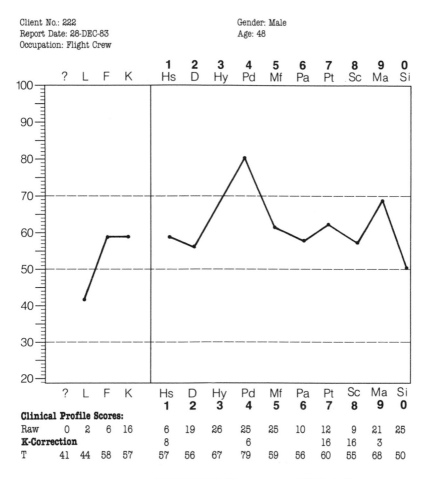

	?	L	F	K	Hs 1	D 2	Hy 3	Pd 4	Mf 5	Pa 6	Pt 7	Sc 8	Ma 9	Si 0
Clinical Profile Scores:														
Raw	0	2	6	16	6	19	26	25	25	10	12	9	21	25
K-Correction					8			6			16	16	3	
T		41	44	58	57	57	56	67	79	59	56	60	55	68	50

Percentage True: 42   F-K (Raw): –10
Average Profile Elevation: 62.3   Disturbance Index (Dsl): 536
(Hs, D, Hy, Pd, Pa, Pt, Sc, Ma)

Welsh Code: 4'93 7-5 12680/   FK/L?:

The Minnesota Multiphasic Personality Inventory
EXTENDED SCORE REPORT

Supplementary Scales:	Raw Score	T Score
Dependency (Dy)	20	51
Dominance (Do)	22	70
Responsibility (Re)	16	40
College Maladjustment (Mt)	14	53
Overcontrolled Hostility (O-H)	10	42
Prejudice (Pr)	13	52

The Minnesota Multiphasic Personality Inventory

EXTENDED SCORE REPORT (*Continued*)

Supplementary Scales:	Raw Score	T Score
Manifest Anxiety (MAS)	12	46
MacAndrew Addiction (MAC)	26	61
Cynicism (CYN)	10	47
Social Status (St)	21	58
Favorable Impression (Fi)	15	65
Depression Subscales (Harris-Lingoes):		
Subjective Depression (D1)	6	47
Psychomotor Retardation (D2)	4	43
Physical Malfunctioning (D3)	3	49
Mental Dullness (D4)	3	55
Brooding (D5)	3	54
Hysteria Subscales (Harris-Lingoes):		
Denial of Social Anxiety (Hy1)	5	59
Need for Affection (Hy2)	6	54
Lassitude-Malaise (Hy3)	6	66
Somatic Complaints (Hy4)	5	59
Inhibition of Aggression (Hy5)	2	46
Psychopathic Deviate Subscales (Harris-Lingoes):		
Familial Discord (Pd1)	6	74
Authority Problems (Pd2)	5	55
Social Imperturbability (Pd3)	10	60
Social Alienation (Pd4a)	8	59
Self Alienation (Pd4b)	6	58
Masculinity-Femininity Subscales (Serkownek):		
Narcissism-Hypersensitivity (Mf1)	7	61
Stereotypic Feminine Interests (Mf2)	5	61
Denial of Stereo. Masculine Interests (Mf3)	4	58
Heterosexual Discomfort-Passivity (Mf4)	2	46
Introspective-Critical (Mf5)	4	55
Socially Retiring (Mf6)	2	28
Paranoia Subscales (Harris-Lingoes):		
Persecutory Ideas (Pa1)	1	46
Poignancy (Pa2)	2	49
Naivete (Pa3)	5	56
Schizophrenia Subscales (Harris-Lingoes):		
Social Alienation (Sc1a)	2	44
Emotional Alienation (Sc1b)	2	48
Lack of Ego Mastery, Cognitive (Sc2a)	1	47
Lack of Ego Mastery, Conative (Sc2b)	2	50
Lack of Ego Mastery, Def. Inhib. (Sc2c)	2	54
Bizarre Sensory Experiences (Sc3)	2	48
Amorality (Ma1)	2	52

Client No.: 222   Report Date: 28-DEC-83

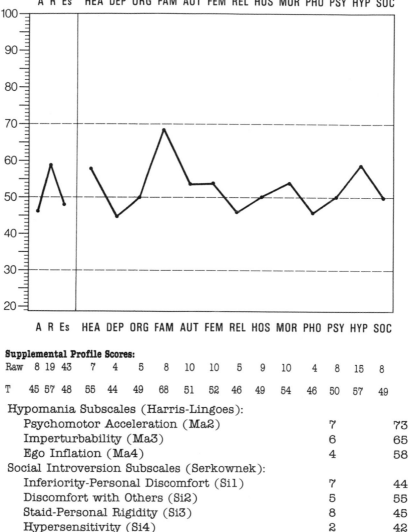

Supplemental Profile Scores:

	A	R	Es	HEA	DEP	ORG	FAM	AUT	FEM	REL	HOS	MOR	PHO	PSY	HYP	SOC
Raw	8	19	43	7	4	5	8	10	10	5	9	10	4	8	15	8
T	45	57	48	55	44	49	68	51	52	46	49	54	46	50	57	49

Hypomania Subscales (Harris-Lingoes):

Psychomotor Acceleration (Ma2)	7	73
Imperturbability (Ma3)	6	65
Ego Inflation (Ma4)	4	58

Social Introversion Subscales (Serkownek):

Inferiority-Personal Discomfort (Si1)	7	44
Discomfort with Others (Si2)	5	55
Staid-Personal Rigidity (Si3)	8	45
Hypersensitivity (Si4)	2	42
Distrust (Si5)	6	58
Physical-Somatic Concerns (Si6)	2	53

CONTENT THEMES

The following Content Themes may serve as a source of hypotheses for further investigations. These content themes summarize similar item responses that appear with greater frequency with this applicant than with most people.

May be overly sensitive in interpersonal relationships.

May be overly self-centered.

May harbor hostility toward others.

May have antisocial attitudes.

May have some unconventional beliefs or attitudes.

May show irresponsible attitudes.

May have problems with authority.

May be experiencing family discord that interferes with his functioning.

May show low energy or lack of enthusiasm.

May show some disregard for the feelings of others.

MMPI ADULT INTERPRETIVE SYSTEM

developed by

Roger L. Greene, Ph.D.
Robert C. Brown, Jr., Ph.D.
and PAR Staff

CLIENT INFORMATION

CLIENT	: Test Report	AGE	: 37
SEX	: Male	MARITAL STATUS	: Married
EDUCATION	: 12 years	DATE OF BIRTH	: 11/11/51
PREPARED FOR	: PAR on 11/11/88	FILE NAME	: REPORT

The interpretive information contained in this report should be viewed as only one source of hypotheses about the individual being evaluated. No decisions should be based solely on the information contained in this report. This material should be integrated with all other sources of information in reaching professional decisions about this individual. This report is confidential and intended for use by qualified professionals only. It should not be released to the individual being evaluated.

CONFIGURAL VALIDITY SCALE INTERPRETATION

There is no information available for the configuration of scores for scales L, F, and K. Interpretation for each of the individual validity scales is presented below.

VALIDITY SCALES

? T = 12

Scores in this range reflect a relatively small number of unanswered items, which in and of itself should not have an impact on the validity of the profile.

L T= 50

L scores in this range are usually obtained by individuals who generally respond frankly and openly to the test items and are willing to admit to minor faults.

PROFILE MATCHES AND SCORES

Scale	Client Profile	Highest Scale Codetype	Best Fit Codetype
Codetype match:		2-8/8-2 (1)	2-8/8-2 (1)
Coefficient of Fit:		.72	.72
Scores:	?	12		
	L	50	51	51
	F	76	80	80
	K	43	48	48
	Hs (1)	87	88	88
	D (2)	95	96	96
	Hy (3)	76	78	78
	Pd (4)	76	78	78
	Mf (5)	52	60	60
	Pa (6)	73	74	74
	Pt (7)	78	82	82
	Sc (8)	96	97	97
	Ma (9)	61	63	63
	Si (0)	68	69	69
	TR (raw)	2	3	3
	Ds-r	72	77	77
	Mp	47	46	46
Mean Clinical Elevation:		80	82	82
Ave age-males:			40	40
Ave age-females:			38	38
% of male codetypes:			1.0	1.0
% of female codetypes:			0.5	0.5
% of males within codetype:			84.2	84.2
% of females within codetype:			15.8	15.8

Configural clinical scale interpretation is provided in the report for the following codetype(s):
2-8/8-2 (1)

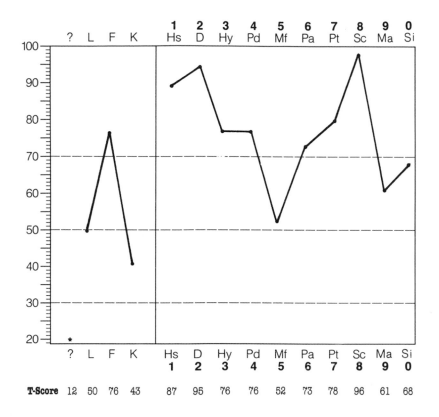

				1	2	3	4	5	6	7	8	9	0
?	L	F	K	Hs	D	Hy	Pd	Mf	Pa	Pt	Sc	Ma	Si
				1	2	3	4	5	6	7	8	9	0
T-Score 12	50	76	43	87	95	76	76	52	73	78	96	61	68

F T= 76

F scores in this range, if they are valid, suggest the increasing probability of serious psychological and emotional problems which are often characteristic of severe neurosis, psychosis, or behavioral problems. Scores in this range also may occur because individuals have had some difficulty reading or understanding the test items (evaluate measures of consistency of item endorsement), or because they have some motivation to over-report psychopathology (evaluate measures of accuracy of item endorsement).

K T= 43

Scores in this range indicate limited personal resources and open acknowledgment of significant psychological distress. These individuals are likely to have a relatively poor self-concept, to be strongly dissatisfied with themselves but lacking the skills necessary to change their situation, to be self-critical, and/or to be extremely open and revealing. Scores in this range may also reflect low ego strength, a lack of insight into one's self-motivation and behavior, and ineffectiveness in dealing with the problems of daily life. Prognosis for psychological intervention is usually guarded.

TEST-TAKING SCALES

TR raw score= 2

Scores in this range indicate that items were endorsed in a consistent manner.

DS-r T= 72

Scores in this range are unremarkable.

Mp T= 50

Scores in this range are unremarkable.

CONFIGURAL CLINICAL SCALE INTERPRETATION

2-8/8-2 (1) Codetype

Clinical Presentation:

This codetype is associated with inconsistent patterns of item endorsement. Scores for validity and test-taking scales should be examined to insure they are within acceptable ranges.

These individuals are often seen as depressed, tense, agitated, anxious, and seclusive. They report a number of physical ailments and worry about their health. They have difficulty with concentration, confused thinking, depression, lack of efficiency, and forgetfulness. Suicidal ideation is prominent and attempts are quite frequent in these individuals; suicide potential should be evaluated.

A significant portion of these patients are psychotic. These individuals often present atypical physical problems which may be delusional. These individuals may experience delusions, ideas of reference, and occasionally auditory hallucinations.

They often feel isolated, apathetic, ineffective, and distant from others. These individuals are often dependent individuals and require much support. At the same time they generally resent those supporting them because of the recognition of their dependency. Their ineffectiveness and attempts to deny unacceptable impulses sometimes produce severe conflict which may lead to dissociative periods of acting out. Sexual conflicts are also quite frequent.

The self-concept of these individuals is quite poor. They generally feel worthless and inadequate. The interpersonal relationships of these individuals are often characterized by numerous difficulties. These individuals tend to withdraw, isolate themselves from others, and keep others at a distance. They feel inadequate in social situations, especially in situations with the opposite sex. Their withdrawal and isolation only serve to exacerbate their symptoms.

Treatment:

The prognosis for individuals who obtain this codetype is generally poor. Their problems are considered chronic and hospitalization may be required. The probability of meaningful long-term change is low.

Possible Diagnoses:
Axis I - Rule Out Mood Disorders
          Dysthymia
          Major Depression
      Rule Out Schizophrenia
Axis II - Rule Out Schizotypal Personality Disorder
          Rule Out Avoidant Personality Disorder
          Rule Out Borderline Personality Disorder

CLINICAL SCALES

Hs (1) T= 87

Scores in this range are frequently obtained by individuals who are expressing excessive concern about the functioning of their bodies and are endorsing multiple vague somatic complaints. These individuals are typically self-centered, dissatisfied, demanding of attention, complaining, and generally negative and pessimistic. They may use their somatic complaints to control and manipulate others. The prognosis for either psychological or medical intervention is guarded. Conservative medical treatment is usually recommended. These individuals are highly skilled in frustrating and sabotaging the help of others, and will often "shop" for physicians and/or therapists. One exception is individuals with multiple bonafide physical disorders of both chronic and acute nature.

D (2) T= 95

Scores in this range are typical for individuals who feel depressed, unhappy, sad, and pessimistic about the future. They often feel guilty and are self-critical. Suicidal ideation and potential should be ruled out. These individuals often feel inadequate, helpless, and lacking in self-confidence. Social withdrawal, poor concentration, appetite and sleep disturbances, and low frustration tolerance are possible. Increasingly higher scores are usually associated with an increase in the number and severity of depressive symptoms.

Hy (3) T= 76

Scores in this range are frequently obtained by individuals who develop physical complaints in response to stress and may use their complaints to avoid responsibility. These individuals are often naive, immature, and self-centered, and deny any psychological problems. They lack insight concerning the causes of their symptoms and their own motives and feelings. They are frequently very demanding of affection and support, and may use indirect and manipulative means to get attention and affection.

Their social relationships are often superficial and immature. They are resistant to psychological interpretations and treatment, and any form of psychological intervention will be difficult. These individuals often look for simplistic, concrete solutions to their problems; solutions that do not require self-examination. Individuals who obtain elevated scores on this scale are unlikely to be seen as psychotic.

Pd (4) T= 76

Scores in this range are typically obtained by individuals who are characterized as angry, belligerent, rebellious, disliking rules and regulations, and hostile toward authority figures. These individuals are likely to be impulsive, unreliable, egocentric, and irresponsible. They often have little regard for social standards. They frequently show poor judgment and seem to have difficulty planning ahead and benefiting from their previous experiences. They make good first impressions but long-term relationships tend to be rather superficial and unsatisfying. Analysis of the Wiggins' Content Scales and/or the Harris-Lingoes Subscales may facilitate interpretation of scores within this range.

Mf (5) T= 52

Scores in this range are typical for males interested in traditional masculine interests and activities.

Pa (6) T= 61

Scores in this range are frequently obtained by individuals who are suspicious, hostile, and feel as if they are being mistreated, or by individuals who are hypersensitive to the reactions of others. The Dependency scale is helpful in distinguishing between these groups of individuals—high scores in the former case and low scores in the latter. They will often blame others for their difficulties. The first group of individuals may manifest psychotic behavior, and a thought disorder may be readily apparent. Ideas of reference and delusions of persecution also may be present.

Pt (7) T = 78

Scores in this range are typically obtained by individuals who are worried, anxious, tense, and experiencing emotional discomfort. They may experience irrational fears and typically ruminate about their problems.

Disabling guilt feelings may be present. Agitation may develop. These individuals worry excessively and may have problems in concentration. Obsessions and compulsions are common.

Sc (8) T= 96

Scores in this range are suggestive of serious psychopathology including confused thinking, distorted perceptions, and other psychotic processes. Difficulties in logic and concentration, impaired judgment, and the presence of a thought disorder should be evaluated. Be sure that measures of consistency and accuracy of item endorsement are within acceptable ranges.

Ma (9) T=61

Scores in this range are often obtained by individuals who are described as pleasant, active, outgoing, and energetic. They are often independent and self-confident. External restrictions on their activities may result in agitation and dissatisfaction.

Si (0) T= 68

Scores in this range usually are obtained by individuals who prefer to be alone or with a small group of friends. They are likely to be reserved in new social situations.

SUPPLEMENTAL SCALES

HARRIS AND LINGOES SUBSCALES

D1 T = 99

High D1 scorers feel depressed, unhappy, and nervous. They lack energy and interest, and are not coping well with their problems. They report difficulties in concentration and attention, lack self-confidence, and feel shy and uneasy in social situations.

D2 T = 97

High D2 scorers are characterized as immobilized. They lack energy to cope with everyday activities, they withdraw from interpersonal relationships, and they deny having hostile and aggressive impulses.

D3 T = 91

High D3 scorers are preoccupied with health and physical functioning, and they typically report a wide variety of specific somatic symptoms and complaints.

D4 T = 98

High D4 scorers lack energy to cope with problems of everyday life. They report difficulties in concentrating and they complain of poor memory and judgment. They lack self-confidence, feel inferior to others, get little enjoyment out of life, and may feel that life is no longer worthwhile.

D5 T = 98

High D5 scorers lack energy and brood and ruminate excessively about life not being worthwhile. They feel inferior and are easily hurt by criticism. At times, they report feeling like they are losing control of their thought processes.

Sc1B T = 94

High Sc1B scorers report feelings of depression and despair, and they may feel life is not worthwhile. They may appear apathetic and frightened. They experience themselves as strange and alien.

Sc2A T = 96

High Sc2A scorers admit to strange thought processes, feelings of unreality, and problems with concentration and attention. At times, they may feel that they are "losing their minds."

Sc2B T = 91

High Sc2B scorers tend to be depressed. They have problems coping with everyday life, feel that life is a strain, and may have given up hope of solving their problems. They respond to stress by regressing and withdrawing into fantasy and daydreaming.

Sc2C T = 99

High Sc2C scorers feel a loss of control over their emotions and impulses. They tend to be restless, hyperactive, and irritable, and they may experience episodes of uncontrollable laughing or crying.

Sc3 T = 98

High Sc3 scorers admit to very unusual experiences which may include hallucinations, unusual thought content, ideas of external influence, and strange bodily experiences. They experience feelings of depersonalization and estrangement.

END OF REPORT

9

The MMPI Restandardization Project

Very shortly after the MMPI gained widespread acceptance, criticisms were made regarding the narrowness of the original standardization groups used to obtain normal values for the scales. The normals used were 724 individuals who were primarily visitors to the University of Minnesota hospitals in the late 1930s and early 1940s, a group consisting almost exclusively of Caucasians, disproportionately of Scandanavian, German, and Irish descent, who were almost exclusively from the Minnesota, North Dakota, South Dakota, Iowa, and Wisconsin area. Dahlstrom et al. (1972) noted that "in 1940, such a Minnesota adult was about 35 years old, was married, lived in a small town or rural area, had eight years of general school, and worked at a skilled or semi-skilled trade (or was married to a man with such an occupational level)." The generalizability of such norms to other areas of the country was repeatedly questioned, and implications of such limited norms have been noted in depth (see Pancoast & Archer, in press).

More recently other criticisms were added. The content and phrasing of several items seemed inappropriate for modern times. Questions were raised concerning possible drift of norms during the 40 or so years since the test was standardized, particularly because cultural attitudes and practices in the 1980s seem so different from the 1940s.

In view of these criticisms, it is a testimony to the robustness of the MMPI that it continues to be the most widely used test of its kind in the world, and it was this robustness and use that prompted a major restandardization project in the 1980s. In conjunction with National Computer Systems and the University of Minnesota Press, several noted psychologists agreed to collaborate on this major project. The psychologists primarily involved in this project up through 1988 have been (in alphabetical order): James Butcher, W. Grant Dahlstrom, John Graham, and Auke Tellegen. These psychologists set about to (a) modernize without changing the scales, (b) make changes at the item level, scale level, and normative level, and (c) maintain continuity with the original MMPI so that research of the last 40 years would be maintained (Butcher, & Graham, 1988).

In 1982, two separate experimental forms of a revised MMPI were developed—one for adults, and one for adolescents (Butcher & Graham, 1988). Besides editing outdated items and removing some others, the restandardization project directors decided to add new items reflecting contemporary issues such as marital and work-related problems. The new adult and adolescent experimental forms thus were created with 154 added items. Although more potential items were generated, due to space considerations only these 154 were added on the answer sheet.

The project directors took approximately 1½ years to modify existing items and to generate the new items. Although in doing so the TR Index was lost, as the 16 repeated items were dropped because "they didn't add to interpretation" (Butcher & Graham, 1988).

THE MMPI—2

The adult version of the revised MMPI was refined, as described later, and is referred to as the MMPI-2. "The whole experimental form of the test booklet did not end up in the final MMPI-2 booklet . . . just 567 items (are) in it" (Dahlstrom, personal communication, 1988). The adolescent version is still under consideration and development, and likely will not be available for several years. Even so, the descriptions that follow provide some information on the adolescent form, though most of the comments focus on the refinement and standardization of the MMPI-2.

Item Revisions

Eighty-two items were edited to improve clarity or to reflect contemporary language use. For example, the word *deportment* is no longer in popular usage, nor is the game "drop the handkerchief." The item "I am bothered by acid stomach several times or more a week" has been changed to read "I am bothered by an upset stomach several times or more a week." The statement "My father was a good man" has been changed to "My father is (was) a good man." Due to the increasing legal challenges of the MMPI based on sexual items, the researchers attempted to make such items less intrusive. For similar reasons, obvious religious items that might appear intrusive were dropped (Dahlstrom, personal communication, 1988).

The following categories are ones in which the items have been rewritten (Butcher & Graham, 1988): (a) outdated language—26 items; (b) sexist language—15 items; (c) minor rewording—14 items; (d) awkward wording—8 items; (e) grammatical improvements—7 items; (f) language simplification—6 items; (g) ambiguous items—4 items; (h) religious content—2 items.

To demonstrate that the rewritten items did not compromise the validity as compared with the original items, the researchers used 337 students (178 males and 199 females) at the University of Minnesota. One-half took the original MMPI two times, 1 week apart, in order to provide a baseline regarding consistency of item endorsement. The second group completed the original MMPI, and then 1 week later took the experimental MMPI with the 82 reworded items.

The percentage of subjects giving the same response to items in the two original versions of the MMPI was compared to the percentage of subjects endorsing the same items in the original and the new form of the MMPI. In the control group, 93% gave the same responses to both MMPIs; in the experimental group, 92% gave the same responses. The researchers also examined each of the reworded categories to see if differences existed in specific item endorsement between groups. No significant differences were found. The results revealed that the new items did not significantly alter the test raw scores. The authors stated, "We have improved items without psychometric costs" (Butcher & Graham, 1988).

Adding New Items

To add new items reflecting contemporary concerns, the authors solicited contributions from various clinicians. Based on their feedback, the researchers decided to add items to the adult form that could be developed into scales measuring (a) suicide potential, (b) potential for therapeutic change, (c) treatment compliance, and (d) type A behavior.

For the adolescent MMPI, a form that still is in the research and development stage, the authors additionally wanted to develop items that could measure adolescent problems in the following areas: (a) use and attitude toward drugs, (b) attitudes towards sex, (c) attitudes toward teachers, (d) peer relationships, (e) school-related problems, and (f) family problems. The authors generated 104 new items specifically for the adolescent form, in addition to the 50 items developed primarily for the adult version. For the adolescent group, the Marks, Seeman, and Haller (1974) norms were used as a comparison. With the aid of Robert Archer, the researchers collected approximately 2,000 adolescent responses that form the basis of their new adolescent norms. These data continue to be analyzed.

The Restandardization Sample

The major criticisms of the MMPI normative sample over the last 40 or so years have focused on its small sample size, consisting of only 724 primarily white, rural persons who were primarily farm laborers or clerical workers with an average eighth-grade education. The present researchers wanted to obtain a sample that was more representative of today's demographic make-up.

Initially in their collection process, the researchers (Butcher, Dahlstrom, Graham, Tellegen, & Kaemmer, 1989) collected subjects from around their respective universities, resulting in an aggregate sample size of approximately 900. Analysis of the demographic composition of these 900 subjects revealed that the sample was not representative of the United States as a whole; minorities were underrepresented, educational levels were high, and age variability did not conform to the 1980 national census data.

The researchers needed (a) more minority subjects, (b) urban rather than suburban subjects, and (c) subjects representative of the U.S. geographic diversity. Their solution was to divide the United States into geographically representative communities and, using local telephone and community census directories, to pick subjects at random. Once identified, subjects were solicited by letters. These letters introduced the subjects to the MMPI, explained what the researchers were hoping to accomplish, and asked them to help in this "important scientific study." The subjects were asked to complete various tests, give a thorough biographic history, and if married, to be part of a marital study. Subjects were paid $15 for their participation, with spouse pairs given an additional $10 to participate.

Response Rates and Characteristics

The letter solicitation resulted in a 10% to 15% response rate, and included subjects from seven states (California, Minnesota, North Carolina, Ohio, Virginia, Washington, and Pennsylvania). In view of the demands on the subject's time of 3 to 4 hours, this was felt to be a "good response rate." As noted elsewhere, these subjects were supplemented with additional samples of native Americans, college students, and military personnel in order to get a demographic composite that more closely matched the 1980 national census. As of June 1988, over 2,600 adult subjects had responded (Butcher & Graham, 1988).

Of the subjects, 56% were female and 44% were male. Age distribution was as follows: 18- to 19-year-olds = 5%; 20- to 29-year-olds = 25%; 30- to 39-year-olds = 19%; 40- to 49-year-olds = 15%; 50- to 60-year-olds = 12%; 60- to 70-year-olds = 11%; 70 and above = 10%.

Eighty-four percent of the sample was white, 11% was Black, 3% was native American, 3% Hispanic, and 1.5% Asian-American. Ages ranged from 18- to 84-years-old. Sixty percent were married, 25% never married, 5% divorced,

3.5% widowed, and 2% separated. Education levels were as follows: 5% had less than a high school education, 22% had completed high school, 26% had some college education, 27% had graduated from college, and 17% had formal education beyond college.

Concurrent Data Collected

To develop a more thorough understanding of this sample, the subjects were given two biographical forms. One was a version of the Holmes and Rahe (1967) "Significant Life Events Form." The second was a biographical background form that measured the following behavior domains: (a) past history, (b) education, (c) occupation, (d) income, (e) alcohol/drug history, (f) previous hospitalizations, and (g) psychiatric care. The second biographical form also measured contemporary difficulties such as recent divorce or death of a significant other.

Another dimension examined was whether or not the respondent was receiving current psychological treatment. Ninety-five percent said they had never been in psychological treatment, whereas 5% said they were currently in treatment. Initially, the researchers were concerned about including such subjects in treatment because they were looking for a normal sample. Upon reflection, they decided to include them because they were, indeed, representative of the population, and instead changed the name from normal sample to community sample. Thus the sample is representative of the community.

Married subjects were further tested in order to measure marital issues. These couples (approximately 900) had been together a median of 13.5 years, and 91% indicated "close or very close" relationships with their partners. They were asked to rate each other on several dimensions using the Spanier (1976) Marital Adjustment Questionnaire. Couples were also given the Katz (1968) adjective checklist. Each married subject took the Marital Adjustment Questionnaire, and each spouse was asked to rate the other on 110 personality variables. This new normative sample contributed an important aspect to the new MMPI.

Comparison of Norm T-scores

The researchers examined how different their new sample of 2,600 people was from Hathaway's original normative group. The new norms for these subjects were plotted on the standard forms. The L scale was found to have a T-score of 48; the F scale was at a T-score of 55; the K scale was at a T-score of 56. Most of the clinical scores were within a five- to seven-point range from the mean of the original norms, though in each case the new norms were higher.

Butcher and Graham (1988) suggested three possible explanations for the higher mean scores with the new sample: (a) The elevated scores could be due to a slightly more deviant sample, (b) the new community sample perhaps was more willing to admit to problems, or (c) the differences in means could be related to omitted items. Graham noted that in the original Hathaway and McKinley study the mean number of items omitted was 30, whereas in the new community sample the mean number of omitted items was "two to three" (Butcher & Graham, 1988). In other words, the present normative group was responding to 20 to 30 more items than Hathaway's original sample, so the mean could be raised due simply to the new subjects answering more questions.

Perhaps the most cogent explanation is that of Pancoast and Archer (1989) who, in their review of MMPI norms since 1940, found that the original MMPI standard norms contained a bias such that subsequent studies of normals consistently showed "noticeable variations from $T = 50$ when profiled on the Minnesota original norms." That is, the original norms of $T = 50$ were apparently inaccurate to begin with, and were "biased on an atypical sample" that "represented an imperfect fit to population mean values at the time they were collected" (Pancoast & Archer, 1989). Thus it is not at all surprising that the MMPI-2 norms would score approximately five T-score points higher when compared to the original Minnesota norms.

Still another explanation for the slight mean variation between normative samples might lie in the statistics used to develop the mean. In the original MMPI, a linear T-transformation was used for transforming raw scores into T-scores. With this kind of transformation, the distribution of raw scores is maintained in that scale's T-score distribution. If the raw scores are skewed, then the skewedness is maintained in the T-score distribution. However, one problem with a linear T-score is that a T of 70 on scale 2 is not necessarily equivalent to a similar T-score on scale 8. In other words, a T-score of 70 on scale 2 will likely have a different percentile rank of T on scale 8.

To solve this problem, Butcher et al. (1989) determined a composite distribution, rather than a linear T transformation. They developed a uniform distribution (omitting scales 5 and 0) so that T-scores are now equivalent. That is, scales "are stretched or shrunken along the whole distribution to fit proportionally the other seven for that gender" (Dahlstrom, personal communication, 1988). This conversion is called a "uniformed T-score transformation." The MMPI-2 will provide conversion tables that will allow use of this "uniformed T-score distribution" as well as the traditional T-score tables. This approach, though statistically interesting, is not without controversy. Various persons have noted that use of such "uniformed T-score transformations" will often produce differences in code-type configurations and in the frequency of occurrence of various code-types (Pancoast & Archer, 1989).

Although the original norms as applied to the new normative sample result in T-scores that suggest slightly more pathology, there actually is no major shift from the norms of Hathaway and McKinley (Butcher & Graham, 1988), and even less so from more recent normative studies (Pancoast & Archer, 1989).

Information about the effects of the new norms on code-types is less clear. Early information suggests that code-type frequency and elevations will change somewhat (Fowler et al., 1988) though the extent of such changes in various populations will not be known for some time until various studies can be carried out. Graham (in Fowler et al., 1988) reported initial data indicating that the new norms tend to produce lower profiles, and that the convergence between code-types using the new norms and code-types using the old norms increases as the profiles become higher in elevation. At elevations over $T = 70$ the convergence between code-type, using old and new norms, was approximately 75%. For profiles over $T = 100$, the concordance was above 90%. Even so, Dahlstrom has predicted that changes in code-type and elevation for the MMPI-2 often will differ substantially from those obtained using the old items and old norms (in Fowler et al., 1988).

Comparisons of Code Elevations and Code-types

Several investigations already have been done to compare data consisting of the new items and norms to the original items and norms to determine if code elevation and code-type remain the same. In addition to the college student populations mentioned earlier, several other sites and populations were used, including the following:

1. The Hazelton Alcohol Treatment Center was chosen because for many years new intakes (approximately 15 per week) had completed MMPIs using the original norms. For over 1 year, 95% of all new intakes were tested using the new MMPI, along with the Beck Depression Inventory.

2. The Hennepin General Hospital in Minnesota has collected data for years in its psychiatric inpatient unit. Researchers thus felt that revised MMPIs taken from this site could be compared to the MMPIs from the same site that used the old items and old norms.

3. A Minnesota state hospital was also used for similar reasons.

4. In Ohio, Graham used two state hospitals, giving patients a full battery of standard psychological tests as well as the MMPI.

5. Five hundred and fifty chronic pain patients at the University of Minnesota Hospital were also tested, constituting one of the largest chronic pain subject samples thus studied.

6. A group of airline pilots was also studied using the new MMPI items and plotting the profile on new norms.

7. Samples from 200 couples in marital therapy were collected and compared with the normative married control sample.

The results of the comparisons between the old MMPI and the new MMPI revealed the following. One hundred and six male Air Force recruits were tested using the new MMPI items and the new norms, and the results were compared to those obtained in the same setting 10 years earlier using the original norms and items. The results were the same regarding code-types and scale elevations (Butcher & Graham, 1988). Modern recruits still obtain elevations at about a T-score of 60 on scales 4 and 9. At the Hazelton Center, 832 male alcoholics who took the revised MMPI were contrasted with 1,720 inpatients tested 10 years earlier using the old MMPI. The new MMPI showed a high degree of overlap in terms of code-type and elevation with the original MMPI results at the Hazelton Treatment Center. Similar findings occurred with female alcoholic inpatients at Hazelton. Both male and female inpatients at Hazelton continued to obtain a 24/42 profile above a T-score of 70 using the new MMPI and new norms.

For thoroughness, other data from similar investigations are needed. Results to date are not sufficient to determine the extent to which clinical validity and usefulness of the knowledge of the MMPI has been compromised by the revisions in MMPI-2. Code-types, using the new norms, may or may not change across the various samples or client populations. Certainly, once the new norms are publicly available, additional clinical research data will need to be collected to empirically verify the extent to which the behavioral and emotional correlates of code-types from the new MMPI will have changed. Much clinical data on specific patients already exists using the original MMPI, and many decisions have been made using those data, so it may be quite some time before professionals can sufficiently understand the comparability of the two tests.

Development of Content Scales

Although Wiggins (1969) developed content scales for the original MMPI, the current researchers wanted a new series of content scales that would be valuable in clinical settings. These scales would incorporate the changes in item content, and would supplement the existing content scales.

As Wiggins had done, the present researchers rationally analyzed individual items to see which "hung together" in content. Using this rational scale construction approach, they generated 22 provisional content scales, which they then refined empirically through examining item convergence, and removing those items lacking convergence. Subsequently, these procedures were repeated, allowing further refinement, and the elimination of item overlap.

This approach has yielded the following new scales:

1. *Anxiety* (23 items), a scale that attempts to separate fear from anxiety.
2. *Fears* (23 items), a scale that measures the number of specific fears of one individual.

3. *Obsessiveness* (16 items), a measure of rumination.
4. *Depression* (33 items), similar to Wiggins *DEP* scale, high scores are characterized as having significant depressive thoughts.
5. *Health Concern* (36 items), similar to Wiggins *HEA* scale, this scale is a measure of the number of physical symptoms an individual reports.
6. *Bizarre Mentation* (24 items), similar to Wiggins *PSY* Scale, this scale measures psychotic thought processes.
7. *Anger* (16 items), a scale reflecting irritability and hotheadedness.
8. *Cynicism* (23 items), a scale measuring misanthropic beliefs.
9. *Antisocial Attitudes* (22 items), a measure of acting out behaviors.
10. *Type A* (19 items), a measure of hard-driving, irritable, fastmoving behaviors.
11. *Low Self Esteem* (24 items), measures poor self-image.
12. *Social Discomfort* (24 items), reflects introverted tendencies.
13. *Family Problems* (25 items), similar to Wiggins *FAM* scale, this scale measures familial discord.
14. *Work Interference* (33 items), indicates behaviors or attitudes likely to contribute to poor work performance.
15. *Negative Treatment Indicators* (26 items), a measure of negative attitudes toward doctors and mental health treatment.

The original Wiggins' scales had alphas ranging from about .50 to about .80; the alpha values for the new scales are higher. The researchers are continuing to investigate other possible new content scales, such as eating disorders and undoubtedly will generate several others.

Existing Special Scales

It is important to note that only some of the existing special scales for the MMPI will continue to be scorable because some of the original items have been eliminated. Scales *A, R, Es,* and *MAC* clearly will be directly usable. The other 400 to 500 special scales listed in *An MMPI Handbook* (Dahlstrom, Welsh, & Dahlstrom, 1975) most probably will not be directly usable (W. G. Dahlstrom, personal communication, 1988). Nevertheless, because the items have been refined, it may be important to cross-validate all of the special scales in a similar fashion to what the present researchers have done.

Future Directions

MMPI research has enjoyed almost 5 decades of uninterrupted flowering. The new standardization project will likely be greeted with mixed feelings by the MMPI community. Many will welcome it as overdue, although some will go through the resistance that is normal when an "old familiar friend" changes in ways that demand new learning and effort in order to fully comprehend the changes.

It appears that the revisions have clearly improved the MMPI, and yet the robustness of this instrument is such that the existing wealth of interpretive data still appears likely to be usable. Initial impressions are that the current code-type interpretations can still be used, although "high points do shift and elevations have shrunk" (Dahlstrom, personal communication, 1988) in at least some situations. Certainly, refinements will occur as researchers compare the old and the new, hopefully providing more precision due to the reduced noise in the system resulting from the revisions and restandardization.

Only after much more research and careful comparisons can the implications of the revised MMPI and the new norms be fully understood. One thing, however, is certain. With the revisions, we can be assured of at least another 50 years of MMPI research literature, with the development of new scales and their corresponding emotional and behavioral correlates.

For now, however, the authors recommend the wisdom of the saying, "Be not the first on whom the new is tried, nor the last to lay the old aside." As Pancoast and Archer (1989) noted, the clinical interpretation literature stems from data gathered on existing adult norms. It is virtually certain that the new norms of the MMPI-2 will result in some diminution of the applicability of the information because it was accumulated based on the orginal MMPI, and thus research "will require an extensive period of time, perhaps spanning as much as a decade." (Pancoast and Archer, 1989, p. 392). The present authors concur with Pancoast and Archer (1989) who encouraged the use of new norms in conjunction with established norms, and who note that "new norms can be endorsed as a substitute for original norms (only) when acceptable research data has accumulated to establish the effects of such a replacement on profile elevation, configuration and correlate patterns in normal and clinical populations." (p. 392).

Appendix A

*Item Composition
of the Standard
Validity and
Clinical Scales*

STANDARD VALIDITY SCALE COMPOSITION*

Scale L

      True: NONE   False: 15, 30, 45, 60, 75, 90, 105, 120, 135, 150, 165, 195, 225, 255, 285

Scale F

      True: 14, 23, 27, 31, 34, 35, 40, 42, 48, 49, 50, 53, 56, 66, 85, 121, 123, 139, 146, 151, 156, 168, 184, 197, 200, 202, 205, 206, 209, 210, 211, 215, 218, 227, 245, 246, 247, 252, 256, 269, 275, 286, 291, 293   False: 17, 20, 54, 65, 75, 83, 112, 113, 115, 164, 169, 177, 185, 196, 199, 220, 257, 258, 272, 276

Scale K

      True: 96   False: 30, 39, 71, 89, 124, 129, 134, 138, 142, 148, 160, 170, 171, 180, 183, 217, 234, 267, 272, 296, 316, 322, 374, 383, 397, 398, 406, 461, 502

STANDARD CLINICAL SCALE COMPOSITION*

Scale 1—Hypochondriasis (Hs)

      True: 23, 29, 43, 62, 72, 108, 114, 125, 161, 189, 273   False: 2, 3, 7, 9, 18, 51, 55, 63, 68, 103, 130, 153, 155, 163, 175, 188, 190, 192, 230, 243, 274, 281

Scale 2—Depression (D)

      True: 5, 13, 23, 32, 41, 43, 52, 67, 86, 104, 130, 138, 142, 158, 159, 182, 189, 193, 236, 259   False: 2, 8, 9, 18, 30, 36, 39, 46, 51, 57, 58, 64, 80, 88, 89, 95, 98, 107, 122, 131, 145, 152, 153, 154, 155, 160, 178, 191, 207, 208, 233, 241, 242, 248, 263, 270, 271, 272, 285, 296

Scale 3—Hysteria (Hy)

      True: 10, 23, 32, 43, 44, 47, 76, 114, 179, 186, 189, 238, 253   False: 2, 3, 6, 7, 8, 9, 12, 26, 30, 51, 55, 71, 89, 93, 103, 107, 109, 124, 128, 129, 136, 137, 141, 147, 153, 160, 162, 163, 170, 172, 174, 175, 180, 188, 190, 192, 201, 213, 230, 234, 243, 265, 267, 274, 279, 289, 292

Scale 4—Psychopathic Deviate (Pd)

True: 16, 21, 24, 32, 33, 35, 38, 42,   False: 8, 20, 37, 82, 91, 96, 107, 134,
61, 67, 84, 94, 102, 106, 110,   137, 141, 155, 170, 171, 173,
118, 127, 215, 216, 224, 239,   180, 183, 201, 231, 235, 237,
244, 245, 284   248, 267, 287, 289, 294, 296

Scale 5—Masculinity-Femininity (Mf)

Male

True: 4, 25, 69, 70, 74, 77, 78, 87,   False: 1, 19, 26, 28, 79, 80, 81, 89,
92, 126, 132, 134, 140, 149,   99, 112, 115, 116, 117, 120,
179, 187, 203, 204, 217, 226,   133, 144, 176, 198, 213, 214,
231, 239, 261, 278, 282, 295,   219, 221, 223, 229, 249, 254,
297, 299   260, 262, 264, 280, 283, 300

Scale 5—Masculinity-Femininity (Mf)

Female

True: 4, 25, 70, 74, 77, 78, 87, 92,   False: 1, 19, 26, 28, 69, 79, 80, 81,
126, 132, 133, 134, 140, 149,   89, 99, 112, 115, 116, 117,
187, 203, 204, 217, 226, 239,   120, 144, 176, 179, 198, 213,
261, 278, 282, 295, 299   214, 219, 221, 223, 229, 231,
                                              249, 254, 260, 262, 264, 280,
                                              283, 297, 300

Scale 6—Paranoia (Pa)

True: 15, 16, 22, 24, 27, 35, 110,   False: 93, 107, 109, 111, 117, 124,
121, 123, 127, 151, 157, 158,   268, 281, 294, 313, 316, 319,
202, 275, 284, 291, 293, 299,   327, 347, 348
305, 317, 338, 341, 364, 365

Scale 7—Psychasthenia (Pt)

True: 10, 15, 22, 32, 41, 67, 76, 86,   False: 3, 8, 36, 122, 152, 164, 178,
94, 102, 106, 142, 159, 182,   329, 353
189, 217, 238, 266, 301, 304,
305, 317, 321, 336, 337, 340,
342, 343, 344, 346, 349, 351,
352, 356, 357, 358, 359, 360,
361

Scale 8—Schizophrenia (Sc)

True: 15, 16, 21, 22, 24, 32, 33, 35,   False: 8, 17, 20, 37, 65, 103, 119,
38, 40, 41, 47, 52, 76, 97, 104,   177, 178, 187, 192, 196, 220,
121, 156, 157, 159, 168, 179,   276, 281, 306, 309, 322, 330
182, 194, 202, 210, 212, 238,
241, 251, 259, 266, 273, 282,
291, 297, 301, 303, 305, 307,
312, 320, 324, 325, 332, 334,
335, 339, 341, 345, 349, 350,
352, 354, 355, 356, 360, 363,
364

Scale 9—Hypomania (Ma)

True: 11, 13, 21, 22, 59, 64, 73, 97,
100, 109, 127, 134, 143, 156,
157, 167, 181, 194, 212, 222,
226, 228, 232, 233, 238, 240,
250, 251, 263, 266, 268, 271,
277, 279, 298

False: 101, 105, 111, 119, 120, 148,
166, 171, 180, 267, 289

Scale 0—Social Introversion (Si)

True: 32, 67, 82, 111, 117, 124, 138,
147, 171, 172, 180, 201, 236,
267, 278, 292, 304, 316, 321,
332, 336, 342, 357, 377, 383,
398, 411, 427, 436, 455, 473,
487, 549, 564

False: 25, 33, 57, 91, 99, 119, 126,
143, 193, 208, 229, 231, 254,
262, 281, 296, 309, 353, 359,
371, 391, 400, 415, 440, 446,
449, 450, 451, 462, 469, 479,
481, 482, 505, 521, 547

Appendix B

Amount and Direction of Basic Scale Item Overlap and the Intercorrelations Resulting From This Overlap

TABLE 1*

Summary of Amount and Direction of the Item Overlap on the Basic Scales of the MMPI

Basic Scales	No. of Items	L	F	K	1 (Hs)	2 (D)	3 (Hy)	4 (Pd)	5-m (Mf)	5-f (Mf)	6 (Pa)	7 (Pt)	8 (Sc)	9 (Ma)	0 (Si)
L	15	9	...	...	...	...	...	...	...	...	1	1	1	...	...
F	64	1	35	...	...	...	...	...	...	...	...	...	...	...	...
K	30	1	1	5	...	2	...	1	2	2	...	2	...	1	8
1	33	...	1	...	8	1	...	...	...	...	...	...	...	...	...
2	60	2	2	6	9	13	...	...	...	...	...	...	1	4	1
3	60	1	1	10	20	13	10	...	...	·1	...	...	...	2	7
4	50	...	5	7	1	7	10	10	2	1	...	...	...	1	6
5-m[a]	60	1	2	1	...	2	4	1	35[b]	5	...	...	1	...	4
5-f[a]	60	1	2	1	...	2	3	2	55	35[b]	...	...	3	...	3
6	40	...	9	2	1	2	4	8	2	2	7	...	...	2	4
7	48	...	1	...	2	13	7	6	1	1	4	9	...	...	1
8	78	...	15	1	4	9	8	10	3	1	13	17	16	...	1
9	46	2	1	4	...	1	4	6	3	3	4	3	11	15	5
0	70	...	...	1	1	7	1	5	5	6	1	8	5	1	26

[a]5-m means male key for scale 5; 5-f means female key for scale 5.

[b]There are thirty-five items scored uniquely on scale 5 as a whole; there are no unique items on either 5-m or 5-f if they are considered as separate scales.

Values in the main diagonal represent number of items scored only on the basic scale (often referred to as nonoverlapping or unique items).

Values above the diagonal represent items that are scored in the opposite direction, while values below the diagonal represent items scored in the same direction on both scales.

*Source: W. G. Dahlstrom, G. S. Welsh, & L. E. Dahlstrom, *An MMPI Handbook,* Vol. I. The University of Minnesota Press, Minneapolis. Copyright 1960, 1972 by the University of Minnesota. Reproduced with permission.

TABLE 2*

Absolute Amount of Item Overlap among the Basic Scales and the Intercorrelations Resulting from This Overlap

Basic Scales[b]	L	F	K	1 (Hs)	2 (D)	3 (Hy)	4 (Pd)	5[a] (Mf)	6 (Pa)	7 (Pt)	8 (Sc)	9 (Ma)	0 (Si)
L	15	.03	.05	.00	.08	.03	.00	.03	−.04	−.04	−.03	.04	.00
F	1	64	.02	.02	.03	.01	.09	.03	.18	.02	.21	.01	.00
K	1	1	30	.00	.09	.24	.16	−.02	.06	−.05	.02	.08	−.15
1	0	1	0	33	.18	.46	.02	.00	.03	.05	.08	.00	.02
2	2	2	4	8	60	.22	.14	.03	.04	.26	.10	−.05	.09
3	1	1	10	20	13	60	.18	.06	.08	.13	.12	.06	−.09
4	0	5	6	1	7	10	50	−.02	.18	.12	.16	.10	−.02
5[a]	1	2	−1	0	2	4	−1	60	.05	.02	.03	.04	.02
6	−1	9	2	1	2	4	8	2	40	.09	.23	.05	−.06
7	−1	1	−2	2	13	7	6	1	4	48	.27	.06	.12
8	−1	15	1	4	8	8	10	2	13	17	78	.18	.05
9	2	1	3	0	−3	3	5	3	2	3	11	46	−.07
0	0	0	−7	1	6	−6	−1	1	−3	7	4	−4	70

aScale 5 Key for males only.

[b]The main diagonal contains the number of items in each scale. The cells below the main diagonal contain the number of overlapping items between each pair of scales (items scored in the same direction minus those scored oppositely).

Cells above the main diagonal contain scale pair correlations.

*Source: Adopted from Wheeler, Little, Lehner (1951), with the use of Guilford's (1936) correlation. Reproduced in *An MMPI Handbook, Vol. I, Clinical Interpretation* by W. Grant Dahlstrom, George Schlager, Welsh and Leona E. Dahlstrom. Copyright © The University of Minnesota 1960, 1972. Reproduced by permission.

Appendix C

T-Score Conversions for Basic Validity and Clinical Scales

TABLE 1

T-score Conversions for Basic Scales without K-corrections for Minnesota Adults*

	Males														Females										
Raw Score	?	L	F	K	1 (Hs)	2 (D)	3 (Hy)	4 (Pd)	5 (Mf)	6 (Pa)	7 (Pt)	8 (Sc)	9 (Ma)	0 (Si)	1 (Hs)	2 (D)	3 (Hy)	4 (Pd)	5 (Mf)	6 (Pa)	7 (Pt)	8 (Sc)	9 (Ma)	0 (Si)	Raw Score
60	58													87										87	60
59												117		86								111		86	59
58												115		85								109		85	58
57												114		84								108		84	57
56												113		83								107		83	56
55							118					111		82		117	112					106		82	55
54							116					110		81		115	110					104		81	54
53							115					109		80		113	109					103		80	53
52							113					107		79		111	107					102		79	52
51									110			106		78					20			101		78	51
50	56						111		108			105		77		109	105		22			99		77	50
49							109		106			103		76		107	103		24			98		76	49
48							107		104		103	102		75		105	101		26		95	97		75	48
47							106		102		102	101		74		103	100		28		94	96		74	47
46						120	104		100		100	99		73		102	98		30		93	94		73	46
45						118	102		98		99	98		72		100	96		32		91	93		72	45
44						116	100		96		98	97		71		98	94		34		90	92		71	44
43						113	98		94		96	95		70		96	93	120	37		89	91		70	43
42						111	96		92		95	94		69		94	91	117	39		88	89		69	42
41				119		108	95		90		93	92		68		92	89	115	41		86	88		68	41

Males

Raw Score	?	L	F	K	1 (Hs)	2 (D)	3 (Hy)	4 (Pd)	5 (Mf)	6 (Pa)	7 (Pt)	8 (Sc)	9 (Ma)	0 (Si)
40	53					106	93	116	88		92	91		67
39						104	91	114	86		91	90	106	66
38						101	89	111	84		89	88	104	65
37						99	87	108	82		88	87	101	64
36						96	86	106	80		86	86	99	63
35						94	84	103	78		85	84	97	62
34						92	82	101	76		84	83	95	61
33					115	89	80	98	74		82	82	93	60
32					113	87	78	96	73	120	81	80	90	58
31			110		110	84	76	93	71	117	79	79	88	56
30	50		108	83	108	82	75	91	69	114	78	78	86	55
29			106	81	106	80	73	88	67	111	77	76	84	54
28			104	79	104	77	71	86	65	108	75	75	81	53
27			102	77	102	75	69	83	63	105	74	74	79	52
26			100	75	100	72	67	81	61	102	73	72	77	51
25			98	74	97	70	65	78	59	100	71	71	75	50
24			96	72	94	68	64	75	57	97	70	70	72	49
23			94	70	92	65	62	73	55	94	68	68	70	48
22			92	68	90	63	60	70	53	91	67	67	68	47
21			90	66	88	60	58	68	51	88	66	65	66	46
20	47		88	64	85	58	56	65	49	85	64	64	63	45
19			86	62	83	56	55	63	47	82	63	63	61	44
18			84	61	81	53	53	60	45	79	61	61	59	43
17			82	59	78	51	51	58	43	76	60	60	57	42
16			80	57	76	48	49	55	41	73	59	59	54	41

Females

Raw Score	0 (Si)	9 (Ma)	8 (Sc)	7 (Pt)	6 (Pa)	5 (Mf)	4 (Pd)	3 (Hy)	2 (D)	1 (Hs)	K	F	L	?
40	67		87	85		43	113	87	90					53
39	66	106	86	84		45	110	86	88					
38	65	104	84	82		47	108	84	86					
37	64	101	83	81		49	106	82	84					
36	63	99	82	80		51	103	80	82					
35	62	97	80	78		53	101	79	80					
34	61	95	79	77		55	99	77	78					
33	60	93	78	76		57	96	75	76	99				
32	58	90	77	75	120	59	94	73	75	97				
31	56	88	75	73	117	61	91	72	73	96		110		
30	55	86	74	72	114	63	89	70	71	94	83	108		50
29	54	84	73	71	111	66	87	68	69	92	81	106		
28	53	81	72	69	108	68	84	66	67	90	79	104		
27	52	79	70	68	105	70	82	64	65	88	77	102		
26	51	77	69	67	102	72	80	63	63	86	75	100		
25	50	75	68	65	100	74	77	61	61	84	74	98		
24	49	72	67	64	97	76	75	59	59	82	72	96		
23	48	70	65	63	94	78	73	57	57	80	70	94		
22	47	68	64	62	91	80	70	56	55	79	68	92		
21	46	66	63	60	88	82	68	54	53	77	66	90		
20	45	63	62	59	85	84	65	52	51	75	64	88		47
19	44	61	60	58	82	86	63	50	49	73	62	86		
18	43	59	59	56	79	88	61	49	47	71	61	84		
17	42	57	58	55	76	90	58	47	46	69	59	82		
16	41	54	57	54	73	92	56	45	44	67	57	80		

319

TABLE 1 (Continued)

T-score Conversions for Basic Scales without K-corrections for Minnesota Adults*

Males

Raw Score	?	L	F	K	1 (Hs)	2 (D)	3 (Hy)	4 (Pd)	5 (Mf)	6 (Pa)	7 (Pt)	8 (Sc)	9 (Ma)	0 (Si)
15		86	78	55	74	46	47	53	39	70	57	57	52	40
14		83	76	53	72	44	45	50	37	67	56	56	50	39
13		80	73	51	69	41	44	47	35	65	54	55	48	38
12		76	70	49	67	39	42	45	34	62	53	53	45	37
11		73	68	48	65	36	40	42	32	59	52	52	43	36
10	44	70	66	46	62	34	38	40	30	56	50	51	41	35
9		66	64	44	60	32	36	37	28	53	49	49	39	34
8		63	62	42	58	29	35	35	26	50	48	48	37	33
7		60	60	40	56			32		47	46	47	34	32
6		56	58	38	53			30		44	45	45	32	30
5		53	55	36	51			27		41	43	44	30	29
4		50	53	35	49			25		38	42	43	28	28
3		46	50	33	47			22		35	41	41	25	27
2		44	48	31	44			20		33	39	40	23	26
1		40	46	29	42					30	38	38		25
0	41	36	44	27	40					27	36	37		

Females

?	L	F	K	1 (Hs)	2 (D)	3 (Hy)	4 (Pd)	5 (Mf)	6 (Pa)	7 (Pt)	8 (Sc)	9 (Ma)	0 (Si)	Raw Score
	86	78	55	65	42	43	53	95	70	52	55	52	40	15
	83	76	53	63	40	42	51		67	51	54	50	39	14
	80	73	51	62	38	40	49		65	50	53	48	38	13
	76	70	49	60	36	38	47		62	49	52	45	37	12
	73	68	48	58	34	36	44		59	47	50	43	36	11
44	70	66	46	56	32	34	42		56	46	49	41	35	10
	66	64	44	54	30	33	40		53	45	48	39	34	9
	63	62	42	52	28	31	37		50	43	47	37	33	8
	60	60	40	50		29	35		47	42	45	34	32	7
	56	58	38	48		27	32		44	41	44	32	30	6
	53	55	36	46		26	30		41	39	43	30	29	5
	50	53	35	45		24	28		38	38	42	28	28	4
	46	50	33	43			25		35	37	40	25	27	3
	44	48	31	41			23		33	36	39	23	26	2
	40	46	29	39			21		30	34	38		25	1
41	36	44	27	37					27	33	37			0

The MMPI user wishing to convert Adult Raw Scores to T-scores with K corrections can do so by inspecting the standard profile sheet.

*Source: W. G. Dahlstrom, G. S. Welsh, & L. E. Dahlstrom, *An MMPI Handbook, Vol. 1, Clinical Interpretation* (Rev.Ed.), 1972, pp 386–387, University of Minnesota Press, Minneapolis. Copyright 1960, 1972 by the University of Minnesota. Reprinted by permission.

Appendix D

MMPI Profile and Answer Sheets

MMPI™

MINNESOTA MULTIPHASIC PERSONALITY INVENTORY™
S.R. Hathaway and J.C. McKinley

PROFILE

"Minnesota Multiphasic Personality Inventory" and "MMPI" are trademarks owned by The University of Minnesota.

MALE

NAME _____

ADDRESS _____

OCCUPATION _____ DATE TESTED ___/___/___

EDUCATION _____ AGE _____

MARITAL STATUS _____

REFERRED BY _____

MMPI Code

FOR RECORDING ADDITIONAL SCALES

Scorer's Initials

Raw Score _____

K to be added _____

Raw Score with K _____

*49 item version

MMPI

MINNESOTA MULTIPHASIC
PERSONALITY INVENTORY ™
S.R. Hathaway and J.C. McKinley

PROFILE

MINNESOTA MULTIPHASIC PERSONALITY INVENTORY
Copyright © THE UNIVERSITY OF MINNESOTA
1943, Renewed 1970. This Profile Form 1948, 1976, 1982. All rights reserved.
Distributed Exclusively by NATIONAL COMPUTER SYSTEMS, INC.
Under License from The University of Minnesota
Printed in the United States of America

"Minnesota Multiphasic Personality Inventory" and "MMPI" are
trademarks owned by The University of Minnesota.

NAME_____
ADDRESS_____
OCCUPATION_____DATE TESTED___/___/___
EDUCATION_____AGE_____
MARITAL STATUS_____REFERRED BY_____

FEMALE

MMPI Code

Scorer's
Initials

NATIONAL
COMPUTER
SYSTEMS

27309

*49 item version

Raw Score _____
K to be added _____
Raw Score with K _____

323

MINNESOTA MULTIPHASIC PERSONALITY INVENTORY**
S.R. Hathaway and J.C. McKinley

HAND-SCORED GROUP FORM ANSWER SHEET

Scores: ? =

Hy =   Pd =

Pa +   Si +

L =   F =   Hs =   D =

Mf =   Ma =   K +

Pt +   Sc +

A +   R =   Es +

Last Name   First   Middle

Birth Date   Age   Sex

MAC +   Testing Date

1	31	61	91	121	151	181	211	241	271
2	32	62	92	122	152	182	212	242	272
3	33	63	93	123	153	183	213	243	273
4	34	64	94	124	154	184	214	244	274
5	35	65	95	125	155	185	215	245	275
6	36	66	96	126	156	186	216	246	276
7	37	67	97	127	157	187	217	247	277
8	38	68	98	128	158	188	218	248	278
9	39	69	99	129	159	189	219	249	279
10	40	70	100	130	160	190	220	250	280
11	41	71	101	131	161	191	221	251	281
12	42	72	102	132	162	192	222	252	282
13	43	73	103	133	163	193	223	253	283
14	44	74	104	134	164	194	224	254	284
15	45	75	105	135	165	195	225	255	285
16	46	76	106	136	166	196	226	256	286
17	47	77	107	137	167	197	227	257	287
18	48	78	108	138	168	198	228	258	288
19	49	79	109	139	169	199	229	259	289
20	50	80	110	140	170	200	230	260	290
21	51	81	111	141	171	201	231	261	291
22	52	82	112	142	172	202	232	262	292
23	53	83	113	143	173	203	233	263	293
24	54	84	114	144	174	204	234	264	294
25	55	85	115	145	175	205	235	265	295
26	56	86	116	146	176	206	236	266	296
27	57	87	117	147	177	207	237	267	297
28	58	88	118	148	178	208	238	268	298
29	59	89	119	149	179	209	239	269	299
30	60	90	120	150	180	210	240	270	300

Printed in the United States of America   27201

324

MMPI

MINNESOTA MULTIPHASIC PERSONALITY INVENTORY™
S.R. Hathaway and J.C. McKinley

FORM R
1985 HAND-SCORED ANSWER SHEET

Last Name   First   Middle

Birth Date   /   /   Age   Sex

Test Date   /   /

Scores:

? _____   Pa _____

L _____   Pt _____

F _____   Sc _____

K _____   Ma _____

Hs _____   Si _____

D _____   A _____

Hy _____   R _____

Pd _____   Es _____

Mf _____   MAC _____

MINNESOTA MULTIPHASIC PERSONALITY INVENTORY
Copyright © THE UNIVERSITY OF MINNESOTA
1943 Renewed 1970. The Answer Sheet 1948, 1976, 1982, 1984
All rights reserved.
Distributed Exclusively by NATIONAL COMPUTER SYSTEMS, INC.
Under License from The University of Minnesota.

"MMPI" and "Minnesota Multiphasic Personality Inventory"
are trademarks owned by The University of Minnesota.
Printed in the United States of America

5-4-3

Distributed by NATIONAL COMPUTER SYSTEMS, INC., P.O. Box 1416, Minneapolis, MN 55440

27394

Appendix E

Adolescent Norms for Males and Females at Ages 17, 16, 15, and 14 and below

Provided in:
Marks, P. A., Seeman, W., and Haller, D. L. (1974). The actuarial use of the MMPI with adolescents and adults (pp. 155–162). Baltimore, MD: William and Wilkins.

Originally published in:
Dahlstrom, W. G., Welsh, G. S,. and Dahlstrom, L. E. (1972). An MMPI handbook: Vol. 1. Clinical Interpretation (pp. 388–399). Minneapolis: University of Minnesota Press. Reproduced with permission.

TABLE 1

T-score Conversions for Basic Scales without K-corrections for Adolescents Age 14 and Below

Males

Raw Score	?	L	F	K	1 (Hs)	2 (D)	3 (Hy)	4 (Pd)	5 (Mf)	6 (Pa)	7 (Pt)	8 (Sc)	9 (Ma)	0 (Si)
0	41	32	36	23	34					23	30	32		
1		37	38	25	37					25	32	33		
2		42	40	27	40					27	33	35		
3		46	42	29	43		20			30	34	36	21	
4		51	44	31	46		22			33	36	37	23	
5		56	46	33	49	21	25	21		35	37	38	25	
6		61	48	35	52	23	27	23		38	38	39	27	
7		66	50	37	55	26	29	25		41	40	40	29	20
8		71	52	39	58	28	31	28	20	44	41	41	31	22
9		76	54	41	61	30	33	30	22	46	43	42	33	23
10	44	80	56	43	64	32	36	32	24	49	44	43	35	24
11		85	58	45	67	35	38	35	27	52	45	44	37	26
12		90	60	48	70	37	40	37	29	55	47	45	39	27
13		95	62	50	73	39	42	39	31	57	48	46	41	28
14		100	64	52	76	41	44	42	34	60	49	47	43	30
15		105	66	54	79	43	47	44	36	63	51	48	45	31
16			68	56	82	46	49	46	38	65	52	50	47	33
17			70	58	84	48	51	49	41	68	54	51	49	34
18			71	60	87	50	53	51	43	71	55	52	50	35
19			73	62	90	52	56	53	46	74	56	53	52	37
20	47		75	64	93	55		56	48	76	58	54	54	38

Females

?	L	F	K	1 (Hs)	2 (D)	3 (Hy)	4 (Pd)	5 (Mf)	6 (Pa)	7 (Pt)	8 (Sc)	9 (Ma)	0 (Si)	Raw Score
41	31	36		36					28	29	32			0
	36	39	22	39					30	30	34			1
	41	41	24	41					32	32	35	20		2
	46	44	27	44			21	120	34	33	36	22		3
	50	46	29	46	20		23	118	36	34	37	24		4
	55	49	31	49	22		25	115	38	36	38	26	20	5
	59	51	33	51	24	20	27	113	40	37	40	28	21	6
	64	54	35	54	26	22	29	111	43	39	41	30	23	7
	69	56	38	56	28	24	31	109	45	40	42	32	24	8
	73	59	40	59	30	27	34	107	47	42	43	35	25	9
44	78	61	42	61	32	29	36	104	49	43	45	37	26	10
	83	64	44	64	34	31	38	102	51	44	46	39	28	11
	87	66	47	66	36	33	40	100	54	46	47	41	29	12
	92	69	49	69	38	35	42	99	56	47	48	43	30	13
	97	71	51	71	41	38	44	97	58	49	49	45	32	14
	101	74	53	74	43	40	46	95	60	50	51	47	33	15
		76	56	76	45	42	49	92	62	52	52	49	34	16
		79	58	79	47	44	51	90	65	53	53	51	35	17
		81	60	81	49	46	53	88	67	54	54	54	37	18
		84	62	84	51	49	55	86	69	56	56	56	38	19
47		86	65	86	53	51	57	84	71	57	57	58	39	20

Males

Raw Score	?	L	F	K	1 (Hs)	2 (D)	3 (Hy)	4 (Pd)	5 (Mf)	6 (Pa)	7 (Pt)	8 (Sc)	9 (Ma)	0 (Si)
21			77	66	96	57	58	58	50	79	59	55	56	40
22			79	68	99	59	60	60	53	82	60	56	58	41
23			81	70	102	61	62	62	55	84	62	57	60	42
24			83	72	105	63	64	65	57	87	63	58	62	43
25			85	74	108	66	67	67	60	90	65	59	64	45
26			87	76	111	68	69	69	62	93	66	60	66	46
27			89	79	114	70	71	72	65	95	67	61	68	47
28			91	81	117	72	73	74	67	98	69	62	70	49
29			93	83	120	75	75	76	69	101	70	63	72	50
30	50		95	85	123	77	78	79	72	104	71	65	74	51
31			97			79	80	81	74	106	73	66	76	53
32			99			81	82	83	76	109	74	67	78	54
33			101			83	84	86	79	112	75	68	80	56
34			103			86	87	88	81	114	77	69	82	57
35			105			88	89	90	83	117	78	70	84	58
36			107			90	91	93	86	120	80	71	86	60
37			109			92	93	95	88		81	72	88	61
38			111			95	95	97	91		82	73	90	62
39			113			97	98	100	93		84	74	92	64
40	53		115			99	100	102	95		85	75	94	65
41			117			101	102	104	98		86	76	96	66
42			119			103	104	106	100		88	77	98	68
43						106	107	109	102		89	78	100	69
44						108	109	111	105		91	80	101	70
45						110	111	113	107		92	81	103	72

Females

Raw Score	?	L	F	K	1 (Hs)	2 (D)	3 (Hy)	4 (Pd)	5 (Mf)	6 (Pa)	7 (Pt)	8 (Sc)	9 (Ma)	0 (Si)
21			89	67	89	55	53	59	81	73	59	58	60	40
22			91	69	91	57	55	61	79	75	60	59	62	42
23			94	71	94	59	58	64	77	78	62	60	64	43
24			96	73	96	62	60	66	75	80	63	62	66	44
25			99	76	99	64	62	68	73	82	64	63	68	45
26			101	78	101	66	64	70	70	84	66	64	70	47
27			104	80	104	68	66	72	68	86	67	65	72	48
28			106	82	106	70	69	74	66	89	69	67	75	49
29			109	85	109	72	71	76	64	91	70	68	77	51
30	50		111	87	111	74	73	79	62	93	72	69	79	52
31			114		113	76	75	81	59	95	73	70	81	53
32			116		116	78	78	83	57	97	74	71	83	54
33			119		118	80	80	85	55	99	76	73	85	56
34						83	82	87	53	102	77	74	87	57
35						85	84	89	51	104	79	75	89	58
36						87	86	92	48	106	80	76	91	59
37						89	89	94	46	108	82	77	94	61
38						91	91	96	44	110	83	79	96	62
39						93	93	98	42	113	84	80	98	63
40	53					95	95	100	40	115	86	81	100	64
41						97	98	102	37		87	82	102	66
42						99	100	104	35		89	84	104	67
43						102	102	107	33		90	85	106	68
44						104	104	109	31		92	86	108	69
45						106	106	111	29		93	87	110	71

TABLE 1 (Continued)

T-score Conversions for Basic Scales without K-corrections for Adolescents Age 14 and Below

Males

Raw Score	?	L	F	K	1 (Hs)	2 (D)	3 (Hy)	4 (Pd)	5 (Mf)	6 (Pa)	7 (Pt)	8 (Sc)	9 (Ma)	0 (Si)
46						112	113	116	109		93	82	105	73
47						115	115	118	112		95	83		75
48						117	118	120	114		96	84		76
49						119	120		117			85		77
50	56								119			86		79
51												87		80
52												88		81
53												89		83
54												90		84
55												91		85
56												92		87
57												93		88
58												95		89
59												96		91
60	58											97		92
61												98		93
62												99		95
63												100		96
64												101		98
65												102		99

Females

Raw Score	?	L	F	K	1 (Hs)	2 (D)	3 (Hy)	4 (Pd)	5 (Mf)	6 (Pa)	7 (Pt)	8 (Sc)	9 (Ma)	0 (Si)
46						108	109	113	26		94	88	113	72
47						110	111	115	24		96	90		73
48						112	113	117	22		97	91		75
49						114	115	119	20			92		76
50	56					116	118					93		77
51						118	120					95		78
52						120						96		80
53												97		81
54												98		82
55												99		83
56												101		85
57												102		86
58												103		87
59												104		88
60	58											106		90
61												107		91
62												108		92
63												109		94
64												110		95
65												112		96

Males

Raw Score	?	L	F	K	1 (Hs)	2 (D)	3 (Hy)	4 (Pd)	5 (Mf)	6 (Pa)	7 (Pt)	8 (Sc)	9 (Ma)	0 (Si)	Raw Score
66												103		100	66
67												104		102	67
68												105		103	68
69												106		104	69
70	62											107		106	70
71												108			71
72												110			72
73												111			73
74												112			74
75												113			75
76												114			76
77												115			77
78												116			78

Females

K	F	L	?	1 (Hs)	2 (D)	3 (Hy)	4 (Pd)	5 (Mf)	6 (Pa)	7 (Pt)	8 (Sc)	9 (Ma)	0 (Si)	Raw Score
											113		97	66
											114		99	67
											115		100	68
											117		101	69
			62								118		102	70
											119			71
											120			72
														73
														74
														75
														76
														77
														78

TABLE 2
T-score Conversions for Basic Scales without K-corrections for Adolescents Age 15

Males

Raw Score	?	L	F	K	1 (Hs)	2 (D)	3 (Hy)	4 (Pd)	5 (Mf)	6 (Pa)	7 (Pt)	8 (Sc)	9 (Ma)	0 (Si)
0	41	32	37	22	36					27	29	33		
1		37	38	24	39					29	31	34		
2		42	40	26	41					31	32	35		
3		46	41	28	44		20			33	34	36	21	
4		50	43	30	46		22			35	35	37	22	
5		55	45	32	48	20	24	22		37	37	38	24	
6		59	46	34	51	22	26	24		40	38	39	26	
7		63	48	37	53	24	28	26	20	42	39	40	28	20
8		67	50	39	55	27	30	28	22	44	41	41	30	21
9		72	52	41	58	29	32	30	24	46	42	42	32	23
10	44	76	53	43	60	31	34	32	26	48	44	43	34	24
11		80	55	45	62	33	36	34	28	50	45	44	36	25
12		85	57	47	65	36	38	37	31	52	46	45	38	27
13		89	58	49	67	38	40	39	33	54	48	46	40	28
14		93	60	51	69	40	42	41	35	56	49	47	42	30
15		98	62	53	72	43	44	43	37	58	51	48	43	31
16			63	55	74	45	46	45	39	60	52	49	45	32
17			65	58	76	47	48	47	41	63	54	50	47	34
18			67	60	79	49	50	49	43	65	55	51	49	35
19			68	62	81	52	52	52	45	67	56	52	51	36
20	47		70	64	84	54	54	54	47	69	58	53	53	38

Females

?	L	F	K	1 (Hs)	2 (D)	3 (Hy)	4 (Pd)	5 (Mf)	6 (Pa)	7 (Pt)	8 (Sc)	9 (Ma)	0 (Si)	Raw Score
41	31	36	21	37				120	26	29	32			0
	36	38	23	39				118	29	31	34			1
	40	41	25	41				115	31	32	35	20		2
	45	43	27	43				113	33	33	36	22		3
	49	45	29	46			21	111	36	35	37	24		4
	53	47	32	48			23	109	38	36	39	26		5
	58	50	34	50	21	21	25	107	40	37	40	29	21	6
	62	52	36	52	24	23	27	105	42	39	41	31	22	7
	66	54	38	55	26	25	30	103	44	40	42	33	23	8
	70	57	40	57	28	27	32	101	47	41	43	35	24	9
44	75	59	42	59	30	29	34	100	49	43	44	37	26	10
	79	61	45	61	32	31	36	98	51	44	45	39	27	11
	83	63	47	64	34	33	38	96	53	45	46	41	28	12
	88	66	49	66	37	35	40	94	55	47	47	42	30	13
	92	68	51	68	39	37	42	92	58	48	48	44	31	14
	96	70	53	70	41	39	44	90	60	49	49	46	32	15
		73	56	72	43	42	46	88	62	51	50	48	33	16
		75	58	75	45	44	48	86	64	52	51	50	35	17
		77	60	77	47	46	51	84	66	53	53	52	36	18
		79	62	79	49	48	53	82	68	55	54	54	37	19
47		82	64	81	52	50	55	79	71	56	55	56	39	20

Males

Raw Score	?	L	F	K	1 (Hs)	2 (D)	3 (Hy)	4 (Pd)	5 (Mf)	6 (Pa)	7 (Pt)	8 (Sc)	9 (Ma)	0 (Si)
21			72	66	86	56	57	56	49	71	59	54	55	39
22			73	68	88	58	59	58	51	73	61	55	57	40
23			75	70	91	61	61	60	53	75	62	56	59	42
24			77	72	93	63	63	62	56	77	64	57	61	43
25			78	74	95	65	65	64	58	79	65	58	63	44
26			80	76	98	67	67	66	60	81	66	59	65	46
27			82	78	100	70	69	69	62	83	68	60	66	47
28			83	81	102	72	71	71	64	86	69	61	68	48
29			85	83	105	74	73	73	66	88	71	62	70	50
30	50		87	85	107	77	75	75	68	90	72	63	72	51
31			88		109	79	77	77	70	92	73	64	74	52
32			90		112	81	79	79	72	94	75	65	76	54
33			92		114	83	81	81	74	96	76	66	78	55
34			93			86	83	84	76	98	78	67	80	56
35			95			88	85	86	79	100	79	68	82	58
36			97			90	87	88	81	102	81	69	84	59
37			98			92	89	90	83	104	82	70	86	60
38			100			95	91	92	85	106	83	71	87	62
39			102			97	94	94	87	109	85	72	89	63
40	53		103			99	96	96	89	111	86	73	91	64
41			105			101	98	99	91		88	74	93	66
42			107			104	100	101	93		89	75	95	67
43			108			106	102	103	95		90	76	97	69
44			110			108	104	105	97		92	77	99	70
45			112			111	106	107	99		93	78	101	71

Females

Raw Score	?	L	F	K	1 (Hs)	2 (D)	3 (Hy)	4 (Pd)	5 (Mf)	6 (Pa)	7 (Pt)	8 (Sc)	9 (Ma)	0 (Si)
21			84	67	84	54	52	57	77	73	58	56	57	40
22			86	69	86	56	54	59	75	75	59	57	59	41
23			89	71	88	58	56	61	73	77	60	58	61	42
24			91	73	90	60	58	63	71	79	62	59	63	44
25			93	75	93	62	60	65	69	82	63	60	65	45
26			95	77	95	65	62	67	67	84	64	61	67	46
27			98	80	97	67	64	69	65	86	66	62	69	48
28			100	82	99	69	66	71	63	88	67	63	70	49
29			102	84	102	71	68	74	61	90	68	64	72	50
30	50		104	86	104	73	70	76	59	93	70	65	74	52
31			107		106	75	72	78	57	95	71	66	76	53
32			109		108	78	74	80	55	97	72	68	78	54
33			111		110	80	76	82	53	99	74	69	80	55
34			114			82	79	84	51	101	75	70	82	57
35			116			84	81	86	49	103	76	71	83	58
36			118			86	83	88	47	106	78	72	85	59
37			120			88	85	90	45	108	79	73	87	61
38						90	87	92	42	110	80	74	89	62
39						93	89	95	40	112	82	75	91	63
40	53					95	91	97	38	114	83	76	93	64
41						97	93	99	36		85	77	95	66
42						99	95	101	34		86	78	96	67
43						101	97	103	32		87	79	98	68
44						103	99	105	30		89	80	100	70
45						106	101	107	28		90	82	102	71

TABLE 2 (Continued)

T-score Conversions for Basic Scales without K-corrections for Adolescents Age 15

Males

Raw Score	?	L	F	K	1 (Hs)	2 (D)	3 (Hy)	4 (Pd)	5 (Mf)	6 (Pa)	7 (Pt)	8 (Sc)	9 (Ma)	0 (Si)
46			114			113	108	109	101		95	79	103	73
47			115			115	110	111	104		96	80		74
48			117			117	112	114	106		98	81		75
49			119			120	114	116	108			82		77
50	56		120				116	118	110			83		78
51							118		112			84		79
52							120		114			85		81
53									116			86		82
54									118			87		83
55									120			88		85
56												89		86
57												90		87
58												91		89
59												92		90
60	58											93		91
61												94		93
62												95		94
63												96		95
64												97		97
65												98		98

Females

Raw Score	?	L	F	K	1 (Hs)	2 (D)	3 (Hy)	4 (Pd)	5 (Mf)	6 (Pa)	7 (Pt)	8 (Sc)	9 (Ma)	0 (Si)
46						108	103	109	26		91	83	104	72
47						110	105	111	24		93	84		73
48						112	107	113	22		94	85		75
49						114	109	115	20			86		76
50	56					116	111	118				87		77
51						119	113					88		79
52							115					89		80
53							118					90		81
54							120					91		82
55												92		84
56												93		85
57												94		86
58												95		88
59												97		89
60	58											98		90
61												99		92
62												100		93
63												101		94
64												102		95
65												103		97

Males

Raw Score	?	L	F	K	1 (Hs)	2 (D)	3 (Hy)	4 (Pd)	5 (Mf)	6 (Pa)	7 (Pt)	8 (Sc)	9 (Ma)	0 (Si)
66												99		99
67												100		101
68												101		102
69												102		103
70	62											103		105
71												104		
72												105		
73												106		
74												107		
75												108		
76												109		
77												110		
78												111		

Females

Raw Score	?	L	F	K	1 (Hs)	2 (D)	3 (Hy)	4 (Pd)	5 (Mf)	6 (Pa)	7 (Pt)	8 (Sc)	9 (Ma)	0 (Si)
66												104		98
67												105		99
68												106		101
69												107		102
70	62											108		103
71												109		
72												110		
73												112		
74												113		
75												114		
76												115		
77												116		
78												117		

TABLE 3
T-score Conversions for Basic Scales without K-corrections for Adolescents Age 16

Males

Raw Score	?	L	F	K	1 (Hs)	2 (D)	3 (Hy)	4 (Pd)	5 (Mf)	6 (Pa)	7 (Pt)	8 (Sc)	9 (Ma)	0 (Si)
0	41	31	35	20	33					34	28	30		
1		35	37	22	36					35	30	32		
2		40	39	24	39					36	31	33		
3		44	40	27	42					37	33	35		
4		49	42	29	45					39	34	36		
5		53	44	31	47	20	21	21		40	36	37	21	
6		58	46	33	50	22	23	23		42	37	38	23	
7		62	47	36	53	24	26	25		43	39	39	25	
8		67	49	38	56	27	28	28	20	45	40	40	28	20
9		71	51	40	59	29	30	30	22	46	42	41	30	21
10	44	76	53	42	62	31	32	32	24	48	43	42	32	22
11		80	54	45	64	33	34	34	27	49	45	43	34	24
12		85	56	47	67	36	37	36	29	51	46	44	36	25
13		89	58	49	70	38	39	38	31	52	48	45	38	27
14		94	60	51	73	40	41	41	35	54	49	46	40	28
15		99	61	54	76	42	43	43	36	55	51	48	43	29
16			63	56	78	45	45	45	39	57	52	49	45	31
17			65	58	81	47	47	47	41	58	54	50	47	32
18			66	60	84	49	50	49	43	60	55	51	49	34
19			68	63	87	51	52	51	46	61	56	52	51	35
20	47		70	65	90	54	54	53	48	63	58	53	53	37

Females

?	L	F	K	1 (Hs)	2 (D)	3 (Hy)	4 (Pd)	5 (Mf)	6 (Pa)	7 (Pt)	8 (Sc)	9 (Ma)	0 (Si)	Raw Score
41	29	35	22	35					21	27	32			0
	34	37	24	37					24	29	33			1
	38	39	26	40					27	30	34			2
	42	41	28	42					29	32	35			3
	47	44	30	44			20	120	32	33	36	21		4
	51	46	33	47		20	23	118	35	34	38	23		5
	56	48	35	49	20	22	25	113	37	36	39	26		6
	60	50	37	51	22	24	27	111	40	37	40	28	20	7
	64	53	39	54	24	26	29	109	42	38	41	30	21	8
	69	55	41	56	26	28	31	106	45	40	42	32	22	9
44	73	57	44	58	28	30	33	104	48	41	43	35	23	10
	78	59	46	61	30	32	36	102	50	42	44	37	24	11
	82	62	48	63	32	34	38	100	53	44	45	39	26	12
	86	64	50	65	34	36	40	98	55	45	46	41	27	13
	91	66	52	67	36	38	42	96	58	46	47	44	28	14
	95	68	55	70	38	40	44	94	61	48	48	46	29	15
		71	57	72	40	42	47	91	63	49	49	48	31	16
		73	59	74	43	44	49	89	66	50	50	50	32	17
		75	61	77	45	46	51	87	68	52	51	53	33	18
		77	63	79	47	48	53	84	71	53	52	55	34	19
47		80	66	81	49	50	55	82	74	54	53	57	36	20

Females

Raw Score	?	L	F	K	1 (Hs)	2 (D)	3 (Hy)	4 (Pd)	5 (Mf)	6 (Pa)	7 (Pt)	8 (Sc)	9 (Ma)	0 (Si)
21			82	68	84	51	52	57	80	76	56	54	59	37
22			84	70	86	53	54	60	77	79	57	55	62	38
23			86	72	88	55	56	62	75	81	58	56	64	39
24			89	74	91	57	57	64	73	84	60	58	66	41
25			91	77	93	59	59	66	70	87	61	59	68	42
26			93	79	95	61	61	68	68	89	62	60	71	43
27			95	81	98	63	63	71	66	92	64	61	73	44
28			98	83	100	65	65	73	64	94	65	62	75	46
29			100	85	102	67	67	75	61	97	66	63	77	47
30			102	88	105	69	69	77	59	99	67	64	80	48
31			104		107	71	71	79	57	102	69	65	82	49
32			107		109	73	73	82	54	105	70	66	84	51
33			109		112	75	75	84	52	107	71	67	86	52
34			111			77	77	86	50	110	73	68	89	53
35			113			79	79	88	47	112	74	69	91	54
36			116			81	81	90	45	115	75	70	93	55
37			118			83	83	92	43	118	77	71	95	57
38			120			85	85	95	40	120	78	72	98	58
39						87	87	97	38		79	73	100	59
40	53					89	89	99	36		81	74	102	60
41						92	91	101	34		82	75	104	62
42						94	93	103	31		83	77	106	63
43						96	95	106	29		85	78	109	64
44						98	97	108	27		86	79	111	65
45						100	99	110	24		87	80	113	67

Males

Raw Score	?	L	F	K	1 (Hs)	2 (D)	3 (Hy)	4 (Pd)	5 (Mf)	6 (Pa)	7 (Pt)	8 (Sc)	9 (Ma)	0 (Si)
21			72	67	93	56	56	56	50	64	59	54	55	38
22			73	70	95	58	58	58	53	66	61	55	58	39
23			75	72	98	60	61	60	55	67	62	56	60	41
24			77	74	101	63	63	62	57	68	64	57	62	42
25			79	76	104	65	65	64	60	70	65	58	64	44
26			80	79	107	67	67	66	62	71	67	59	66	45
27			82	81	109	69	69	69	65	73	68	61	68	46
28			84	83	112	71	71	71	67	74	70	62	70	48
29			86	85	115	74	74	73	69	76	71	63	73	49
30	50		87	88	118	76	76	75	72	77	73	64	75	51
31			89			78	78	77	74	79	74	65	77	52
32			91			80	80	79	76	80	76	66	79	54
33			92			83	82	82	79	82	77	67	81	55
34			94			85	85	84	81	83	79	68	83	56
35			96			87	87	86	84	85	80	69	85	58
36			98			89	89	88	86	86	82	70	88	59
37			99			92	91	90	88	88	83	71	90	61
38			101			94	93	92	91	89	85	72	92	62
39	53		103			96	96	95	93	91	86	74	94	63
40			105			98	98	97	95	92	87	75	96	65
41			106			101	100	99	98		89	76	98	66
42			108			103	102	101	100		90	77	100	68
43			110			105	104	103	103		92	78	103	69
44			112			107	106	105	105		93	79	105	71
45			113			110	109	107	107		95	80	107	72

TABLE 3 (Continued)

T-score Conversions for Basic Scales without K-corrections for Adolescents Age 16

Males

Raw Score	?	L	F	K	1 (Hs)	2 (D)	3 (Hy)	4 (Pd)	5 (Mf)	6 (Pa)	7 (Pt)	8 (Sc)	9 (Ma)	0 (Si)
46				115		112	111	110	110		96	81	109	73
47				117		114	113	112	112		98	82		75
48				118		116	115	114	114		99	83		76
49				120		119	117	116	117			84		78
50	56						120	118	119			85		79
51												86		81
52												88		82
53												89		83
54												90		85
55												91		86
56												92		88
57												93		89
58												94		90
59												95		92
60	58											96		93
61												97		95
62												98		96
63												99		98
64												101		99
65												102		100

Females

Raw Score	?	L	F	K	1 (Hs)	2 (D)	3 (Hy)	4 (Pd)	5 (Mf)	6 (Pa)	7 (Pt)	8 (Sc)	9 (Ma)	0 (Si)
46						102	101	112	22		89	81	115	68
47						104	103	114	20		90	82		69
48						106	105	116			91	83		70
49						108	107	119				84		72
50	56					110	109					85		73
51						112	111					86		74
52						114	113					87		75
53						116	115					88		77
54						118	117					89		78
55						120	119					90		79
56												91		80
57												92		82
58												93		83
59												94		84
60	58											95		85
61												97		86
62												98		88
63												99		89
64												100		90
65												101		91

Males

Raw Score	?	L	F	K	1 (Hs)	2 (D)	3 (Hy)	4 (Pd)	5 (Mf)	6 (Pa)	7 (Pt)	8 (Sc)	9 (Ma)	0 (Si)	Raw Score
66												103		102	66
67												104		103	67
68												105		105	68
69												106		106	69
70	62											107		107	70
71												108			71
72												109			72
73												110			73
74												111			74
75												112			75
76												114			76
77												115			77
78												116			78

Females

Raw Score	?	L	F	K	1 (Hs)	2 (D)	3 (Hy)	4 (Pd)	5 (Mf)	6 (Pa)	7 (Pt)	8 (Sc)	9 (Ma)	0 (Si)	Raw Score
66												102		93	66
67												103		94	67
68												104		95	68
69												105		96	69
70	62											106		98	70
71												107			71
72												108			72
73												109			73
74												110			74
75												111			75
76												112			76
77												113			77
78												114			78

339

TABLE 4
T-score Conversions for Basic Scales without K-corrections for Adolescents Age 17

Males

Raw Score	?	L	F	K	1 (Hs)	2 (D)	3 (Hy)	4 (Pd)	5 (Mf)	6 (Pa)	7 (Pt)	8 (Sc)	9 (Ma)	0 (Si)
0	41	30	32	20	35						27	31		
1		34	34	23	38					22	28	32		
2		38	36	25	40					25	30	33		
3		43	39	27	43	21	21			28	32	34		
4		47	41	29	45	23	23			31	33	35	20	
5		51	43	31	48	24				34	35	36	22	
6		55	45	34	50	26	25	20		37	36	37	24	
7		59	47	36	53	28	27	23	20	40	38	38	26	
8		63	50	38	55	30	29	25	22	43	39	39	28	
9		68	52	40	58	32	30	27	24	46	41	40	31	20
10	44	72	54	42	60	34	32	29	26	49	42	41	33	21
11		76	56	45	63	35	34	32	29	52	44	43	35	23
12		80	58	47	65	37	36	34	31	55	45	44	37	24
13		81	60	49	68	39	38	36	33	58	47	45	39	26
14		88	63	51	70	41	40	39	35	61	48	46	41	27
15		93	65	53	73	43	42	41	37	64	50	47	43	29
16			67	56	75	44	44	43	40	67	52	48	45	30
17			69	58	78	46	46	46	42	70	53	49	48	32
18			71	60	80	48	48	48	44	72	55	50	50	33
19			73	62	83	50	49	50	46	75	56	51	52	35
20	47		76	64	85	52	51	52	48	78	58	52	54	36

Females

Raw Score	?	L	F	K	1 (Hs)	2 (D)	3 (Hy)	4 (Pd)	5 (Mf)	6 (Pa)	7 (Pt)	8 (Sc)	9 (Ma)	0 (Si)
0	41	28	32		31					21	25			
1		33	35	21	34					24	27	29		
2		37	37	23	36				120	27	28	31		
3		41	40	26	38				117	30	30	32	22	
4		45	42	28	41			17	115	33	31	33	24	
5		49	45	31	43			19	113	35	33	35	26	
6		54	47	33	45			21	111	38	34	36	28	
7		58	49	36	48	20	21	24	108	41	36	37	30	
8		62	52	38	50	22	23	26	106	44	37	38	32	
9		66	54	41	52	24	25	28	104	47	39	40	34	
10	44	70	57	44	55	26	27	31	102	50	40	41	37	21
11		74	59	46	57	28	29	33	100	53	42	43	39	22
12		79	62	49	59	30	31	35	98	56	43	44	41	23
13		83	64	51	61	32	33	37	96	59	44	45	43	25
14		87	67	54	64	35	35	40	94	61	46	46	45	26
15		91	69	56	66	37	37	42	92	64	47	47	47	27
16			72	59	68	39	39	44	89	67	49	48	50	29
17			74	61	71	41	41	47	87	70	50	49	52	30
18			77	64	73	43	43	49	85	73	52	50	54	31
19			79	66	75	45	45	51	83	76	53	52	56	33
20	47		81	69	77	47	47	54	80	79	55	53	58	34

340

Males

Raw Score	?	L	F	K	1 (Hs)	2 (D)	3 (Hy)	4 (Pd)	5 (Mf)	6 (Pa)	7 (Pt)	8 (Sc)	9 (Ma)	0 (Si)
21			78	67	88	54	53	55	50	81	59	53	56	38
22			80	69	90	55	55	57	53	84	61	55	58	39
23			82	71	93	57	57	59	55	87	62	56	60	41
24			84	73	95	59	59	62	57	90	64	57	62	42
25			87	75	98	61	61	64	59	93	65	58	65	44
26			89	78	100	63	63	66	61	96	67	59	67	45
27			91	80	103	64	65	69	63	99	69	60	69	47
28			93	82	105	66	67	71	66	102	70	61	71	49
29			95	84	108	68	68	73	68	105	72	62	73	50
30	50		97	86	110	70	70	75	70	108	73	63	75	52
31			100		113	72	72	78	72	111	75	64	77	53
32			102		115	73	74	80	74	114	76	66	79	55
33			104		118	75	76	82	77	117	78	67	82	56
34			106			77	78	85	79	120	79	68	84	58
35			108			79	80	87	81		81	69	86	59
36			110			81	82	89	83		82	70	88	61
37			113			83	84	91	85		84	71	90	62
38			115			84	86	94	87		86	72	92	64
39			117			86	87	96	90		87	73	94	65
40	53		119			88	89	98	92		89	74	96	67
41						90	91	101	94		90	75	99	68
42						92	93	103	96		92	77	101	70
43						93	95	105	98		93	78	103	71
44						95	97	108	100		95	79	105	73
45						97	99	110	103		96	80	107	74

Females

Raw Score	?	L	F	K	1 (Hs)	2 (D)	3 (Hy)	4 (Pd)	5 (Mf)	6 (Pa)	7 (Pt)	8 (Sc)	9 (Ma)	0 (Si)
21			84	71	80	50	49	56	78	82	56	54	60	35
22			86	74	82	52	51	58	76	84	58	55	63	37
23			89	76	84	54	53	61	74	87	59	56	65	38
24			91	79	87	56	55	63	71	90	60	57	67	39
25			94	81	89	58	57	65	69	93	62	58	69	41
26			96	84	91	60	59	67	67	96	63	60	71	42
27			99	86	93	62	61	70	65	99	65	61	73	43
28			101	89	96	65	63	72	62	102	66	62	76	45
29			104	91	98	67	65	74	60	105	68	63	78	46
30	50		106	94	100	69	67	77	58	108	69	64	80	47
31			109		103	71	69	79	56	110	71	65	82	49
32			111		105	73	71	81	53	113	72	66	84	50
33			113		107	75	73	84	51	116	74	68	86	51
34			116			78	75	86	49	119	75	69	89	53
35			118			80	77	88	47		77	70	91	54
36						82	79	91	44		78	71	93	55
37						84	81	93	42		79	72	95	57
38						86	83	95	40		81	73	97	58
39						88	85	98	38		82	74	99	59
40	53					90	87	100	36		84	76	101	61
41						93	89	102	33		85	77	104	62
42						95	91	104	31		87	78	106	63
43						97	93	107	29		88	79	108	65
44						99	95	109	27		90	80	110	66
45						101	97	111	24		91	81	112	67

341

TABLE 4 (Continued)
T-score Conversions for Basic Scales without K-corrections for Adolescents Age 17

Males

Raw Score	?	L	F	K	1 (Hs)	2 (D)	3 (Hy)	4 (Pd)	5 (Mf)	6 (Pa)	7 (Pt)	8 (Sc)	9 (Ma)	0 (Si)
46						99	101	112	105		98	81	109	76
47						101	103	114	107		99	82		77
48						102	105	117	109		101	83		79
49						104	107	119	111			84		80
50	56					106	108		114			85		82
51						108	110		116			86		83
52						110	112		118			88		85
53						112	114		120			89		86
54						113	116					90		88
55						115	118					91		89
56						117	120					92		91
57						118						93		92
58												94		94
59												95		95
60	58											96		97
61												97		98
62												99		100
63												100		101
64												101		103
65												102		104

Females

?	L	F	K	1 (Hs)	2 (D)	3 (Hy)	4 (Pd)	5 (Mf)	6 (Pa)	7 (Pt)	8 (Sc)	9 (Ma)	0 (Si)	Raw Score
					103	99	114	22		93	82	114	69	46
					105	101	116	20		94	84		70	47
					108	103	118			95	85		71	48
					110	105					86		73	49
56					112	107					87		74	50
					114	109					88		75	51
					116	111					89		77	52
					118	113					90		78	53
					120	115					92		79	54
					123	117					93		81	55
					125						94		82	56
					127						95		83	57
					129						96		85	58
					131						97		86	59
58					133						98		87	60
											100		89	61
											101		90	62
											102		91	63
											103		93	64
											104		94	65

Males

Raw Score	?	L	F	K	1 (Hs)	2 (D)	3 (Hy)	4 (Pd)	5 (Mf)	6 (Pa)	7 (Pt)	8 (Sc)	9 (Ma)	0 (Si)
66												103		106
67												104		107
68												105		109
69												106		110
70	62											107		112
71												108		
72												109		
73												111		
74												112		
75												113		
76												114		
77												115		
78												116		

Females

Raw Score	?	L	F	K	1 (Hs)	2 (D)	3 (Hy)	4 (Pd)	5 (Mf)	6 (Pa)	7 (Pt)	8 (Sc)	9 (Ma)	0 (Si)	Raw Score
66												105		95	66
67												106		97	67
68												108		98	68
69												109		99	69
70	62											110		101	70
71												111			71
72												112			72
73												113			73
74												114			74
75												116			75
76												117			76
77												118			77
78												119			78

343

Appendix F

Item Composition of Special Scales With Direction of Scoring

HARRIS (1955) SUBSCALES*

Scale 2—Depression

D₁—Subjective Depression (32 items)
    True: 32, 41, 43, 52, 67, 86, 104,
        138, 142, 158, 159, 182, 189,
        236, 259
    False: 2, 8, 46, 57, 88, 107, 122, 131,
        152, 160, 191, 207, 208, 242,
        272, 285, 296

D₂—Psychomotor Retardation (15 items)
    True: 41, 52, 182, 259
    False: 8, 30, 39, 57, 64, 89, 95, 145,
        207, 208, 233

D₃—Physical Malfunctioning (11 items)
    True: 130, 189, 193, 288
    False: 2, 18, 51, 153, 154, 155, 160

D₄—Mental Dullness (15 items)
    True: 32, 41, 86, 104, 159, 182, 259,
        290
    False: 8, 9, 46, 88, 122, 178, 207

D₅—Brooding (10 items)
    True: 41, 67, 104, 138, 142, 158,
        182, 236
    False: 88, 107

Scale 3—Hysteria

Hy₁—Denial of Social Anxiety (6 items)
    True: None
    False: 141, 172, 180, 201, 267, 292

Hy₂—Need for Affection (12 items)
    True: 253
    False: 26, 71, 89, 93, 109, 124, 136,
        162, 234, 265, 289

Hy₃—Lassitude-Malaise (15 items)
    True: 32, 43, 76, 189, 238
    False: 2, 3, 8, 9, 51, 107, 137, 153,
        160, 163

Hy₄—Somatic Complaints (17 items)
    True: 10, 23, 44, 47, 114, 186
    False: 7, 55, 103, 174, 175, 188, 190,
        192, 230, 243, 274

Hy₅—Inhibition of Aggression (7 items)
    True: None
    False: 6, 12, 30, 128, 129, 147, 170

Scale 4—Psychopathic Deviate

Pd₁—Familial Discord (11 items)
    True: 21, 42, 212, 216, 224, 245
    False: 96, 137, 235, 237, 527**

Pd₂—Authority Problems (11 items)
    True: 38, 59, 118, 520**
    False: 37, 82, 141, 173, 289, 294,
        429**

Pd₃—Social Imperturbability (12 items)
    True: 64, 479,** 520,** 521**
    False: 82, 141, 171, 180, 201, 267,
        304,** 352**

Pd₄ₐ—Social Alienation (18 items)
    True: 16, 24, 35, 64, 67, 94, 110,
        127, 146, 239, 244, 284,
        305,** 368,** 520**
    False: 20, 141, 170

Pd₄ᵦ—Self-Alienation (15 items)
    True: 32, 33, 61, 67, 76, 84, 94, 102,
        106, 127, 146, 215, 368
    False: 8, 107

Scale 6—Paranoia

Pa₁—Persecutory Ideas (17 items)
    True: 10, 16, 24, 35, 121, 123, 127,
        151, 157, 202, 275, 284, 291,
        293, 338, 364
    False: 347

Pa₂—Poignancy (9 items)
    True: 24, 158, 299, 305, 317, 341,
        365
    False: 111, 268

Pa₃—Naiveté (9 items)
    True: 314
    False: 93, 109, 117, 124, 313, 316,
        319, 348

Scale 8—Schizophrenia

Sc₁ₐ—Social Alienation (21 items)
    True: 16, 21, 24, 35, 52, 121, 157,
        212, 241, 282, 305, 312, 324,
        325, 352, 364
    False: 65, 220, 276, 306, 309

Sc₁ᵦ—Emotional Alienation (11 items)
    True: 76, 104, 202, 301, 339, 355,
        360, 363
    False: 8, 196, 322

Sc₂ₐ—Lack of Ego Mastery, Cognitive (10 items)
    True: 32, 33, 159, 168, 182, 335,
        345, 349, 356
    False: 178

Scale 8—Schizophrenia (Continued)	*Scale 9—Hypomania*

Sc$_{2B}$—Lack of Ego Mastery, Conative (14 items)
　　　　True:　32, 40, 41, 76, 104, 202, 259,
　　　　　　　301, 335, 339, 356
　　　　False:　8, 196, 322
Sc$_{2C}$—Lack of Ego Mastery, Defective Inhibition (11 items)
　　　　True:　22, 97, 156, 194, 238, 266,
　　　　　　　291, 303, 352, 354, 360
　　　　False:　None
Sc$_3$—Bizarre Sensory Experiences (20 items)
　　　　True:　22, 33, 47, 156, 194, 210, 251,
　　　　　　　273, 291, 332, 334, 341, 345,
　　　　　　　350
　　　　False:　103, 119, 187, 192, 281, 330

Ma$_1$—Amorality (6 items)
　　　　True:　143, 250, 271, 277, 298
　　　　False:　289
Ma$_2$—Psychomotor Acceleration (11 items)
　　　　True:　13, 97, 100, 134, 181, 228,
　　　　　　　238, 266, 268
　　　　False:　111, 119
Ma$_3$—Imperturbability (8 items)
　　　　True:　167, 222, 240
　　　　False:　105, 148, 171, 180, 267
Ma$_4$—Ego Inflation (9 items)
　　　　True:　11, 59, 64, 73, 109, 157, 212,
　　　　　　　232, 233
　　　　False:　None

*Source: W. G. Dahlstrom, G. S. Welsh, & L. E. Dahlstrom, An MMPI Handbook, Vol. I. The University of Minnesota Press, Minneapolis. Copyright 1960, 1972 by the University of Minnesota. Reproduced with permission.

**These items are not scored on the Pd Scale, but were included by Harris and Lingoes. Graham (1987) recommended retaining these items in the subscales because of their inclusion in past research and scoring.

Wiggins (1966) Content Scales*

Scale
Abbreviations

SOC　Social maladjustment (27 items)
　　　　True:　52, 171, 172, 180, 201, 267,　　*False:*　57, 91, 99, 309, 371, 391, 449,
　　　　　　　292, 304, 377, 384, 453, 455,　　　　　　450, 479, 482, 502, 520, 521,
　　　　　　　509　　　　　　　　　　　　　　　　　547
DEP　Depression (33 items)
　　　　True:　41, 61, 67, 76, 94, 104, 106,　　*False:*　8, 79, 88, 207, 379, 407
　　　　　　　158, 202, 209, 210, 217, 259,
　　　　　　　305, 337, 338, 339, 374, 390,
　　　　　　　396, 413, 414, 487, 517, 518,
　　　　　　　526, 543
FEM　Feminine interests (30 items)
　　　　True:　70, 74, 77, 78, 87, 92, 126,　　*False:*　1, 81, 219, 221, 223, 283, 300,
　　　　　　　132, 140, 149, 203, 261, 295,　　　　　　423, 434, 537, 552, 563
　　　　　　　463, 538, 554, 557, 562
MOR　Poor morale (23 items)
　　　　True:　84, 86, 138, 142, 244, 321,　　*False:*　122, 264
　　　　　　　357, 361, 375, 382, 389, 395,
　　　　　　　397, 398, 411, 416, 418, 431,
　　　　　　　531, 549, 555
REL　Religious fundamentalism (12 items)
　　　　True:　58, 95, 98, 115, 206, 249, 258,　　*False:*　491
　　　　　　　373, 483, 488, 490

Wiggins (1966) Content Scales* *(Continued)*

Scale
Abbreviations

AUT   Authority conflict (20 items)
　　　True: 59, 71, 93, 116, 117, 118, 124,   *False:* 294
　　　　　　250, 265, 277, 280, 298, 313,
　　　　　　316, 319, 406, 436, 437, 446
PSY   Psychoticism (48 items)
　　　True: 16, 22, 24, 27, 33, 35, 40, 48,   *False:* 198, 347, 464
　　　　　　50, 66, 73, 110, 121, 123, 127,
　　　　　　136, 151, 168, 184, 194, 197,
　　　　　　200, 232, 275, 278, 284, 291,
　　　　　　293, 299, 312, 317, 334, 341,
　　　　　　345, 348, 349, 350, 364, 400,
　　　　　　420, 433, 448, 476, 511, 551
ORG   Organic symptoms (36 items)
　　　True: 23, 44, 108, 114, 156, 159,   *False:* 46, 68, 103, 119, 154, 174,
　　　　　　161, 186, 189, 251, 273, 332,   　　　175, 178, 185, 187, 188, 190,
　　　　　　335, 541, 560   　　　192, 243, 274, 281, 330, 405,
　　　　　　　　　　496, 508, 540
FAM   Family problems (16 items)
　　　True: 21, 212, 216, 224, 226, 239,   *False:* 65, 96, 137, 220, 527
　　　　　　245, 325, 327, 421, 516
HOS   Manifest hostility (27 items)
　　　True: 28, 39, 80, 89, 109, 129, 139,   *False:* none
　　　　　　145, 162, 218, 269, 282, 336,
　　　　　　355, 363, 368, 393, 410, 417,
　　　　　　426, 438, 447, 452, 468, 469,
　　　　　　495, 536
PHO   Phobias (27 items)
　　　True: 166, 182, 351, 352, 360, 365,   *False:* 128, 131, 169, 176, 287, 353,
　　　　　　385, 388, 392, 473, 480, 492,   　　　367, 401, 412, 522, 539
　　　　　　494, 499, 525, 553
HYP   Hypomania (25 items)
　　　True: 13, 134, 146, 181, 196, 228,
　　　　　　234, 238, 248, 266, 268, 272,
　　　　　　296, 340, 342, 372, 381, 386,
　　　　　　409, 439, 445, 465, 500, 505,
　　　　　　506
HEA: Poor health (28 items)
　　　True: 10, 14, 29, 34, 72, 125, 279,   *False:* 2, 18, 36, 51, 55, 63, 130, 153,
　　　　　　424, 519, 544   　　　155, 163, 193, 214, 230, 462,
　　　　　　　　　　474, 486, 533, 542

*Source: J. S. Wiggins, Substantive dimensions of self-report in the MMPI item pool, *Psychological Monographs,* 1966, 80 (22 whole No. 630). Copyright 1966 by the American Psychological Association. Reprinted by permission.

Wiener (1946) and Harmon Subtle-Obvious Subscales*

Abbreviation

D-O. Depression, obvious. (40 items)
    True: 23, 32, 41, 43, 52, 67, 86, 104,   *False:* 2, 8, 9, 18, 36, 46, 51, 57, 88,
        138, 142, 158, 159, 182, 189,   95, 107, 122, 131, 152, 153,
        236, 259, 290   154, 178, 207, 242, 270, 271,
        272, 285

D-S. Depression, subtle (20 items)
    True: 5, 130, 193   *False:* 30, 39, 58, 64, 80, 89, 98, 145,
        155, 160, 191, 208, 233, 241,
        248, 263, 296

Hy-O. Hysteria, obvious (32 items)
    True: 10, 23, 32, 43, 44, 47, 76, 114,   *False:* 2, 3, 7, 8, 9, 51, 55, 103, 107,
        179, 186, 189, 238   128, 137, 153, 163, 174, 175,
        188, 192, 230, 243, 274

Hy-S. Hysteria, subtle (28 items)
    True: 253   *False:* 6, 12, 26, 30, 71, 89, 93, 109,
        124, 129, 136, 141, 147, 160,
        162, 170, 172, 180, 190, 201,
        213, 234, 265, 267, 279, 289,
        292

Pd-O. Psychopathic deviate, obvious (28 items)
    True: 16, 24, 32, 33, 35, 38, 42, 61,   *False:* 8, 20, 37, 91, 107, 137, 287,
        67, 84, 94, 106, 110, 118, 215,   294
        216, 224, 244, 245, 284

Pd-S. Psychopathic deviate, subtle (22 items)
    True: 21, 102, 127, 239   *False:* 82, 96, 134, 141, 155, 170,
        171, 173, 180, 183, 201, 231,
        235, 237, 248, 267, 289, 296

Pa-O. Paranoia, obvious (23 items)
    True: 16, 24, 27, 35, 110, 121, 123,   *False:* 281, 294, 347
        151, 158, 202, 275, 284, 291,
        293, 305, 317, 326, 338, 341,
        364

Pa-S. Paranoia, subtle (17 items)
    True: 15, 127, 157, 299, 365   *False:* 93, 107, 109, 111, 117, 124,
        268, 313, 316, 319, 327, 348

Ma-O. Hypomania, obvious (23 items)
    True: 13, 22, 59, 73, 97, 100, 156,   *False:* 111, 119, 120
        157, 167, 194, 212, 226, 238,
        250, 251, 263, 266, 277, 279,
        298

Ma-S. Hypomania, subtle (23 items)
    True: 11, 21, 64, 109, 127, 134, 143,   *False:* 101, 105, 148, 166, 171, 180,
        181, 222, 228, 232, 233, 240,   267, 289
        268, 271

MAC—MacAndrew (1965) Alcoholism Scale (51 items)*

True: 6, 27, 34, 50, 56, 57, 58, 61,   *False:* 86, 120, 130, 149, 173, 179,
81, 94, 116, 118, 127, 128,   278, 294, 320, 335, 356, 378,
140, 156, 186, 215, 224, 235,   460
243, 251, 263, 283, 309, 413,
419, 426, 445, 446, 477, 482,
483, 488, 500, 507, 529, 562

O-H—Overcontrolled Hostility Scale. Megargee, Cook, and Mendelsohn (1967) (31 items)*

True: 78, 91, 229, 319, 338, 373,   *False:* 1, 30, 81, 90, 102, 109, 129,
394, 425, 488, 559   130, 141, 165, 181, 183, 290,
329, 382, 396, 439, 446, 475,
501, 534

Es—Ego Strength. Barron (1953) (68 items)*

True: 2, 36, 51, 95, 109, 153, 174,   *False:* 14, 22, 32, 33, 34, 43, 48, 58,
181, 187, 192, 208, 221, 231,   62, 82, 94, 100, 132, 140, 189,
234, 253, 270, 355, 367, 380,   209, 217, 236, 241, 244, 251,
410, 421, 430, 458, 513, 515   261, 341, 344, 349, 359, 378,
384, 389, 420, 483, 488, 489,
494, 510, 525, 541, 544, 548,
554, 555, 559, 561

*Source: *An MMPI Handbook, Vol. I, Clinical Interpretation* by W. G. Dahlstrom, G. S. Welsh and L. E. Dahlstrom, Copyright The University of Minnesota 1960, 1972. Reproduced by permission.

A—Anxiety Scale. Welsh (1956) (39 items)*

True: 32, 41, 67, 76, 94, 138, 147,   *False:* 379
236, 259, 267, 278, 301, 305,
321, 337, 343, 344, 345, 356,
359, 374, 382, 383, 384, 389,
396, 397, 411, 414, 418, 431,
443, 465, 499, 511, 518, 544,
555

R—Repression Scale. Welsh (1956) (40 items)*

True: none

False: 1, 6, 9, 12, 39, 51, 81, 112,
126, 131, 140, 145, 154, 156,
191, 208, 219, 221, 271, 272,
281, 282, 327, 406, 415, 429,
440, 445, 447, 449, 450, 451,
462, 468, 472, 502, 516, 529,
550, 556

Source: An MMPI Handbook, Vol. I, Clinical Interpretation by W. G. Dahlstrom, G. S. Welsh and L. E. Dahlstrom. Copyright The University of Minnesota 1960, 1972. Reproduced by permission.

Tryon, Stein, and Chu Cluster Scales*

Cluster Scales

I—Social Introversion versus Interpersonal poise and outgoingness (26 items)

    True: 52, 86, 138, 171, 172, 180, 201, 267, 292, 304, 317, 321, 371, 377, 509

    False: 57, 79, 264, 309, 353, 415, 449, 479, 482, 521, 547

II—Body symptoms versus lack of physical complaints (33 items)

    True: 10, 14, 23, 29, 44, 47, 62, 72, 108, 114, 125, 161, 189, 191, 263, 544

    False: 2, 3, 18, 36, 51, 55, 68, 103, 153, 160, 163, 175, 190, 192, 230, 243, 330

III—Suspicion and mistrust versus absence of suspicion (25 items)

    True: 71, 89, 112, 136, 244, 265, 278, 280, 284, 316, 319, 348, 368, 383, 390, 404, 406, 426, 436, 438, 447, 455, 469, 507, 558

    False: none

IV—Depression and apathy versus positive and optimistic outlook (28 items)

    True: 41, 61, 67, 76, 84, 104, 142, 168, 236, 259, 301, 339, 357, 361, 384, 396, 397, 411, 414, 418, 487, 526, 549

    False: 8, 46, 88, 107, 379

V—Resentment and aggression versus lack of resentment and aggression (21 items)

    True: 28, 39, 94, 97, 106, 129, 139, 145, 147, 148, 162, 234, 336, 375, 381, 382, 416, 443, 468, 536

    False: none

VI—Autism and disruptive thought versus absence of such disturbance (23 items)

> True: 15, 31, 33, 40, 100, 134, 241,   *False:* 329
>   297, 342, 345, 349, 356, 358,
>   359, 374, 389, 425, 459, 511,
>   545, 559, 560

VII—Tension, worry, and fears versus absence
of such complaints (36 items)

> True: 13, 22, 32, 43, 102, 158, 166,   *False:* 131, 152, 242, 407
>   182, 186, 217, 238, 303, 322,
>   335, 337, 338, 340, 351, 360,
>   365, 388, 431, 439, 442, 448,
>   473, 492, 494, 499, 506, 543,
>   555

Source: An MMPI Handbook, Vol. I, Clinical Interpretation by W. G. Dahlstrom, G. S. Welsh
and L. E. Dahlstrom. Copyright The University of Minnesota 1960, 1972. Reproduced by permission.

Serkownek Subscales for Scales 5 and 0*

Scale 5 subscales

Mf_1—Narcissism—Hypersensitivity (18 items)

> True: 25, 89,[AB] 117, 179,[A] 187,[A]   *False:* 79, 133,[A] 187,[A] 198, 214, 262,
>   226, 239,[AB] 278, 282, 297,[A]   264
>   299

Mf_2—Stereotypic Feminine Interests (14 items)

> True: 4, 70, 74, 77, 78, 87, 92,[AB]   *False:* 300
>   132, 140,[AB] 149, 204, 261,
>   295

Mf_3—Denial of Stereotypic Masculine Interests
(8 items)

> True: none   *False:* 1, 81, 144, 176, 219, 221, 223,
>   283

Mf_4—Heterosexual Discomfort—Passivity (4
items)

> True: 69[A]   *False:* 19, 80, 231[A]

Mf_5—Introspective—Critical (7 items)

> True: 204   *False:* 92,[AB] 99, 115, 249, 254, 264

Mf_6—Socially Retiring (9 items)

> True: none   *False:* 89, 99, 112, 116, 117, 126,[A]
>   140,[AB] 203,[A] 229[A]

Scale 0 subscales

Si$_1$—Inferiority—personal   discomfort   (27 items)

    True: 32, 67, 82, 138, 147, 171, 172,   *False:* 57, 309, 353, 371
        180, 201, 236, 267, 278, 292,
        304, 321, 336, 359,[A] 377, 383,
        411, 455, 549, 564

Si$_2$—Discomfort with others (14 items)

    True: 357, 377, 427, 469,[AB] 473,   *False:* 449, 450, 462, 479, 481,[A] 521,
        487, 505[A]   547

Si$_3$—Staid—personal rigidity (16 items)

    True: none   *False:* 33,[AB] 91, 99, 143, 208, 229,
                    231, 254, 400, 415, 440, 446,
                    449, 450, 469,[AB] 505[A]

Si$_4$—Hypersensitivity (10 items)

    True: 25, 32, 126,[A] 138, 236, 278,   *False:* none
        391,[A] 427, 487, 549

Si$_5$—Distrust (12 items)

    True: 117, 124, 147, 278, 316, 359,[A] *False:* none
        383, 398, 411, 436, 481,[A]
        482[A]

Si$_6$—Physical—somatic concerns (10 items)

    True: 33,[AB] 236, 332   *False:* 119, 193, 262, 281, 309, 449,
                   451

[A]These items are scored opposite the main scale direction to remain consistent with their factor loadings.

[B]These items appear on more than one subscale in opposite scored directions. That is, each item is scored as true on one subscale and false on another.

___. Underlined items are scored opposite for males and females.

*Source: K. Serkownek, Subscales for Scales 5 and 0 of the Minnesota Multiphasic Personality Inventory. Unpublished materials, Umsqua Counseling, 770 S.E. Kane, Roseburg, Oregon 97470.

Friedman Overlap Scales (FOS)*

Psychotic Overlap Scale (POS)—18 items

    True: 16, 21, 24, 35, 97, 121, 127,   *False:* 111, 119
        156, 157, 194, 202, 212, 251,
        291, 341, 364

Neurotic Overlap Scale (NOS)—30 items

    True: 10, 23, 43, 67, 86, 114, 142,   *False:* 2, 3, 7, 9, 18, 30, 36, 51, 55,
        189   89, 122, 152, 153, 155, 160,
                   163, 175, 188, 190, 230, 243,
                   274

Friedman Overlap Scales (FOS)* *(Continued)*

Maladjustment Overlap Scale (MOS)—35 items
<table>
<tr><td>True:</td><td>13, 15, 22, 32, 41, 47, 52, 76,</td><td>False:</td><td>8, 93, 103, 107, 124, 178, 180,</td></tr>
<tr><td></td><td>104, 158, 159, 179, 182, 238,</td><td></td><td>192, 267, 281, 289</td></tr>
<tr><td></td><td>259, 266, 273, 301, 305, 317,</td><td></td><td></td></tr>
<tr><td></td><td>349, 352, 356, 360</td><td></td><td></td></tr>
</table>

*Source: Friedman, A. F., Gleser, G. C., Smeltzer, D. J. and Wakefield, J. A. (1983). MMPI overlap item scales for differentiating psychotics, neurotics and nonpsychiatric groups. *Journal of Consulting and Clinical Psychology,* 51, 629–631. All items on scales are from the group booklet form of the MMPI.

Ds—Dissimulation Scale. Gough (1954) (74 items)
<table>
<tr><td>True:</td><td>10, 14, 16, 19, 23, 24, 29, 31,</td><td>False:</td><td>68, 83, 88, 96, 137, 207, 257,</td></tr>
<tr><td></td><td>35, 42, 44, 47, 50, 53, 73, 93,</td><td></td><td>306, 405, 466, 524, 528</td></tr>
<tr><td></td><td>97, 104, 125, 179, 206, 210,</td><td></td><td></td></tr>
<tr><td></td><td>211, 212, 216, 226, 241, 246,</td><td></td><td></td></tr>
<tr><td></td><td>247, 297, 303, 320, 325, 328,</td><td></td><td></td></tr>
<tr><td></td><td>341, 344, 352, 360, 375, 388,</td><td></td><td></td></tr>
<tr><td></td><td>419, 422, 433, 438, 443, 453,</td><td></td><td></td></tr>
<tr><td></td><td>458, 459, 471, 475, 476, 480,</td><td></td><td></td></tr>
<tr><td></td><td>481, 485, 518, 519, 525, 535,</td><td></td><td></td></tr>
<tr><td></td><td>541, 543, 545, 565</td><td></td><td></td></tr>
</table>

*Source: H. G. Gough (1954). Some common misconceptions about neuroticism. *Journal of Consulting Psychology,* 18, 287–292.

Ds—Dissimulation Scale-revised (40 items)*
<table>
<tr><td>True:</td><td>10, 23, 24, 29, 31, 32, 44, 47,</td><td>False:</td><td>68, 83, 88, 96, 257, 306</td></tr>
<tr><td></td><td>93, 97, 104, 125, 210, 212,</td><td></td><td></td></tr>
<tr><td></td><td>226, 241, 247, 303, 325, 352,</td><td></td><td></td></tr>
<tr><td></td><td>360, 375, 388, 422, 438, 453,</td><td></td><td></td></tr>
<tr><td></td><td>459, 475, 481, 518, 525, 535,</td><td></td><td></td></tr>
<tr><td></td><td>541, 543</td><td></td><td></td></tr>
</table>

*Source: H. G. Gough (1957). *California Psychological Inventory Manual.* Palo Alto, Calif., Consulting Psychologists Press.

Appendix G

*T-Score
Conversions for
Special Scales*

TABLE 1
T-Score Conversions for Harris-Lingoes Subscales of Basic Scales for Minnesota Adults

Males

Raw Score	D_1	D_2	D_3	D_4	D_5	Hy_1	Hy_2	Hy_3	Hy_4	Hy_5	Pd_1	Pd_2	Pd_3	Pd_{4A}	Pd_{4B}	Pa_1	Pa_2	Pa_3	Sc_{1A}	Sc_{1B}	Sc_{2A}	Sc_{2B}	Sc_{2C}	Sc_3	Ma_1	Ma_2	Ma_3	Ma_4	Raw Score
32	122																												32
31	119																												31
30	117																												30
29	114																												29
28	111																												28
27	108																												27
26	105																												26
25	102																												25
24	99																												24
23	96																												23
22	93																												22
21	91																												21
20	88																		120					121					20
19	85																		116					117					19
18	82													95					111					113					18
17	79								106					91			117		107					109					17
16	76								102					88			113		103					105					16
15	73	103		114				104	98					84	93		108		99					101					15
14	70	98		109				100	94					81	89		104		94			115		97					14
13	67	92		104				95	91					77	85		99		90			110		93					13
12	65	87		100			79	91	87				68	74	81		95		86			105		89					12
11	62	81	104	95			75	87	83		103	92	64	70	77		90		82			99	112	85			102		11
10	59	76	98	90	92		71	83	79		98	86	60	66	74		86		77	118	103	94	106	81			95		10

Raw Score	D_1	D_2	D_3	D_4	D_5	Hy_1	Hy_2	Hy_3	Hy_4	Hy_5	Pd_1	Pd_2	Pd_3	Pd_{4A}	Pd_{4B}	Pa_1	Pa_2	Pa_3	Sc_{1A}	Sc_{1B}	Sc_{2A}	Sc_{2B}	Sc_{2C}	Sc_3	Ma_1	Ma_2	Ma_3	Ma_4	Raw Score
9	56	70	91	85	87		66	79	75		92	80	56	63	70	82	95	76	73	109	97	88	99	77	87			89	9
8	53	65	84	80	82		62	74	71		86	74	52	59	66	77	88	71	69	101	91	83	93	73	80	77		83	8
7	50	59	77	75	76		58	70	67	82	80	67	48	56	62	73	81	66	65	92	85	77	86	69	73	71		77	7
6	47	54	70	70	71	64	54	66	63	75	74	61	44	52	58	68	75	61	60	83	78	72	80	65	66	65	81	71	6
5	44	48	63	65	65	59	50	62	59	68	69	55	40	49	54	64	68	56	56	74	72	66	73	60	59	59	74	65	5
4	41	43	56	60	60	53	46	57	55	60	63	49	35	45	51	59	62	51	52	66	66	61	67	56	52	53	67	58	4
3	39	37	49	55	54	47	42	53	51	53	57	43	31	42	47	55	55	46	48	57	60	55	60	52	45	47	59	52	3
2	36	32	42	50	49	42	38	49	47	46	51	37	27	38	43	50	49	41	44	48	53	50	54	48	38	42	52	46	2
1	33	26	35	45	44	36	34	45	43	39	45	30	23	35	39	46	42	36	39	39	47	45	47	44	31	36	45	40	1
0	30	21	29	40	38	31	30	41	39	31	39	24	19	31	35	41	36	31	35	31	41	39	41	40	24	30	37	34	0

Females

Raw Score	D_1	D_2	D_3	D_4	D_5	Hy_1	Hy_2	Hy_3	Hy_4	Hy_5	Pd_1	Pd_2	Pd_3	Pd_{4A}	Pd_{4B}	Pa_1	Pa_2	Pa_3	Sc_{1A}	Sc_{1B}	Sc_{2A}	Sc_{2B}	Sc_{2C}	Sc_3	Ma_1	Ma_2	Ma_3	Ma_4	Raw Score
32	109																												32
31	106																												31
30	104																												30
29	101																												29
28	99																												28
27	96																												27
26	94																												26
25	91																												25
24	89																												24
23	86																												23
22	84																												22
21	81																												21
20	79																		117				118						20
19	76													96					113				114						19
18	74																		109				110						18

TABLE 1 (Continued)

Females

Raw Score	D_1	D_2	D_3	D_4	D_5	Hy_1	Hy_2	Hy_3	Hy_4	Hy_5	Pd_1	Pd_2	Pd_3	Pd_{4A}	Pd_{4B}	Pa_1	Pa_2	Pa_3	Sc_{1A}	Sc_{1B}	Sc_{2A}	Sc_{2B}	Sc_{2C}	Sc_3	Ma_1	Ma_2	Ma_3	Ma_4	Raw Score
17	71													92		124			105					106					17
16	69													89		119			101					102					16
15	66	97		110				97	86					85	93	114			97					98					15
14	64	92		106				93	83					81	90	110			93			110		94					14
13	61	86		101				90	79					78	86	105			88			105		91					13
12	59	81		96			81	86	76				69	74	82	100			84			100		87					12
11	56	76	99	91			77	82	73		103	106	66	70	78	95			80			95	102	83		98			11
10	54	71	93	87	88		73	78	69		98	98	62	67	74	90			76	120	104	90	96	79		92			10
9	51	66	87	82	83		69	74	66		92	91	58	63	70	85	97	78	72	111	98	85	91	75		85	88		9
8	49	61	80	77	77		64	70	63		86	84	54	59	67	80	90	73	68	103	91	80	85	71		79	81	82	8
7	46	56	74	72	72		60	67	59	74	80	76	50	56	63	75	83	68	64	94	85	74	80	67		73	75	76	7
6	44	51	67	68	66		56	63	56	67	74	69	47	52	59	71	76	62	60	85	79	69	74	63	89	66	69	70	6
5	41	45	61	63	61		51	59	53	60	69	62	43	49	55	66	69	57	55	76	72	64	69	59	81	60	63	64	5
4	39	40	55	58	55		47	55	49	54	63	54	39	45	51	61	62	52	51	67	66	59	63	55	72	53	57	58	4
3	36	35	48	54	50		43	51	46	47	57	47	35	41	47	56	55	47	47	58	60	54	58	51	64	47	51	52	3
2	34	30	42	49	45		39	47	43	41	51	40	31	38	44	51	49	42	43	50	53	49	52	47	55	41	45	46	2
1	31	25	36	44	39		34	44	39	34	45	32	28	34	40	46	42	37	39	41	47	44	46	43	47	34	39	40	1
0	29	20	29	39	34		30	40	36	27	39	25	24	30	36	41	35	32	35	32	41	39	41	39	38	28	33	34	0

*W. G. Dahlstrom, G. S. Welsh, and L. E. Dahlstrom, *An MMPI Handbook, Vol. I*, The University of Minnesota Press, Minneapolis. Copyright 1960, 1972 by the University of Minnesota. Reproduced with permission.

TABLE 2
T-Score Conversions for Wiggins Content Scales

	Adult Males (N = 225)												
Raw Score	SOC	DEP	FEM	MOR	REL	AUT	PSY	ORG	FAM	HOS	PHO	HYP	HEA
0	32	36	25	34	29	26	36	37	34	31	35	23	37
1	34	38	27	36	32	29	38	40	38	33	38	25	40
2	36	40	30	38	36	31	40	42	43	35	40	28	42
3	38	42	33	40	39	34	41	45	47	37	43	30	45
4	40	44	36	42	42	36	43	47	51	39	46	32	48
5	43	46	39	44	46	39	45	49	56	41	48	34	50
6	45	48	41	46	49	41	46	52	60	43	51	37	53
7	47	50	44	48	52	44	48	54	64	45	54	39	55
8	49	52	47	50	56	46	50	56	68	47	56	41	58
9	51	54	50	52	59	49	52	59	73	49	59	44	61
10	53	56	52	54	62	51	53	61	77	51	62	46	63
11	55	58	55	56	65	54	55	63	81	53	64	48	66
12	57	60	58	58	69	56	57	66	86	55	67	50	68
13	59	62	61	60		59	59	68	90	57	70	53	71
14	61	64	64	62		61	60	70	94	59	72	55	74
15	63	66	66	64		64	62	73	99	61	75	57	76
16	65	68	69	66		66	64	75	103	63	78	59	79
17	67	69	72	68		69	65	77		65	80	62	81
18	70	71	75	70		71	67	80		67	83	64	84
19	72	73	77	72		74	69	82		69	86	66	87
20	74	75	80	74		76	71	84		71	88	68	89
21	76	77	83	76			72	87		73	91	71	92
22	78	79	86	78			74	89		75	94	73	94
23	80	81	89	80			76	91		77	96	75	97
24	82	83	91				78	94		79	99	77	99
25	84	85	94				79	96		82	102	80	102
26	86	87	97				81	98		84	104		105
27	88	89	100				83	101		86	107		107
28		91	102				85	103					110
29		93	105				86	106					
30		95	108				88	108					
31		97					90	110					
32		99					91	113					
33		101					93	115					
34							95	117					
35							97	120					
36							98						
37							100						
38							102						
39							104						
40							105						

TABLE 3
T-Score Conversions for Wiggins Content Scales

					Adult Females *(N = 315)*									
Raw *Score*	*SOC*	*DEP*	*FEM*	*MOR*	*REL*	*AUT*	*PSY*	*ORG*	*FAM*	*HOS*	*PHO*	*HYP*	*HEA*
0	30	33		30	24	28	35	35	34	31	30	17	35
1	32	35		32	27	31	37	37	38	34	32	19	37
2	34	37		34	31	34	39	39	42	36	34	22	40
3	36	39	01	36	35	36	41	42	46	38	36	24	42
4	38	41	04	38	38	39	43	44	50	40	39	27	45
5	40	43	07	40	42	42	45	46	54	42	41	30	48
6	42	45	10	42	46	45	47	48	58	44	43	32	50
7	44	47	13	44	49	47	49	50	62	47	45	35	53
8	46	49	15	46	53	50	51	52	66	49	48	37	55
9	48	51	18	48	57	53	53	55	70	51	50	40	58
10	50	53	21	50	60	55	55	57	74	53	52	43	60
11	52	54	24	52	64	58	57	59	78	55	55	45	63
12	53	56	27	54	68	61	59	61	82	57	57	48	65
13	55	58	30	56		63	61	63	86	59	59	50	68
14	57	60	33	58		66	63	66	90	62	61	53	71
15	59	62	36	60		69	64	68	94	64	64	56	73
16	61	64	39	62		71	66	70	98	66	66	58	76
17	63	66	42	64		74	68	72		68	68	61	78
18	65	68	45	66		77	70	74		70	70	63	81
19	67	70	48	68		79	72	77		72	73	66	83
20	69	72	51	70		82	74	79		75	75	69	86
21	71	74	53	72			76	81		77	77	71	89
22	73	76	56	74			78	83		79	80	74	91
23	75	78	59	76			80	85		81	82	76	94
24	77	80	62				82	87		83	84	79	96
25	79	82	65				84	90		85	86	82	99
26	81	84	68				86	92		87	89		101
27	83	86	71				88	94		90	91		104
28		88	74				90	96					106
29		90	77				92	98					
30		92	80				94	101					
31		94					96	103					
32		96					98	105					
33		98					100	107					
34							102	109					
35							104	112					

Adult Females
(N = 315)

Raw Score	SOC	DEP	FEM	MOR	REL	AUT	PSY	ORG	FAM	HOS	PHO	HYP	HEA
36							106	114					
37							108						
38							110						
39							112						
40							114						
41							116						
42							118						
43							120						

*Source: J. S. Wiggins, Content Scales: Basic data for scoring and interpretation, unpublished materials, 1971. Reproduced by permission.

TABLE 4
T-Score Conversions for Wiggins Content Scales

College Males[a]
(N = 291)

Raw Score	SOC	DEP	FEM	MOR	REL	AUT	PSY	ORG	FAM	HOS	PHO	HYP	HEA
0	35	36	25	36	32	28	34	38	36	29	34	15	35
1	37	38	27	38	35	30	36	41	39	31	37	18	39
2	38	40	30	40	38	33	39	44	43	33	41	21	42
3	40	42	33	42	42	35	41	47	46	36	44	24	46
4	42	44	36	45	45	38	43	50	50	38	47	26	50
5	44	46	39	47	48	40	46	53	53	40	51	29	53
6	46	48	41	49	51	43	48	56	56	42	54	32	57
7	48	50	44	51	54	45	50	59	60	44	58	34	60
8	49	53	47	53	57	48	53	62	63	46	61	37	64
9	51	55	50	55	60	50	55	65	67	48	64	40	68
10	53	57	52	57	63	53	57	68	70	50	68	42	71
11	55	59	55	60	66	55	60	71	73	53	71	45	75
12	57	61	58	62	69	58	62	74	77	55	74	48	79
13	59	63	61	64		60	64	77	80	57	78	51	82
14	60	65	64	66		63	66	80	84	59	81	53	86
15	62	67	66	68		65	69	83	87	61	85	56	90
16	64	69	69	70		68	71	86	90	63	88	59	93
17	66	71	72	73		70	73	89		65	91	61	97
18	68	73	75	75		73	76	92		67	95	64	101
19	70	75	77	77		75	78	95		70	98	67	104
20	71	78	80	79		78	80	98		72	101	69	108

361

TABLE 4 (*Continued*)
T-Score Conversions for Wiggins Content Scales

| | College Males[a] (N = 291) | | | | | | | | | | | | |
Raw Score	SOC	DEP	FEM	MOR	REL	AUT	PSY	ORG	FAM	HOS	PHO	HYP	HE
21	73	80	83	81			83	101		74	105	72	112
22	75	82	86	83			85	104		76	108	75	115
23	77	84	89	86			87	107		78	112	78	119
24	79	86	91				90	110		80	115	80	
25	81	88	94				92	113		82	118	83	
26	83	90	97				94	116		84			
27	84	92	100				96	119		87			
28		94	102				99						
29		96	105				101						
30		98	108				103						
31		100					106						
32		103					108						
33		105					110						
34							113						
35							115						
36							117						
37							120						

Source: J. S. Wiggins, Content Scales: Basic data for scoring and interpretation, unpublished materials 1971. Reproduced by permission.

[a]Tables 4 and 5 are a "state university undergraduate" normative group of 291 men and 316 women. I represents the combined samples of: (a) 100 University of Illinois men (Skrzypek & Wiggins, 1966) and 8: University of Illinois women (Baker, 1967), (b) 95 University of Oregon men and 108 University of Orego women (Goldberg & Rorer, 1963), and (c) 96 University of Minnesota men and 125 University of Minnesot: women (Goldberg & Rorer, 1963).

TABLE 5
T-Score Conversions for Wiggins Content Scales

College Females
(N = 316)

Raw Score	SOC	DEP	FEM	MOR	REL	AUT	PSY	ORG	FAM	HOS	PHO	HYP	HEA
0	36	35		33	29	32	34	38	35	29	31	13	35
1	38	38		35	32	35	37	41	39	32	34	16	39
2	40	40		38	36	38	40	44	42	35	36	19	42
3	42	42	01	40	39	41	42	48	46	38	39	21	46
4	43	45	04	42	42	44	45	51	50	41	42	24	50
5	45	47	07	45	46	47	48	54	53	44	44	27	53
6	47	49	10	47	49	50	50	58	57	47	47	30	57
7	49	51	13	50	52	53	53	61	60	50	50	33	60
8	51	54	15	52	56	56	56	65	64	53	52	36	64
9	53	56	18	54	59	59	58	68	68	56	55	38	67
10	55	58	21	57	62	62	61	71	71	59	57	41	71
11	57	61	24	59	66	65	64	75	75	61	60	44	74
12	59	63	27	61	69	67	66	78	78	64	63	47	78
13	61	65	30	64		70	69	81	82	67	65	50	81
14	63	67	33	66		73	72	85	86	70	68	53	85
15	65	70	36	68		76	74	88	89	73	70	55	88
16	67	72	39	71		79	77	91	93	76	73	58	92
17	69	74	42	73		82	80	95		79	76	61	95
18	71	77	45	76		85	83	98		82	78	64	99
19	73	79	48	78		88	85	101		85	81	67	103
20	74	81	51	80		91	88	105		88	84	70	106
21	76	83	53	83			91	108		91	86	72	110
22	78	86	56	85			93	112		94	89	75	113
23	80	88	59	87			96	115		97	91	78	117
24	82	90	62				99	118		100	94	81	120
25	84	93	65				101			103	97	84	
26	86	95	68				104			105	99		
27	88	97	71				107			108	102		
28		99	74				109						
29		102	77				112						
30		104	80				115						
31		106					118						
32		109					120						
33		111											

Source: J. S. Wiggins, Content Scales: Basic data for scoring and interpretation, unpublished materials, 1971. Reproduced by permission.

TABLE 6
T-Score Conversions for Wiener-Harmon Subtle-Obvious Scales

Raw Score	Adult Males T Scores									
	D-O	D-S	HY-O	HY-S	PD-O	PD-S	PA-O	PA-S	MA-O	MA-S
39	120									
38	118									
37	115									
36	113									
35	111									
34	109									
33	106									
32	104		115							
31	102		113							
30	100		110							
29	97		108							
28	95		105	83	111					
27	93		103	81	108					
26	91		101	79	105					
25	88		98	77	103					
24	86		96	74	100					
23	84		94	72	97		120		109	103
22	82		91	70	94	101	117		106	99
21	79		89	68	92	97	113		102	96
20	77	84	86	66	89	94	110		99	92
19	75	81	84	64	86	90	106		95	88
18	73	77	82	61	83	86	103		92	84
17	70	73	79	59	81	82	100	97	88	80
16	68	70	77	57	78	78	96	93	85	76
15	66	66	75	55	75	74	93	89	82	72
14	64	63	72	53	72	70	89	84	78	68
13	61	59	70	50	70	66	86	80	75	64
12	59	56	67	48	67	62	82	76	71	61
11	57	52	65	46	64	58	79	71	68	57
10	55	49	63	44	61	54	76	67	64	53
9	52	45	60	42	59	50	72	63	61	49
8	50	41	58	39	56	46	69	58	57	45
7	48	38	56	37	53	42	65	54	54	41
6	46	34	53	35	50	38	62	50	50	37
5	43	31	51	33	48	34	58	46	47	33
4	41	27	48	31	45	31	55	41	44	29
3	39	24	46	29	42	27	51	37	40	26
2	37	20	44	26	39	23	48	33	37	22
1	34	16	41	24	37	19	45	28	33	18
0	32	13	39	22	34	15	41	24	30	14

Adult Females
T Scores

Raw Score	D-O	D-S	HY-O	HY-S	PD-O	PD-S	PA-O	PA-S	MA-O	MA-S
39	111									
38	108									
37	106									
36	104									
35	102									
34	100									
33	98									
32	96		104							
31	94		102							
30	92		99							
29	90		97							
28	88		95	85	115					
27	86		93	83	112					
26	84		91	81	109					
25	82		89	78	106					
24	80		87	76	104					
23	78		85	74	101		132		109	105
22	76		83	71	98	105	128		106	101
21	73		80	69	95	101	124		102	97
20	71	83	78	66	92	97	120		99	93
19	69	79	76	64	89	93	115		96	89
18	67	76	74	62	86	89	111		92	85
17	65	72	72	59	84	84	107	103	89	81
16	63	68	70	57	81	80	103	99	86	77
15	61	64	68	55	78	76	99	94	83	73
14	59	61	66	52	75	72	95	89	79	69
13	57	57	64	50	72	68	91	85	76	66
12	55	53	61	47	69	64	87	80	73	62
11	53	50	59	45	66	60	83	75	69	58
10	51	46	57	43	63	55	79	71	66	54
9	49	42	55	40	61	51	75	66	63	50
8	47	39	53	38	58	47	71	61	59	46
7	45	35	51	36	55	43	67	57	56	42
6	43	31	49	33	52	39	63	52	53	38
5	41	27	47	31	49	35	59	47	50	34
4	38	24	45	28	46	31	55	43	46	30
3	36	20	42	26	43	27	50	38	43	26
2	34	16	40	24	41	22	46	33	40	22
1	32	13	38	21	38	18	42	29	36	18
0	30	9	36	19	35	14	38	24	33	14

TABLE 7
T-Score Conversions For Special Scales*

| | | Adult Males T Scores | | | | | |
| | | | | | | | |

Raw Score	MAC	Es	A	R	Ds-r	Ds	OH
74						148	
73						146	
72						145	
71						143	
70						142	
69						140	
68		103				139	
67		101				137	
66		99				136	
65		98				134	
64		96				133	
63		94				131	
62		92				130	
61		91				128	
60		89				127	
59		87				125	
58		85				123	
57		84				122	
56		82				120	
55		80				119	
54		78				117	
53		77				116	
52		75				114	
51	138	73				113	
50	135	71				111	
49	132	70				110	
48	130	68				108	
47	127	66				107	
46	124	65				105	
45	121	63				103	
44	118	61				102	
43	116	59				100	
42	113	58				99	
41	110	56				97	
40	107	54		123	128	96	
39	104	52	88	120	126	94	
38	102	51	86	118	123	93	
37	99	49	85	115	121	91	
36	96	47	84	113	119	90	
35	93	45	82	110	116	88	
34	90	44	81	107	114	87	
33	88	42	79	105	112	85	
32	85	40	78	102	110	84	

Raw Score	MAC	Es	A	R	Ds-r	Ds	OH
31	82	38	77	100	107	82	108
30	79	37	75	97	105	80	105
29	76	35	74	95	103	79	102
28	74	33	73	92	100	77	98
27	71	31	71	90	98	76	95
26	68	30	70	87	96	74	92
25	65	28	69	84	93	73	89
24	63	26	67	82	91	71	86
23	60	24	66	79	89	70	83
22	57	23	65	77	86	68	80
21	54	21	63	74	84	67	77
20	51	19	62	72	82	65	74
19	49	17	60	69	80	64	71
18	46	16	59	66	77	62	68
17	43	14	58	64	75	60	64
16	40	12	56	61	73	59	61
15	37	11	55	59	70	57	58
14	35	9	54	56	68	56	55
13	32	7	52	54	66	54	52
12	29	5	51	51	63	53	49
11	26	4	50	48	61	51	46
10	23	2	48	46	59	50	43
9	21	0	47	43	56	48	40
8	18	-2	46	41	54	47	37
7	15	-3	44	38	52	45	33
6	12	-5	43	36	49	44	30
5	9	-7	41	33	47	42	27
4	7	-9	40	31	45	40	24
3	4	-10	39	28	43	39	21
2	1	-12	37	25	40	37	18
1	-2	-14	36	23	38	36	15
0	-5	-16	35	20	36	34	12

Source: T-Score conversions were constructed by Dr. James A. Wakefield, Jr., from data provided by Dahlstrom, Welsh and Dahlstrom (1975).

TABLE 8
T-Score Conversions For Special Scales

		Adult Females T Scores					
Raw Score	MAC	Es	A	R	Ds-r	Ds	OH
69						138	
68						137	
67						135	
66						134	
65						132	
64						131	
63						129	
62						128	
61						126	
60						125	
59						123	
58		89				122	
57		88				120	
56		86				119	
55		84				117	
54		82				116	
53		81				114	
52		79				113	
51		77				111	
50		76				110	
49		74				108	
48		72				106	
47		70				105	
46		69				103	
45	129	67				102	
44	126	65				100	
43	123	63				99	
42	120	62				97	
41	117	60				96	
40	114	58			120	94	
39	112	56			118	93	
38	109	55			115	91	
37	106	53			113	90	
36	103	51	78		111	88	
35	100	49	77		109	87	
34	97	48	76		107	85	
33	94	46	74		105	84	
32	92	44	73		103	82	

Raw Score	MAC	Es	A	R	Ds-r	Ds	OH
31	89	42	72	104	101	81	
30	86	41	71	101	98	79	
29	83	39	69	98	96	78	
28	80	37	68	95	94	76	
27	77	36	67	93	92	75	95
26	74	34	66	90	90	73	91
25	72	32	64	87	88	72	88
24	69	30	63	84	86	70	85
23	66	29	62	81	84	69	82
22	63	27	60	78	82	67	79
21	60	25	59	75	79	66	76
20	57	23	58	73	77	64	72
19	54	22	57	70	75	63	69
18	52	20	55	67	73	61	66
17	49	18	54	64	71	60	63
16	46	16	53	61	69	58	60
15	43	15	52	58	67	56	57
14	40	13	50	55	65	55	53
13	37	11	49	53	62	53	50
12	34	9	48	50	60	52	47
11	32	8	47	47	58	50	44
10	29	6	45	44	56	49	41
9	26	4	44	41	54	47	38
8	23	2	43	38	52	46	34
7	20	1	41	35	50	44	31
6	17	−1	40	33	48	43	28
5	14	−3	39	30	46	41	25
4	12	−4	38	27	43	40	22
3	9	−6	36	24	41	38	19
2	6	−8	35	21	39	37	15
1	3	−10	34	18	37	35	12
0	0	−11	33	15	35	34	9

Source: T-Score conversions were constructed by Dr. James A. Wakefield, Jr., from data provided in Dahlstrom, Welsh and Dahlstrom (1975).

TABLE 9 A
T-Score Conversions For Subscales of Scale 5 (MF)

Adult Males (M) and Females (F)
T Scores

Raw Score	MF_1-M	MF_1-F	MF_2-M	MF_2-F	MF_3-M	MF_3-F	MF_4-M	MF_4-F	MF_5-M	MF_5-F	MF_6-M	MF_6-F
18	122	113										
17	116	108										
16	111	102										
15	105	97										
14	100	92	121	84								
13	94	86	115	78								
12	89	81	108	72								
11	83	75	101	66								
10	78	70	94	60								
9	72	64	88	54							77	81
8	67	59	81	48	88	66					70	74
7	61	53	74	42	81	57			81	82	63	66
6	56	48	68	36	73	49			72	73	56	59
5	50	43	61	30	66	40			64	64	49	52
4	45	37	54	24	58	31	70	68	55	55	42	44
3	39	32	48	18	51	22	58	53	46	46	35	37
2	34	26	41	12	43	13	46	38	37	37	28	30
1	28	21	34	6	36	5	33	23	29	29	21	22
0	23	15	27	0	28	0	21	8	20	20	14	15

TABLE 9 B
T-Score Conversions For Subscales of Scale 0 (Si)

Adult Males (M) and Females (F)
T Scores

Raw Score	Si_1-M	Si_1-F	Si_2-M	Si_2-F	Si_3-M	Si_3-F	Si_4-M	Si_4-F	Si_5-M	Si_5-F	Si_6-M	Si_6-F
27	132	126										
26	128	122										
25	123	118										
24	119	113										
23	114	109										
22	110	105										
21	106	101										
20	101	96										
19	97	92										
18	92	88										
17	88	84										
16	84	80			88	82						
15	79	75			82	76						
14	75	71	112	110	77	70						
13	70	67	106	103	71	65						
12	66	63	100	97	66	59			96	99		
11	62	58	93	91	61	53			90	92		
10	57	54	87	85	55	47	103	91	84	86	122	119
9	53	50	81	79	50	41	95	84	77	79	113	111
8	48	46	74	73	44	35	88	77	71	73	105	102
7	44	42	68	66	39	29	80	70	64	66	96	94
6	40	37	62	60	34	23	73	63	58	60	87	86
5	35	33	55	54	28	18	65	56	52	53	79	77
4	31	29	49	48	23	12	58	49	45	47	70	69

TABLE 9 B (*Continued*)
T-Score Conversions For Subscales of Scale 0 (Si)

								Adult Males (M) and Females (F) T Scores								
Raw Score	Si_1-M	Si_1-F	Si_2-M	Si_2-F	Si_3-M	Si_3-F	Si_4-M	Si_4-F	Si_5-M	Si_5-F	Si_6-M	Si_6-F
3	26	25	43	42	17	6	50	42	39	40	62	60
2	22	21	37	35	12	0	43	35	32	34	53	52
1	18	16	30	29	7	-6	35	28	26	27	44	44
0	13	12	24	23	1	-12	28	21	20	21	36	35

Source: K. Serkownek, Subscales for Scales 5 and 0 of the Minnesota Multiphasic Personality Inventory. Unpublished materials, Umpqua Counseling, 770 S.E. Kane, Roseburg, Oregon 97470.

TABLE 10
T-Score Conversions For Friedman Overlap Scales

Raw Score	Adult Males (M) and Females (F) T Scores					
	1 POS-M	POS-F	2 NOS-M	NOS-F	3 MOS-M	MOS-F
35					140	123
34					137	121
33					134	118
32					131	115
31					127	112
30			99	92	124	110
29			97	90	121	107
28			95	88	118	104
27			93	86	115	102
26			90	84	112	99
25			88	82	108	96
24			86	79	105	94
23			83	77	102	91
22			81	75	99	88
21			79	73	96	85
20			76	71	93	83
19			74	69	90	80
18	183	166	72	67	86	77
17	175	159	70	65	83	75
16	167	152	67	62	80	72
15	159	145	65	60	77	69
14	151	138	63	58	74	66
13	143	130	60	56	71	64
12	134	123	58	54	68	61
11	126	116	56	52	64	58
10	118	109	53	50	61	56
9	110	102	51	48	58	53
8	102	95	49	45	55	50
7	94	88	47	43	52	48
6	86	80	44	41	49	45
5	77	73	42	39	46	42
4	69	66	40	37	42	39
3	61	59	37	35	39	37
2	53	52	35	33	36	34
1	45	45	33	31	33	31
0	37	38	30	28	30	29

T-Score conversions provided by Dr. James A. Wakefield, Jr.
[1]POS - Psychotic Overlap Scale
[2]NOS - Neurotic Overlap Scale
[3]MOS - Maladjustment Overlap Scale

Appendix H

Nichols Critical Items List Caldwell Critical Items List

Nichols Critical Items List*

Health/Somatic/Neurological

Ill Health

True		False				
NONE		36	51	131	153	160

[a]MINN.	Males: M, 1.20; SD, 1.22.	Females:	M, 1.35, SD, 1.27.
[b]MEDICAL	Males: M, 2.61; SD, 1.47.	Females:	M, 2.92, SD, 1.35.

Neurasthenia

True			False		
189	409	544	163	188	330

MINN.	Males: M, 1.37; SD, 1.17.	Females:	M, 1.94, SD, 1.14.
MEDICAL	Males: M, 2.85; SD, 1.74.	Females:	M, 3.37, SD, 1.58.

Pain & Discomfort

True			False				
44	72	161	55	68	190	243	532

MINN.	Males: M, 1.05; SD, 1.27.	Females:	M, 1.41, SD, 1.41.
MEDICAL	Males: M, 2.13; SD, 1.88.	Females:	M, 2.85, SD, 1.95.

Head Complaints

True				False
44	108	114	161	190

MINN.	Males: M, 0.63; SD, 0.98.	Females:	M, 0.69, SD, 0.93.
MEDICAL	Males: M, 0.92; SD, 1.30.	Females:	M, 1.34, SD, 1.48.

Cardiorespiratory

True	False			
34	55	130	193	230

MINN.	Males: M, 0.92; SD, 1.00.	Females:	M, 1.24, SD, 1.18.
MEDICAL	Males: M, 1.18; SD, 1.12.	Females:	M, 1.30, SD, 1.15.

Vascular

True				False			
47	246	530		7	190	523	528

MINN.   Males: M, 1.16; SD, 1.28.   Females: M, 1.68, SD, 1.42.
MEDICAL Males: M, 1.37; SD, 1.28.   Females: M, 2.12, SD, 1.46.

Upper Gastrointestinal

True						False			
10	23	29	72	125	424	2	130	405	533

MINN.   Males: M, 1.40; SD, 1.62.   Females: M, 1.37, SD, 1.60.
MEDICAL Males: M, 1.70; SD, 1.82.   Females: M, 2.15, SD, 2.06.

Lower Gastrointestinal

True	False		
14	18	63	542

MINN.   Males: M, 0.62; SD, 0.84.   Females: M, 0.77, SD, 0.90.
MEDICAL Males: M, 0.94; SD, 1.04.   Females: M, 1.34, SD, 1.15.

Genitourinary

True	False		
519	462	474	486

MINN.   Males: M, 0.58; SD, 0.83.   Females: M, 0.91, SD, 1.00.
MEDICAL Males: M, 0.76; SD, 0.93.   Females: M, 0.81, SD, 0.92.

Sweating

True		False
191	263	NONE

MINN.   Males: M, 0.68; SD, 0.73.   Females: M, 0.54, SD, 0.74.
MEDICAL Males: M, 0.52; SD, 0.70.   Females: M, 0.51, SD, 0.71.

Motor

True		
22	186	194

False					
103	119	187	192	330	540

MINN.	Males: M, 1.16; SD, 1.36.	Females:	M, 1.53, SD, 1.52.
MEDICAL	Males: M, 1.78; SD, 1.81.	Females:	M, 2.18, SD, 1.93.

Sensory

True				
62	210	273	334	541

False				
185	274	281	496	508

MINN.	Males: M, 1.53; SD, 1.43.	Females:	M, 1.96, SD, 1.60.
MEDICAL	Males: M, 2.25; SD, 1.75.	Females:	M, 2.35, SD, 1.71.

Memory & Concentration

True						
32	156	159	335	342	356	560

False	
178	188

MINN.	Males: M, 1.42; SD, 1.52.	Females:	M, 1.80, SD, 1.76.
MEDICAL	Males: M, 2.60; SD, 2.44.	Females:	M, 2.58, SD, 2.42.

Losses of Consciousness

True			
22	156	194	251

False		
154	174	175

MINN.	Males: M, 1.02; SD, 1.13.	Females:	M, 1.38, SD, 1.22.
MEDICAL	Males: M, 1.20; SD, 1.38.	Females:	M, 1.63, SD, 1.43.

Anxiety & Depression

Acute Tension-Anxiety State

True						
5	13	16	29	43	72	186
238	335	337	352	506	543	555

False						
2	3	9	152	230	242	287
407						

MINN.	Males: M, 3.96; SD, 3.05.	Females:	M, 5.14, SD, 3.88.
MEDICAL	Males: M, 6.94; SD, 4.52.	Females:	M, 7.96, SD, 4.50.

Phrenophobia

True	False
168 182	NONE

| MINN. | Males: M, 0.06; SD, 0.26. | Females: | M, 0.07, SD, 0.27. |
| MEDICAL | Males: M, 0.31; SD, 0.62. | Females: | M, 0.33, SD, 0.62. |

Depressed State

True	False
41 76 84 104 142 158 168 236 252 259 301 397 418 431 526	2 3 107 178 318 379

| MINN. | Males: M, 3.82; SD, 3.14. | Females: | M, 4.77, SD, 3.42. |
| MEDICAL | Males: M, 5.82; SD, 4.93. | Females: | M, 6.67, SD, 4.93. |

Sleep Disturbance

True	False
5 31 43 211 227 340 359 559	3 152

| MINN. | Males: M, 1.63; SD, 1.44. | Females: | M, 2.49, SD, 1.80. |
| MEDICAL | Males: M, 2.72; SD, 1.99. | Females: | M, 3.28, SD, 2.07. |

Suicidal Ideation

True	False
104 106 139 202 209 252 339 413 517 526 565	88

| MINN. | Males: M, 1.24; SD, 1.51. | Females: | M, 0.91, SD, 1.21. |
| MEDICAL | Males: M, 0.91; SD, 1.62. | Females: | M, 0.87, SD, 1.65. |

Thinking Disturbance

Unusual Experience

True	False
27 50 134 168 278 335 341 356 420	119 464

| MINN. | Males: M, 2.16; SD, 1.68. | Females: | M, 2.28, SD, 1.51. |
| MEDICAL | Males: M, 2.28; SD, 1.87. | Females: | M, 2.32, SD, 1.79. |

Active Psychotic Experience

True	False
33 48 66 184 291 334 345 349 350 476	NONE

MINN.	Males: M, 1.42; SD, 1.57.	Females:	M, 1.17, SD, 1.44.
MEDICAL	Males: M, 0.87; SD, 1.35.	Females:	M, 0.83, SD, 1.28.

Active Persecutory Experience

True	False
35 110 121 123 151 197 200 275 284 293 364	347

MINN.	Males: M, 1.03; SD, 1.66.	Females:	M, 0.80, SD, 1.20.
MEDICAL	Males: M, 0.86; SD, 1.49.	Females:	M, 0.64, SD, 1.27.

Miscellaneous

Assaultive Impulse

True	False
39 97 145 234 381	399

MINN.	Males: M, 1.89; SD, 1.65.	Females:	M, 1.90, SD, 1.64.
MEDICAL	Males: M, 1.69; SD, 1.63.	Females:	M, 1.49, SD, 1.46.

Delinquency

True	False
38 56 118 419	294

MINN.	Males: M, 1.11; SD, 1.23.	Females:	M, 0.45, SD, 0.81.
MEDICAL	Males: M, 1.43; SD, 1.41.	Females:	M, 0.60, SD, 0.96.

Substance Abuse

True	False
156 215 251 505	137 460 466

MINN.	Males: M, 0.95; SD, 1.04.	Females:	M, 0.86, SD, 0.91.
MEDICAL	Males: M, 1.31; SD, 1.39.	Females:	M, 0.96, SD, 1.20.

Sexual Problems

True					False				
69	74 (Males)	85	179	297	320	20	37	74 (Females)	133	430
470	519								

MINN.	Males: M, 1.91; SD, 1.39.	Females:	M, 2.13, SD, 1.42. (Based on 11 items)
MEDICAL	Males: M, 1.73; SD, 1.68.	Females:	M, 1.62, SD, 1.54. (Based on 12 items)

*Source: David S. Nichols, unpublished materials, Dammasch State Hospital, P.O. Box 38, Wilsonville, OR 97070

[a]Means and standard deviations are based on the revised Minnesota Normal Adults (Hathaway and Briggs, 1957) and were provided by David S. Nichols and Roger L. Greene.

[b]Means and standard deviations based on general medical patient sample (9,700 men, 6,580 women).

Caldwell Critical Items

Content Area

I. Distress and depression (11 items)
        True: 5, 27, 86, 142, 158, 168, 182,
                259, 337
        False: 152, 178

II. Suicidal thoughts (5 items)
        True: 139, 202, 209, 339
        False: 88

III. Ideas of reference, persecution, and delusions (10 items)
        True: 35,[a] 110, 121, 123, 151, 200,
                275, 293, 331,[a] 364
        False: 347

IV. Peculiar experiences and hallucinations (9 items)
        True: 33, 48, 66, 184, 291, 323,[a]
                334, 345, 349, 350
        False: none

V. Sexual difficulties (7 items)
        True: 69, 74,[b] 179, 297
        False: 20, 37,[a] 74,[c] 133, 302[a]

VI. Authority problems (5 items)
        True: 38,[a] 59, 118, 205, 311[a]
        False: 294

Caldwell Critical Items (Continued)

VII. Alcohol and drugs (4 items)
      True: 156, 215, 251
      False: 460

VIII. Family discord (7 items)
      True: 21,[a] 212, 216, 245, 308[a]
      False: 96, 137, 237

IX. Somatic concerns (10 items)
      True: 23, 114, 125, 189
      False: 2, 9, 55, 153, 175, 243

Source: From A. B. Caldwell, "MMPI Critical Items" unpublished materials, 1969 (available from *Caldwell Report,* 1545 Sawtelle Blvd., Los Angeles, Calif. 90025).
[a]Repeated item
[b]Male only
[c]Female only

References

Aaronson, B. S. (1958). Age and sex influence on MMPI profile peak distributions in an abnormal population. *Journal of Consulting Psychology, 22,* 203–206.

Adams, D. K., & Horn, J. L. (1965). Nonoverlapping keys for the MMPI scales. *Journal of Consulting Psychology, 29,* 284.

American Psychiatric Association. (1980). *Diagnostic and statistical manual of mental disorders* (3rd ed.). Washington, DC: Author.

American Psychological Association. (1977). *Standards for providers of psychological services.* Washington, DC: Author.

American Psychological Association. (1981). Ethical principles of psychologists. *American Psychologist, 36*(b), 633–638.

American Psychological Association. (1985). *Standards for education and psychological testing.* Washington, DC: Author.

American Psychological Association. (1986). Committee on psychological tests and assessment (CPTA). *Guidelines for computer-based tests and interpretations.* Washington, DC: Author.

Anastasi, A. (1982). *Psychological testing* (5th ed.). New York: Macmillan.

Anderson, H. E., & Bashaw, W. L. (1966). Further comments on the internal structure of the MMPI. *Psychological Bulletin, 66,* 211–213.

Anthony, N. (1971). Comparison of clients' standard, exaggerated and matching MMPI profiles. *Journal of Consulting and Clinical Psychology, 36,* 100–103.

Apfeldorf, M., & Hunley, P. J. (1981). The MacAndrew MMPI alcoholism scale: Alcoholism and drug addictiveness. *Journal of Studies on Alcohol, 42,* 80–86.

Applied Innovations, Inc. (1986). *MMPI software manual.* Wakefield, RI.

Archer, R. P. (1987). *Using the MMPI with adolescents.* Hillsdale, NJ: Lawrence Erlbaum Associates.

Austin, A. W. (1959). A factor study of the MMPI psychopathic deviate scale. *Journal of Consulting Psychology, 23,* 550–554.

Austin, A. W. (1961). A note on the MMPI psychopathic deviate scale. *Educational and Psychological Measurement, 21,* 895–897.

Baker, J. N. (1967). Effectiveness of certain MMPI dissimulation scales under "real-life" conditions. *Journal of Consulting Psychology, 14,* 286–292.

Ball, J. C., & Carroll, D. (1960). Analysis of MMPI cannot say score on an adolescent population. *Journal of Clinical Psychology, 16,* 30–31.

Ball, J. C. (1962). *Social deviancy and adolescent personality.* Lexington, KY: University of Kentucky Press.

Barron, F. (1953). An ego strength scale which predicts response to psychotherapy. *Journal of Consulting Psychology, 17,* 327–333.

Beckwith, J. B., Hammond, S. B., & Campbell, I. M. (1983). Homogeneous scales for the neurotic triad of the MMPI. *Journal of Personality Assessment, 47(6),* 604–613.

Bem, S. L. (1974). The measurement of psychological androgyny. *Journal of Consulting and Clinical Psychology, 42,* 152–162.

Blanchard, J. S. (1981). Readability of the MMPI. *Perceptual and Motor Skills, 52,* 985–986.

Block, J. (1965). *The challenge of response sets: Unconfounding meaning, acquiescene, and social desirability in the MMPI.* New York: Appleton-Century-Crofts.

Blum, G. S. (1950). *The blacky pictures.* New York: Psychological Corp.

Boerger, A. R. (1975). *The utility of some alternative approaches to MMPI scale construction.* Unpublished doctoral dissertation, Kent State University, Kent, OH.

Bond, J. A. (1986). Inconsistent responding to repeated MMPI items: Is its major cause really carelessness? *Journal of Personality Assessment, 50,* 50–64.

Bond, J. A. (1987). The process of responding to personality items: Inconsistent responses to repeated presentation of identical items. *Personality and Individual Differences, 8,* 409–417.

Buck, J. A., & Graham, J. R. (1978). The 4–3 MMPI people type: A failure to replicate. *Journal of Consulting and Clinical Psychology, 46,*344.

Buechley, R., & Ball, H. (1952). A new test of "validity" for the group MMPI. *Journal of Consulting Psychology, 16,* 299–301.

Burkhart, B. R., Gynther, M. D., & Fromuth, M. E. (1980). The relative predictive validity of subtle vs. obvious items on the MMPI depression scale. *Journal of Clinical Psychology, 36,* 748–751.

Buros, O. K. (Ed.). (1978). *The eighth mental measurements yearbook.* Highland Park, NJ: Gryphon Press.

Butcher, J. N. (1979). Use of the MMPI in personnel selection. In J. N. Butcher (Ed.), *New developments in the use of the MMPI* (pp. 165–201). Minneapolis, MN: University of Minnesota Press.

Butcher, J. N. (1984). Interpreting defensive profiles. In J. N. Butcher & J. R. Graham (Eds.), *Clinical applications of the MMPI. No. 3* (pp. 5–7). Minneapolis: University of Minnesota, Department of Professional Development and Conference Services, Continuing Education and Extension.

Butcher, J. N. (1985). Why use the MMPI? In J. N. Butcher & J. R. Graham (Eds.), *Clinical applications of the MMPI: 1* (pp. 1–2). Minneapolis: University of Minnesota Department of Conferences.

Butcher, J. N. (1987). *Computerized psychological assessment: A practitioner's guide.* New York: Basic Books.

Butcher, J. N., & Graham, J. R. (1988). *The MMPI restandardization project.* University of Minnesota Continuing Education Project. Tampa, FL.

Butcher, J. N., Dahlstrom, W. G., Graham, J. R., Tellegen, A., & Kaemmer, B. (1989). *Manual for the restandardized Minnesota Multiphasic Personality Inventory: MMPI-2. An administrative and interpretive guide.* Minneapolist, MN: University of Minnesota Press.

Butcher, J. N., & Owen, P. L. (1978). Objective personality inventories: Recent research and some contemporary issues. In B. Wolman (Ed.), *Clinical diagnosis of mental disorders* (pp. 475, 546). New York: Plenum.

Butcher, J. N., & Pancheri, P. (1976). *A handbook of cross-national MMPI research.* Minneapolis: University of Minnesota Press.

Butcher, J. N., & Tellegen, A. (1978). Common methodological problems in MMPI research. *Journal of Consulting and Clinical Psychology, 46,* 620–628.

Caldwell, A. B. (1969). *MMPI critical items.* Unpublished Mimeograph (available from Caldwell Report, 1545 Sawtelle Blvd., Ste. 14, Los Angeles, CA 90025).

Caldwell, A. B. (1977). *Questions people ask when taking the MMPI.* Special Bulletin No. 3 (available from Caldwell Report, 1545 Sawtelle Blvd., Ste. 14, Los Angeles, CA 90025).

Caldwell, A. B. (1988). *MMPI supplemental scale manual.* (Caldwell Report, 1545 Sawtelle Boulevard, Los Angeles, CA 90025).

Calvin, J. (1975). *A replicated study of the concurrent validity of the Harris subscales for the MMPI.* Unpublished doctoral dissertation, Kent State University, Kent, OH.

Carkhuff, R. R., Barnett, L., & McCall, J. N. (1965). *The counselor's handbook: Scale and profile interpretations of the MMPI.* Urbana, IL: R. W. Parkinson and Associates.

Carson, R. C. (1969). Interpretive manual to the MMPI. In J. N. Butcher (Ed.), *MMPI research developments and clinical applications.* New York: McGraw-Hill.

Cattell, R. B., Eber, H. W., & Tatsuoka, M. M. (1970). *Handbook for the sixteen personality factor questionnaire.* Champaign, IL: Institute for Personality and Ability Testing.

Christian, W. L., Burkhart, B. R., & Gynther, M. D. (1978). Subtle-obvious ratings of MMPI items: New interest in an old concept. *Journal of Consulting and Clinical Psychology, 46,* 1178–1186.

Chu, C. (1966). *Object cluster analysis of the MMPI.* Unpublished doctoral dissertation, University of California, Berkeley.

Clayton, M. R., & Graham, J. R. (1979). Predictive validity of Barron's Es scale: The role of symptom acknowledgment. *Journal of Consulting and Clinical Psychology, 47,* 424–425.

Clopton, J. R. (1978). MMPI scale development methodology. *Journal of Personality Assessment, 42,* 148–151.

Clopton, J. R. (1982). Scale development methodology reconsidered. *Journal of Personality Assessment, 46,* 143–146.

Clopton, J. R., & Klein, G. L. (1978). An initial look at the redundancy of specialized MMPI scales. *Journal of Consulting and Clinical Psychology, 46,* 1436–1438.

Clopton, J. R., & Neuringer, C. (1977). MMPI cannot say scores: Normative data and degree of profile distortion. *Journal of Personality Assessment, 41,* 511–513.

Cochran, M. L. (1975). Abbreviated MMPI booklet forms: The 300 and 366 item scales with K-corrections. *Journal of Clinical Psychology, 31,* 298–300.

Colligan, R. C., & Offord, K. P. (1987a). The MacAndrew alcoholism scale applied to a contemporary normative sample. *Journal of Clinical Psychology, 43,* 291–293.

Colligan, R. C., & Offord, K. P. (1987b). Resiliency reconsidered: Contemporary MMPI normative data for Barron's ego strength scale. *Journal of Clinical Psychology, 43,* 467–472.

Colligan, R. C., & Offord, K. P. (1988). Contemporary norms for the Wiggins content scales: A 45-year update. *Journal of Clinical Psychology, 44,* 23–32.

Colligan, R. C., Osborne, D., & Offord, K. P. (1980). Linear transformation and the interpretation of MMPI T-scores. *Journal of Clinical Psychology, 36,* 162–165.

Colligan, R. C., Osborne, D., Swenson, W. M., & Offord, K. P. (1983). *The MMPI: A contemporary normative study.* New York: Praeger.

Colligan, R. C., Osborne, D., Swenson, W. M., & Offord, K. P. (1984). The MMPI: Development of contemporary norms. *Journal of Clinical Psychology, 40,* 100–107.

Comrey, A. L. (1958). A factor analysis of items on the MMPI psychopathic deviate scale. *Educational and Psychological Measurement, 18,* 91–98.

Conley, J. J. (1981). An MMPI typology of male alcoholics: Admission, discharge, and outcome comparisons. *Journal of Personality Assessment, 45,* 33–39.

Crumpton, E., Cantor, J. M., & Batiste, C. A. (1960). A factor analytic study of Barron's ego-strength scale. *Journal of Clinical Psychology, 16,* 283–291.

Dahlstrom, W. G., & Dahlstrom, L. (Eds.). (1980). *Basic readings on the MMPI: A new selection on personality measurement*. Minneapolis: University of Minnesota Press.

Dahlstrom, W. G., Lachar, D., & Dahlstrom, L. E. (1986). *MMPI patterns of American minorities*. Minneapolis: University of Minnesota Press.

Dahlstrom, W. G., Welsh, G. S., & Dahlstrom, L. E. (1972). *An MMPI handbook: Vol. 1. Clinical interpretation*. Minneapolis: University of Minnesota Press.

Dahlstrom, W. G., Welsh, G. S., & Dahlstrom, L. E. (1975). *An MMPI handbook: Vol. 2. Research applications*. Minneapolis: University of Minnesota Press.

Dahlstrom, W. G., & Welsh, G. S. (1960). *An MMPI handbook: A guide to use in clinical practice and research*. Minneapolis: University of Minnesota Press.

Dean, E. F. (1972). A lengthened mini: The midi-mult. *Journal of Clinical Psychology, 28,* 68–71.

Drake, L. E. (1946). A social I.E. scale for the Minnesota multiphasic personality inventory. *Journal of Applied Psychology, 30,* 51–54.

Drake, L. E., & Oetting, E. R. (1959). *An MMPI codebook for counselors*. Minneapolis: University of Minnesota Press.

Drake, L. E., & Thiede, W. B. (1948). Further validation of the social I.E. scale for the Minnesota multiphasic personality inventory. *Journal of Educational Research, 41,* 551–556.

Dubinsky, S., Gamble, D. J., & Rogers, M. L. (1985). A literature review of subtle-obvious items on the MMPI. *Journal of Personality Assessment, 49,* 62–68.

Duckworth, J. (1979). *MMPI interpretation manual for counselors and clinicians*. Muncie, IN: Accelerated Development Inc.

Duckworth, J., & Anderson, W. (1986). *The MMPI interpretation manual for counselors and clinicians*. Muncie, IN: Accelerated Development Inc.

Duckworth, J. C., & Barley, W. D. (1988). Within-normal-limit profiles. In R. L. Greene (Ed.), *The MMPI: Use with specific populations* (pp. 278–315). Philadelphia: Grune & Stratton.

Edwards, A. L. (1959). *Edwards personal preference schedule*. New York: Psychological Corporation.

Edwards, A. L. (1966). A comparison of 57 MMPI scales and 57 experimental scales matched with the MMPI scales in terms of item social desirability scale values and probabilities of endorsement. *Educational and Psychological Measurement, 26,* 15–27.

Edwards, A. L., Diers, C. J., & Walker, J. N. (1962). Response-sets and factor loadings on sixty-one personality scales. *Journal of Applied Psychology, 46,* 220–225.

Edwards, A. L., Klockars, A. J., & Abbott, R. D. (1970). Social desirability and the TSC MMPI scales. *Multivariate Behavioral Research, 5,* 153–156.

Ehrenworth, N. V., & Archer, R. P. (1985). A comparison of clinical accuracy ratings of interpretive approaches for adolescent MMPI responses. *Journal of Personality Assessment, 49,* 413–421.

Eichman, W. J. (1962). Factored scales for the MMPI: A clinical and statistical manual. *Journal of Clinical Psychology, 18,* 363–395.

Erdberg, P. (1979). A systematic approach to providing feedback from the MMPI. In C. S. Newmark (Ed.), *MMPI clinical and research trends* (pp. 328–342). New York: Praeger.

Evans, C., & McConnell, T. R. (1941). A new measure of introversion-extroversion. *Journal of Psychology, 12,* 111–124.

Evans, R. G. (1984a). Normative data for two MMPI critical item sets. *Journal of Clinical Psychology, 40,* 512–515.

Evans, R. G. (1984b). The test–retest index and high F MMPI profiles. *Journal of Clinical Psychology, 40,* 516–518.

Evans, R. G., & Dinning, W. D. (1983). Response consistency among high F scale scores on the MMPI. *Journal of Clinical Psychology, 39,* 246–248.

Eysenck, H. J. (1967). *The biological basis of personality*. Springfield, IL: Thomas.

Eysenck, H. J., & Eysenck, M. W. (1985). *Personality and individual differences.* New York: Plenum.

Eysenck, H. J., & Eysenck, S. B. G. (1975). *Manual: Eysenck personality questionnaire* (junior and adult). San Diego: Edits.

Eysenck, H. J., Wakefield, J. A., & Friedman, A. F. (1983). Diagnosis and clinical assessment: The DSMIII. *Annual Review of Psychology, 34,* 167–193.

Faschingbauer, T. R. (1974). A 166-item written short form of the group MMPI: The FAM. *Journal of Consulting and Clinical Psychology, 42,* 645–655.

Finney, J. C., Smith, D. F., Skeeters, D. E., & Auvenshine, C. D. (1971). MMPI alcoholism scales: Factor structure and content analysis. *Quarterly Journal of Studies on Alcohol, 32,* 1055–1060.

Foerstner, S. B. (1986). *The factor structure and factor stability of selected Minnesota multiphasic personality inventory (MMPI) subscales: Harris and Lingoes subscales, Wiggins content scales, Wiener subscales, and Serkownek subscales.* Unpublished doctoral dissertation. University of Akron.

Fowler, R. D. (1966). *The MMPI notebook: A guide to the clinical use of the automated MMPI.* Nutley, NJ: Roche Psychiatric Service Institute.

Fowler, R. D. (1969). Automated interpretation of personality test data. In J. N. Butcher (Ed.), *MMPI: Research developments and clinical applications.* New York: McGraw-Hill.

Fowler, R. D. (Chair), Butcher, J. N., Tellegen, A; Graham, J. R; & Dahlstrom, W. G. (1988). *Symposium: Revision and restandardization of the MMPI: Rationale, normative sample, new norms, and initial validation.* Paper presented to the American Psychological Association Annual Convention, Atlanta, Ga.

Friedman, A. F. (1982). Review of extraversion and introversion: An interactional perspective by Larry W. Morris. *Journal of Personality Assessment, 46,* 185–187.

Friedman, A. F. (1984). Review of Eysenck personality questionnaire. In D. J. Keyser & R. C. Sweetland (Eds.), *Test Critiques.* Kansas City, MO: Test Corporation of America.

Friedman, A. F., Gleser, G. C., Smeltzer, D. J., Wakefield, J. A., & Schwartz, M. S. (1983). MMPI overlap item scales for differentiating psychotics, neurotics, and nonpsychiatric groups. *Journal of Consulting and Clinical Psychology, 51,* 629–631.

Friedman, A. F., Sasek, J., & Wakefield, J. A., Jr. (1976). Subjective ratings of Cattell's 16 personality factors. *Journal of Personality Assessment, 40,* 302–305.

Friedman, A. F., Wakefield, J. A., Jr., Boblitt, W. E., & Surman, G. (1976). Validity of psychoticism scale of the EPQ. *Psychological Reports, 39,* 1309–1310.

Fulkerson, S. C., & Willage, D. E. (1980). Decisional ambiguity as a source of "cannot say" responses on personality questionnaires. *Journal of Personality Assessment, 44,* 381–386.

Fuller, C. G., & Malony, H. N., Jr. (1984). A comparison of English and Spanish (Nunez) translations of the MMPI. *Journal of Personality Assessment, 48,* 130–131.

Gallagher, B. J., & Jones, B. J. (1987). The attitudes of psychiatrists toward etiological theories of schizophrenia: 1975–1985. *Journal of Clinical Psychology, 43,* 438–443.

Gearing, M. L. (1979). The MMPI as a primary differentiator and predictor of behavior in prison: A methodological critque and review of the recent literature. *Psychological Bulletin, 86,* 926–963.

Gentry, T. A., Wakefield, J. A., & Friedman, A. F. (1985). MMPI scales for measuring Eysenck's personality factors. *Journal of Personality Assessment, 49,* 146–149.

Giannetti, R. A., Johnson, J. H., Klingler, D. E., & Williams, T. A. (1978). Comparison of linear and configural MMPI diagnostic methods with an uncontaminated criterion. *Journal of Consulting and Clinical Psychology, 46,* 1046–1052.

Gilberstadt, H., & Duker, J. (1965). *A handbook for clinical and actuarial MMPI interpretation.* Philadelphia: Saunders.

Goldberg, L. R. (1965). Diagnosticians vs. diagnostic signs: The diagnosis of psychosis vs. neurosis from the MMPI. *Psychological Monographs, 79* (9, whole No. 602).

Goldberg, L. R. (1969). The search for configural relationships in personality assessment: The diagnosis of psychosis vs. neurosis from the MMPI. *Multivariate Behavioral Research, 4,* 523–536.

Goldberg, L. R., & Rorer, L. D. (1963). test–retest item statistics for original and reversed MMPI items. *Oregon Research Institute Monograph, 3*(1).

Goodson, J. H., & King, G. D. (1976). A clinical and actuarial study on the validity of the Goldberg index for the MMPI. *Journal of Clinical Psychology, 32,* 328–335.

Gough, H. G. (1947). Simulated patterns on the MMPI. *Journal of Abnormal and Social Psychology, 42,* 215–255.

Gough, H. G. (1950). The F minus K dissimulation index for the MMPI. *Journal of Consulting Psychology, 14,* 408–413.

Gough, H. G. (1954). Some common misconceptions about neuroticism. *Journal of Consulting Psychology, 18,* 287–292.

Gough, H. G. (1957; revised 1987). *Manual for the California psychological inventory.* Palo Alto, CA: Consulting Psychologists Press.

Gough, H. G. (1987). *California psychological inventory: Administrators guide.* Palo Alto, CA: Consulting Psychologists Press.

Graham, J. R. (1977). *The MMPI: A practical guide.* New York: Oxford University Press.

Graham, J. R. (1985). Interpreting the MacAndrew alcoholism scale. In J. N. Butcher & J. R. Graham (Eds.), *Clinical applications of the MMPI* (pp. 27–28). Minneapolis: University of Minnesota Department of Conferences.

Graham, J. R. (1987). *The MMPI: A practical guide.* New York: Oxford University Press.

Graham, J. R., Schroeder, H. E., & Lilly, R. S. (1971). Factor analysis of items on the social introversion and masculinity-femininity scales on the MMPI. *Journal of Clinical Psychology, 27,* 367–370.

Graham, J. R., & Tisdale, M. J. (1983). *Interpretation of low 5 scores for women of high educational levels.* Paper presented at the 18th Annual Symposium on Recent Developments in the Use of the MMPI, Minneapolis, Minnesota.

Gravitz, M. A. (1968). Normative findings for the frequency of MMPI critical items. *Journal of Clinical Psychology, 24,* 220.

Gray, J. A. (1972). The psychophysiological nature of introversion-extroversion: A modification of Eysenck's theory. In V. D. Nebylitsyn & J. A. Gray (Eds.), *The biological basis of individual behavior.* New York: Academic Press.

Grayson, H. M. (1951). A psychological admissions testing program and manual. Los Angeles, CA: Veterans Administration Center, Neuropsychiatric Hospital.

Grayson, H. M., & Olinger, L. B. (1957). Simulation of normalcy by psychiatric patients on the MMPI. *Journal of Consulting Psychology, 21,* 73–77.

Greene, R. L. (1978). An empirically derived MMPI carelessness scale. *Journal of Clinical Psychology, 34,* 407–410.

Greene, R. L. (1979). Response consistency on the MMPI: The TR index. *Journal of Personality Assessment, 43,* 1, 69–71.

Greene, R. L. (1980). *The MMPI: An interpretive manual.* New York: Grune & Stratton.

Greene, R. L. (1982). Some reflections on "MMPI short forms: A review." *Journal of Personality Assessment, 46,* 486–487.

Greene, R. L. (1985). New norms, old norms, what norms for the MMPI? Review of *The MMPI: A Contemporary Normative Study* (1983) by Colligan, R. C., Osborne, D., Swenson, W. M. and Offord, K. P. *Journal of Personality Assessment, 49,* 108–110.

Greene, R. L. (1987). Ethnicity and MMPI performance: A review. *Journal of Consulting and Clinical Psychology, 55,* 497–512.

Greene, R. L. (1988). The relative efficacy of F–K and the obvious and subtle scales to detect overreporting of psychopathology on the MMPI. *Journal of Clinical Psychology, 44,* 152–159.

Greene, R. L., & Garvin, R. D. (1988). Substance abuse/dependence. In R. L. Greene (Ed.), *The MMPI: Use with specific populations* (pp. 159–197). Philadelphia: Grune & Stratton.

Greene, R. L., & Nichols, D. S. (1987, July). *Preliminary factor analysis of the MMPI item pool in a psychiatric population, segregated by sex and race.* Paper presented at the 10th International Conference on Personality Assessment, Brussels, Belgium.

Grow, R., McVaugh, W., & Eno, T. D. (1980). Faking and the MMPI. *Journal of Clinical Psychology, 36,* 910–917.

Guilford, J. P. (1936). *Psychometric methods.* New York: McGraw-Hill.

Guilford, J. P. (1952). When not to Factor Analyze. *Psychological Bulletin, 49,* 26–37.

Gulas, I. (1973). MMPI 2-point codes for a "normal" college population: A replication study. *Journal of Psychology, 84,* 319–322.

Gynther, M. D. (1963). A note on the Meehl-Dahlstrom rules for discriminating psychotic from neurotic MMPI profiles. *Journal of Clinical Psychology, 19,* 226.

Gynther, M. D. (1972). Review of the MMPI. In O. K. Buros (Ed.), *Seventh mental measurements yearbook* (p. 104). Highland Park, NJ: Gryphon Press.

Gynther, M. D. (1979a). Ethnicity and personality: An update. In J. N. Butcher (Ed.), *New developments in the use of the MMPI.* Minneapolis: University of Minnesota Press.

Gynther, M. D. (1979b). Aging and personality. In J. N. Butcher (Ed.), *New developments in the use of the MMPI.* Minneapolis: University of Minnesota Press.

Gynther, M. D., & Brilliant, P. J. (1968). The diagnostic utility of Welsh's A–R categories. *Journal of Projective Techniques and Personality assessment, 32,* 572–574.

Gynther, M. D., Burkhardt, B. R., & Hovanitz, C. A. (1979). Do face-valid items have more predictive validity than subtle items? The case of the MMPI Pd scale. *Journal of Consulting and Clinical Psychology, 47,* 295–300.

Haertzen, C. A., & Hill, H. E. (1963). Assessing subjective effects of drugs: An index of carelessness and confusion for use with the addiction research center inventory (ARCI). *Journal of Clinical Psychology, 19,* 407–412.

Harris, R., & Lingoes, J. (1955). *Subscales for the Minnesota multiphasic personality inventory.* Mimeographed materials, The Langley Porter Clinic.

Harris, R., & Lingoes, J. (1968). *Subscales for the Minnesota multiphasic personality inventory.* Mimeographed materials, The Langley Porter Clinic.

Hartshorne, H., & May, M. A. (1928). *Studies in Deceit.* New York: MacMillan.

Hathaway, S. R. (1939). The personality inventory as an aid in the diagnosis of psychopathic inferiors. *Journal of Consulting Psychology, 3,* 112–117.

Hathaway, S. R. (1947). A coding system for MMPI profiles. *Journal of Consulting Psychology, 11,* 334–337.

Hathaway, S. R. (1956). Scales 5 (masculinity-femininity), 6 (paranoia), and 8 (schizophrenia). In G. S. Welsh & W. G. Dahlstrom (Eds.), *Basic readings on the MMPI in psychology and medicine* (pp. 104–111). Minneapolis: University of Minnesota Press.

Hathaway, S. R. (1964). MMPI: Professional use by professional people. *American Psychologist, 19,* 204–210.

Hathaway, S. R., & Briggs, P. I. (1957). Some normative data on new MMPI scales. *Journal of Clinical Psychology, 13,* 364–368.

Hathaway, S. R., & McKinley, J. C. (1940). A multiphasic personality schedule (Minnesota): I. Construction of the Schedule. *Journal of Psychology, 10,* 249–254.

Hathaway, S. R., & McKinley, J. C. (1942). A multiphasic personality schedule (Minnesota): III The Measurement of Symptomatic Depression. *Journal of Psychology, 14,* 73–84.

Hathaway, S. R., & McKinley, J. C. (1943). *The Minnesota multiphasic personality inventory* (rev. ed.). Minneapolis: University of Minnesota Press.

Hathaway, S. R., & McKinley, J. C. (1967). *The Minnesota multiphasic personality inventory manual.* New York: Psychological Corp.

Hathaway, S. R., & McKinley, J. C. (1983). *The Minnesota multiphasic personality inventory manual*. New York: Psychological Corp.

Hathaway, S. R., & Meehl, P. E. (1951). *An atlas for the clinical use of the MMPI*. Minneapolis: University of Minnesota Press.

Henrichs, T. F. (1964). Objective configural rules for discriminating MMPI profiles on a psychiatric population. *Journal of Clinical Psychology, 20,* 157–159.

Henrichs, T. F. (1966). A note on the extension of MMPI configural rules. *Journal of Clinical Psychology, 22,* 51–52.

Hoffman, H., & Jackson, D. N. (1976). Substantive dimensions of psychopathology derived from MMPI content scales and the differential personality inventory. *Journal of Consulting and Clinical Psychology, 31,* 408–410.

Hoffman, H., Loper, R. G., & Kammeier, M. L. (1974). Identifying future alcoholics with MMPI alcoholism scales. *Quarterly Journal of Studies on Alcohol, 35,* 490–498.

Holmes, C. B., Dungan, D. S., & McLaughlin, T. P. (1982). Validity of five MMPI alcoholism scales. *Journal of Clinical Psychology, 38,* 661–664.

Holmes, T. H., & Rahe, R. H. (1967). The social readjustment rating scale. *Journal of Psychosomatic Research, 11,* 213–218.

Hovanitz, C. A., & Jordan-Brown, L. (1986). The validity of MMPI subtle and obvious items in psychiatric patients. *Journal of Clinical Psychology, 42,* 100–108.

Hovey, H. B., & Lewis, E. G. (1967). Semiautomatic interpretation of the MMPI. *Journal of Clinical Psychology, 23,* 123–134.

Huber, N. A., & Danahy, S. (1975). Use of the MMPI in predicting completion and evaluating changes in a long-term alcoholism treatment program. *Journal of Studies on Alcohol, 36,* 1230–1237.

Hugo, J. (1971). Abbreviation of the Minnesota multiphasic personality inventory through multiple regression. (Doctoral dissertation, University of Alabama, 1971). *Dissertation Abstracts International, 32,* 123B.

Hunsley, J., Hanson, R. K., & Parker, C. H. K. (1988). A summary of the reliability and stability of MMPI scales. *Journal of Clinical Psychology, 44,* 44–46.

Jacobi, J. (1968). *The psychology of C. G. Jung*. New Haven, CT: Yale University Press.

Katz, M. M. (1968). A phenomenological typology of schizophrenia. In Katz, M. M., Cole, J. O., & Barton, W. E. (Eds.), *The role and methodology of classification in psychiatry and psychopathology* (Public Health Service Publication No. 1584). Washington, DC: U.S. Government Printing Office.

Kendrick, S., & Hatzenbuehler, L. (1982). The effects of oral administration by a live examiner on the MMPI: A split-half design. *Journal of Clinical Psychology, 38,* 788–792.

Kimlicka, T. M., Sheppard, P. L., Wakefield, J. A., & Cross, H. J. (1987). Relationship between psychological androgyny and self-actualization tendencies. *Psychological Reports, 61,* 443–446.

Kimlicka, T. M., Wakefield, J. A., & Friedman, A. F. (1980). Comparison of factors from the Bem sex-role inventory for male and female college students. *Psychological Reports, 46,* 1011–1017.

Kimlicka, T. M., Wakefield, J. A., & Goad, N. A. (1982). Sex-roles of ideal opposite sexed persons for college males and females. *Journal of Personality Assessment, 46,* 519–521.

Kincannon, J. C. (1968). Prediction of the standard MMPI scale scores from 71 items: The mini-mult. *Journal of Consulting and Clinical Psychology, 32,* 319–325.

Koss, M. P. (1979). MMPI item content: Recurring issues. In J. N. Butcher (Ed.), *New developments in the use of the MMPI*, (pp. 3–38). Minneapolis: University of Minnesota Press.

Koss, M. P., & Butcher, J. N. (1973). A comparison of psychiatric patients self-report with other sources of clinical information. *Journal of Research in Personality, 7,* 225–236.

Koss, M. P., Butcher, J. N., & Hoffman, N. G. (1976). The MMPI critical items: How well do they work? *Journal of Consulting and Clinical Psychology, 44*, 921–928.

Kranitz, L. (1972). Alcoholics, heroin addicts and non-addicts: Comparisons on the MacAndrew alcoholism scale on the MMPI. *Quarterly Journal of Studies on Alcohol, 33*, 807–809.

Lachar, D. (1974). *The MMPI: Clinical assessment and automated interpretation.* Los Angeles: Western Psychological Services.

Lachar, D., & Alexander, R. S. (1978). Veridicality of self-report: Replicated correlates of the Wiggins MMPI content scales. *Journal of Consulting and Clinical Psychology, 46*, 1349–1356.

Lachar, D., Berman, W., Grisell, J. L., & Schoff, K. (1976). The MacAndrew alcoholism scale as a general measure of substance misuse. *Journal of Studies on Alcohol, 37*, 1609–1615.

Lachar, D., & Wroebel, T. A. (1979). Validation of clinician's hunches: Construction of a new MMPI critical item set. *Journal of Consulting and Clinical Psychology, 47*, 277–284.

Lane, P. J., & Kling, J. S. (1979). Construct validation of the overcontrolled-hostility scale of the MMPI. *Journal of Consulting and Clinical Psychology, 47*, 781–782.

Lane, J. B., & Lachar, D. (1979). Correlates of broad MMPI categories. *Journal of Clinical Psychology, 35*, 560–566.

Lanyon, R. I. (1968). *A handbook of MMPI group profiles.* Minneapolis: University of Minnesota Press.

Lanyon, R. I., & Goodstein, L. D. (1971). *Personality assessment.* New York: Wiley.

Lawton, M. P., & Kleban, M. H. (1965). Prisoners' faking on the MMPI. *Journal of Clinical Psychology, 21*, 269–271.

Lewak, R. W., Marks, P. A., & Nelson, G. E. (1988). *The MMPI feedback manual.* Manuscript submitted for publication.

Lewak, R., & Nelson, G. (1986). *The MMPI: Questions and answers.* Del Mar Psychiatric Clinic, 240 9th Street, Del Mar, CA 92014.

MacAndrew, C. (1965). The differentiation of male alcoholic out-patients from nonalcoholic psychiatric patients by means of the MMPI. *Quarterly Journal of Studies on Alcohol, 26*, 238–246.

MacAndrew, C. (1981). What the MAC scale tells us about men alcoholics. *Journal of Studies on Alcohol, 42*, 604–625.

McKinley, J. C., & Hathaway, S. R. (1940). A multiphasic personality schedule (Minnesota): II. A differential study of hypochondriasis. *Journal of Psychology, 10*, 255–268.

McKinley, J. C., & Hathaway, S. R. (1942). A multiphasic personality schedule (Minnesota): IV. Psychasthenia. *Journal of Applied Psychology, 26*, 614–624.

McKinley, J. C., & Hathaway, S. R. (1943). The identification and measurement of the psychoneuroses in medical practice. *Journal of the American Medical Association, 122*, 161–167.

McKinley, J. C., & Hathaway, S. R. (1944). The MMPI: V. hysteria, hypomania, and psychopathic deviate. *Journal of Applied Psychology, 28*, 153–174.

McLachlan, J. F. (1974). Test–retest stability of long and short MMPI scales over two years. *Journal of Clinical Psychology, 30*, 189–191.

McLaughlin, J. F., Helmes, E., & Howe, M. G. (1983). Note on the reliability of three MMPI short forms. *Journal of Personality Assessment, 47*, 357–358.

Maloney, M. P., & Ward, M. P. (1976). *Psychological Assessment: A conceptual approach.* New York: Oxford University Press.

Marks, P. A., & Seeman, W. (1963). *The actuarial description of abnormal personality: An atlas for use with the MMPI.* Baltimore, MD: Williams & Wilkins.

Marks, P. A., Seeman, W., & Haller, D. (1974). *The actuarial use of the MMPI with adolescents and adults.* Baltimore, MD: Williams & Wilkins.

Matarazzo, J. D. (1986). Computerized clinical psychological test interpretations: Unvalidated plus all mean and no sigma. *American Psychologist, 41*, 14–24.

Meehl, P. E. (1946). Profile analysis of the MMPI in differential diagnosis. *Journal of Applied Psychology, 30*, 517–524.

Meehl, P. E. (1954). *Clinical versus statistical prediction: A theoretical analysis and a review of the evidence*. Minneapolis: University of Minnesota Press.

Meehl, P. E. (1956). Wanted—A good cookbook. *American Psychologist, 11,* 262–272.

Meehl, P. E. (1970). Psychology and criminal law. *Univ. of Richmond Law Review, 5,* 1–30.

Meehl, P. E. (1973). *Psychodiagnosis: Selected papers*. Minneapolis: University of Minnesota Press.

Meehl, P. E., & Dahlstrom, W. G. (1960). Objective configural rules for discriminating psychotic from neurotic MMPI profiles. *Journal of Consulting Psychology, 24,* 375–387.

Meehl, P. E., & Hathaway, S. R. (1980). The K factor as a suppressor variable in the MMPI. In W. G. Dahlstrom & L. Dahlstrom (Eds.), *Basic readings on the MMPI: A new selection on personality measurement,* (pp. 83–121). Minneapolis: University of Minnesota Press. (Original work published 1946)

Mees, H. L. (1959). Preliminary steps in the construction of factor scales for the MMPI. (Doctoral dissertation, University of Washington, 1960). *Dissertation Abstracts International, 20,* 2905.

Megargee, E. I., Cook, P. E., & Mendelsohn, G. A. (1967). The development and validation of an MMPI scale of assaultiveness in overcontrolled individuals. *Journal of Abnormal Psychology, 72,* 519–528.

Meyer, R. G. (1983). *The clinician's handbook: The psychopathology of adulthood and late adolescence*. Boston: Allyn & Bacon.

Miller, H. R., & Streiner, D. L. (1985). The Harris-Lingoes subscales: Fact or fiction. *Journal of Clinical Psychology 41*(1), 45–51.

Miller, H. R., & Streiner, D. L. (1986). Differences in MMPI profiles with the norms of Colligan et al. *Journal of Consulting and Clinical Psychology, 54,* 843–845.

Moreland, K. L. (1985). *Test-retest reliability of 80 MMPI scales*. Unpublished materials (available from NCS Professional Assessment Services, P.O. Box 1416, Minneapolis, MN 55440).

Murray, H. A. (1943). *Thematic apperception test manual*. Cambridge, MA: Harvard University Press.

Newmark, C. S., Chassin, P., Evans, D. L., & Gentry, L. (1984). "Floating" MMPI profiles revisited. *Journal of Clinical Psychology, 40,* 199–201.

Nichols, D. S. (1974). The Goldberg rules in the detection of MMPI codebook modal diagnoses. *Journal of Clinical Psychology, 30,* 186–188.

Nichols, D. S. (1988). Mood disorders. In R. L. Greene (Ed.), *The MMPI: Use with specific populations* (pp. 74–109). Philadelphia: Grune & Stratton.

Nunez, R. (1967). Inventario multifasico de la personalidad. MMPI-Espanol Mexico: El Manual Moderno, S.A.

O'Leary, M. R., Chaney, E. F., Brown, L. S., & Schuckit, M. A. (1978). The use of the Goldberg indices with alcoholics: A cautionary note. *Journal of Clinical Psychology, 34,* 988–990.

Osborne, D. (1979). Use of the MMPI with medical patients. In J. N. Butcher (Ed.), *New developments in the use of the MMPI* (pp. 141–163). Minneapolis: University of Minnesota Press.

Overall, J. E., & Gomez-Mont, F. (1974). The MMPI-168 for psychiatric screening. *Educational and Psychological Measurement, 34,* 315–319.

Ownby, R. L. (1987). *Psychological reports: A guide to report writing in professional psychology*. Brandon, VT: Clinical Psychology.

Pancoast, D. L., & Archer, R. P. (1989). Original Adult MMPI norms in normal samples: A review with implications for future developments. *Journal of Personality Assessment, 53,* 376–395.

Pancoast, D. L., Archer, R. P., & Gordon, R. A. (1988). The MMPI and clinical diagnosis: A comparison of classification system outcomes with discharge diagnoses. *Journal of Personality Assessment, 52,* 81–90.

Parsons, O. A., Yourshaw, S., & Borstelmann, L. (1968). Self-ideal-self-discrepancies on the MMPI: Consistencies over time and geographic region. *Journal of Counseling Psychology, 15,* 160–166.

Payne, F. D., & Wiggins, J. S. (1972). MMPI profile types and the self-report of psychiatric patients. *Journal of Abnormal Psychology, 79,* 1–8.

Pepper, L. J., & Strong, P. N. (1958). *Judgmental subscales for the Mf scale of the MMPI.* Unpublished materials, Hawaii Department of Health, Honolulu, HI.

Persons, R. W., & Marks, P. A. (1971). The violent 4–3 MMPI personality type. *Journal of Consulting and Clinical Psychology, 36,* 189–196.

Peteroy, E. T., Pirrello, P. E., & Adams, N. (1982). The relationship between two Wiggins content scales and length of hospitalization. *Journal of Clinical Psychology, 38,* 344–346.

Peterson, D. R. (1954). The diagnosis of subclinical schizophrenia. *Journal of Consulting Psychology, 18,* 198–200.

Pfost, K. S., Kunce, J. T., & Stevens, M. J. (1984). The relationship of MacAndrew alcoholism scale scores to MMPI profile type and degree of elevation. *Journal of Clinical Psychology, 40,* 852–855.

Preng, K. W., & Clopton, J. R. (1986). Application of the MacAndrew alcoholism scale to alcoholics with psychiatric diagnoses. *Journal of Personality Assessment, 50,* 113–122.

Rathus, S. A., Fox, J. A., & Ortins, J. B. (1980). The MacAndrew scale as a measure of substance abuse and delinquency among adolescents. *Journal of Clinical Psychology, 36,* 579–583.

Reynolds, W. M., & Sundberg, N. D. (1976). Recent research trends in testing. *Journal of Personality Assessment, 40,* 228–333.

Rodgers, D. A. (1972). Review of the MMPI. In O. K. Buros (Ed.), *Seventh mental measurements yearbook.* Highland Park, NJ: Gryphon Press.

Rogers, R., Dolmetsch, R., & Cavanaugh, J. L. (1983). Identification of random responses on MMPI protocols. *Journal of Personality Assessment, 47,* 364–368.

Rome, H. P., Swenson, W. M., Mataya, P., McCarthy, C. E., Pearson, J. S., Keating, F. R., & Hathaway, S. R. (1962). Symposium on automation procedures in personality assessment. *Proceedings of the Staff Meetings of the Mayo Clinic, 37,* 61–82.

Rosen, A. (1962). Development of MMPI scales based on a reference group of psychiatric patients. *Psychological Monographs, 76,* (8) (whole No. 527).

Roy, R. E. (1984). The Goldberg neurotic-psychotic rule and MMPI 2-7-8 patients. *Journal of Personality Assessment, 48,* 398–402.

Sawyer, J. (1966). Measurement and prediction, clinical and statistical. *Psychological Bulletin, 66,* 178–200.

Schuerger, J. M., Foerstner, S. B., Serkownek, K., & Ritz, G. (1987). History and validities of the Serkownek subscales for MMPI scales 5 and 0. *Psychological Reports, 61,* 227–235.

Seeman, W. (1952). "Subtlety" in structured personality tests. *Journal of Consulting Psychology, 16,* 278–283.

Serkownek, K. (1975). *Subscales for scales 5 and 0 of the Minnesota multiphasic personality inventory.* Unpublished materials, c/o Unique Counseling, 770 S.E. Kane, Roseberg, Oregon 97470.

Sherer, M., Haygood, J. M., & Alfano, A. M. (1984). Stability of psychological test results in newly admitted alcoholics. *Journal of Clinical Psychology, 40,* 855–857.

Shure, G. H., & Rogers, M. S. (1965). Note of caution on the factor analysis of the MMPI. *Psychological Bulletin, 63,* 14–18.

Sines, J. O. (1977). M-F: Bipolar and probably multidimensional. *Journal of Clinical Psychology, 33,* 1038–1041.

Skrzypek, G. J., & Wiggins, J. S. (1966). Contrasted groups versus repeated measurement designs in the evaluation of social desirability scales. *Educational and Psychological Measurement, 26,* 131–138.

Spanier, G. B. (1976). Measuring dyadic adjustment: New scales for assessing the quality of marriage and similar dyads. *Journal of Marriage and the Family, 38,* 15–28.

Spera, J., & Robertson, M. (1974). *A 104-item MMPI: The maximult.* Paper presented at the annual meeting of the American Psychological Association, New Orleans.

Stein, K. B. (1968). The TSC scales: The outcome of a cluster analysis of the 550 MMPI items. In P. McReynolds (Ed.), *Advances in psychological assessment* (Vol. 1, pp. 80–104). Palo Alto, CA: Science and Behavior Books.

Stein, K. B. (1970). The TSC scales: Social undesirability or personal maladjustment? A reply to Edwards, Klockans, and Abbott. *Multivariate Behavioral Research,* 157–158.

Stein, K. B., & Chu, G. L. (1967). Dimensionality of Barron's ego-strength scale. *Journal of Consulting Psychology, 31,* 153–161.

Streiner, D. L., & Miller, H. R. (1986). Can a short form of the MMPI ever be developed? *Journal of Clinical Psychology, 42,* 109–113.

Swain-Holcomb, B., & Thorne, B. M. (1984). A comparison of male and female alcoholics with an MMPI classification system. *Journal of Personality Assessment, 48,* 392–397.

Swenson, W. M., Pearson, J. S., & Osborne, D. (1973). *An MMPI source book: Basic item, scale and pattern data on 50,000 medical patients.* Minneapolis: University of Minnesota Press.

Tallent, N. (1983). *Psychological report writing* (2nd ed.). Engelwood Cliffs, NJ: Prentice-Hall.

Taulbee, E. S. (1958). A validation of MMPI scale pairs in psychiatric diagnosis. *Journal of Clinical Psychology, 14*(3), 316.

Taulbee, E. S., & Sisson, B. D. (1957). Configurational analysis of MMPI profiles. *Journal of Consulting Psychology, 21,* 413–417.

Terman, L. M., & Miles, C. C. (1936). *Sex and personality: Studies in masculinity and femininity.* New York: McGraw-Hill.

Todd, A. L., & Gynther, M. D. (1988). Have MMPI Mf scale correlates changed in the past 30 years? *Journal of Clinical Psychology, 44,* 505–510.

Tryon, R. C. (1966). Unrestricted cluster and factor analysis with application to the MMPI and Holzinger-Harman problems. *Multivariate Behavioral Research, 1,* 229–244.

Uecker, A. E. (1970). Differentiating male alcoholics from other psychiatric inpatients: Validity of the MacAndrew alcoholism scale. *Quarterly Journal of Studies on Alcohol, 31,* 379–380.

University of Minnesota Press. (1983). *Minnesota multiphasic personality inventory.* Revised Manual for Administering and Scoring. Minneapolis, MN.

Van de Riet, V. W., & Wolking, W. D. (1969). Interpretive hypotheses for the MMPI. Gainesville: University of Florida, mimeo.

Wakefield, J. A., Jr. (1979). *Using personality to individualize instruction.* San Diego: Edits.

Wakefield, J. A., Jr., Bradley, P. E., Doughtie, E. B., & Kraft, I. A. (1975). Influence of overlapping and nonoverlapping items on the theoretical interrelationships of MMPI scales. *Journal of Consulting and Clinical Psychology, 43,* 851–856.

Wakefield, J. A., Jr., & Goad, N. A. (1982). *Psychological differences: Causes, consequences, and uses in education and guidance.* San Diego: Edits.

Wakefield, J. A., Sasek, J., Friedman, A. F., & Bowden, J. D. (1976). Androgyny and other measures of masculinity-femininity. *Journal of Consulting and Clinical Psychology, 44,* 766–770.

Wakefield, J. A., Jr., Wood, K. A., Wallace, R. F., & Friedman, A. F. (1978). A curvilinear relationship between extraversion and performance for adult retardates. *Psychological Reports, 43,* 387–392.

Wakefield, J. A., Jr., Yom, B. L., Bradley, P. E., Doughtie, E. B., Cox, J. A., & Kraft, I. A. (1974). Eysenck's personality dimensions: A Model for the MMPI. *British Journal of Social and Clinical Psychology, 13,* 413–420.

Walters, G. D. (1988). Schizophrenia. In R. L. Greene (Ed.), *The MMPI: Use with specific populations* (pp. 50–73). Philadelphia: Grune & Stratton.

Walters, G. D. (1985). Scale 4 (Pd.) of the MMPI and the diagnosis antisocial personality. *Journal of Personality Assessment, 49,* 474–476.

Walters, G. D., & Greene, R. L. (1983). Factor structure of the overcontrolled-hostility scale of the MMPI. *Journal of Clinical Psychology, 39,* 560–562.

Walters, G. D., Greene, R. L., & Solomon, G. S. (1982). Empirical correlates of the overcontrolled-hostility scale and the MMPI 4-3 high-point pair. *Journal of Consulting and Clinical Psychology, 50,* 213–218.

Walters, G. D., Solomon, G. S., & Greene, R. L. (1982). The relationship between the over-controlled-hostility scale and the MMPI 4-3 high point pair. *Journal of Clinical Psychology, 38,* 613–615.

Walters, G. D., White, T. W., & Green, R. L. (1988). Use of the MMPI to identify malingering and exaggeration of psychiatric symptomatology in male prison inmates. *Journal of Consulting and Clinical Psychology, 56,* 111–117.

Ward, L. C., & Ward, J. W. (1980). MMPI readability reconsidered. *Journal of Personality Assessment, 44,* 387–389.

Ward, L. C., Ward, J. W., & Moore, C. W. (1983). Prediction of Wiggins content scale scores from 168- and 399-item abbreviations on the MMPI. *Journal of Personality Assessment, 47,* 359–363.

Watson, C. G., Plemel, D., Vassar, P., Manifold, V., Kucala, T., & Anderson, D. (1987). The comparative validities of six MMPI repression scales. *Journal of Clinical Psychology, 43,* 472–477.

Webb, J. T. (1970, April). *The relation of MMPI two-point codes to age, sex and education in a representative nationwide sample of psychiatric outpatients.* Paper presented at the Southeastern Psychological Association Convention, Louisville, KY.

Webb, J. T. (1971). Regional and sex differences in MMPI scale high-point frequencies of psychiatric patients. *Journal of Clinical Psychology, 27,* 483–486.

Webb, J. T., McNamara, K. M., & Rodgers, D. A. (1986, 1981). *Configural interpretations of the MMPI and CPI.* Columbus, OH: Ohio Psychology Publishing.

Welsh, G. S. (1948). An extension of Hathaway's MMPI profile coding system. *Journal of Consulting Psychology,* 343–344.

Welsh, G. S. (1956). Factor dimensions A and R. In G. S. Welsh & W. G. Dahlstrom (Eds.), *Basic readings on the MMPI in psychology and medicine* (pp. 264–281). Minneapolis: University of Minnesota Press.

Welsh, G. S. (1965). MMPI profiles and factors A and R. *Journal of Clinical Psychology, 21,* 43–47.

Wheeler, W. M., Little, K. B., & Lehner, G. F. J. (1951). The internal structure of the MMPI. *Journal of Consulting Psychology, 15,* 134–141.

White, W. C. (1975). Validity of the overcontrolled-hostility (O-H) scale: A brief report. *Journal of Personality Assessment, 39,* 587–590.

Wiederstein, M. (1986). *Construct validity for measuring Eysenck's dimensions of psychoticism and neuroticism with the MMPI.* Unpublished doctoral dissertation, California School of Professional Psychology, Fresno, CA.

Wiener, D. N., & Harmon, L. R. (1946). *Subtle and obvious keys for the MMPI: Their development.* (Advisement bulletin No. 16). Minneapolis, MN: Regional Veterans Administration Office.

Wiggins, J. S. (1966). Substantive dimensions of self-report on the MMPI item pool. *Psychological Monograph, 80* (22, whole No. 630).

Wiggins, J. S. (1969). Content dimensions in the MMPI. In J. N. Butcher (Ed.), *MMPI: Research developments and clinical applications* (pp. 127–180). New York: McGraw-Hill.

Willcockson, J. C., Bolton, B., & Dana, R. H. (1983). A comparison of six MMPI short forms: Codetype correspondence and indices of psychopathology. *Journal of Clinical Psychology, 39,* 968–969.

Williams, C. L. (1983). Further investigation of the Si scale of the MMPI: Reliabilities, correlates and subscale Utility. *Journal of Clinical Psychology, 39,* 951–957.

Williams, C. L. (1985). Use of the MMPI with adolescents. In J. N. Butcher & J. R. Graham (Eds.), *Clinical applications of the MMPI* (pp. 37–39). Minneapolis: University of Minnesota Department of Conferences.

Wong, M. R. (1984). MMPI scale 5: Its meaning, or lack thereof. *Journal of Personality Assessment, 48,* 279–284.

Woodworth, R. S. (1920). *Personal data sheet.* Chicago: Stoelting.

Author Index

Subject Index